iOS Programming
THE BIG NERD RANCH GUIDE

JOE CONWAY & AARON HILLEGASS

BiG
nerD
ranch

iOS Programming: The Big Nerd Ranch Guide

by Joe Conway and Aaron Hillegass

Big Nerd Ranch, Inc.
154 Krog Street
Suite 100
Atlanta, GA 30307
(404) 478-9005
http://www.bignerdranch.com/
book-comments@bignerdranch.com

The 10-gallon hat with propeller logo is a trademark of Big Nerd Ranch, Inc.

Exclusive worldwide distribution of the English edition of this book by

Pearson Technology Group
800 East 96th Street
Indianapolis, IN 46240 USA
http://www.informit.com

ISBN-10 0321773772
ISBN-13 978-0321773777

First printing, July 2011

Acknowledgments

While our names appear on the cover, many people helped make this book a reality. We would like to take this chance to thank them.

- The other instructors who teach the iOS Bootcamp fed us with a never-ending stream of suggestions and corrections. They are Scott Ritchie, Brian Hardy, Mikey Ward, Christian Keur, Alex Silverman, and Alex von Below.

- Our tireless editor, Susan Loper, took our distracted mumblings and made them into readable prose.

- Several technical reviewers helped us find and fix flaws. They are Bill Monk, Mark Miller, and Jonathan Saggau.

- Ellie Volckhausen designed the cover. (The photo is of the bottom bracket of a bicycle frame.)

- Chris Loper at IntelligentEnglish.com designed and produced the EPUB and Kindle versions.

- The amazing team at Pearson Technology Group patiently guided us through the business end of book publishing.

The final and most important thanks goes to our students whose questions inspired us to write this book and whose frustrations inspired us to make it clear and comprehensible.

Table of Contents

Introduction

An aspiring iOS developer faces three basic hurdles:

- *You must learn the Objective-C language*. Objective-C is a small and simple extension to the C language. After the first four chapters of this book, you will have a working knowledge of Objective-C.

- *You must master the big ideas*. These include things like memory management techniques, delegation, archiving, and the proper use of view controllers. The big ideas take a few days to understand. When you reach the halfway point of this book, you will understand these big ideas.

- *You must master the frameworks*. The eventual goal is to know how to use every method of every class in every framework in iOS. This is a project for a lifetime: there are over 3000 methods and more than 200 classes available in iOS. To make things even worse, Apple adds new classes and new methods with every release of iOS. In this book, you will be introduced to each of the subsystems that make up the iOS SDK, but we will not study each one deeply. Instead, our goal is get you to the point where you can search and understand Apple's reference documentation.

We have used this material many times at our iOS Development Bootcamp at Big Nerd Ranch. It is well-tested and has helped hundreds of people become iOS application developers. We sincerely hope that it proves useful to you.

Prerequisites

This book assumes that you are already motivated to learn to write iOS apps. We won't spend any time convincing you that the iPhone, the iPad, and the iPod touch are compelling pieces of technology.

We also assume that you know the C programming language and something about object-oriented programming. If this is not true, you should probably start with an introductory book on C and Objective-C, such as *Objective-C Programming: The Big Nerd Ranch Guide*.

What's Changed in the Second Edition?

First, we changed the title from *iPhone Programming* to *iOS Programming*. As this change implies, the second edition includes more iPad-specific information. For instance, we've added new chapters on **UIPopovercontroller** and **UISplitViewController**, which exist only on the iPad.

Core Data has matured considerably since the first edition, so we decided a chapter on using SQLite directly was unnecessary. The Core Data chapter was moved earlier in the book to reflect its increased importance.

You'll find new chapters on push notifications and blocks. We've also added a chapter dedicated to the static analyzer and the Instruments profiling tool.

This edition assumes that the reader is using Xcode 4. For more information on getting Xcode 4, see the final section of this introduction.

Besides these obvious changes, we made thousands of tiny improvements that were inspired by questions from our readers and our students. Every page of this book is just a little better than the corresponding page from the first edition.

Our Teaching Philosophy

This book will teach you the essential concepts of iOS programming. At the same time, you'll type in a lot of code and build a bunch of applications. By the end of the book, you'll have knowledge *and* experience. However, all the knowledge shouldn't (and, in this book, won't) come first. That's sort of the traditional way we've all come to know and hate. Instead, we take a learn-while-doing approach. Development concepts and actual coding go together.

Here's what we've learned over the years of teaching iOS programming:

- We've learned what ideas people must have to get started programming, and we focus on that subset.

- We've learned that people learn best when these concepts are introduced *as they are needed*.

- We've learned that programming knowledge and experience grow best when they grow together.

- We've learned that "going through the motions" is much more important than it sounds. Many times we'll ask you to start typing in code before you understand it. We get that you may feel like a trained monkey typing in a bunch of code that you don't fully grasp. But the best way to learn coding is to find and fix your typos. Far from being a drag, this basic debugging is where you really learn the ins and outs of the code. That's why we encourage you to type in the code yourself. You could just download it, but copying and pasting is not programming. We want better for you and your skills.

What does this mean for you, the reader? To learn this way takes some trust. And we appreciate yours. It also takes patience. As we lead you through these chapters, we will try to keep you comfortable and tell you what's happening. However, there will be times when you'll have to take our word for it. (If you think this will bug you, keep reading – we've got some ideas that might help.) Don't get discouraged if you run across a concept that you don't understand right away. Remember that we're intentionally *not* providing all the knowledge you will ever need all at once. If a concept seems unclear, we will likely discuss it in more detail later when it becomes necessary. And some things that aren't clear at the beginning will suddenly make sense when you implement them the first (or the twelfth) time.

People learn differently. It's possible that you will love how we hand out concepts on an as-needed basis. It's also possible that you'll find it frustrating. In case of the latter, here are some options:

- Take a deep breath and wait it out. We'll get there, and so will you.

- Check the index. We'll let it slide if you look ahead and read through a more advanced discussion that occurs later in the book.

- Check the online Apple documentation. This is an essential developer tool, and you'll want plenty of practice using it. Consult it early and often.

- If it's Objective-C or object-oriented programming concepts that are giving you a hard time (or if you think they will), you might consider backing up and reading our *Objective-C Programming: The Big Nerd Ranch Guide*.

How To Use This Book

This book is based on the class we teach at Big Nerd Ranch. As such, it was designed to be consumed in a certain manner.

Set yourself a reasonable goal, like "I will do one chapter every day." When you sit down to attack a chapter, find a quiet place where you won't be interrupted for at least an hour. Shut down your email, your Twitter client, and your chat program. This is not a time for multi-tasking; you will need to concentrate.

Do the actual programming. You can read through a chapter first, if you'd like. But the real learning comes when you sit down and code as you go. You will not really understand the idea until you have written a program that uses it and, perhaps more importantly, debugged that program.

A couple of the exercises require supporting files. For example, in the first chapter you will need an icon for your Quiz application, and we have one for you. You can download the resources and solutions to the exercises from `http://www.bignerdranch.com/solutions/iOSProgramming.zip`.

There are two types of learning. When you learn about the Civil War, you are simply adding details to a scaffolding of ideas that you already understand. This is what we will call "Easy Learning". Yes, learning about the Civil War can take a long time, but you are seldom flummoxed by it. Learning iOS programming, on the other hand, is "Hard Learning," and you may find yourself quite baffled at times, especially in the first few days. In writing this book, we have tried to create an experience that will ease you over the bumps in the learning curve. Here are two things you can do to make the journey easier:

- Find someone who already knows how to write iOS applications and will answer your questions. In particular, getting your application onto the device the first time is usually very frustrating if you are doing it without the help of an experienced developer.

- Get enough sleep. Sleepy people don't remember what they have learned.

How This Book Is Organized

In this book, each chapter addresses one or more ideas of iOS development followed by hands-on practice. For more coding practice, we issue challenges towards the end of each chapter. We encourage you to take on at least some of these. They are excellent for firming up the concepts introduced in the chapter and making you a more confident iOS programmer. Finally, most chapters conclude with one or two "For the More Curious" sections that explain certain consequences of the concepts that were introduced earlier.

Chapter 1 introduces you to iOS programming as you build and deploy a tiny application. You'll get your feet wet with Xcode and the iOS simulator along with all the steps for creating projects and files. The chapter includes a discussion of Model-View-Controller and how it relates to iOS development.

Chapters 2 and 3 provide an overview of Objective-C and memory management. Although you won't create an iOS application in these two chapters, you will build and debug a tool called RandomPossessions to ground you in these concepts. (You will reuse this tool and its related class in the Homepwner application introduced in Chapter 10.)

In Chapters 4 and 5, you will learn about the Core Location and MapKit frameworks and create a mapping application called Whereami. You will also get plenty of experience with the important design pattern of delegation and working with protocols, frameworks, object diagrams, and the Apple documentation.

Chapters 6 and 7 focus on the iOS user interface with the Hypnosister and HypnoTime applications. You will get lots of practice working with views and view controllers as well as implementing scrolling, zooming, and navigating between screens using a tab bar.

Chapter 8 covers the accelerometer. You will learn how to obtain, filter, and use the data from the accelerometer to handle motion events, including shakes. You will use accelerometer data to add a new feature to the HypnoTime application.

In Chapter 9, you will create a smaller application named HeavyRotation while learning about notifications and how to implement autorotation in an application. You will also use autoresizing to make HeavyRotation iPad-friendly.

Chapter 10 introduces the largest application in the book – Homepwner. (By the way, "Homepwner" is not a typo; you can find the definition of "pwn" at www.urbandictionary.com.) This application keeps a record of your possessions in case of fire or other catastrophe. Homepwner will take nine chapters total to complete.

In Chapters 10, 11, and 16, you will build experience displaying lists of information. You will learn about table views, their view controllers, and their data sources. You will learn how to display data in a table, how to allow the user to edit the table, and how to improve the interface.

Chapter 12 builds on the navigation experience gained in Chapter 7. You will learn how to use **UINavigationController**, and you will give Homepwner a drill-down interface and a navigation bar.

In Chapter 13, you'll learn how to take pictures with the camera and how to display and store images in Homepwner. You'll use **NSDictionary** and **UIImagePickerController**.

In Chapter 14, you'll learn about **UIPopoverController** for the iPad and modal view controllers. In addition, you will make Homepwner a universal application – an application that runs natively on both the iPhone and the iPad.

Chapter 15 delves into ways to save and load data. In particular, you will archive data in the Homepwner application using the NSCoding protocol. The chapter also shows you how to work with multitasking and transitions between application states, such as active, background, and suspended.

Chapter 17 is an introduction to Core Data. You will change the Homepwner application to store and load its data using an **NSManagedObjectContext**.

Chapter 18 introduces the concepts and techniques of internationalization and localization. You will learn about **NSLocale**, strings tables, and **NSBundle** as you localize Homepwner. This chapter will complete the Homepwner app.

In Chapter 19, you will use **NSUserDefaults** to save user preferences in a persistent manner.

In Chapter 20, you'll create a drawing application named TouchTracker. You'll learn how to add multi-touch capability and more about touch events. You'll also get experience with the first responder and responder chain concepts and more practice with **NSDictionary**.

In Chapter 21, You'll learn about the Instruments application while debugging performance and memory issues in TouchTracker. It will also discuss Xcode schemes and the static analyzer.

Chapters 22 and 23 introduce layers and the Core Animation framework with a brief return to the HypnoTime application to implement animations. You will learn about implicit animations and animation objects, like **CABasicAnimation** and **CAKeyframeAnimation**.

Chapter 24 covers two important features of Objective-C: blocks and categories.

Chapter 25 ventures into the wide world of web services as you create the Nerdfeed application. This application fetches and parses an RSS feed from a server using **NSURLConnection** and **NSXMLParser**. Nerdfeed will also display a web page in a **UIWebView**.

In Chapter 26, you will learn about **UISplitViewController** and add a split view user interface to Nerdfeed to take advantage of the iPad's larger screen size.

Chapter 27 will show you how to play audio and video as you build an application called MediaPlayer. You will learn about playing audio and video, where to keep these resources, streaming limits, and the low-level audio API. You will also enable MediaPlayer to play music while in the background state and learn guidelines and other uses for background execution.

Chapter 28 includes building a Cocoa application for the Mac desktop. You will also write an iOS application that uses Bonjour to locate the desktop app on the network. Once the desktop application is located, you will talk to it via HTTP.

In Chapter 29, you'll extend the desktop app so that it can send push notifications to your iOS device.

Style Choices

This book contains a lot of code. We have attempted to make that code and the designs behind it exemplary. We have done our best to follow the idioms of the community, but at times we have wandered from what you might see in Apple's sample code or code you might find in other books. You may not understand these points now, but it is best that we spell them out before you commit to reading this book:

- There is an alternative syntax for calling accessor methods known as *dot-notation*. In this book, we will explain dot-notation, but we will not use it. For us and for most beginners, dot-notation tends to obfuscate what is really happening.

- In our subclasses of **UIViewController**, we always change the designated initializer to **init**. It is our opinion that the creator of the instance should not need to know the name of the XIB file that the view controller uses, or even if it has a XIB file at all.

- We will always create view controllers programmatically. Some programmers will instantiate view controllers inside XIB files. We've found this practice leads to projects that are difficult to comprehend and debug.

- We will nearly always start a project with the simplest template project: the window-based application. The boilerplate code in the other template projects doesn't follow the rules that precede this one, so we think they make a poor basis upon which to build.

We believe that following these rules makes our code easier to understand and easier to maintain. After you have worked through this book (where you *will* do it our way), you should try breaking the rules to see if we're wrong.

Typographical Conventions

To make this book easier to read, certain items appear in certain fonts. Class names, method names, and function names appear in a bold, fixed-width font. Class names start with capital letters, and method names start with lowercase letters. In this book, method and function names will be formatted the same for simplicity's sake. For example, "In the **loadView** method of the **RexViewController** class, use the **NSLog** function to print the value to the console."

Variables, constants, and types appear in a fixed-width font but are not bold. So you'll see, "The variable fido will be of type float. Initialize it to M_PI."

Applications and menu choices appear in the Mac system font. For example, "Open Xcode and select New Project... from the File menu."

All code blocks will be in a fixed-width font. Code that you need to type in is always bold. For example, in the following code, you would type in everything but the first and last lines. (Those lines are already in the code and appear here to let you know where to add the new stuff.)

```
@interface QuizAppDelegate : NSObject <UIApplicationDelegate> {
    int currentQuestionIndex;

    // The model objects
    NSMutableArray *questions;
    NSMutableArray *answers;

    // The view objects
    IBOutlet UILabel *questionField;
    IBOutlet UILabel *answerField;
    UIWindow *window;
}
```

Necessary Hardware and Software

You can only develop iOS apps on an Intel Mac. You will need to download Apple's iOS SDK, which includes Xcode (Apple's Integrated Development Environment), the iOS simulator, and other development tools.

You should join Apple's iOS Developer Program, which costs $99/year, for three reasons:

• Downloading the latest developer tools is free for members.

• Only signed apps will run on a device, and only members can sign apps. If you want to test your app on your device, you will need to join.

• You can't put an app in the store until you are a member.

If you are going to take the time to work through this entire book, membership in the iOS Developer Program is, without question, worth the cost. Go to http://developer.apple.com/programs/ios/ to join.

What about iOS devices? Most of the applications you will develop in the first half of the book are for the iPhone, but you will be able to run them on an iPad. On the iPad screen, iPhone applications appear in an iPhone-sized window. Not a compelling use of the iPad, but that's okay when you're starting with iOS. In these first chapters, you'll be focused on learning the fundamentals of the iOS SDK, and these are the same across iOS devices. Later in the book, we'll look at some iPad-only options and how to make applications run natively on both iOS device families.

Excited yet? Good. Let's get started.

1
A Simple iOS Application

In this chapter, you are going to write your first iOS application. You probably won't understand everything that you are doing, and you may feel stupid just going through the motions. But going through the motions is enough for now. Mimicry is a powerful form of learning; it is how you learned to speak, and it is how you'll start iOS programming. As you become more capable, you can experiment and challenge yourself to do creative things on the platform. For now, just do what we show you. The details will be explained in later chapters.

When you are writing an iOS application, you must answer two basic questions:

- How do I get my objects created and configured properly? (Example: "I want a button here entitled Show Estimate.")

- How do I deal with user interaction? (Example: "When the user presses the button, I want this piece of code to be executed.")

Most of this book is dedicated to answering these questions.

When an iOS application starts, it puts a *window* on the screen. You can think of the window as the background on which everything else appears: buttons, labels, etc. Anything that can appear on the window is a *view*.

The iOS SDK is an object-oriented library, and the window and views are represented by objects. The window is an instance of the class **UIWindow**. Each view is an instance of one of several subclasses of **UIView**. For example, a button is an instance of **UIButton**, which inherits from **UIView**.

There are two ways you can place a view on the window:

- programmatically create the view and add it to the **UIWindow**

- visually choose and position the view using the interface builder

For your first iOS application, you will visually place views on the window. This application, called Quiz, will show a user a question and then reveal the answer when the user presses a button. Pressing another button will show a new question (Figure 1.1).

Figure 1.1   Your first application: Quiz

Creating an Xcode Project

Open Xcode and, from the File menu, select New and then New Project....

A new workspace window will appear, and a sheet will slide from its toolbar with several application templates to choose from. On the lefthand side, select Application from the iOS section. From the choices that appear, select Window-based Application (the most basic template) and press the Next button (Figure 1.2).

Figure 1.2   Creating a new project

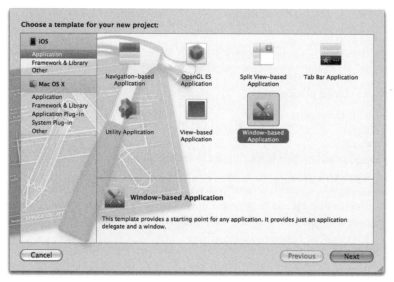

On the next pane (Figure 1.3), name this product Quiz. In the Company Identifier field, enter com.bignerdranch (or replace bignerdranch with your company name). From the pop-up menu labeled Device Family, select iPhone. Uncheck the two checkboxes and press Next.

Figure 1.3   Naming a new project

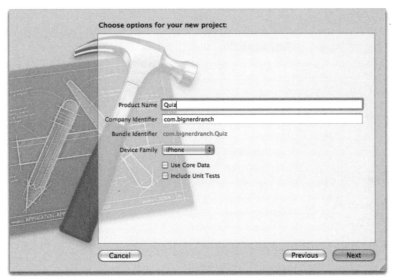

(Even though we're building this application for the iPhone, it will run on the iPad. It will run in an iPhone-sized window that does not make the most of the iPad screen, but that's okay for now. For the applications in the first half of this book, we will stick with the iPhone device family template. In these chapters, you'll be focused on learning the fundamentals of the iOS SDK, and these are the same across iOS devices. Later, we will look at some iPad-only options and how to make applications run natively on both iOS device families.)

Save the project in the directory where you plan to store all of the exercises in this book. (You can uncheck the box to create a local git repository, but it doesn't hurt anything to keep it on.)

Once the project is created, it will open in the Xcode workspace window (Figure 1.4). Take a look at the lefthand side of this window. This area is called the navigator area, and it displays different *navigators* – tools that show you different pieces of your project. You can choose which navigator to use by selecting one of the icons in the navigator selector, the bar just above the navigator area. The navigator currently open is the *project navigator*. (If the project navigator is not visible, click the 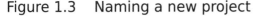 icon in the navigator selector.)

Figure 1.4   Xcode workspace window

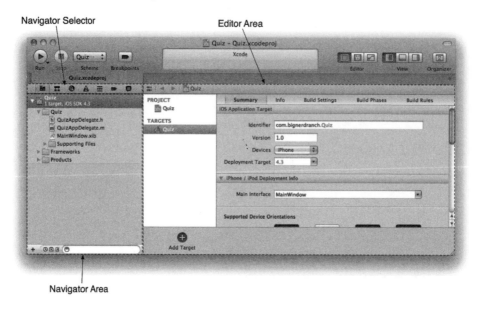

(Feeling overwhelmed by the number of buttons, views, and gadgets in the workspace? Don't worry – in this chapter, we'll cover a few in detail, and we'll cover others later as they are needed. In the meantime, you can mouse over any of the buttons to see a brief description of what it does.)

The project navigator shows you the files that make up your project (Figure 1.5). These files can be grouped into folders to help you organize your project. A few groups have been created by the template for you; you can rename them whatever you want or add new ones. The groups are purely for the organization of files and do not correlate to the filesystem in any way.

Figure 1.5   Quiz application's files in the project navigator

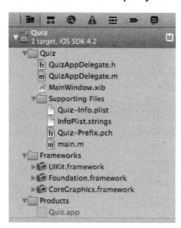

In the project navigator, find a file named MainWindow.xib. This file contains the interface for your Quiz application. Click on MainWindow.xib to open it in the editor area.

Building Interfaces

In many GUI builders on other platforms, you describe what you want an application to look like and then press a button to generate a bunch of code. Xcode's interface builder is different. It is an object editor: you create and configure objects, like windows, buttons, and labels, and then save them into an archive. The archive is a XIB (pronounced "zib") file.

A XIB file is an XML representation of the archived objects. When you build a project, the XIB file is compiled into a NIB file. Developers manipulate XIB files (they're easier to work with), and applications use NIB files (they're smaller and easier to parse). However, most iOS developers use the words XIB and NIB interchangeably.

When you build an application, the compiled NIB file is copied into the application's *bundle*. An iOS application is really a directory containing the executable and any resources the executable uses. We refer to this directory as the *bundle*. Then, when your application reads in the NIB file, the objects in the archive are brought to life. Your first application will have only one NIB file created from MainWindow.xib that is loaded when the application first launches. A complex application can have many NIB files that are read in as they are needed.

When you select a XIB file in the project navigator, the editor area displays an outline view and a canvas (Figure 1.6). The outline view is on the lefthand side of the editor area, and it shows the objects in the XIB file. You can shrink the outline view into a dock by clicking the disclosure button in the bottom left corner of the view. The dock shows fewer details and is useful when screen real estate is running low. However, for learning purposes, it is easier to see what is going on in the outline view.

Figure 1.6   Editing a XIB in Xcode

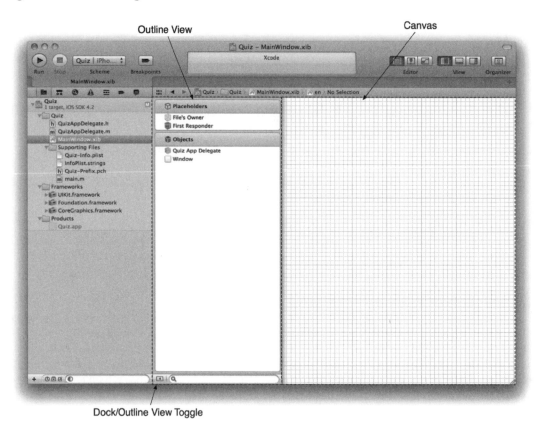

The outline view shows that `MainWindow.xib` contains four objects:

File's Owner

An instance of **UIApplication**. The event queue for your application is managed by this object.

First Responder

This object doesn't have much use in iOS right now; it is more of a relic from Desktop Cocoa. You can ignore it.

QuizAppDelegate

An instance of **QuizAppDelegate**, an object created by Xcode specifically for this project. You will be editing the source code for this class. (We'll talk more about classes and objects in Chapter 2.)

Window

An instance of **UIWindow** that represents the application's window.

The canvas portion of the editor area is for viewing and manipulating the layout of your interface. Click on the Window object in the outline view to display it on the canvas (Figure 1.7). You can move the window by dragging in the blue-shaded area around it. Note that moving the window doesn't change anything about it; it just re-organizes the canvas. You can also close the window by clicking on the x in its top left corner. Again, this doesn't delete the window; it just removes it from the canvas. You can get it back by selecting it again in the outline view.

Figure 1.7   Canvas with Window object displayed

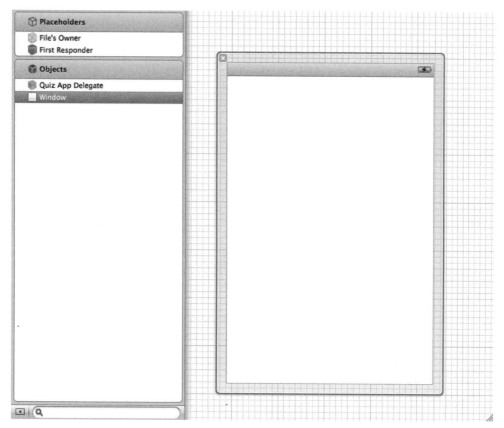

The window object in Figure 1.7 is the foundation of your user interface and appears exactly as it will in your application. Flip back to Figure 1.1, and you'll see that Quiz needs four additional interface elements: two text labels and two buttons.

To add these elements, you need to get to the *utilities area*. In the top-right corner of Xcode's toolbar, find the ▢▢▢ buttons labeled View. These buttons toggle the navigator, debug area, and utilities. Click the right button to show the utilities area (Figure 1.4).

The utilities area appears to the right of the editor area and has two sections: the *inspector* and the *library*. The top section is the inspector, which contains settings for the file that is currently displayed in the editor area. The bottom section is the library, which lists items you can add to a file or project. You can change the relative sizes of these sections by dragging the line between them.

At the top of each section is a selector for different types of inspectors and libraries (Figure 1.8). From the library selector, select the 🔘 icon to reveal the *object library*. This library contains the objects you can add to a XIB file.

Figure 1.8   Xcode utilities area

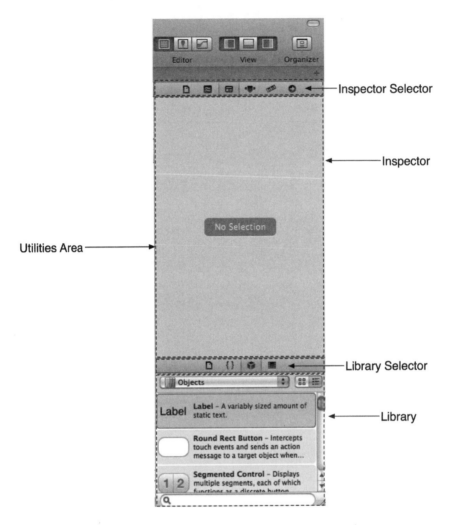

Scroll down the list or use the search bar at the bottom of the library to find Label. Then select the label and drag it onto the window object on the canvas. Position this label in the center of the window, near the top. Drag another label onto the window and position it in the center closer to the bottom. Then find Round Rect Button in the library and drag two buttons onto the window. Position one below each label. You can resize an object by selecting it and then dragging its corners and edges. Make all four objects wide enough that they span most of the window.

Now let's give the buttons helpful titles. You can edit the title of a button simply by double-clicking it. Change the top button to Show Question and the bottom button to Show Answer. You can edit the text of a label the same way; leave the top label blank and have the bottom label display ???. Your window should look like the one in Figure 1.9.

Figure 1.9   Adding buttons and labels to the window

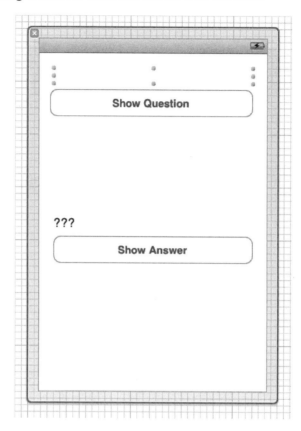

The labels and buttons are objects (of type **UILabel** and **UIButton**), and objects have instance variables that specify their behavior and appearance. For example, when you entered a title for the top button, you set that button's `title` instance variable. You can edit a few of these instance variables directly on the canvas, but most must be edited in the utilities area. For example, labels have a `textAlignment` instance variable. The default is left-aligned, but we want this text to be centered. Select the bottom label and then click the 🖝 icon in the inspector selector.

This inspector is the *attributes inspector*, and here you can set the instance variables of the selected object. Near the top of this inspector is a segmented control for alignment. Select the centered text option, as shown in Figure 1.10.

Figure 1.10   Centering the label text

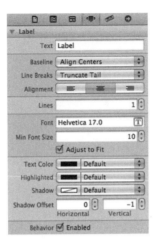

Notice the ??? is now centered in the bottom label. Now center the text in the top label. (There's no text now, but there will be in the running application.)

Your application's interface now looks like it should, but before we start writing code, let's dive into some programming theory.

Model-View-Controller

You may hear iOS programmers mention the Model-View-Controller pattern. What this means is every object you create is exactly one of the following: a model object, a view object, or a controller object.

View objects are visible to the user. In Quiz, the buttons, labels, and window are all view objects. Views are usually standard **UIView** subclasses (**UIButton**, **UISlider**), but you will sometimes write custom view classes. These typically have names like **DangerMeterView** or **IncomeGraphView**.

Model objects hold data and know nothing about the user interface. In this application, the model objects will be two arrays of strings: the questions array and the answers array. Figure 1.11 displays the object diagram of the Quiz application's model objects.

Figure 1.11   Diagram of model objects in Quiz

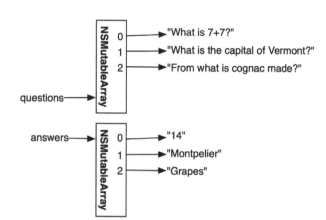

Model objects typically use standard collection classes (**NSArray**, **NSDictionary**, **NSSet**) and standard value types (**NSString**, **NSDate**, **NSNumber**). But there can be custom classes, which typically have names that sound like data-bearing objects, such as **InsurancePolicy** or **PlayerHistory**.

View and model objects are the factory workers of an application – they focus only on performing specific tasks. For example, an instance of **UILabel** (a view object) knows how to display text in a given font within a given rectangle. An **NSString** instance (a model object) knows how to store a character string. But the label doesn't know *what* text to display, and the string doesn't know *what* characters to store.

This is where *controller objects* come in. Controllers are the managers in an application. They keep the view and model objects in sync, control the "flow" of the application, and save the model objects out to the filesystem (Figure 1.12). Controllers are the least reusable classes that you will write, and they tend to have names like **ScheduleController** and **ScoreViewController**.

Figure 1.12   MVC Pattern

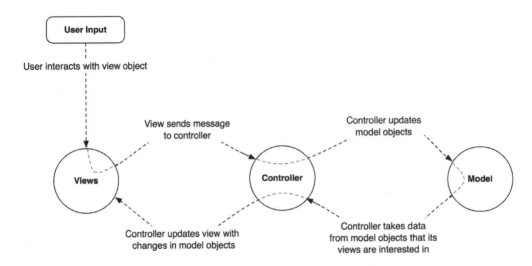

When you create a new iOS project from a template, the template automatically makes a controller object for you. For Quiz, this controller is the **QuizAppDelegate**. Most applications have more than one controller object, but a simple application like Quiz only needs one.

One of the **QuizAppDelegate**'s tasks will be showing the user a new question when the Show Question button is tapped. Tapping this button will trigger a method in the **QuizAppDelegate**. This method will retrieve a new question from an array of questions and place that question in one of the labels. These interactions are laid out in the object diagram for Quiz (Figure 1.13).

Figure 1.13   Object diagram for Quiz

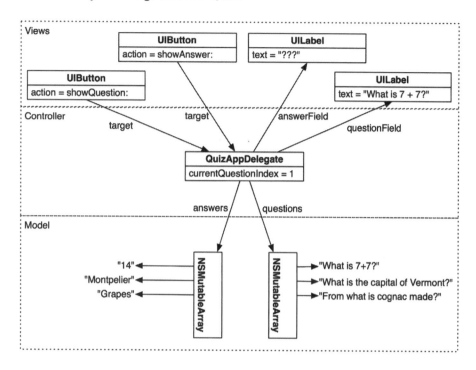

This diagram is the big picture of Quiz. It's okay if it doesn't make perfect sense yet; it will make more by the end of the chapter. We'll talk about object diagrams again in Chapter 5.

Declarations

To manage its relationships and responsibilities, **QuizAppDelegate** needs five instance variables and two methods. In this section, you will declare these in the **QuizAppDelegate** header file, QuizAppDelegate.h.

Declaring instance variables

Here are the five instance variables **QuizAppDelegate** needs:

questions	a pointer to an **NSMutableArray** containing instances of **NSString**
answers	a pointer to another **NSMutableArray** containing instances of **NSString**
currentQuestionIndex	an int that holds the index of the current question in the questions array
questionField	a pointer to the **UILabel** object where the current question will be displayed

answerField   a pointer to the **UILabel** object where the current answer will be
                                           displayed

In the project navigator, select QuizAppDelegate.h. Inside the curly braces, add the following
declarations for the five instance variables. (Notice the bold type? In this book, code that you need to
add is always bold; the code that's not bold is there to tell you where to type in the new stuff.)

```
@interface QuizAppDelegate : NSObject <UIApplicationDelegate>

{
    int currentQuestionIndex;

    // The model objects
    NSMutableArray *questions;
    NSMutableArray *answers;

    // The view objects - don't worry about this IBOutlet macro,
    // we'll talk about it shortly
    IBOutlet UILabel *questionField;
    IBOutlet UILabel *answerField;
}
@property (nonatomic, retain) IBOutlet UIWindow *window;

@end
```

(Scary syntax? Feelings of dismay? Don't panic – you will learn more about the Objective-C language
in the next chapter. For now, just keep going.)

Declaring methods

Each of the buttons needs to trigger a method in the **QuizAppDelegate**. A method is a lot like a
function – a list of instructions to be executed. Declare two methods in QuizAppDelegate.h after the
line that starts with @property. (We will explain @property in Chapter 3; you can ignore it for now.)

```
@interface QuizAppDelegate : NSObject <UIApplicationDelegate>
{
    int currentQuestionIndex;

    // The model objects
    NSMutableArray *questions;
    NSMutableArray *answers;

    // The view objects
    IBOutlet UILabel *questionField;
    IBOutlet UILabel *answerField;
}
@property (nonatomic, retain) IBOutlet UIWindow *window;

- (IBAction)showQuestion:(id)sender;
- (IBAction)showAnswer:(id)sender;

@end
```

Save QuizAppDelegate.h.

What do IBOutlet and IBAction do in the declarations you just entered? They allow you to connect
your controller and view objects in the XIB file.

Making Connections

When the Quiz application loads its interface from MainWindow.xib, the objects that make up the interface are floating around in memory. The **QuizAppDelegate** (a controller object) needs to know where the labels (view objects) are in memory so that it can tell them what to display. The buttons (view objects that the user interacts with) need to know where the **QuizAppDelegate** is so that they can report when they are tapped. Your objects need *connections*. A connection lets an object know where another object is in memory.

Figure 1.14 shows the connections for Quiz. Some have already been made by the template (between the window outlet of **QuizAppDelegate** and the **UIWindow** instance, for example), and some were made implicitly (dragging a view object onto the window sets up a connection between the view and the window). However, you still have a few more connections to make to get your objects communicating properly.

Figure 1.14   Current connections and needed connections

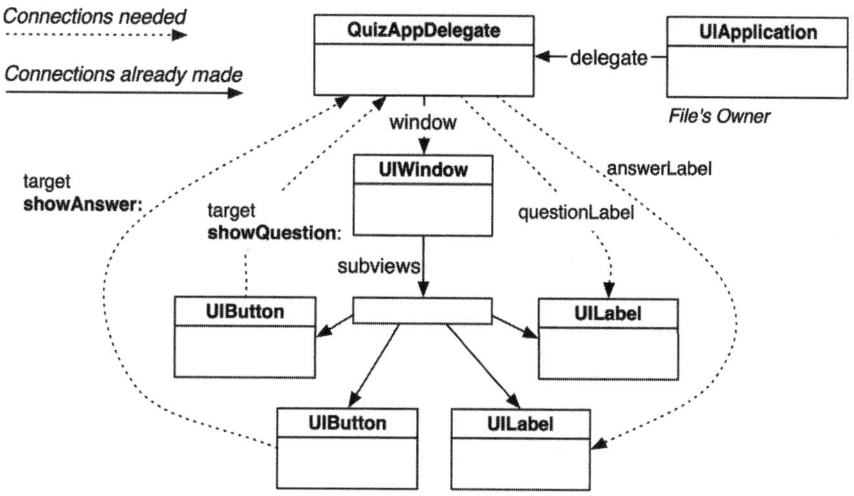

Here are the missing connections:

- **QuizAppDelegate**, the controller object, must have pointers to the **UILabel** instances so it can tell them what to display.

- The **UIButton** instances must have pointers to the **QuizAppDelegate** so they can send messages to the controller when tapped.

Setting pointers

Let's start with the connections to the **UILabel** instances. The instance of **QuizAppDelegate** has a pointer called questionField. You want questionField to point to the instance of **UILabel** at the top of the window. In MainWindow.xib, right-click or Control-click on the **QuizAppDelegate** in the outline view to bring up the connections panel (Figure 1.15). Then drag from the circle beside questionField to the **UILabel**.

Figure 1.15   Setting questionField

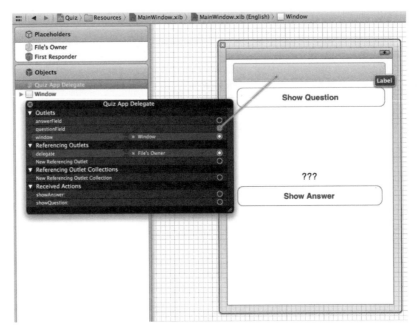

(If you do not see questionField here, double-check your QuizAppDelegate.h file for typos. Did you end each line with a semicolon? Have you saved the file since you added questionField?)

When the XIB file is loaded (for MainWindow.xib, this is when the application launches), the **QuizAppDelegate**'s questionField pointer will now automatically point to this instance of **UILabel**.

Next, drag from the circle beside answerField to the other **UILabel** (Figure 1.16).

Figure 1.16   Setting answerField

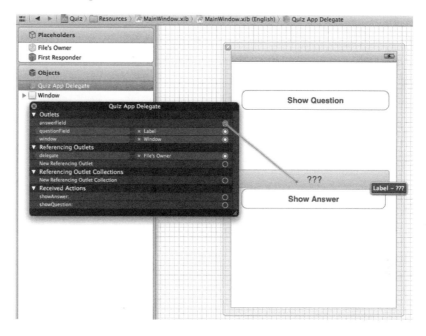

Notice that you drag *from* the object with the pointer *to* the object that you want that pointer to point at. Also, notice that the pointers that appear in the connections panel are the ones that have been decorated with IBOutlet in QuizAppDelegate.h.

Setting targets and actions

When a **UIButton** is tapped, it sends a message to another object. The object that is sent the message is called the *target*. The message is called the *action*, and it is the name of the method that tapping the button should trigger. So the button needs answers to two questions: "Who's the target?" and "What's the action?" For the Show Question button, the target should be **QuizAppDelegate**, and the action should be **showQuestion:**.

To set an object's target and action, you Control-drag from the object to its target. When you release the mouse, the target is set, and a pop-up menu appears that lets you choose the action. Select the Show Question button and Control-drag (or right-drag) to the **QuizAppDelegate**. Once **QuizAppDelegate** is highlighted, release the mouse button and choose **showQuestion:** from the pop-up menu, as shown in Figure 1.17. Notice that the choices in this menu are the methods you decorated with IBAction in QuizAppDelegate.h.

Figure 1.17   Setting Show Question target/action

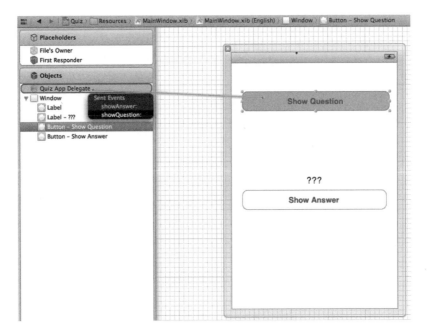

Now set the target and action of the Show Answer button. Control-drag from the button to the QuizAppDelegate and choose showAnswer: from the pop-up menu (Figure 1.18).

Figure 1.18   Setting Show Answer target/action

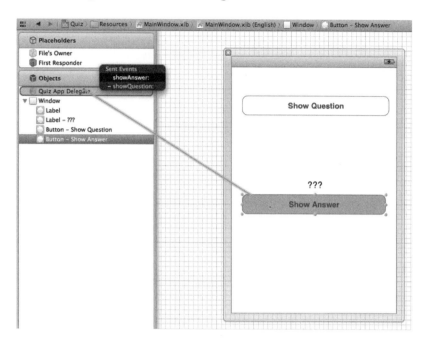

Summary of connections

There are now six connections between your **QuizAppDelegate** and other objects. You've set its pointers answerField and questionField to point at the labels. That's two. The **QuizAppDelegate** is the target for both buttons. That's four. The project's template made two additional connections. First, the **UIApplication** object (File's Owner in this XIB file) has a pointer called delegate which points at the **QuizAppDelegate**; we'll discuss this somewhat complex relationship in Chapter 4. Second, the window pointer of your **QuizAppDelegate** was set to the instance of **UIWindow**. That makes six.

You can check these connections in the *connections inspector*. Select the **QuizAppDelegate** in the outline view and then click the ⊙ icon in the inspector selector to reveal the connections inspector in the utilities area. (Figure 1.19).

Figure 1.19   Checking connections in the Inspector

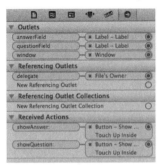

Your XIB file is complete. The view objects and the one controller object have been created, the views have been configured, and all the necessary connections have been made. Save your XIB file, and let's move on to writing the methods.

Implementing Methods

Methods and instance variables are declared in the header file (in this case, `QuizAppDelegate.h`), but the actual code for the methods is placed in the implementation file (in this case, `QuizAppDelegate.m`). Select `QuizAppDelegate.m` from the project navigator and type in the following **init** method. This method creates two arrays and fills them with questions and answers.

```
@implementation QuizAppDelegate

- (id)init
{
    // Call the init method implemented by the superclass
    self = [super init];
    if(self) {
        // Create two arrays and make the pointers point to them
        questions = [[NSMutableArray alloc] init];
        answers = [[NSMutableArray alloc] init];

        // Add questions and answers to the arrays
        [questions addObject:@"What is 7 + 7?"];
        [answers addObject:@"14"];

        [questions addObject:@"What is the capital of Vermont?"];
        [answers addObject:@"Montpelier"];

        [questions addObject:@"From what is cognac made?"];
        [answers addObject:@"Grapes"];
    }

    // Return the address of the new object
    return self;
}
```

In the declarations in `QuizAppDelegate.h`, neither `questions` or `answers` is labeled `IBOutlet`. The objects that `questions` and `answers` point to are created and configured programmatically in the code above instead of by the XIB file.

After the **init** method, add the two action methods.

```
- (IBAction)showQuestion:(id)sender
{
    // Step to the next question
    currentQuestionIndex++;

    // Am I past the last question?
    if (currentQuestionIndex == [questions count]) {

        // Go back to the first question
        currentQuestionIndex = 0;
    }

    // Get the string at that index in the questions array
    NSString *question = [questions objectAtIndex:currentQuestionIndex];

    // Log the string to the console
    NSLog(@"displaying question: %@", question);

    // Display the string in the question field
    [questionField setText:question];

    // Clear the answer field
    [answerField setText:@"???"];
}
- (IBAction)showAnswer:(id)sender
{
    // What is the answer to the current question?
    NSString *answer = [answers objectAtIndex:currentQuestionIndex];

    // Display it in the answer field
    [answerField setText:answer];
}
```

You will use the default implementations for the rest of the methods, so leave them alone.

Flip back to Figure 1.13. This diagram should make a bit more sense now that you have created all of the objects and connected them in the XIB file.

Build and Run on the Simulator

Now you are ready to build the application and run it on the simulator. You can click the iTunes-esque play button in the top left corner of the workspace, but you'll be doing this often enough that it's easier to remember and use the keyboard shortcut, Command-R. Either way, make sure that the Simulator option is selected in the pop-up menu next to the play button (Figure 1.20).

Figure 1.20   Running the application

If there are any errors or warnings, you can view them in the *issue navigator* by selecting the ▲ icon in the navigator selector (Figure 1.21). The keyboard shortcut for the issue navigator is Command-4. In fact, the shortcut for any navigator is Command plus the navigator's position in the selector. For example, the project navigator is Command-1.

Figure 1.21   Issue navigator with errors and warnings

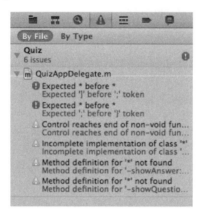

You can click on any issue in the issue navigator, and it will take you to the source file and the line of code where the issue occurred. Find and fix any issues you have (i.e., code typos!) by comparing your code with the book's and then build the application again. Repeat this process until your application compiles.

Once your application has compiled, it will launch in the iOS simulator. But before you play with it, you'll want the console visible so that you can see the output of the log statements. To see the console, reveal the *debug area* by clicking the middle button in the ⬛⬛⬛ group at the top right of the workspace window.

The console is on the righthand side of the debug area, and the variables view is on the left. You can toggle these panels on and off with the ⬛⬛⬛ control in the top-right corner of the debug area. You can also resize the area and its panels by dragging their frames (Figure 1.22).

Figure 1.22   Debug area expanded

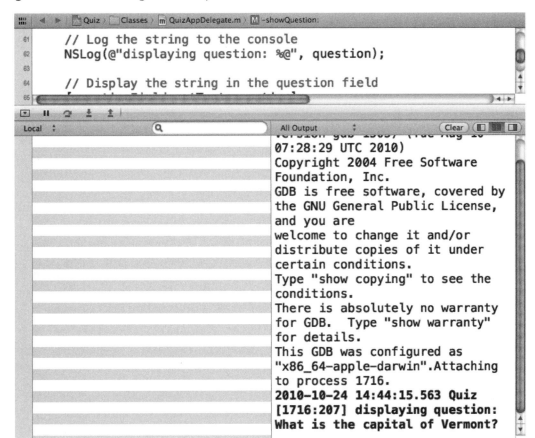

Play around with the Quiz application. You should be able to tap the Show Question button and see a new question in the top label; tapping Show Answer should show the right answer. If your application isn't working as expected, double-check your connections in MainWindow.xib and check the console output when you tap the buttons.

Deploying an Application

Now that you've written your first iOS application and run it on the simulator, it's time to deploy it to a device.

To install an application on your development device, you need a developer certificate from Apple. Developer certificates are issued to registered iOS Developers who have paid the developer fee. This certificate grants you the ability to sign your code, which allows it to run on a device. Without a valid certificate, devices will not run your application.

Apple's Developer Program Portal (http://developer.apple.com) contains all the instructions and resources to get a valid certificate. The interface for the set-up process is continually being updated by

Apple, so it is fruitless to describe it in detail. Instead, use the Development Provisioning Assistant, a step-by-step guide available on the program portal.

Work through the Development Provisioning Assistant, *paying careful attention to each screen.* At the end, you will have added the required certificates to Keychain Access and the provisioning profile to Xcode.

If you're curious about what exactly is going on here, there are four important items in the provisioning process:

Developer Certificate	This certificate file is added to your Mac's keychain using Keychain Access. It is used to digitally sign your code.
App ID	The application identifier is a string that uniquely identifies your application on the App Store. Application identifiers typically look like this: `com.bignerdranch.AwesomeApp`, where the name of the application follows the name of your company.
	The App ID in your provisioning profile must match the *bundle identifier* of your application. A development profile, like you just created, will have a wildcard character (*) for its App ID and therefore will match any bundle identifier. To see the bundle identifier for the Quiz application, select the project in the project navigator. Then select the Quiz target and the Summary pane.
Device ID (UDID)	This identifier is unique for each iOS device.
Provisioning Profile	This is a file that lives on your development device and on your computer. It references a Developer Certificate, a single App ID, and a list of the device IDs for the devices that the application can be installed on. This file is suffixed with `.mobileprovision`.

When an application is deployed to a device, Xcode uses a provisioning profile on your computer to access the appropriate certificate. This certificate is used to sign the application binary. Then, the development device's UDID is matched to one of the UDIDs contained within the provisioning profile, and the App ID is matched to the bundle identifier. The signed binary is then sent to your development device where it is confirmed by the same provisioning profile on the device and finally launched.

Open Xcode and plug your development device (iPhone, iPod touch, or iPad) into your computer. This will automatically open the Organizer window, which you can re-open by clicking the ▣ button from the top right corner of the workspace. You can select Devices from the top of the Organizer window to view all of the provisioning information.

To run the Quiz application on your device, you must tell Xcode to deploy to the device instead of the simulator. Locate the pop-up button named Scheme in the top left of the workspace window. Choose iOS Device from the list. (If iOS Device is not an option, find the choice that reads something like "Joe Conway's iPad.") Build and run your application (Command-R), and it will appear on your device.

Application Icons

Once the Quiz application is installed on your development device, return to the device's Home screen, and you'll see that its icon is a plain white tile. Let's give Quiz a better icon.

An *application icon* is a simple image that represents the application on the iOS desktop. Different devices require different sizes icons, and these requirements are shown in Table 1.1.

Table 1.1. Application icon sizes by device

Device	Application icon size
iPhone/iPod touch without Retina display	57x57 pixels
iPhone/iPod touch with Retina display	114x114 pixels
iPad	72x72 pixels

If you supply a single application icon image at 57x57 pixels, that image will be scaled up on devices where a larger icon is needed. This is never good. A scaled-up icon will be pixellated and scream, "We're amateurs!" to your customers. Therefore, any application you deploy to the App Store should have an icon for every device class on which it can run.

We have prepared two icon image files (sizes 57x57 and 114x114) for the Quiz application. You can download these icons (along with resources for other chapters) from http://www.bignerdranch.com/solutions/iOSProgramming.zip. Unzip iOSProgramming.zip and find the Icon.png and the Icon@2x.png files in the Resources directory of the unzipped folder. (If you open these images, you'll see that they aren't glossy and don't have rounded corners like other application icons. These effects are applied for you by the OS.)

Now you're going to add these icons to your application bundle as *resources*. In general, there are two kinds of files in an application: code and resources. Code is used to create the application itself (like QuizAppDelegate.h and QuizAppDelegate.m). Resources are things like images and sounds that are used by the application at runtime. XIB files, which are read in at runtime, are also resources.

In the project navigator, select the Quiz project, which is at the top of the list and slightly shaded. Then, in the editor area, select Quiz from under the Targets heading. Finally, select Summary from the top of the editor area (Figure 1.23).

Figure 1.23   Adding the smaller icon in the Summary panel

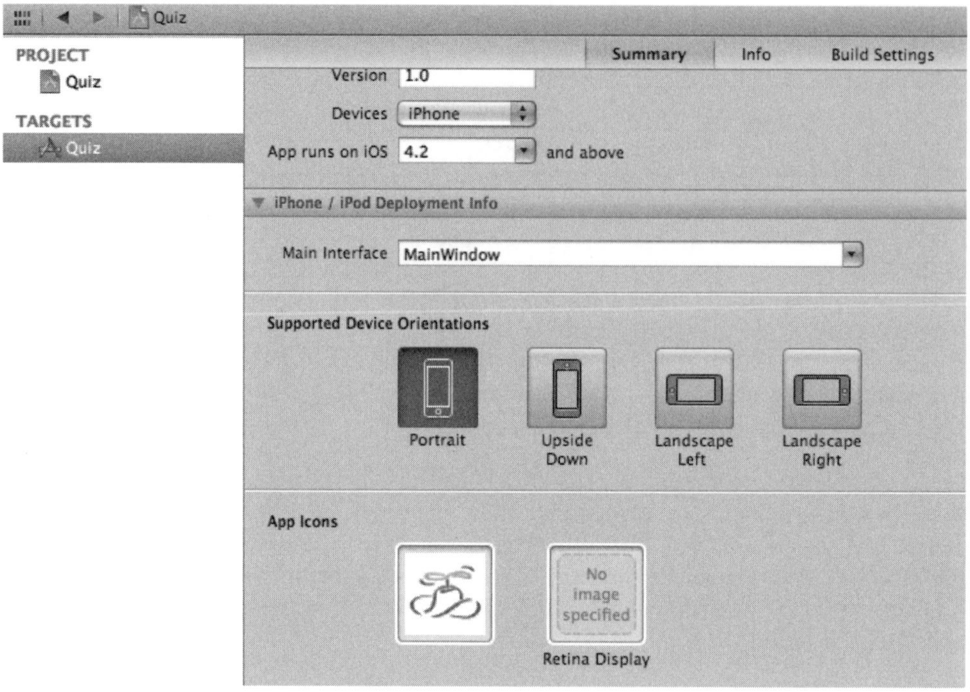

This panel is where you can set a number of options for the application, including its icon. Drag the Icon.png file from Finder onto the tile in the App Icons section. A drop-down sheet will appear. You'll see this sheet any time you add a file to a project (Figure 1.24).

Figure 1.24   Adding a resource to a project

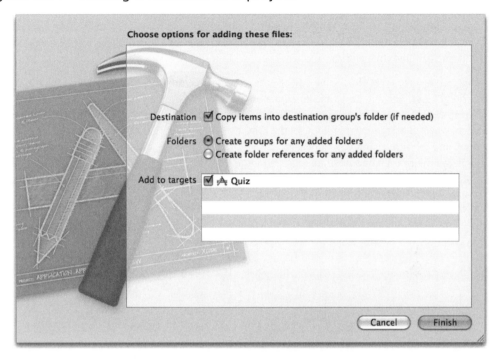

The first check box asks if you want to copy this file into your project's directory on the filesystem. Make sure this box is checked to keep all the files for this project in a single directory. You can ignore the Folders section because you are only adding a single file. Also make sure the Quiz target is checked. This specifies to the project to include this file in the application bundle on building. Click Finish.

Next, drag the Icon@2x.png file from Finder onto the tile labeled Retina Display. (Note that there isn't a tile here for the iPad because Quiz is an iPhone application.)

Build and run the application again. After you exit the application, you should see the Quiz application with the BNR logo.

When you dragged the image files onto the icon tiles, two things happened. First, the image files were added to your project. (You can verify this by returning to the project navigator, where you'll find Icon.png and Icon@2x.png in the list of files.) Second, two entries were made in the Quiz-Info.plist file. When you add an icon, the Icon files value is updated with the names of the files you added. You can verify this by selecting Quiz-Info.plist and viewing it in the editor area. You can also select the Info item next to Summary to see the same information.

Launch Images

Another item you can set for an application in the Summary panel is the *launch image*, which appears while an application is loading. (If you don't supply a launch image, the user will see a black screen during this period.) The launch image has a specific role on iOS: it conveys to the user that the application is indeed launching and depicts the user interface that the user will interact with once the application has finished launching. Therefore, a good launch image is a content-less screenshot of the application. For example, the Weather application's interface is a rounded square with the name of a city and its current temperature; Weather's launch image is just that rounded square. (Keep in mind that the launch image is replaced when the application puts its window onto the screen; it does not become the background image of the application.)

Xcode can grab a screenshot from your device, and you can use this screenshot as the launch image for Quiz. To get a screenshot, build and run Quiz on a device. Open the Organizer window in Xcode and locate your device from the device list. (It will be the one with a green dot next to it.) Underneath your device, select the Screenshots item. In the bottom righthand corner of the editor area, click New Screenshot, and the screenshot will appear in the editor area. You can either drag this image onto the Launch Images tile or click the Save as Launch Image button at the bottom of the Organizer window (Figure 1.25). (For most applications, you will first have to edit the screenshot in an image-editing application to get the right look.)

Figure 1.25   Taking a screenshot with Xcode

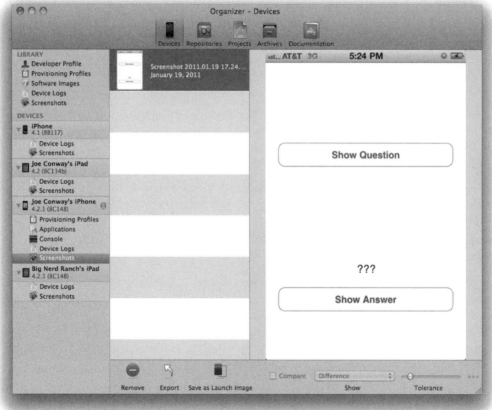

Build and run the application. As the application launches, you will briefly see the launch image.

A launch image must fit the screen of the device it is being launched on. Table 1.2 shows the different size images you will need for each type of device.

Table 1.2. Launch image sizes by device

Device	Launch image size
iPhone/iPod touch without Retina display	320x480 pixels
iPhone/iPod touch with Retina display	640x960 pixels
iPad	1024x768 pixels

(Note that Table 1.2 lists the screen resolutions of the devices; the real status bar is overlaid on top of the status bar in the launch image.)

Just like with application icons, there are tiles for different-sized images to support different devices. And also, just like with icons, if you provide only one image, that image will be scaled to fit the device's screen. So provide an image for every possible device.

One thing the launch image should *not* do is display a splash screen for your company or application. While many applications (especially games) use splash screens as launch images, here is the argument against it: the amount of time it takes to load any application depends on the hardware it is running on. Right now, iOS devices aren't very powerful, and a large application may take a few seconds to load. This gives the user ample time to ingest the launch image. However, as iOS devices become more powerful, that launch image may only appear for a fraction of a second. This would appear as a disconcerting flash to users, and they would wonder, "Have I pressed something wrong? How do I go back to that screen?" There are infinite ways of expressing your creativity on the platform from within an application – the launch image isn't one of them.

Congratulations! You have written your first application and installed it on your device. Now it is time to dive into the big ideas that make it work.

2

Objective-C

iOS applications are written in the Objective-C language using the Cocoa Touch library. Objective-C is a simple extension of the C language and Cocoa Touch is a collection of Objective-C classes. This book assumes you know some C and understand the ideas of object-oriented programming. If C or object-oriented programming makes you feel uneasy, we recommend starting with *Objective-C Programming: The Big Nerd Ranch Guide*.

In this chapter, you will learn the basics of Objective-C and create a command line tool called RandomPossessions. You'll reuse parts of this tool in an iOS application starting in Chapter 10, so even if you're familiar with Objective-C, you should still go through this chapter in order to create RandomPossessions.

Objects

Let's say you need a way to represent a party. Your party has a few attributes that are unique to it, like a name, a date, and a list of invitees. You can also ask the party to do things like send an email reminder to all the invitees, print name tags, or cancel the party altogether.

In C, you would define a *structure* to hold the data that describes a party. The structure would have data members – one for each of the party's attributes. Each data member would have a name and a type.

To create an individual party, you would use the function `malloc` to allocate a chunk of memory large enough to hold the structure. You would write C functions to set the value of its attributes and have it perform actions.

In Objective-C, instead of using a structure to represent a party, you use a *class*. A class is like a cookie-cutter that produces objects. The `Party` class creates objects, and these objects are instances of the `Party` class. Each instance of the `Party` class can hold the data for a single party (Figure 2.1).

Figure 2.1   A class and its instances

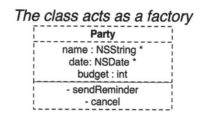

An instance of **Party**, like all objects, is a chunk of data stored in memory, and it stores the values for its attributes in *instance variables*. So an instance of **Party** might have the following instance variables: name, date, budget.

A C structure is a chunk of memory, and so is an object. A C structure has data members, each with a name and a type. Similarly, an object has instance variables, each with a name and a type.

But there is an important difference between a structure in C and a class in Objective-C – a class has *methods*. A method is similar to a function: it has a name, a return type, and a list of parameters that it expects. A method also has access to an object's instance variables. If you want an object to run the code in one of its methods, you send that object a *message*.

Using Instances

An instance of a class (an object) has a life span: it is created, sent messages, and then destroyed when it is no longer needed.

Creating objects

To create an object, you send an **alloc** message to a class. In response, that class creates an object in memory and gives you a pointer to it. Creating an object looks like this:

```
NSMutableArray *arrayInstance = [NSMutableArray alloc];
```

Here an instance of type **NSMutableArray** is created, and you are returned a pointer to it in the variable arrayInstance. When you have a pointer to an instance, you can send messages to it. The first message you *always* send to a newly allocated instance is an initialization message. Although sending an **alloc** message to a class creates an instance, the instance isn't valid until it has been initialized.

```
[arrayInstance init];
```

Because an object must be allocated *and* initialized before it can be used, we always combine these two messages in one line.

```
NSMutableArray *arrayInstance = [[NSMutableArray alloc] init];
```

The code to the right of the assignment operator (=) says, "Create an instance of **NSMutableArray** and send it the message **init**." Both **alloc** and **init** return a pointer to the newly created object so that you have a reference to it. (A pointer holds the location of an object in memory, not the object itself. It "points to" the object.) Typically, you use the assignment operator to store the pointer in a variable.

Combining two messages in a single line of code is called a *nested message send*. The innermost brackets are evaluated first, so the message **alloc** is sent to the class **NSMutableArray** first. This returns a new, uninitialized instance of **NSMutableArray** that is then sent the message **init**.

Sending messages

What do you do with an instance that has been initialized? You send it more messages.

Let's take a closer look at message anatomy. First of all, a message is always contained in square brackets. Within a pair of square brackets, a message has three parts:

receiver   a pointer to the object being asked to execute a method

selector   the name of the method to be executed

arguments   the values to be supplied as the parameters to the method

One such message you can send an **NSMutableArray** instance is **addObject:**

```
[arrayInstance addObject:anotherObject];
```

Sending the **addObject:** message to arrayInstance (the receiver) triggers the **addObject:** method (named by the selector) and passes in anotherObject (an argument).

The **addObject:** message has only one argument, but Objective-C methods can take a number of arguments or none at all. The message **init**, for instance, has no arguments.

Another message you can send an **NSMutableArray** instance is **replaceObjectsInRange:withObjectsFromArray:range:**. This message takes three arguments. Each argument is paired with a label in the selector, and each label ends with a colon. The selector is all of the labels taken together (Figure 2.2).

Figure 2.2   Parts of a message send

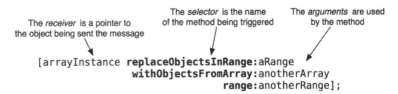

This pairing of labels and arguments is an important feature of Objective-C. In other languages, this method would look like this:

```
arrayInstance.replaceObjectsInRangeWithObjectsFromArrayRange(aRange,
                                                             anotherArray,
                                                             anotherRange);
```

In these languages, it isn't completely obvious what each of the arguments sent to this function are. In Objective-C, however, each argument is paired with the appropriate label.

```
[arrayInstance replaceObjectsInRange:aRange
                withObjectsFromArray:anotherArray
                               range:anotherRange];
```

It takes some getting used to, but eventually, Objective-C programmers appreciate the clarity of arguments being interposed into the selector. The trick is to remember that for every pair of square brackets, there is only one message being sent. Even though **replaceObjectsInRange:withObjectsFromArray:range:** has three labels, it is still only one message, and sending that message results in only one method being executed.

Notice the distinction being made between a *message* and a *method*: a method is a chunk of code that can be executed and a message is the act of asking a class or object to execute a method. However, the name of a message always matches the name of the method to be executed.

In Objective-C, the name of a method is what makes it unique. Therefore, a class cannot have two methods with the same name and different types for their arguments or return type. However, two methods can have the same individual labels, as long as the name of each method differs when taken as a whole. For example, the class **NSString** has two methods **rangeOfString:options:** and **rangeOfString:options:range:**.

Destroying objects

To destroy an object, you send it the message **release**.

```
[arrayInstance release];
```

This line of code destroys the object pointed to by the arrayInstance variable. (It's actually a bit more complicated than that, and you'll learn about the details of memory management in the next chapter.) It is important to note that although you destroyed the object, the variable arrayInstance still has a value – the address of where the **NSMutableArray** instance used to exist. If you send a message to arrayInstance now, it will cause a problem because that object no longer exists.

However, if arrayInstance is set to nil, the problem goes away. (nil is the zero pointer. C programmers know it as NULL. Java programmers know it as null.)

```
arrayInstance = nil;
```

Now there is no danger of sending a message to the outdated memory address. Sending a message to nil is okay in Objective-C – nothing happens. In a language like Java, sending messages to nil is illegal, so you see this sort of thing a lot:

```
if (rover != nil) {
    [rover doSomething];
}
```

In Objective-C, this check is unnecessary because a message sent to nil is ignored. (A corollary: if your program isn't doing anything when you think it should be doing something, an unexpected nil pointer is often the culprit.)

Writing the RandomPossessions Tool

Before you dive into the UIKit, the set of libraries for creating iOS applications, you're going to write a command line tool that will let you focus on the Objective-C language. Open Xcode and select File → New → New Project.... In the lefthand table in the Mac OS X section, click Application and then select Command Line Tool from the upper panel, as shown in Figure 2.3. Click the Next button.

Figure 2.3   Creating a command line tool

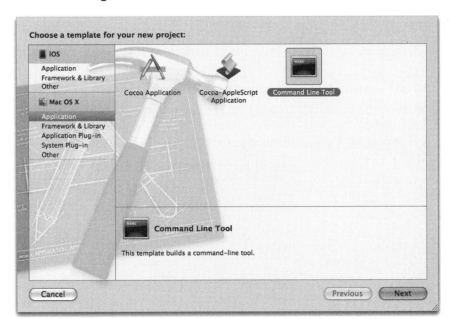

On the next panel, name the product RandomPossessions and choose Foundation as its type (Figure 2.4). Click Next, and you will be prompted to save the project. Save it some place safe – you will be reusing parts of this code in future projects.

Figure 2.4   Naming the project

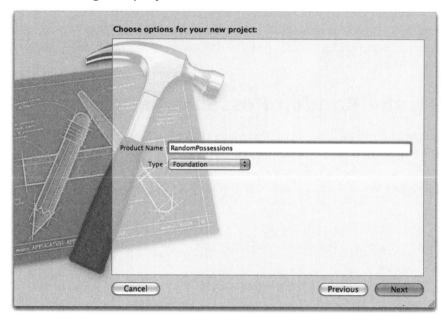

One source file (main.m) has been created for you in the RandomPossessions group of the project navigator (Figure 2.5).

Figure 2.5   Project navigator for command line tool template

Click on this file to open it in the editor area, and you'll see that some code has already been written for you – most notably, a **main** function that is the entry point of any C (or Objective-C) application.

Time to put your knowledge of Objective-C basics to the test. Delete the line of code that **NSLog**s "Hello, World!" and replace it with lines that create and destroy an instance of an **NSMutableArray**.

```
#import <Foundation/Foundation.h>
int main (int argc, const char * argv[])
{
    NSAutoreleasePool *pool = [[NSAutoreleasePool alloc] init];

    // Create a mutable array, store its address in items variable
    NSMutableArray *items = [[NSMutableArray alloc] init];
```

```
    // Release the array
    [items release];

    // Don't leave items pointing at freed memory!
    items = nil;


    [pool drain];
    return 0;
}
```

Once you have an instance of **NSMutableArray**, you can send it messages, like **addObject:** and **insertObject:atIndex:**. In this code, the receiver is the items variable that points at the newly instantiated **NSMutableArray**. Add a few strings to the array instance.

```
int main (int argc, const char * argv[])
{
    NSAutoreleasePool *pool = [[NSAutoreleasePool alloc] init];

    NSMutableArray *items = [[NSMutableArray alloc] init];

    // Send the message addObject: to the NSMutableArray pointed to
    // by the variable items, passing a string each time.
    [items addObject:@"One"];
    [items addObject:@"Two"];
    [items addObject:@"Three"];

    // Send another message, insertObject:atIndex:, to that same array object
    [items insertObject:@"Zero" atIndex:0];

    [items release];
    items = nil;

    [pool drain];
    return 0;
}
```

When this application executes, it creates an **NSMutableArray** and fills it with four **NSString** instances. However, you need to confirm that you added the strings. In main.m, after adding the final object to the array, loop through every item in the array and print each one to the console.

```
int main (int argc, const char * argv[])
{
    NSAutoreleasePool *pool = [[NSAutoreleasePool alloc] init];

    NSMutableArray *items = [[NSMutableArray alloc] init];
    [items addObject:@"One"];
    [items addObject:@"Two"];
    [items addObject:@"Three"];
    [items insertObject:@"Zero" atIndex:0];


    // For every item in the array as determined by sending count to the items array
    for(int i = 0; i < [items count]; i++) {
        // We get the ith object from the array and pass it as an argument to NSLog,
        // which implicitly sends the description message to that object
        NSLog(@"%@", [items objectAtIndex:i]);
    }
```

```
    [items release];
    items = nil;

    [pool drain];
    return 0;
}
```

Click the Run button. It may seem like nothing has happened because the program exits right away, but the *log navigator* tells another story.

The log navigator stores the build results and console output from each build of your application. To reveal the log navigator, select the 🖹 icon or use the keyboard shortcut Command-7. Select Debug RandomPossessions at the top of the log navigator to see your console output in the editor area (Figure 2.6).

Figure 2.6   Console output

NSString

Now let's go back and take a closer look at some of the code in your main function. First, notice the @"One" argument in the first **addObject:** message sent to items.

```
[items addObject:@"One"];
```

In Objective-C, when you want a hard-coded string, you prefix a character string with an @ symbol. This creates an instance of **NSString** (another Objective-C class) that holds the character string.

But, wait – aren't instances created by sending **alloc** to a class? That is the way most objects are created, but the @ prefix is a special case for the **NSString** class. It is convenient shorthand for creating strings.

The following code shows three such uses, and each is completely valid Objective-C, where **length** is an instance method on **NSString**:

```
NSString *myString = @"Hello, World!";
int len = [myString length];

len = [@"Hello, World!" length];

myString = [[NSString alloc] initWithString:@"Hello, World!"];
len = [myString length];
```

Next, let's look at the function **NSLog** we used to print to the console. **NSLog** takes a variable number of arguments and prints a string to the console. The first argument is required and must be an **NSString** instance. This instance is called the *format string*, and it contains text and a number of tokens. Each additional argument passed to the function replaces a token in the format string. The tokens (also called format specifications) must be prefixed with a percent symbol (%), and they specify the type of the argument they correspond to. Here's an example:

```
int a = 1;
float b = 2.5;
char c = 'A';
NSLog(@"Integer: %d Float: %f Char: %c", a, b, c);
```

The order of the arguments matters: the first token is replaced with the second argument (the format string is always the first argument), the second token is replaced with the third argument, and so on. The console output would be

```
Integer: 1 Float: 2.5 Char: A
```

In C, there is a function called **printf** that does the same thing. However, **NSLog** adds one more token to the available list: %@. When %@ is encountered in the format string, instead of the token being replaced by the corresponding argument, that argument is sent the message **description**. This method returns an **NSString** that replaces the token. Because the argument is sent a message, that argument must be an object. As we'll see shortly, every object implements the method **description**, so any object will work.

NSArray and NSMutableArray

What exactly is this **NSMutableArray** you've been using? An array is a collection object (also called a container). The Cocoa Touch frameworks provide a handful of collection objects, such as **NSDictionary** and **NSSet**, and each has a slightly different use. An array is an ordered list of objects that can be accessed by an index. Other languages might call it a list or a vector. An **NSArray** is immutable, which means you cannot add or remove objects after the array is instantiated. You can, however, retrieve objects from the array. **NSArray**'s mutable subclass, **NSMutableArray**, lets you add and remove objects dynamically.

In Objective-C, an array does not actually *contain* the objects that belong to it; instead it holds a pointer (a reference) to each object. When an object is added to an array,

```
[array addObject:object];
```

the address of that object in memory is stored inside the array.

So, to recap, in your command line tool, you created an instance of **NSMutableArray** and added four instances of **NSString** to it, as shown in Figure 2.7.

Figure 2.7   NSMutableArray instance

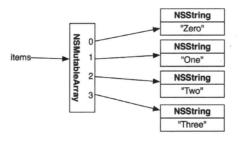

Arrays can only hold references to Objective-C objects. This means primitives and C structures cannot be added to an array. For example, you cannot have an array of ints. Also, because arrays only hold a pointer to an object, *a single array can contain objects of different types*. This is different from most strongly-typed languages where an array can only hold objects of its declared type.

You can ask an array how many objects it is currently storing by sending it the message **count**. This information is important because if you ask for an object from an array at an index that is greater than the number of objects in the array, an exception will be thrown. (Exceptions are very bad; they will most likely cause your application to crash. We'll talk more about exceptions at the end of this chapter.)

```
int numberOfObjects = [array count];
```

When an object is added to an array with the message **addObject:**, it is added at the end of the array. You can also insert objects at a specific index – as long as that index is less than or equal to the current number of objects in the array.

```
int numberOfObjects = [array count];
[array insertObject:object
           atIndex:numberOfObjects];
```

Note that you cannot add nil to an array. If you need to add "holes" to an array, you must use **NSNull**. **NSNull** is an object that represents nil and is used specifically for this task.

```
[array addObject:[NSNull null]];
```

To retrieve the pointer to an object later, you send the message **objectAtIndex:** to the array

```
NSString *object = [array objectAtIndex:0];
```

For readers who know something about retain counts: an object added to an array is sent the message **retain**. When an object is removed from an array, it is sent the message **release**. When an array is deallocated, all of its objects are sent the message **release**. If you don't know what retain, release, and deallocate mean, that's okay; you'll learn about them in the next chapter.

Subclassing an Objective-C Class

Classes exist in a hierarchy, and every class has exactly one superclass – except for the root class of the entire hierarchy: **NSObject** (Figure 2.8). A class inherits the behavior of its superclass, which means, at minimum, every class inherits the methods and instance variables defined in **NSObject**. As the top superclass, **NSObject**'s role is to implement the basic behavior of every object in Cocoa Touch. Two of the methods **NSObject** implements are **alloc** and **description**. (We sometimes say "**description** is a method *on* **NSObject**" and mean the same thing.)

Figure 2.8   Class hierarchy

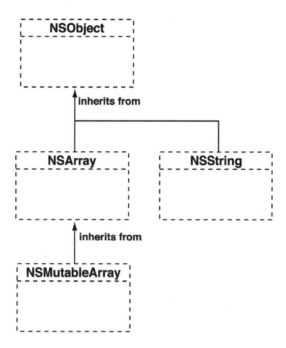

A subclass can add methods and instance variables to extend the behavior of its superclass. For example, **NSMutableArray** extends **NSArray**'s ability to hold pointers to objects by adding the ability to dynamically add and remove objects.

A subclass can also override methods of its superclass. For example, **NSString** overrides the **description** method of **NSObject**. Sending the **description** message to an **NSObject** returns information about that instance. By default, **description** returns the object's class and its address in memory, like this: <QuizAppDelegate: 0x4b222a0>.

A subclass of **NSObject** can override this method to return something that better describes an instance of that subclass. For example, **NSString** overrides **description** to return the string itself. **NSArray** overrides **description** to return the description of every object in the array.

In this exercise, you're going to create a subclass of **NSObject** named Possession. An instance of the **Possession** class will represent an item that a person owns in the real world. Click File → New → New File.... Select Cocoa Touch from the iOS section in the lefthand table. Then select Objective-C class from the upper panel and hit Next, as shown in Figure 2.9.

Figure 2.9   Creating a class

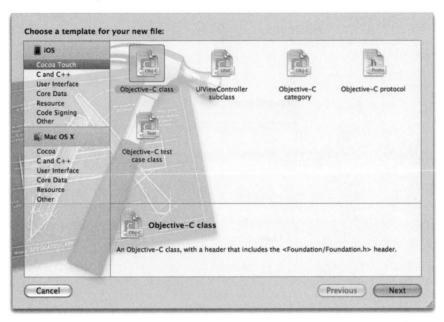

On the next panel, select NSObject as the superclass and click Next, as shown in Figure 2.10.

Figure 2.10   Choosing a superclass

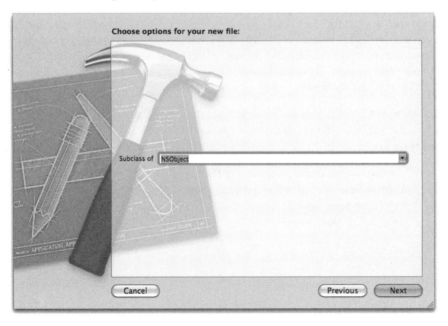

Name the class **Possession** (Figure 2.11). When creating a new class for a project, you want to save the files that describe it inside the project's source directory on the filesystem. By default, the current project directory is already selected for you. You can also choose the group in the project navigator that these files will be added to. Because these groups are simply for organizing and because this project is very small, the group doesn't matter, so just stick with the default. Make sure the checkbox is selected for the RandomPossessions target. This ensures that this class will be compiled when the project is built. Click Save.

Figure 2.11   Saving a new class

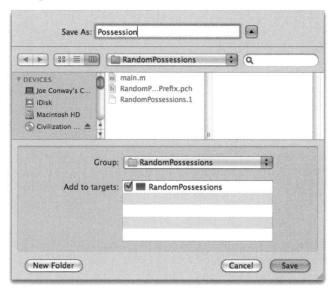

Creating the **Possession** class generated two files: `Possession.h` and `Possession.m`. Locate those files in the project navigator. `Possession.h` is the *header file* (also called an interface file). This file declares the name of the new class, its superclass, the instance variables that each instance of this class has, and any methods this class implements. `Possession.m` is the implementation file, and it contains the code for the methods that the class implements. Every Objective-C class has these two files. You can think of the header file as a user manual for an instance of a class and the implementation file as the engineering details that define how it really works.

Open `Possession.h` in the editor area by clicking on it in the project navigator. The file currently looks like this:

```
#import <UIKit/UIKit.h>

@interface Possession : NSObject
{

}
@end
```

Let's break down this interface declaration to figure out what it means. First, note that the C language retains all of its keywords, and any additional keywords added by Objective-C are distinguishable by the @ prefix. To declare a class in Objective-C, you use the keyword `@interface` followed by the name of this new class. After a colon comes the name of the superclass. **Possession**'s superclass is **NSObject**. Objective-C only allows single inheritance, so you will only ever see the following pattern:

```
@interface ClassName : SuperclassName
```

Next comes the space for declaring instance variables. Instance variables must be declared *inside* the curly brace block immediately following the class and superclass declaration. After the closing curly brace, you declare any methods that this class implements. Finally, the @end keyword finishes off the declaration for the new class.

Instance variables

So far, the **Possession** class doesn't add anything to its superclass **NSObject**. What it needs are some possession-like instance variables. A possession, in our world, is going to have a name, a serial number, a value, and a date of creation. In Possession.h, add instance variables to the **Possession** class:

```
#import <Foundation/Foundation.h>

@interface Possession : NSObject
{
    NSString *possessionName;
    NSString *serialNumber;
    int valueInDollars;
    NSDate *dateCreated;
}
@end
```

Now every instance of **Possession** has a spot for a simple integer. It also has spots to hold references to two **NSString** instances and one **NSDate** instance. (A reference is another word for pointer; the asterisk (*) denotes that the variable is a pointer.) Figure 2.12 shows an example of a **Possession** instance after its instance variables have been given values.

Figure 2.12   A Possession instance

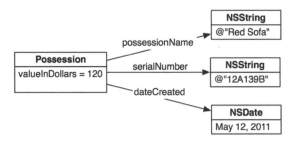

Notice that Figure 2.12 shows a total of four objects: the **Possession**, two **NSString**s and the **NSDate**. Each of these objects is its own object and exists independently of the others. The **Possession** only has pointer to the three other objects. These pointers are the instance variables of **Possession**.

For example, every **Possession** has a pointer instance variable named possessionName. This **Possession**'s possessionName points to an **NSString** instance whose contents are "Red Sofa." The "Red Sofa" string does not live inside the **Possession**, though. The **Possession** instance knows where the "Red Sofa" **NSString** lives in memory and stores its address as possessionName. One way to think of this relationship is "the **Possession** calls this string its possessionName. "

The story is different for the instance variable valueInDollars. This instance variable is *not* a pointer to another object; it is just an int. Non-pointer instance variables are stored inside the object itself. This is not an easy idea to understand at first. Throughout this book, we will make use of object diagrams like this one to drive home the difference between an object and a pointer to an object.

Accessor methods

Now that you have instance variables, you need a way to get and set their values. In object-oriented languages, we call methods that get and set instance variables *accessors*. Individually, we call them *getters* and *setters*. Without these methods, one object cannot access the instance variables of another object.

Accessor methods look like this:

```
// Getter
- (NSString *)possessionName
{
    // Return a pointer to the object this Possession calls its possessionName
    return possessionName;
}

// Setter
- (void)setPossessionName:(NSString *)newPossessionName
{
    // Change the instance variable to point at another string,
    // this Possession will now call this new string its possessionName
    possessionName = newPossessionName;
}
```

Then, if you wanted to access a **Possession**'s possessionName, you would send it one of the following messages:

```
// Create a new Possession instance
Possession *p = [[Possession alloc] init];

// Set possessionName to a new NSString
[p setPossessionName:@"Red Sofa"];

// Get the pointer of the Possession's possessionName
NSString *str = [p possessionName];

// Print that object
NSLog(@"%@", str); // This would print "Red Sofa"
```

In Objective-C, the name of a setter method is **set** plus the name of the instance variable it is changing – in this case, **setPossessionName:**. In other languages, the name of the getter method would likely be **getPossessionName**. However, in Objective-C, the name of the getter method is just the name of the instance variable. Some of the cooler parts of the Cocoa Touch library make the assumption that your classes follow this convention; therefore, stylish Cocoa Touch programmers always do so.

In Possession.h, declare accessor methods for the instance variables of **Possession**. You will need getters and setters for valueInDollars, possessionName, and serialNumber. For dateCreated, you only need a getter method.

```
#import <Foundation/Foundation.h>

@interface Possession : NSObject
{
    NSString *possessionName;
    NSString *serialNumber;
    int valueInDollars;
    NSDate *dateCreated;
}
- (void)setPossessionName:(NSString *)str;
- (NSString *)possessionName;

- (void)setSerialNumber:(NSString *)str;
- (NSString *)serialNumber;

- (void)setValueInDollars:(int)i;
- (int)valueInDollars;

- (NSDate *)dateCreated;
@end
```

(For those of you with some experience in Objective-C, we'll talk about properties in the next chapter.)

Now that these accessors have been declared, they need to be defined in the implementation file. Open Possession.m in the editor area by selecting it in the project navigator.

At the top of any implementation file, you must import the header file of that class. The implementation of a class needs to know how it has been declared. (Importing a file is the same as including a file in the C language except you are ensured that the file will only be included once.)

After the import statements is an implementation block that begins with the @implementation keyword followed by the name of the class that is being implemented. All of the method definitions in the implementation file are inside this implementation block. Methods are defined until you close out the block with the @end keyword.

We're going to skip memory management until the next chapter, so the accessor methods for **Possession** are very simple: setter methods assign the appropriate instance variable to point at the incoming object, and getter methods return a pointer to the object the instance variable points at. (For valueInDollars, we're just assigning the passed-in value to the instance variable for the setter and returning the value in the getter.) Edit Possession.m:

```
#import "Possession.h"

@implementation Possession

- (void)setPossessionName:(NSString *)str
{
    possessionName = str;
}
- (NSString *)possessionName
{
    return possessionName;
}

- (void)setSerialNumber:(NSString *)str
{
    serialNumber = str;
}
```

```
- (NSString *)serialNumber
{
    return serialNumber;
}

- (void)setValueInDollars:(int)i
{
    valueInDollars = i;
}

- (int)valueInDollars
{
    return valueInDollars;
}

- (NSDate *)dateCreated
{
    return dateCreated;
}

@end
```

Build your application (select Product → Build or use the shortcut Command-B) to ensure that there are no compiler errors or warnings.

Now that your accessors have been declared and defined, you can send messages to **Possession** instances to get and set their instance variables. Let's test this out. In main.m, import the header file for **Possession** and create a new **Possession** instance. After it is created, log its instance variables to the console.

```
#import "Possession.h"

int main (int argc, const char * argv[])
{
    NSAutoreleasePool *pool = [[NSAutoreleasePool alloc] init];

    NSMutableArray *items = [[NSMutableArray alloc] init];
    [items addObject:@"One"];
    [items addObject:@"Two"];
    [items addObject:@"Three"];
    [items insertObject:@"Zero" atIndex:0];

    for(int i = 0; i < [items count]; i++) {
        NSLog(@"%@", [items objectAtIndex:i]);
    }

    Possession *p = [[Possession alloc] init];
    NSLog(@"%@ %@ %@ %d", [p possessionName], [p dateCreated],
                          [p serialNumber], [p valueInDollars]);

    [items release];
    items = nil;

    [pool drain];
    return 0;
}
```

Build and run the application. Check the console by selecting the most recent entry in the log navigator. You should see the previous console output followed by a line that has three "(null)" strings and a 0. (When an object is created, all of its instance variables are set to 0. For primitives like int, the value is 0; for pointers to objects, that pointer points to nil.)

To give this **Possession** some substance, you need to create new objects and pass them as arguments to the setter methods for this instance. In main.m, type in the following code:

```
// Notice we omitted some of the surrounding code. The bold code is the code to add,
// the non-bold code is existing code that shows you where to type in the new stuff.

Possession *p = [[Possession alloc] init];

// This creates a new NSString, "Red Sofa", and gives it to the Possession
[p setPossessionName:@"Red Sofa"];

// This creates a new NSString, "A1B2C", and gives it to the Possession
[p setSerialNumber:@"A1B2C"];

// We send the value 100 to be used as the valueInDollars of this Possession
[p setValueInDollars:100];

NSLog(@"%@ %@ %@ %d", [p possessionName], [p dateCreated],
                     [p serialNumber], [p valueInDollars]);
```

Build and run the application. Now you should see values for everything but the dateCreated, which we'll take care of shortly.

Instance methods

Not all instance methods are accessors. You will regularly find yourself wanting to send messages to instances that perform other tasks. One such message is **description**. You can implement this method for **Possession** to return a string that describes a **Possession** instance. Because **Possession** is a subclass of **NSObject** (the class that originally declares the **description** method), when you re-implement this method in the **Possession** class, you are *overriding* it. When overriding a method, all you need to do is define it in the implementation file; you do not need to declare it in the header file because it has already been declared by the superclass.

In Possession.m, override the **description** method. This new code can go anywhere between @implementation and @end, as long as it's not inside the curly brackets of an existing method.

```
- (NSString *)description
{
    NSString *descriptionString =
        [[NSString alloc] initWithFormat:@"%@ (%@): Worth $%d, recorded on %@",
                          possessionName,
                          serialNumber,
                          valueInDollars,
                          dateCreated];

    return descriptionString;

}
```

Now whenever you send the message **description** to an instance of **Possession**, it will return an **NSString** that describes that instance. (To those of you familiar with Objective-C and managing memory, don't panic – you will fix the problem with this code in the next chapter.) In main.m, substitute this new method into the **NSLog** that prints out the instance variables of the **Possession**.

```
[p setValueInDollars:100];

// Remember, an NSLog with %@ as the token will print the
// description of the corresponding argument
NSLog(@"%@", p);
```

Build and run the application and check your results in the log navigator. You should see a log statement that looks like this:

```
Red Sofa (A1B2C): Worth $100, recorded on (null)
```

What if you want to create an entirely new instance method, one that you are not overriding from the superclass? You declare the new method in the header file and define it in the implementation file. A good method to begin with is an object's initializer.

Initializers

At the beginning of this chapter, we discussed how an instance is created: its class is sent the message **alloc**, which creates an instance of that class and returns a pointer to it, and then that instance is sent the message **init**, which gives its instance variables initial values. As you start to write more complicated classes, you will want to create initialization methods like **init** that take arguments that the object can use to initialize itself. For example, the **Possession** class would be much cleaner if we could pass one or more of its variables as part of the initialization process.

To cover the different possible initialization scenarios, many classes have more than one initialization method, or initializer. Each initializer begins with the word **init**. Naming initializers this way doesn't make these methods different from other instance methods; it is only a naming convention. However, the Objective-C community is all about naming conventions, which you should strictly adhere to. (Seriously. Disregarding naming conventions in Objective-C results in problems that are worse than most beginners would imagine.)

For each class, regardless of how many initialization methods there are, one method is chosen as the *designated initializer*. For **NSObject**, there is only one initializer, **init**, so it is the designated initializer. The designated initializer makes sure that every instance variable of an object is valid. ("Valid" has different meanings, but in this context it means "when you send messages to this object after initializing it, you can predict the outcome and nothing bad will happen.")

Typically, the designated initializer has parameters for the most important and frequently used instance variables of an object.

The **Possession** class has four instance variables, but only three are writeable. Therefore, **Possession**'s designated initializer needs to accept three arguments. In Possession.h, declare the designated initializer:

```
    NSDate *dateCreated;
}

- (id)initWithPossessionName:(NSString *)name
            valueInDollars:(int)value
            serialNumber:(NSString *)sNumber;

- (void)setPossessionName:(NSString *)str;
```

This method's name, or selector, is **initWithPossessionName:valueInDollars:serialNumber:**. This selector has three labels (**initWithPossessionName:**, **valueInDollars:**, and **serialNumber:**), which tells you the method accepts three arguments.

These arguments each have a type and a parameter name. In the declaration, the type follows the label in parentheses. The parameter name then follows the type. So the label **initWithPossessionName:** is expecting a pointer to an instance of type **NSString**. Within the body of that method, you can use name to reference the **NSString** object pointed to.

id

Take another look at the initializer's declaration. Its return type is id, which is defined as "a pointer to any object." (This is a lot like void * in C and is pronounced "eye-dee.") **init** methods are always declared to return id.

Why not make the return type Possession * – a pointer to a **Possession**? After all, that is the type of object that is returned from this method. A problem will arise, however, if **Possession** is ever subclassed. The subclass would inherit all of the methods from **Possession**, including this initializer and its return type. An instance of the subclass could then be sent this initializer message, but what would be returned? Not a **Possession**, but an instance of the subclass. You might think, "No problem. Override the initializer in the subclass to change the return type." But remember – in Objective-C, you cannot have two methods with the same selector and different return types (or arguments). By specifying that an initialization method returns "any object," we never have to worry what happens with a subclass.

isa

As programmers, we always know the type of the object that is returned from an initializer. (How do we know this? It is an instance of the class we sent **alloc** to.) Not only do we know the type of the object, *the object itself* knows its type.

Every object has an instance variable called isa. When an instance is created by sending **alloc** to a class, that class sets the isa instance variable of the returned object to point back at the class that created it (Figure 2.13). We call it the isa pointer because an object "is a" instance of that class.

Figure 2.13   The isa pointer

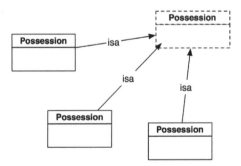

The isa pointer is where Objective-C holds much of its power. At runtime, when a message is sent to an object, that object goes to the class named in its isa pointer and says, "I was sent this message. Run the code for the matching method." This is different than most compiled languages, where the method to be executed is determined at compile time.

Implementing the designated initializer

Now that you have declared the designated initializer in `Possession.h`, you need to implement it. Open `Possession.m`. Recall that the definitions for methods go within the implementation block in the implementation file, and add the designated initializer there.

```
@implementation Possession

- (id)initWithPossessionName:(NSString *)name
            valueInDollars:(int)value
             serialNumber:(NSString *)sNumber
{
    // Call the superclass's designated initializer
    [super init];

    // Give the instance variables initial values
    [self setPossessionName:name];
    [self setSerialNumber:sNumber];
    [self setValueInDollars:value];
    dateCreated = [[NSDate alloc] init];

    // Return the address of the newly initialized object
    return self;
}
```

In the designated initializer, the first thing you always do is call the superclass's designated initializer using `super`. The last thing you do is return a pointer to the successfully initialized object using `self`. So to understand what's going on in an initializer, you will need to know about `self` and `super`.

self

Inside a method, `self` is an implicit local variable. There is no need to declare it, and it is automatically set to point to the object that was sent the message. (Most object-oriented languages have this concept, but some call it `this` instead of `self`.) Typically, `self` is used so that an object can send a message to itself:

```
- (void)chickenDance
{
    [self pretendHandsAreBeaks];
    [self flapWings];
    [self shakeTailFeathers];
}
```

In the last line of an **init** method, you always return the newly initialized object, so the caller can assign it to a variable:

```
return self;
```

super

Often when you are overriding a method in a subclass, you want it to add something to what the existing method of the superclass already does. To make this easier, there is a compiler directive in Objective-C called `super`:

```
- (void)someMethod
{
    [self doMoreStuff];
    [super someMethod];
}
```

How does super work? Usually when you send a message to an object, the search for a method of that name starts in the object's class. If there is no such method, the search continues in the superclass of the object. The search will continue up the inheritance hierarchy until a suitable method is found. (If it gets to the top of the hierarchy and no method is found, an exception is thrown.) When you send a message to super, you are sending a message to self but demanding that the search for the method begin at the superclass.

In the case of **Possession**'s designated initializer, we send the **init** message to super. This calls **NSObject**'s implementation of **init**. If an initializer message fails, it will return nil. Therefore, it is a good idea to save the return value of the superclass's initializer into the self variable and confirm that it is not nil before doing any further initialization. In Possession.m, edit your designated initializer to confirm the initialization of the superclass.

```
- (id)initWithPossessionName:(NSString *)name
            valueInDollars:(int)value
              serialNumber:(NSString *)sNumber
{
    // Call the superclass's designated initializer
    self = [super init];

    // Did the superclass's designated initializer succeed?
    if (self) {
        // Give the instance variables initial values
        [self setPossessionName:name];
        [self setSerialNumber:sNumber];
        [self setValueInDollars:value];
        dateCreated = [[NSDate alloc] init];
    }

    // Return the address of the newly initialized object
    return self;
}
```

Other initializers and the initializer chain

A class can have more than one initializer. For example, **Possession** could have an initializer that takes an **NSString** for the possessionName, but not the serialNumber or valueInDollars. Instead of replicating all of the code in the designated initializer, this other initializer would simply call the designated initializer. It would pass the information it was given for the possessionName and pass default values for the other two arguments.

Possession's designated initializer is **initWithPossessionName:valueInDollars:serialNumber:**. However, it has another initializer, **init**, that it inherits it from its superclass **NSObject**. If **init** is sent to an instance of **Possession**, none of the stuff you put in the designated initializer will be called. Therefore, you must link **Possession**'s implementation of **init** to its designated initializer. In Possession.m, override the **init** method to call the designated initializer with default values.

```
- (id)init
{
    return [self initWithPossessionName:@"Possession"
                          valueInDollars:0
                           serialNumber:@""];
}
```

Using initializers as a chain like this reduces the chance for error and makes maintaining code easier. For classes that have more than one initializer, the programmer who created the class chooses which initializer is designated. You only write the core of the initializer once in the designated initializer, and other initialization methods simply call that core with default values. This relationship is shown in Figure 2.14; the designated initializers are white, and the additional initializer is gray.

Figure 2.14 Initializer chain

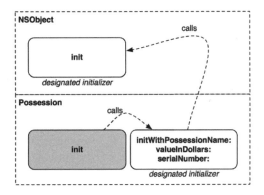

Let's form some simple rules for initializers from these ideas.

• A class inherits all initializers from its superclass and can add as many as it wants for its own purposes.

• Each class picks one initializer as its *designated initializer*.

• The designated initializer calls the superclass's designated initializer.

• Any other initializer a class has calls the class's designated initializer.

• If a class declares a designated initializer that is different from its superclass, you must override the superclass' designated initializer to call the new designated initializer.

Class methods

Methods come in two flavors: instance methods and class methods. *Instance methods* (like **init**) are sent to instances of the class, and *class methods* (like **alloc**) are sent to the class itself. Class methods typically either create new instances of the class or retrieve some global property of the class. Class methods do not operate on an instance or have any access to instance variables.

Syntactically, class methods differ from instance methods by the first character in their declaration. An instance method uses the - character just before the return type, and a class method uses the + character.

One common use for class methods is to provide convenient ways to create instances of that class. For the **Possession** class, it would be nice if you could create a random possession so that you could easily test your class without having to think up a bunch of clever names. Declare a class method in Possession.h that will create a random possession.

```
@interface Possession : NSObject
{
    NSString *possessionName;
    NSString *serialNumber;
    int valueInDollars;
    NSDate *dateCreated;
}

+ (id)randomPossession;

- (id)initWithPossessionName:(NSString *)name
              valueInDollars:(int)value
                serialNumber:(NSString *)sNumber;
```

Notice the order of the declarations for the methods. Class methods come first, followed by initializers, followed by any other methods. This is a convention that makes your header files easier to read.

Class methods that return an instance of their type create an instance (with **alloc** and **init**), configure it, and then return it. In Possession.m, implement **randomPossession** to create, configure, and return a **Possession** instance (make sure this method is between the @implementation and @end):

```
+ (id)randomPossession
{
    // Create an array of three adjectives
    NSArray *randomAdjectiveList = [NSArray arrayWithObjects:@"Fluffy",
                                                             @"Rusty",
                                                             @"Shiny", nil];

    // Create an array of three nouns
    NSArray *randomNounList = [NSArray arrayWithObjects:@"Bear",
                                                        @"Spork",
                                                        @"Mac", nil];

    // Get the index of a random adjective/noun from the lists
    // Note: The % operator, called the modulo operator, gives
    // you the remainder. So adjectiveIndex is a random number
    // from 0 to 2 inclusive.
    int adjectiveIndex = rand() % [randomAdjectiveList count];
    int nounIndex = rand() % [randomNounList count];

    NSString *randomName = [NSString stringWithFormat:@"%@ %@",
                [randomAdjectiveList objectAtIndex:adjectiveIndex],
                [randomNounList objectAtIndex:nounIndex]];

    int randomValue = rand() % 100;

    NSString *randomSerialNumber = [NSString stringWithFormat:@"%c%c%c%c%c",
                                        '0' + rand() % 10,
                                        'A' + rand() % 26,
```

```
                                        '0' + rand() % 10,
                                        'A' + rand() % 26,
                                        '0' + rand() % 10];

        // Once again, ignore the memory problems with this method
        Possession *newPossession =
            [[self alloc] initWithPossessionName:randomName
                                  valueInDollars:randomValue
                                    serialNumber:randomSerialNumber];
        return newPossession;
}
```

This method creates two arrays using the method **arrayWithObjects:**. **arrayWithObjects:** takes a list of objects terminated by nil. nil is not added to the array; it just indicates the end of the argument list.

Then **randomPossession** creates a string from a random adjective and noun, another string from random numbers and letters, and a random integer value. It then creates an instance of **Possession** and sends it the designated initializer with these randomly-created objects and int as parameters.

In this method, you also use **stringWithFormat:**, which is a class method of **NSString**. This message is sent directly to **NSString**, and the method returns an **NSString** instance with the passed-in parameters. In Objective-C, class methods that return an object of their type (like **stringWithFormat:** and **randomPossession**) are called *convenience methods*.

Notice the use of self in **randomPossession**. Because **randomPossession** is a class method, self refers to the **Possession** class itself instead of an instance. Class methods should use self in convenience methods instead of their class name so that a subclass can be sent the same message. In this case, if you create a subclass of **Possession**, you can send that subclass the message **randomPossession**. Using self (instead of **Possession**) will allocate an instance of the class that was sent the message and set the instance's isa pointer to that class as well.

Testing your subclass

Open main.m. Currently, in the **main** function, you are adding **NSString** instances to an **NSMutableArray** instance and then printing them to the console. Now you will add **Possession** instances to the array and log them instead. Delete the code that previously created a single **Possession** and change your **main** function to look just like this:

```
#import <Foundation/Foundation.h>
#import "Possession.h"

int main (int argc, const char * argv[])
{
    NSAutoreleasePool * pool = [[NSAutoreleasePool alloc] init];

    NSMutableArray *items = [[NSMutableArray alloc] init];

    for (int i = 0; i < 10; i++) {
        Possession *p = [Possession randomPossession];
        [items addObject:p];
    }

    for (int i = 0; i < [items count]; i++) {
        NSLog(@"%@", [items objectAtIndex:i]);
    }
```

```
    [items release];
    items = nil;

    [pool drain];
    return 0;
}
```

Build and run your application and then check the output in the log navigator. All you did was replace what objects you added to the array, and the code runs perfectly fine with a different output (Figure 2.15). Creating this class was a success.

Figure 2.15   Application result

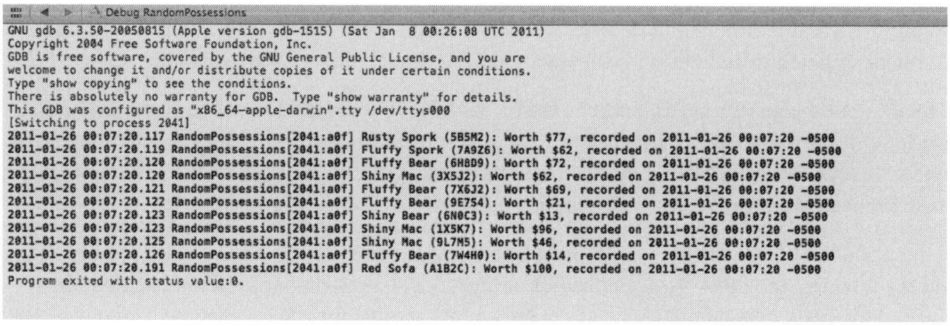

Check out the `#import` statements at the top of `main.m`. Why did you have to import the class header `Possession.h` when you didn't you have to import, say, `NSMutableArray.h`? **NSMutableArray** comes from the Foundation framework, so it is included when you import `Foundation/Foundation.h`. On the other hand, your class exists in its own file, so you have to explicitly import it into `main.m`. Otherwise, the compiler won't know it exists and will complain loudly.

Exceptions and the Console Window

In a language like C, we have functions, and when we call a function, code is executed. If we try and call a function that doesn't exist, the compiler says, "I can't do that, Joe," and the code will fail to compile. This is known as a compile-time error.

Objective-C, being a dynamically typed language, isn't able to figure out at compile time whether an object will respond to a message. (An object only responds to a message if its class implements the associated method.) The compiler will warn you if it thinks you are sending a message to an object that won't respond, but the code will still compile. If, for some reason (and there are many), you end up sending a message to an object that doesn't respond, your application will throw an exception, also known as a run-time error.

In `main.m`, add the following line of code after you create your array:

```
NSMutableArray *items = [[NSMutableArray alloc] init];
[items doSomethingWeird];
```

The class **NSMutableArray** does not implement a method called **doSomethingWeird**, and sending this message to an instance of **NSMutableArray** is going to throw an exception. Build and run your application.

The application will immediately throw an exception, and the debugger will suspend execution at the point of the exception. The debug area will appear (if not, select the center View button at the top right of the workspace window), and the console will show the following:

```
2009-07-19 01:34:53.602 RandomPossessions[25326:10b]
*** -[NSCFArray doSomethingWeird]: unrecognized selector sent to instance 0x104b40
```

This is what an exception looks like. What exactly is it saying? At the beginning of every output statement, the date, time, and name of the application are printed out. You can ignore that information and focus on what comes after the "***." That line tells us that an *unrecognized selector* was sent to an instance. You know that selector means message. You sent a message to an object, and the object does not implement that method.

The type of the receiver and the name of the message are also in this output, which makes it easier to debug. An instance of **NSCFArray** was sent the message **doSomethingWeird**. (The - at the beginning tells you the receiver was an instance of **NSCFArray**. A + would mean the class was the receiver.)

(What does **NSCFArray** mean? The **CF** stands for Core Foundation. We'll get into that in Chapter 4. For now, you can just drop the **CF** out of the name. An **NSArray**, the superclass of **NSMutableArray** is the type of the object that was sent this bad message.)

Remove the line of code you added and take away this very important lesson: always check the console output for errors when you run your application. Run-time errors are just as important as compile-time errors.

Some languages use try and catch blocks to handle exceptions. While Objective-C has this ability, we don't use it very often in application code. Typically, an exception is a programmer error and should be fixed in the code instead of handled at runtime.

Fast Enumeration

The newest version of Objective-C added a few syntax changes to the language. One if these is *fast enumeration*. Before Objective-C 2.0, iterating through an **NSArray** looked like this:

```
for (int i = 0; i < [items count]; i++) {
    Possession *item = [items objectAtIndex:i];
    NSLog(@"%@", item);
}
```

Now you can write that code segment much more succinctly with fast enumeration in `main.m`.

```
for (Possession *item in items)
    NSLog(@"%@", item);

[items release];
items = nil;
```

```
    [pool drain];
    return 0;
}
```

Now that we have covered the basics of Objective-C, the next chapter will discuss memory management in Cocoa Touch.

Challenge

Create a bug in your program by asking for the eleventh item in the array. Run it and note the exception that gets thrown.

3

Memory Management

Understanding memory management in the Cocoa Touch framework is a major roadblock for newcomers. Unlike Objective-C on the Mac, Objective-C on iOS has no garbage collector. Thus, it is your responsibility to clean up after yourself.

Memory Management Basics

This book assumes you are coming from a C background, so the words "pointer," "allocate," and "deallocate" shouldn't scare you. If your memory is a little fuzzy, here's a review.

An iOS device has a limited amount of random access memory. Random access memory (RAM) is much faster to write to and read from than a hard drive, so when an application is executing, all of the memory it consumes is taken from RAM. When an operating system like iOS launches your application, it reserves a heaping pile of the system's unused RAM for your application. Not-so-coincidentally, the memory reserved for your application is called *the heap*. The heap is your application's playground; it can do whatever it wants with it, and it won't affect the rest of the OS or any other application.

When your application creates an instance of a class, it goes to the giant heap of memory it was given and takes a little scoop. As your application runs, you create objects and start using more and more of the heap. Most objects are not permanently necessary, and when an object is no longer needed, the memory it was consuming should be returned to the heap. Then that memory can be reused for an object you create later.

This dynamic use, return, and reuse of memory requires proper management. Two major problems occur when memory is not managed properly:

premature deallocation   A chunk of memory is returned to the heap before a part of the program is finished using it.

memory leak   A chunk of memory is no longer needed by any part of a program, but it is not freed up to be used for something else.

Managing memory in C

In the C programming language, you explicitly ask the heap for a certain number of bytes. This is called *allocation*, and it is the first stage of the heap life cycle shown in Figure 3.1. To allocate memory, you use a function like `malloc`. If you want 100 bytes from the heap, you do something like this:

```
void function(void)
{
    char *buffer = malloc(100);
}
```

You then have 100 bytes with which you can perform a task like writing a string to these bytes and then printing that string (which requires reading from those bytes). The location of the first of the 100 bytes is stored in the pointer buffer. You use this pointer to access the 100 bytes (Figure 3.1).

Figure 3.1   Heap allocation life cycle

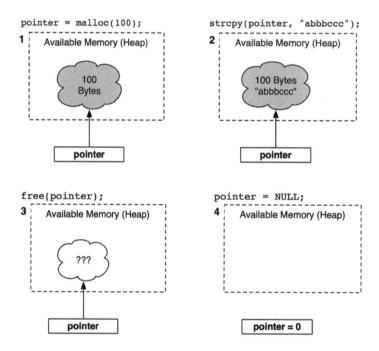

When you don't need those bytes anymore, you give them back to the heap by using the **free** function. This is called *deallocation*.

```
void function(void)
{
    char *buffer = malloc(100);

    // Do something with buffer

    free(buffer);
}
```

Calling **free** returns the 100 bytes (starting at the address stored in buffer) to the heap. If another **malloc** function is executed, any of these 100 bytes is fair game to be returned. Those bytes could be divvied up into smaller sections, or they could become part of a larger allocation. Because you don't know what will become of those bytes when they are returned to the heap, it isn't safe to access them through the buffer pointer anymore.

Managing memory with objects

Even though at the base level an object is also a certain number of bytes allocated from the heap, you never explicitly call **malloc** or **free** with objects.

Every class knows how many bytes of memory it needs to allocate for an instance. When you create an instance of a class by sending it the **alloc** message, the correct number of bytes is allocated from the heap. Like with **malloc**, you are returned a pointer to this memory. However, when using Objective-C, we think in terms of objects rather than raw memory. While our pointer still points to a spot in memory, we don't need to know the details of that memory; we just know we have an object.

Of course, once you allocate memory, you need a way to return it. Every object implements the method **dealloc**. When an object receives this message, it returns its memory to the heap.

So, **malloc** is replaced with the class method **alloc**, and the function **free** is replaced with the instance method **dealloc**. However, you never explicitly send a **dealloc** message to an object; an object is responsible for sending **dealloc** to itself. That begs the question: if an object is in charge of destroying itself, how does it know when it is safe and right to do so? This is where reference counting comes into play.

Reference Counting

In the Cocoa Touch framework, Apple has adopted *manual reference counting* to manage memory and avoid premature deallocation and memory leaks.

To understand reference counting, imagine a puppy. When the puppy is born, it has an owner. That owner later gets married, and the new spouse also becomes an owner of that dog. The dog is alive because they feed it. Later on, the couple gives the dog away. The new owner of the dog decides he doesn't like the dog and lets it know by kicking it out of the house. Having no owner, the dog runs away and, after a series of unfortunate events, ends up in doggy heaven.

What is the moral of this story? As long as the dog had an owner to care for it, it was fine. When it no longer had an owner, it ran away and ceased to exist. This is how reference counting works. When an object is created, it has an owner. Throughout its existence, it can have different owners, and it can have more than one owner at a time. When it has zero owners, it deallocates itself and goes to instance heaven.

Using retain counts

An object never knows *who* its owners are. It only knows *how many* it currently has. It keeps track of this number in its *retain count* (Figure 3.2).

Figure 3.2   Retain count for a dog

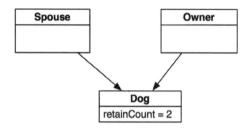

When an object is created – and therefore has one owner – its retain count is set to one. When an object gains an owner, it is sent the message **retain**, and its retain count is incremented. When an object loses an owner, it is sent the message **release**, and its retain count is decremented. When that retain count reaches zero, the object sends itself the message **dealloc**, which returns all of the memory it occupied to the heap.

Imagine how you would write the code to implement this scheme yourself:

```
- (id)retain
{
    retainCount++;
    return self;
}
- (void)release
{
    retainCount--;
    if (retainCount == 0)
        [self dealloc];
}
```

Let's consider how retain counts work between objects by imagining you have a grocery list. You created it, so you own it. Later, you give that grocery list to your friend to do the shopping. You don't need to keep the grocery list anymore, so you release it. Your friend is smart, so he retained the list as soon as he got it. Therefore, the grocery list will still exist whenever your friend needs it, and he is now the sole owner of the list.

Here is your code:

```
- (void)createAndGiveAwayTheGroceryList
{
    // Create a list
    GroceryList *g = [[GroceryList alloc] init];

    // (The retain count of g is 1)

    // Share it with your friend who retains it
    [smartFriend takeGroceryList:g];

    // (The retain count of g is 2)

    // Give up ownership
    [g release];
```

```
    // (The retain count of g is 1)
    // But we don't really care here, as this method's
    // responsibility is finished.
}
```

Here is your friend's code:

```
- (void)takeGroceryList:(GroceryList *)x
{
    // Take ownership
    [x retain];

    // Hold onto a pointer to the object
    myList = x;
}
```

Retain counts can still go wrong in the two classic ways: leaks and premature deallocation. Continuing with the grocery list example, say you create and give a grocery list to your friend. He retains it, but you don't release it. Your friend finishes the shopping and releases the list. By now, you've forgotten where the list is, and since you never released it, its retain count is greater than zero – and now always will be. At this moment, nobody knows where this list is, but it still exists. This is a leak.

Think of the grocery list as an **NSArray**. You have a pointer to this **NSArray** in the method where you created it. If you leave the scope of the method without releasing the **NSArray**, you'll lose the pointer along with the ability to release the **NSArray** later. (You can't send a release message unless you know *where* to send it.) Even if every other owner releases the **NSArray**, it will never be deallocated, and the application can't use that memory for something else.

Consider the other way this process can go wrong – premature deallocation. You create a grocery list and give it to a friend who doesn't bother to retain it. When you release the list, it is deallocated because you were its only owner. Later, when your friend tries to use the list, he can't find it because it doesn't exist anymore.

This situation is worse that it sounds. Not only is your friend unable to do the shopping, but there are also application-level consequences to premature deallocation. When an object attempts to access another object that doesn't exist, your application accesses bad memory, starts to fail, and eventually crashes. On the other hand, if an object retains the objects it needs, then those objects are guaranteed to exist, and this type of disaster is avoided.

Reference counting is all about responsibility: if something creates an object, it is an owner of that object. Same goes for retaining an existing object. Releasing an object relinquishes that ownership. If something takes ownership of an object, it is responsible for relinquishing its ownership when it can no longer send messages to that object – when it no longer has a pointer to that object.

Let's make these ideas more concrete with an example from the RandomPossessions tool you wrote in the last chapter. Open RandomPossessions.xcodeproj and then open main.m in the editor area. In the **main** function, you created an instance of **NSMutableArray** named items. You know two things about this instance: the **main** function owns it, and it has a retain count of one. As an owner, it is **main**'s responsibility to send this instance the message **release** when it no longer needs it. The last time you reference items in this function is when you print out all of its entries, so you can release it after that:

```
for (Possession *item in items) {
    NSLog(@"%@", item);
}
[items release];
items = nil;
```

When the message **release** is sent, the object pointed to by items decrements its retain count. In this case, the object is deallocated because **main** was its only owner. If another object had retained items, it wouldn't have been deallocated.

Using autorelease

You created items in **main**, use it there, and release it there. But what happens when you want to create an object to give out, not to own and use yourself?

This is often the case with convenience methods – class methods that return instances of the class. In the **Possession** class, you implemented a convenience method called **randomPossession** that returns an instance of **Possession** with random parameters. The **Possession** class owns this instance because it was created inside of a **Possession** class method, and the instance has a retain count of one.

However, the **Possession** class itself has no use for this instance; **randomPossession** is called by **main** where it returns the newly created **Possession** instance.

Should you release the **Possession** in **main**?

```
for(int i = 0; i < 10; i++)
{
    Possession *p = [Possession randomPossession];
    [items addObject:p];

    // Don't do this!
    [p release];
}
```

This is a very bad idea. The responsibility that is the core of reference counting includes not releasing objects that don't belong to you. That's like cancelling your friend's party. Or taking your neighbor's dog to the pound. If you don't own it, you shouldn't release it, and **main** does not own this **Possession** instance – it did not allocate it or retain it; it only has a pointer to it, courtesy of the **randomPossession** convenience method.

Releasing the possession is the responsibility of the **Possession** class, and it must be done in **randomPossession** before the pointer to it is lost when the scope of the method runs out. But where in **randomPossession** can you safely release the new **Possession** instance?

```
+ (id)randomPossession
{
    ... Create random variables ...
    Possession *newPossession = [[self alloc]
                    initWithPossessionName:randomName
                            valueInDollars:randomValue
                              serialNumber:randomSerialNumber];


    // If we release newPossession here,
    // the object is deallocated before it is returned.
```

```
    return newPossession;

    // If we release newPossession here, this code is never executed.
}
```

What can you do? You need some way of saying "Don't release this object yet, but I don't want to be an owner of it anymore." Fortunately, you can mark an object for future release by sending it the message **autorelease**. When an object is sent **autorelease**, it is not immediately released; instead, it is added to an instance of **NSAutoreleasePool**. This **NSAutoreleasePool** keeps track of all the objects that have been autoreleased. Periodically, the autorelease pool is drained; it sends the message **release** to the objects in the pool and then removes them.

An object marked for autorelease after its creation has two possible destinies: it can either continue its death march to deallocation or another object can retain it. If another object retains it, its retain count is now 2. (It is owned by the retaining object, and it has not been sent **release** by the autorelease pool.) Sometime in the future, the autorelease pool will release it, which will set its retain count back to 1.

Sometimes the idea of "the object will be released some time in the future" confuses developers. When an iOS application is running, there is a run loop that is continually cycling. This run loop checks for events, like a touch or a timer firing. Whenever an event occurs, the application breaks from the run loop and processes that event by calling the methods you have written in your classes. When your code is finished executing, the application returns to the loop. At the end of the loop, all autoreleased objects are sent the message **release**, as shown in Figure 3.3. So, while you are executing a method, which may call other methods, you can safely assume that an autoreleased object will not be released.

Figure 3.3   Autorelease pool draining

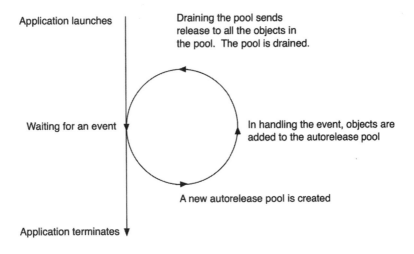

The return value for **autorelease** is the instance that is sent the message, so you can nest **autorelease** messages.

```
// Because autorelease returns the object being autoreleased, we can do this:
NSObject *x = [[[NSObject alloc] init] autorelease];
```

At the end of **randomPossession** in Possession.m, autorelease the newly created instance so that the receiver of this object can choose to retain it or just let it be destroyed.

```
Possession *newPossession =
    [[self alloc] initWithPossessionName:randomName
                          valueInDollars:randomValue
                            serialNumber:randomSerialNumber];

    return [newPossession autorelease];
}
```

Now, in main.m, when the **main** function asks the **Possession** class for a random possession, the class returns an autoreleased instance of **Possession**. At this point, nothing owns this instance. When the **Possession** is added to the items array, the array retains it, and it has a retain count of one.

```
for(int i = 0; i < 10; i++)
{
    // Get a new Possession instance - no one owns it as it's been autoreleased
    Possession *p = [Possession randomPossession];

    // Add p to the items array, it will retain that Possession
    [items addObject:p];
}
```

When will items release the **Possession**? When an **NSMutableArray** is deallocated, the objects it contains are released. Thus, when **main** (the sole owner of items) releases items, the **NSMutableArray** that items points to will release all its **Possession** instances (Figure 3.4). We've made sure these **Possession** instances had only items as an owner, so these instances will also be deallocated.

Figure 3.4   Deallocating an NSMutableArray

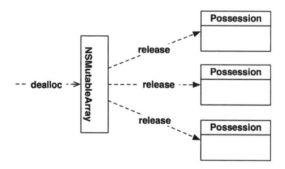

Here are three memory management facts to remember when working with instances of **NSMutableArray**:

- When an object is added to an **NSMutableArray**, that object is sent the message **retain**; the array becomes an owner of that object and has a pointer to it.

- When an object is removed from an **NSMutableArray**, that object is sent the message **release**; the array relinquishes ownership of that object and no longer has a pointer to it.

- When an **NSMutableArray** is deallocated, it sends the message **release** to all of its entries.

Now let's turn to another place in RandomPossessions where you should use autorelease. In Possession.m, you override the **description** method of **Possession**'s superclass. This method creates and returns an instance of **NSString**. Change the **description** method so that it returns an autoreleased string.

```
- (NSString *)description
{
    NSString *descriptionString =
        [[NSString alloc] initWithFormat:@"%@ (%@): Worth $%d, Recorded on %@",
                            possessionName,
                            serialNumber,
                            valueInDollars,
                            dateCreated];
    return [descriptionString autorelease];
}
```

You can make this even simpler by using a convenience method. **NSString**, like many other classes in the iOS SDK, includes convenience methods that return autoreleased objects – just like **randomPossession** does now. Modify **description** to use the convenience method **stringWithFormat:**. This ensures that the **NSString** instance that **description** creates and returns is autoreleased.

```
- (NSString *)description
{
    return [NSString stringWithFormat:@"%@ (%@): Worth $%d, Recorded on %@",
                            possessionName,
                            serialNumber,
                            valueInDollars,
                            dateCreated];
}
```

Accessors and memory management

Up to this point, our examples of ownership have been ownership by creation. When you want to own an object that you didn't create, you must retain it. For example, if an object has instance variables that point to other objects, that object should retain them. You can retain an object pointed to by an instance variable in the setter method for that variable.

Let's look at the instance variables of the **Possession**. Every instance of **Possession** has three instance variables that are pointers to other objects (possessionName, serialNumber, and dateCreated). Right now, the setter methods in **Possession** simply assign the incoming value to the instance variable:

```
- (void)setPossessionName:(NSString *)str
{
    possessionName = str;
}
```

Not good enough. If we give an **NSString** to a **Possession** for its possessionName, and the **Possession** doesn't retain it, then when we release the string, it will be destroyed. This is premature deallocation because the **Possession** still needs that string as its possessionName. The **Possession** will eventually send messages to or give out its possessionName. It will be embarrassing (and application-crashing) if the object that the variable points to doesn't exist.

Therefore, in a setter method, an object should retain the objects pointed to by its instance variables to make sure the objects continue to exist. Open `Possession.m` in the editor area. Modify the method `setPossessionName:` so that the **Possession** retains the string passed to it:

```
- (void)setPossessionName:(NSString *)str
{
    [str retain];
    possessionName = str;
}
```

The **Possession** will increment the retain count of the string passed to it, and no matter what happens to that string elsewhere in code, it will still exist until the **Possession** releases it.

Now let's look at what happens if you use the setter method to change the `possessionName`. For example, imagine we named a possession "White Sofa," and then a keen friend points out that it is actually off-white:

```
Possession *p = [[Possession alloc] init];
[p setPossessionName:@"White Sofa"];

// Wait, no it isn't...
[p setPossessionName:@"Off-white Sofa"];
```

Stepping through this code, p retains the string "White Sofa" and sets its `possessionName` to point at that string. Then, it retains the string "Off-white Sofa" and sets its `possessionName` to point at that string instead. This is a leak: the **Possession** lost its pointer to the "White Sofa" string but never released its ownership of it (Figure 3.5).

Figure 3.5   Sending a setter message more than once

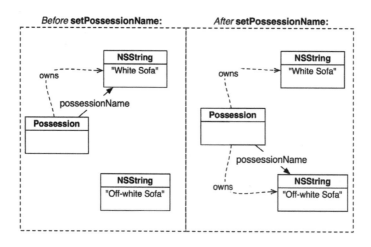

Therefore, in a setter method, you retain the new object, release the object you currently have, and then make the assignment. Add the following line of code to this setter method in `Possession.m`.

```
- (void)setPossessionName:(NSString *)str
{
    [str retain];
    [possessionName release];
}
```

```
        possessionName = str;
}
```

You must retain the new object before releasing the current one. More often than you might imagine, possessionName and str will point at the same object. If you reverse the retain and release statements, you would release the object that you had planned to retain as the possessionName. Oops.

Now write the matching code for the method **setSerialNumber:** in Possession.m.

```
- (void)setSerialNumber:(NSString *)str
{
    [str retain];
    [serialNumber release];
    serialNumber = str;
}
```

What happens in these setter methods if the incoming argument or the current instance variable points to nil? If you pass nil as an argument in **setPossessionName:**, the **Possession** releases its current possessionName and sets its possessionName to nil. The result is the **Possession** has no possessionName. If you send **setPossessionName:** to a **Possession** that has no possessionName, you will send the **release** message to nil, which has no effect.

Note that we've only been changing setter methods. Getter methods do not need additional memory management. However, the object that sends the getter message may need to retain what is returned.

What about the other two instance variables? The dateCreated instance variable does not have a setter method; it is created and given its value in the designated initializer. Therefore, the instance of **Possession** already owns it, and it is ensured to exist. The valueInDollars instance variable needs no memory management because valueInDollars is a primitive and not an object.

Implementing dealloc

In the previous section, you released the object pointed to by possessionName when changing the name of a **Possession**. It is just as important to release the objects pointed to by a **Possession**'s instance variables when the **Possession** is being deallocated.

When the retain count of a **Possession** instance hits zero, it will send itself the message **dealloc**. When the **Possession** instance is destroyed, its instance variables that are pointers to other objects are also destroyed (but not the objects they point to). Thus, you must ask yourself if the **Possession** owns these objects, and if it does, you must release them before these pointers are destroyed.

You own the objects pointed to by possessionName and serialNumber by virtue of retaining them in their setter methods. You also own dateCreated because you allocated it in the designated initializer for **Possession**.

Having established that you own these objects, you must release them before you lose your pointers to them. You can do this at the beginning of the **dealloc** method of **Possession**. In Possession.m, override **dealloc** to release the instance variables that the **Possession** owns.

```
- (void)dealloc
{
    [possessionName release];
    [serialNumber release];
    [dateCreated release];
    [super dealloc];
}
```

Always call the superclass implementation of **dealloc** at the end of the method. When an object is deallocated, it should release all of its own instance variables first. Then, because you call the superclass's implementation, it goes up its class hierarchy and releases any instance variables of its superclass. In the end, the implementation of **dealloc** in **NSObject** returns the object's memory to the heap.

Why send **release** to instance variables and not **dealloc**? One object should never send **dealloc** to another. Always use **release** and let the object check its own retain count and decide whether to send itself **dealloc**.

Simplifying accessors with properties

Now that you've added memory management to your setter methods, let's look at a shortcut for creating accessor (both setter and getter) methods called properties. A *property* declares accessors for you in a header file. In Possession.h, replace the accessor declarations with properties.

```
@interface Possession : NSObject
{
    NSString *possessionName;
    NSString *serialNumber;
    int valueInDollars;
    NSDate *dateCreated;
}
+ (id)randomPossession;

- (id)initWithPossessionName:(NSString *)name
              valueInDollars:(int)value
                serialNumber:(NSString *)sNumber;

- (id)initWithPossessionName:(NSString *)name;


@property NSString *possessionName;
@property NSString *serialNumber;
@property int valueInDollars;
@property NSDate *dateCreated;


@end
```

Notice that properties are declared in the method area and not in the curly brackets with the instance variables. They also are, by convention, declared after class methods and initializers but before other instance methods.

Properties replace the accessor declarations, which saves a few lines of typing in the header file. But that's not all. You can also use properties to automatically generate the implementations of the accessor methods. You generate the accessors by *synthesizing* the property in the implementation file. But before we get to the actual synthesizing, we need to talk about *property attributes*.

Every property has a set of attributes that tailors the accessor methods it can generate. These attributes are listed in the property declaration. There are three categories of attributes:

atomicity	We will always use nonatomic for this attribute. There is rarely a reason to use the default, atomic, and the discussion of why is outside the scope of this book.

writability
By default, a property is `readwrite`. A `readwrite` property will generate a setter and getter method. The other option, `readonly`, only generates a getter method.

memory management
This attribute category only applies to the setter method. By default, a property is `assign`. In this case, a property's setter method only assigns the incoming argument to its instance variable. The other options are `retain` and `copy`, where the incoming argument is either retained or copied and then assigned to the instance variable. (We'll talk more about `copy` in a moment.)

In `Possession.h`, add attributes to the property declarations to match the current accessor implementations.

```
// The generated accessor methods for this property will be a getter
// and a setter that retains the incoming object and releases the old object.
@property (nonatomic, retain) NSString *possessionName;

// Ditto to the previous property
@property (nonatomic, retain) NSString *serialNumber;

// The generated accessor methods for this property will be a getter and a setter
// that simply assigns the incoming value to the ivar valueInDollars.
@property (nonatomic) int valueInDollars;

// The only generated accessor method for this property will be a getter.
@property (nonatomic, readonly) NSDate *dateCreated;
```

Now we can synthesize the properties in the implementation file. In `Possession.m`, remove all of the accessor method implementations and synthesize the properties instead.

```
@implementation Possession
@synthesize possessionName, serialNumber, valueInDollars, dateCreated;
```

Build and run the application. Everything should work the same as before.

Let's review what's changed here. Before, you explicitly declared and implemented all of your accessor methods. Now you've replaced the accessor declarations with property declarations and the accessor implementations with an `@synthesize` statement. The **Possession** keeps the same behavior with significantly less typing. In programming, whenever you can specify details and let the system do the work, it not only saves you typing, but it also helps prevent typos and other errors.

(So why did we make you type in all the accessors first instead of going straight to properties? It's important to understand what properties actually do. Too many new developers use properties without understanding the code behind them, and it trips them up later.)

There are a couple of additional points to make about properties. First, you do not have to synthesize a property. You can declare a property in the header file and implement the accessor methods yourself. This is useful for situations where you want to customize the accessors. You can also synthesize a property and implement one of the accessor methods; this overrides the method you replaced without affecting its partner.

Second, the name of a property does not have to match the name of the instance variable. In a synthesize statement, you can point a property at an instance variable of another name.

```
// This is just an example, don't type this code in.
@interface Possession : NSObject
{
    ...
}
@property (nonatomic, assign) NSString *name;
@end

@implementation Possession

@synthesize name = possessionName;
// This is equivalent to
// - (void)setName:(NSString *)str
// {
//      possessionName = str;
// }
// - (NSString *)name
// {
//      return possessionName;
// }
@end
```

This links the **name** property to the possessionName instance variable; therefore, when sending the message **name** to an instance of **Possession**, the value of possessionName is returned.

Finally, you don't even need an instance variable at all. When you synthesize a property, the compiler looks for an instance variable of the same name and if it finds one, it uses that instance variable. If a matching instance variable is not found, one is automatically created for you.

copy and mutableCopy

There are times when instead of retaining an object, you want to copy an object. When you send the message **copy** to an instance, a brand new instance is created that has the same values as the original instance. Copying an object gives you a brand new object with a retain count of one, and the retain count of the original object is unchanged. The object that sent the **copy** message is the owner of the new object.

You typically want to make a copy of an object if it is *mutable*. For example, an **NSMutableArray** is a mutable array. There is also an **NSMutableString**, a mutable subclass of **NSString**. Since **NSMutableString** "is a" **NSString**, it is conceivable that you could have an instance of **NSMutableString** as the possessionName of a **Possession**.

Imagine what would happen if an **NSMutableString** was set as the possessionName of a **Possession**. Another object that had a pointer to this string could change it, which would also change the name of the **Possession**. The **Possession** would have no idea this had happened.

```
NSMutableString *str = [[NSMutableString alloc] initWithString:@"White Sofa"];

// This is okay, as NSMutableString is a NSString since it is a subclass
[possession setPossessionName:str];

[str appendString:@" - Stained"];
// possession's name is now "White Sofa - Stained"
```

Typically, you do not want this behavior. Changing an object's instance variables without using an accessor is usually bad form. You can use **copy** to prevent the possibility of instance variables being changed behind your back.

In general, if a class has a mutable subclass, properties that are of the type of that class should have the attribute copy instead of retain. Then you will have a copy of the object that is all yours.

In Possession.h, change the memory management attribute of the two **NSString** properties to copy.

```
@property (nonatomic, copy) NSString *possessionName;
@property (nonatomic, copy) NSString *serialNumber;
```

The generated setter methods for these properties now look like this:

```
- (void)setPossessionName:(NSString *)str
{
    id t = [str copy];
    [possessionName release];
    possessionName = t;
}
```

When you copy an object, the copy returned is immutable. For instance, if you copy an **NSMutableArray**, the new object is simply an **NSArray**. (If you want a copy that can change, you must send the message **mutableCopy** instead.) Keep in mind, not all classes have mutable subclasses, and not all objects can be copied.

Congratulations! You've implemented retain counts and fixed the memory management problems in RandomPossessions. Your application now manages its memory like a champ!

Keep this code around because you are going to use it in later chapters.

Retain count rules

Let's make a few rules about retain counts to carry with us. In these rules, we use the word "you" to mean "an instance of whatever class you are currently working on." It is a useful form of empathy: you imagine that you are the object you are writing. So, for example, "If you retain the string, it will not be deallocated." really means "If an instance of the class that you are currently working on retains the string it will not be deallocated."

Here, then, are the rules. (Implementation details are in parentheses.)

- If you create an object using a method whose name starts with **alloc** or **new** or contains **copy**, then you have taken ownership of it. (That is, assume that the new object has a retain count of 1 and is *not* in the autorelease pool.) You have a responsibility to release the object when you no longer need it. Here are some of the common methods that convey ownership: **alloc** (which is always followed by an **init** method), **copy**, and **mutableCopy**.

- An object created through *any* other means – like a convenience method – is *not* owned by you. (That is, assume it has a retain count of one and is already in the autorelease pool, and thus doomed unless it is retained before the autorelease pool is drained.)

- If you don't own an object and you want to ensure its continued existence, take ownership by sending it the message **retain**. (This increments the retain count.)

- When you own an object and no longer need it, send it the message **release** or **autorelease**. (**release** decrements the retain count immediately. **autorelease** causes the message **release** to get sent when the autorelease pool is drained.)

- As long as an object has at least one owner, it will continue to exist. (When its retain count goes to zero, it is sent the message **dealloc**.)

One of the tricks to understanding memory management is to think locally. The **Possession** class does not need to know anything about other objects that also care about its possessionName or serialNumber. As long as a **Possession** instance retains objects it wants to keep, you won't have any problems. Programmers new the language sometimes make the mistake of trying to keep tabs on objects throughout an application. Don't do this. If you follow these rules and always think local to a class, you never have to worry what the rest of an application is doing with an object.

Earlier in this chapter, we made changes to the accessor methods of **Possession** so they would properly handle memory management. Before that, the application ran perfectly fine. Why? The objects that were created and set as the instance variables of the **Possession** instances were never released. Therefore, it didn't matter if we retained them. However, in a real application, there are many more moving parts, and objects will be created and released. With proper memory management in place, this **Possession** class will now stand up in a real-world application.

For the More Curious: More on Memory Management

Throughout the book, we include "For the More Curious" sections that go into deeper explanations of topics presented in the chapter. These sections are not absolutely essential to get you where you're going, but we hope you'll find them interesting and useful. Because these sections are more in-depth than the chapter, they are often (but not always) more advanced. If you read through one of these sections and feel stupid, don't worry; everyone felt stupid the first couple of times these concepts were presented to them.

In this chapter, we talked about the heap and how every object lives inside this part of memory. There are actually two more parts of memory that serve different purposes: the data segment and the stack. The data segment is where the application executable lives, and all of the instructions that make up your methods and functions live here. This area in memory never changes after an application is launched. The code is loaded into memory once and isn't modified. When you create a literal **NSString** like so,

```
NSString *foo = @"A string";
```

the memory for this string lives in the data segment as well. We still treat it as an object, though, and if another object wants to keep this string, it must copy or retain it.

The stack is an area of memory reserved for handling the calling of functions. (A method is really just a function under the hood.) When you call a function, a chunk of the stack is reserved specifically for that function. We call this chunk a *stack frame*. The stack frame holds the address of the function that called it so that when the function ends, it can return to the previous function. It also contains any of the arguments passed to the function and a space to store the return value of a function. Additionally, it reserves memory for the local variables of a function.

```
- (void)fido
{
    int x = 5;
    NSString *str = [[NSString alloc] init];

    // The variable "str" is a local variable and it lives in the stack frame
    // The string it points to lives on the heap.
}
```

Figure 3.6 Pointer on the stack, object on the heap

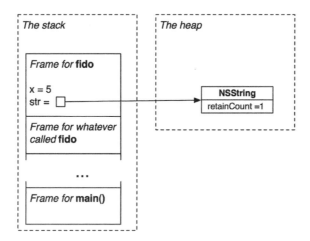

When a function exits, the stack frame is destroyed along with all of the local variables it had.

We also made a distinction between instance variables that are pointers to objects and instance variables that are primitives. When we add instance variables to a class, we are increasing the size in memory of an instance of that class by the amount of memory that instance variable needs to store its information.

A pointer instance variable is simply four bytes: the amount needed to hold an address of another object that lives on the heap. A primitive's memory is stored inside that instance, so adding a double, for example, would add 8 bytes to the size of that instance.

A **Possession** has three pointers instance variables and one int, which are each 4 bytes. Therefore, the **Possession** is 16 bytes plus the amount of bytes an **NSObject** needs. Let's pretend an **NSObject** is also 4, for a total of 20 bytes needed per **Possession**.

So, when instantiating a **Possession**, 20 bytes are allocated from the heap. Even if the **NSString** that is the possessionName of that **Possession** is 100 bytes (because it has 100 characters), the **Possession** itself remains 20 bytes. This can help us understand the difference between pointers to objects and objects themselves.

4

Delegation and Core Location

In this chapter, we will introduce delegation, a recurring design pattern of Cocoa Touch development and the Core Location framework, which provides the location-finding features of iOS. In addition, we will also take a quick look at how to use the debugger that Xcode provides to find and fix problems in your code.

To learn about delegation, you're going to write an application called Whereami that uses delegation over and over again. This application will display an interactive map and allow the user to tag the current location with a pin and a title. This exercise spans two chapters. At the end of this chapter, the application won't look like much, but the final product – and the clearer understanding of delegation – will be worth it.

From the File menu, select New and then New Project.... On the next window, select Application from the iOS section and create a Window-based Application. Name the project Whereami and select iPhone as the device family.

Projects, targets, and frameworks

Let's look more closely at the what this new project actually is. A *project* is a file that contains a list of references to other files (source code, resources, frameworks, and libraries) as well as a number of settings that lay out the rules for items within the project. Projects end in .xcodeproj, as in Whereami.xcodeproj.

A project always has at least one target. A *target* uses the files in the project to build a particular product. When you build and run, you build and run the target, not the project.

The *product* the target builds is typically an application, although it can be a compiled library or a unit test bundle. When you create a new project and choose a template, Xcode automatically creates a target for you. When you created the Whereami project, you selected an iOS application, so Xcode created an iOS application target and named it Whereami.

In the project navigator, select the Whereami project (the item at the very top). Notice that the Whereami project and the Whereami target are listed in the editor area. Select the Whereami target to see the details and settings that define this target. (We won't discuss all of these now, but we'll come back to different ones as we need them.) From the choices at the top of the editor area, select Build Phases (Figure 4.1). The target's build phases are a series of steps, and these steps lead, in this case, to an iOS application.

Figure 4.1   Build phases of the Whereami target

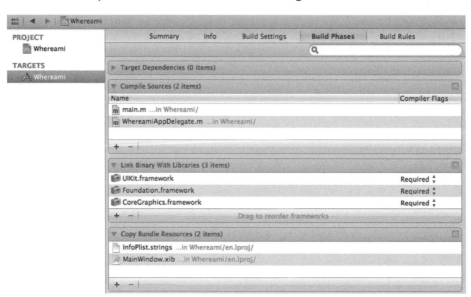

The essential build phases for creating an iOS application are Compile Sources, Link Binary With Libraries, and Copy Bundle Resources. We'll look at these phases in detail at the end of the chapter. For now, let's focus on Link Binary With Libraries and *frameworks*.

A *framework* is a collection of related classes that you can add to a target. Cocoa Touch is a collection of frameworks. One of the benefits of Cocoa Touch being organized into frameworks is that you only have to add the frameworks that a target needs.

To see what frameworks are already linked to your target, click the disclosure button next to Link Binary With Libraries. Right now, there are three. The UIKit framework contains classes that make up the iOS user interface, the Foundation framework includes classes like **NSString** and **NSArray**, and Core Graphics enables the graphics library that we will dig into starting in Chapter 6.

Whereami also needs the Core Location framework, which includes the classes related to finding a device's location. To add this framework to your target, click the plus (+) button in the bottom left corner of the Link Binary With Libraries section. A sheet that displays the available frameworks will appear (Figure 4.2). Select CoreLocation.framework from this list and click Add.

Figure 4.2   Adding the Core Location framework

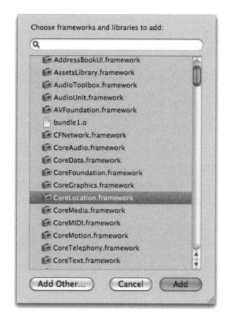

CoreLocation.framework will now appear in the Link Binary With Libraries phase and in the project navigator. In the project navigator, you can move the framework to the Frameworks group to keep your project tidy, but you don't have to.

Make sure you remember how to add a framework to a project – you will have to do it fairly frequently!

Core Location

The Core Location framework contains the classes that enable applications to determine the device's geographical location. No matter what type of iOS device is being used, the Core Location code you write does not change.

The classes in the Core Location framework are all prefixed with **CL**. In fact, every framework in Cocoa Touch has its own prefix – UIKit classes are prefixed with **UI**, Foundation classes with **NS**, etc. Prefixing class names is a convention that prevents namespace collisions. For example, pretend that both Foundation and Core Location have classes called **Object**. If you wrote an application that used both frameworks, any instantiation of an **Object** would leave the compiler in a quandary – *which* **Object** does this code refer to? Note that prefixes aren't just for frameworks. Objective-C programmers typically include prefixes of two or three letters in the names of classes they create for the same reason.

In addition to adding the Core Location framework to your target, you also have to import the framework's header file into files that need to know about Core Location classes. Every framework has a header file that imports the header file of every class in that framework. This file is always the name of the framework suffixed with .h.

Open `WhereamiAppDelegate.h` and import the Core Location header file at the top. Also, add an instance variable to hold a pointer to an instance of **CLLocationManager** – one of the classes in the Core Location framework.

```
#import <UIKit/UIKit.h>
#import <CoreLocation/CoreLocation.h>

@interface WhereamiAppDelegate : NSObject <UIApplicationDelegate>
{
    CLLocationManager *locationManager;
}
@property (nonatomic, retain) IBOutlet UIWindow *window;
@end
```

CLLocationManager is the class that interfaces with the location hardware of the device. An instance of **CLLocationManager** has a number of properties that specify its behavior. We're going to set two of them: `distanceFilter` and `desiredAccuracy`.

The `distanceFilter` property determines how far the device must move in meters before **CLLocationManager** will tell your application that the location has changed. The `desiredAccuracy` property tells the location manager how accurate the location-finding should be. This is important because there is a tradeoff between the accuracy of the location and the amount of battery life and time required to determine the location. Moreover, the accuracy ultimately depends on the type of device the user has, the availability of cellular towers and satellites, and the availability of known wireless access points.

Once its properties are set, the **CLLocationManager** is told to start working. It then does its thing while the rest of the application continues with other tasks – like accepting user input or updating the interface.

Open `WhereamiAppDelegate.m`, and in the **application:didFinishLaunchingWithOptions:** method, instantiate a **CLLocationManager** to track the device's location. For this application, you will set its properties to request the most accurate location data as often as possible.

```
- (BOOL)application:(UIApplication *)application
    didFinishLaunchingWithOptions:(NSDictionary *)launchOptions
{
    // Create location manager object
    locationManager = [[CLLocationManager alloc] init];

    // We want all results from the location manager
    [locationManager setDistanceFilter:kCLDistanceFilterNone];

    // And we want it to be as accurate as possible
    // regardless of how much time/power it takes
    [locationManager setDesiredAccuracy:kCLLocationAccuracyBest];

    // Tell our manager to start looking for its location immediately
    [locationManager startUpdatingLocation];

    // This line may say self.window, don't worry about that
    [[self window] makeKeyAndVisible];
    return YES;
}
```

Receiving updates from CLLocationManager

If you build and run this code right now, the location manager will get your current location, but you won't see this information anywhere. Your application has to retrieve the location from the location manager. You might guess that there is a property on **CLLocationManager** called currentLocation that we can access to retrieve the location. It's a good guess, but there isn't. You could try polling the location manager to get the location, but the amount of time it takes to determine the current location is too variable for polling to be efficient.

The best solution is for the location manager to take matters into its own hands. Whenever it finds the current location, it sends the message **locationManager:didUpdateToLocation:fromLocation:**. Who is sent this message? The location manager's *delegate* – and we get to decide who that is.

Every **CLLocationManager** has a delegate property, and we can set this property to point to the object that should receive the "location found" message. For Whereami, this object is the **WhereamiAppDelegate** (Figure 4.3).

Figure 4.3   Whereami object diagram

In WhereamiAppDelegate.m, update the **application:didFinishLaunchingWithOptions:** method to set the delegate property of the location manager to be the instance of **WhereamiAppDelegate**.

```
- (BOOL)application:(UIApplication *)application
    didFinishLaunchingWithOptions:(NSDictionary *)launchOptions
{
    locationManager = [[CLLocationManager alloc] init];

    // There will be a warning from this line of code; ignore it for now
    [locationManager setDelegate:self];

    [locationManager setDistanceFilter:kCLDistanceFilterNone];
```

One of the arguments of the **locationManager:didUpdateToLocation:fromLocation:** message is an instance of a class named **CLLocation**. When a **CLLocationManager** has enough data to produce a new location, it creates an instance of **CLLocation**, which contains the latitude and longitude of the device (Figure 4.4). It also contains the accuracy of its reading and, depending on the device, the elevation above sea level.

Figure 4.4   A CLLocation object

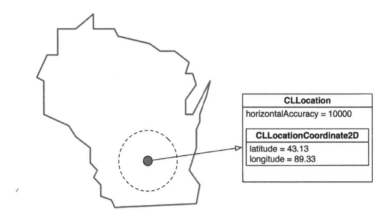

Because the **CLLocationManager** sends **locationManager:didUpdateToLocation:fromLocation:** to the instance of **WhereamiAppDelegate**, you implement this method in WhereamiAppDelegate.m. (Be very careful that there are no typos or capitalization errors, or it won't be called. The selector of the message the location manager sends must exactly match the selector of the method implemented.)

```
- (void)locationManager:(CLLocationManager *)manager
    didUpdateToLocation:(CLLocation *)newLocation
           fromLocation:(CLLocation *)oldLocation
{
    NSLog(@"%@", newLocation);
}
```

You also need to know if the **CLLocationManager** fails to find its location and why. If it fails, **CLLocationManager** sends a different message to its delegate – **locationManager:didFailWithError:**. In WhereamiAppDelegate.m, implement this method.

```
- (void)locationManager:(CLLocationManager *)manager
       didFailWithError:(NSError *)error
{
    NSLog(@"Could not find location: %@", error);
}
```

Build and run the application. You can choose whether to build to the simulator or to a device by selecting the appropriate item from the Scheme pop-up button next to the Run and Stop buttons. After giving permission for the application to use location services and waiting a few seconds while the location is found, your console should display the description of the location object, which looks something like this:

```
<+37.33168900, -122.03073100> +/- 100.00m (speed -1.00 mps / course -1.00)
```

Delegation

When you set the delegate property of the **CLLocationManager** and implemented the two methods in **WhereamiAppDelegate**, you were using a design pattern called *delegation*. This is a very common pattern in Cocoa Touch, and many classes have a delegate property.

Delegation is an object-oriented approach to *callbacks*. A callback is a function that is supplied in advance of an event and is called every time the event occurs. Some objects need to make a callback for more than one event. For instance, the location manager wants to "callback" when it finds a new location and when it encounters an error.

However, there is no built-in way for two (or more) callback functions to coordinate and share information. This is the problem addressed by delegation – we supply a single delegate to receive all of the event messages for a particular object. This delegate object can then store, manipulate, act on, and relay the related information as it sees fit.

Let's take a moment to compare delegation with another object-oriented approach to callbacks: target-action pairs. (You used this approach in Chapter 1 with the **UIButton**s in your Quiz application.) In a target-action pair, you have a target object that you send an action message to when an event occurs. The target must implement the action message, and, for each event, a new target-action pair must be created. With delegation, on the other hand, you set the delegate once and can then send it messages for different events. The delegate will implement the method for each event it wants to hear about (Figure 4.5).

Figure 4.5   Target-Action vs. Delegation

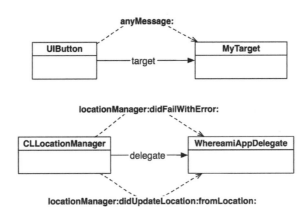

Also, with a target-action pair, you can send the target any action message you choose. Delegation, however, does not offer this flexibility; an object can only send its delegate a specific set of messages listed in a *protocol*.

Protocols

For every object that can have a delegate, there is a corresponding *protocol* that declares the messages that the object can send its delegate. The delegate implements methods from the protocol for events it is interested in. When a class implements methods from a protocol, it is said to *conform to* the protocol.

The protocol for **CLLocationManager**'s delegate looks like this:

```
// Note that a few methods have been omitted
// from the real declaration of this protocol
// so we can focus on what is going on
```

```
@protocol CLLocationManagerDelegate <NSObject>

@optional

- (void)locationManager:(CLLocationManager *)manager
    didUpdateToLocation:(CLLocation *)newLocation
           fromLocation:(CLLocation *)oldLocation;

- (void)locationManager:(CLLocationManager *)manager
        didUpdateHeading:(CLHeading *)newHeading;

- (BOOL)locationManagerShouldDisplayHeadingCalibration:(CLLocationManager *)manager;

- (void)locationManager:(CLLocationManager *)manager
          didEnterRegion:(CLRegion *)region;

- (void)locationManager:(CLLocationManager *)manager
        didFailWithError:(NSError *)error;
@end
```

This protocol, like all protocols, is declared with the directive @protocol followed by its name, CLLocationManagerDelegate. The NSObject in angled brackets refers to the NSObject protocol and tells us that CLLocationManagerDelegate includes all of the methods in the NSObject protocol. The methods specific to CLLocationManagerDelegate are declared next, and then the protocol is closed with an @end directive.

Note that a protocol is not a class; it is simply a list of methods. You cannot create instances of a protocol, it cannot have instance variables, and these methods are not implemented anywhere in the protocol. Instead, the implementation is left to each class that conforms to the protocol.

We call protocols used for delegation *delegate protocols*, and the naming convention for a delegate protocol is the name of the delegating class plus the word Delegate. Not all protocols are delegate protocols, however, and we will see an example of a different kind of protocol in the next chapter.

All of the protocols we've mentioned so far are part of the iOS SDK, but you can also write your own protocols. We'll do that later in Chapter 14 and Chapter 26.

Protocol methods

In the CLLocationManagerDelegate protocol, we see two types of methods: methods that handle information updates and methods that handle requests for input. For example, the location manager's delegate implements the **locationManager:didEnterRegion:** method if it wants to hear from the location manager that the device has entered a particular region. On the other hand, **locationManagerShouldDisplayHeadingCalibration:** is the message a location manager sends its delegate to ask if it should display the heading calibration. The method returns a BOOL value, which is the delegate's answer.

Methods declared in a protocol can be required or optional. By default, protocol methods are required. If a protocol has optional methods, these are preceded by the directive @optional. Looking back at the CLLocationManagerDelegate protocol, you can see that all of its methods are optional. This is typically true of delegate protocols.

Before sending an optional method, the object first asks its delegate by sending another message, **respondsToSelector:**. Every object implements this method, which checks at runtime whether an object implements a given method. You can turn a selector into a value you can pass as an argument with the @selector() directive. For example, **CLLocationManager** could implement a method that looks like this:

```
- (void)finishedFindingLocation:(CLLocation *)newLocation
{
    // locationManager:didUpdateToLocation:fromLocation:
    // is an optional method, so we check first.
    SEL updateMethod = @selector(locationManager:didUpdateToLocation:fromLocation:);

    if ([[self delegate] respondsToSelector:updateMethod]) {
        // If the method is implemented, then we send the message.
        [[self delegate] locationManager:self
                    didUpdateToLocation:newLocation
                        fromLocation:oldLocation];
    }
}
```

If a method in a protocol is required, then the message will be sent without checking first. This means that if the delegate does not implement that method, an unrecognized selector exception will be thrown, and the application will crash.

To prevent this from happening, the compiler will insist that a class implement the required methods in a protocol. But, in order for the compiler to know to check for these methods, the class must explicitly state that it conforms to a protocol. This is done in the class header file: the protocols that a class conforms to are added to a comma-delimited list inside angled brackets in the interface declaration following the superclass.

In WhereamiAppDelegate.h, declare that **WhereamiAppDelegate** conforms to the CLLocationManagerDelegate protocol.

```
@interface WhereamiAppDelegate : NSObject
    <UIApplicationDelegate, CLLocationManagerDelegate>
```

Build the application again. (Now that you've declared that **WhereamiAppDelegate** conforms to the CLLocationManagerDelegate protocol, the warning from the line of code where you set the delegate of the locationManager disappears.)

Notice the UIApplicationDelegate protocol in this declaration. The method **application:didFinishLaunchingWithOptions:** is from the UIApplicationDelegate protocol. It's a message that the **UIApplication** can send its delegate when the application is done launching and is about to start accepting user input. For Whereami, the delegate of the **UIApplication** is the instance of **WhereamiAppDelegate**. (The template set this property for you.) So, that delegate method is declared in the UIApplicationDelegate protocol and implemented in WhereamiAppDelegate.m.

Delegation, controllers, and memory management

From the perspective of the model-view-controller pattern, **WhereamiAppDelegate** is a controller object. It is typically the case that delegates are controller objects.

Delegates are never retained by their delegating objects. Why? Consider **WhereamiAppDelegate**. It owns locationManager and is also the delegate of locationManager. If the locationManager retained the **WhereamiAppDelegate**, these two objects would own each other and create something called a retain cycle. We will discuss retain cycles in more depth in Chapter 6, but the idea is if two objects retain each other, then they will never be deallocated.

To avoid retain cycles, delegate properties use the assign attribute instead of retain or copy. We call this a "weak reference," where an object has a pointer to another object but does not retain it.

```
@property (nonatomic, assign) id delegate;
```

Remember that the point of owning an object is that you can rely on its existence and will never get caught sending messages to an object that doesn't exist. So, if an object cannot retain its delegate, then the delegate must be responsible and tell the object when it is being deallocated.

In this application, however, the **WhereamiAppDelegate** instance never gets deallocated. Check for yourself – place an **NSLog** in **WhereamiAppDelegate**'s **dealloc**, and you'll never see it. Some controller objects are made to exist the entire time an application is running, and this is always the case for the **AppDelegate**. For classes like this, we typically don't bother writing **dealloc** methods. When you first begin programming for iOS, it may be difficult to determine whether a controller will be destroyed. When you aren't sure, you should implement **dealloc** – it never hurts to do so.

So let's go ahead and examine what **WhereamiAppDelegate**'s **dealloc** method would look like if we were to implement it. We know it needs to remove itself as the location manager's delegate. But there is one other important thing it must do – release the locationManager instance variable.

```
- (void)dealloc
{
    if([locationManager delegate] == self)
        [locationManager setDelegate:nil];

    [locationManager release];
    [window release];
    [super dealloc];
}
```

As you learned in the last chapter, releasing instance variables when an object is deallocated is important for freeing up memory and avoiding memory leaks. The object pointed to by locationManager is owned by the instance of **WhereamiAppDelegate** because you **alloc**'ed it in **application:didFinishLaunchingWithOptions:**. So, if the **WhereamiAppDelegate** was ever going to be destroyed, it would need to release locationManager in **dealloc**.

Note that the possibility of not implementing **dealloc** is for controller objects only; model and view objects should *always* have **dealloc** methods. Also, keep in mind that each of your applications so far has only had a single controller object, the **AppDelegate**. Soon, you'll build applications that have multiple controllers, some of which will definitely need to be deallocated. We will return to this discussion once we start building more complicated applications.

Using the Debugger

When an application is launched from Xcode, the debugger is attached to that application. The debugger monitors the current state of the application, like what method it is currently executing and the values of the variables that are accessible from that method. Using the debugger can help you understand what an application is actually doing, which, in turn, helps you find and fix bugs.

One way to use the debugger is to set a *breakpoint*. Setting a breakpoint on a line of code pauses the execution of the application at that line (before it executes). This is useful when your application is not doing what you expected and you need to look at what is really happening.

In `WhereamiAppDelegate.m`, find the first line of code in
`application:didFinishLaunchingWithOptions:` where you instantiate the **`CLLocationManager`**. Set a breakpoint by clicking the gutter (the lightly shaded bar on the left side of the editor area) next to that line of code. The blue indicator shows you where the application will "break" the next time you run it (Figure 4.6).

Figure 4.6   A breakpoint

```
- (BOOL)application:(UIApplication *)application
    didFinishLaunchingWithOptions:(NSDictionary *)launchOptions
{
    // Create location manager object -
    // it will send its messages to our WhereamiAppDelegate
    locationManager = [[CLLocationManager alloc] init];
    [locationManager setDelegate:self];

    // We want all results from the location manager
    [locationManager setDistanceFilter:kCLDistanceFilterNone];
```

Build and run the application. The application will start and then stop before the first line of **`application:didFinishLaunchingWithOptions:`** is executed. Notice the green indicator that appears on the same line as the breakpoint. This indicator shows you the current point of execution.

Now our application is temporarily frozen in time, and we can examine it more closely. In the navigator area, click the ☰ icon to open the *debug navigator*. This navigator shows a *stack trace* of where the breakpoint stopped execution. The slider at the bottom of the debug navigator expands and collapses the stack. Drag it to the right to see all of the methods in the stack trace. (Figure 4.7).

Figure 4.7   The debug navigator

The method where the break occurred is at the top of the stack trace. It was called by the method just below it, which was called by the method just below it, and so on. This chain of method calls continues all the way back to **main**. Notice that the two methods that you implemented are in black text and the methods Apple implemented are in gray.

Select the method at the top of the stack. This will display the implementation of **application:didFinishLaunchingWithOptions:** in the editor area. Below the editor area, check out the variables view to the left of the console. This area shows the variables available within the scope of this method along with their current values (Figure 4.8).

Figure 4.8   Debug area with Variables View

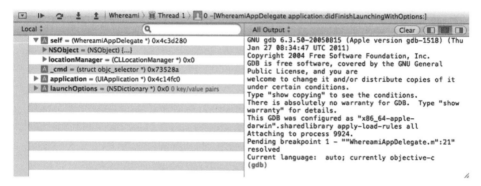

(If you don't see the variables view, find the ⬛⬛⬛ control above the console. Click the center button to see both the console and the variables view.)

In the variables view, a variable that is a pointer to an object shows the object's address in memory. (There are some exceptions, like **NSString**, where the actual string is shown instead.) A variable that is a primitive, like int, shows its actual value.

Now click the disclosure button next to self. The first item under self is its superclass. In the context of this method, self is a pointer to the instance of **WhereamiAppDelegate**, so its superclass is **NSObject**. Clicking the disclosure button next to **NSObject** shows what self inherits from its superclass.

After the superclass, you can check out the object's instance variables, which for **WhereamiAppDelegate**, is just locationManager. The breakpoint is set to the line that creates the instance of **CLLocationManager** and assigns it to locationManager. That line of code has yet to be executed, so locationManager is still set to nil (0x0).

In addition to giving you a snapshot of the application at a given point, the debugger also allows you to "step through" your code line by line and watch the behavior of your application as each line executes. The buttons that control the execution are on the *debugger bar*. This bar sits between the editor area and the debug area (Figure 4.9).

Click the button to step over a line. This will execute just the current line of code, which instantiates the **CLLocationManager**. Notice that the green execution indicator moves to the next line. Even more interesting, the variables view shows that the value of locationManager has changed to a valid address in memory – this object is now alive and well.

Figure 4.9 Debugger bar

At this point, you could continue stepping through the code to see what happens. Or you could click the button to continue executing your code normally. Or you could step into a method. Stepping into a method takes you to the method that is called by the line of code that currently has the green execution indicator. Once you're in the method, you have the chance to step through its code in the same way.

Let's add a method that we can step into and out of. Declare the following method in WhereamiAppDelegate.h.

```
#import <UIKit/UIKit.h>
#import <CoreLocation/CoreLocation.h>

@interface WhereamiAppDelegate : NSObject
    <UIApplicationDelegate, CLLocationManagerDelegate>
{
    CLLocationManager *locationManager;
}
@property (nonatomic, retain) IBOutlet UIWindow *window;

- (void)doSomethingWeird;

@end
```

In WhereamiAppDelegate.m, implement this method to log some stuff to the console.

```
- (void)doSomethingWeird
{
    NSLog(@"Line 1");
    NSLog(@"Line 2");
    NSLog(@"Line 3");
}
```

Next in `WhereamiAppDelegate.m`, send this message to the instance of **WhereamiAppDelegate** in **application:didFinishLaunchingWithOptions:**.

```
- (BOOL)application:(UIApplication *)application
    didFinishLaunchingWithOptions:(NSDictionary *)launchOptions
{
    // Create location manager object -
    // it will send its messages to our WhereamiAppDelegate
    locationManager = [[CLLocationManager alloc] init];

    [self doSomethingWeird];
```

Finally, drag your breakpoint to this newly-implemented line. Build and run the application.

When the execution halts, click the button to step into this method. The execution indicator will jump *inside* the **doSomethingWeird** method to the first line of its implementation. Now click the button to step over a line. The line of code that logs Line 1 will execute, and you will see its text in the console.

The execution indicator is now at the statement that logs Line 2. If you've decided that you've seen enough of this fascinating method, you can click the button to step out of it. Notice that the rest of the log statements appear in the console, and the execution indicator is now back in **application:didFinishLaunchingWithOptions:** – right after the call to **doSomethingWeird**. This behavior is important to understand: when you step out of a method, you don't cancel its execution; the method will finish normally and return to the code that called it.

To remove the breakpoint, simply drag it off the gutter. Or click the ➡ icon in the navigator selector to reveal the breakpoint navigator and see all the breakpoints in your project. From there, you can select a breakpoint and delete it.

Sometimes, a new developer will set a breakpoint and forget about it. Then, when the application is run, execution stops, and it looks like the application has crashed. If you can't make out why an application of yours has "crashed," make sure you aren't stopped on a forgotten breakpoint.

While you can set breakpoints to break on a particular line, the debugger will break on any line that causes your application to crash or that causes an exception to be thrown. Let's introduce an exception to see this happen. In `WhereamiAppDelegate.m`, delete the entire implementation of **doSomethingWeird** (not just the code inside the method's brackets, but the method signature, too). Leave the line in **application:didFinishLaunchingWithOptions:** that sends the **doSomethingWeird** message and leave the declaration in the header file.

Now **WhereamiAppDelegate** no longer implements this method, and when it sends this message to self, an exception will be thrown. Build and run the application.

Immediately after launch, the application will blow up. The debugger will show you where (look for the green execution indicator), and the console will show you why. Notice that the stack trace is a bit longer this time, and the method that caused the exception is not at the top of the stack trace. This will sometimes be the case: your code supplies bad data (like an unrecognized selector) to a method, and then somewhere within that method's implementation, the application crashes. To find the source of the error, look for your methods in the stack trace. The culprit may not be at the top, but it will certainly be one of yours.

Also notice that the compiler warned you that the method definition was not found for **doSomethingWeird**. This means you declared a method in the header file but did not implement it. Remove the declaration of **doSomethingWeird** from `WhereamiAppDelegate.h` and build again. This time, you will see a different warning at the point where **doSomethingWeird** is sent to self. Now the compiler is telling you that this method doesn't exist at all.

Remove the line of code that sends **doSomethingWeird** to self. Your application should run correctly again. Build and run to make sure before heading to the next chapter.

Challenge: Heading

Most chapters in this book will finish with a challenge that encourages you to take the application another step further and prove to yourself what you've learned. We suggest that you tackle as many of these challenges as you can to cement your knowledge and move from *learning* iOS development from us to *doing* iOS development on your own.

In addition, these challenges usually require poking around in the Apple documentation – an essential skill for an iOS developer. We will talk more about the documentation in the next chapter. In the meantime, you can get to the "doc" by selecting Documentation and API Reference from Xcode's Help menu. For the following challenge, you'll want to search for CLLocationManager.

Using delegation, retrieve the heading information from the **CLLocationManager** and print it to the console. (Hint: You need to implement at least one more delegate method and send another message to the location manager.)

For the More Curious: Build Phases, Compiler Errors, and Linker Errors

Building an application in Xcode takes several steps. We call these steps *build phases*, and you saw them earlier in this chapter when you were adding the Core Location framework to the Whereami target (Figure 4.1). Here is what each build phase does:

Compile Sources
: This build phase contains the source code files that are compiled when this target is built. By default, any time you add a source code file to a project, it is added to this build phase.

Link Binary With Libraries
: After your source code has been compiled, it is linked with the frameworks (libraries). This allows your code to use classes from these frameworks.

Copy Bundle Resources
: After your code is compiled and linked, an executable is created and placed inside an application bundle, which is really just a folder. Then, the files listed in the Copy Bundle Resources phase are added to the bundle alongside the executable. These resources are the data files that your application uses at runtime, like MainWindow.xib and any images or sounds that are part of the application. By default, when you add a file to a project that is not source code, it is added to this build phase.

We usually see errors during the Compile Sources phase, but sometimes we get errors during the Link Binary With Libraries phase. Errors generated during these phases are easier to diagnose and correct if you understand what the phases do.

Preprocessing

The Compile Sources build phase can be broken into two steps: preprocessing and compiling. The goal of the preprocessing phase is to create an *intermediate file* for each implementation file (.m). The intermediate file is still Objective-C code like the implementation file, but, as we will see, the intermediate file can get very large.

To create an intermediate file, the preprocessor resolves all the preprocessor directives in the implementation file. Preprocessor directives are statements prefixed with the pound symbol (#), like #import. The resolution of a #import statement replaces the import statement with the contents of the imported file. (You can view the contents of imported files by Command-clicking the import statement.)

For example, consider WhereamiAppDelegate.m, which imports WhereamiAppDelegate.h. The intermediate file created for WhereamiAppDelegate.m contains all the code from WhereamiAppDelegate.h and WhereamiAppDelegate.m. But, it doesn't stop there. WhereamiAppDelegate.h imports two files, UIKit.h and CoreLocation.h. These two files import more header files, which import more header files, and so on. The intermediate file for WhereamiAppDelegate.m is all of the code in all of these files (Figure 4.10).

Figure 4.10   Preprocessor creates intermediate files

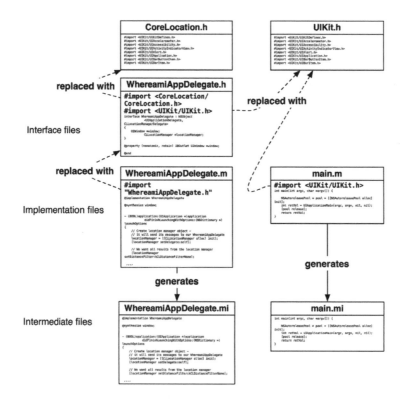

Compiling

Once the preprocessor has finished, the generated intermediate files are compiled. Compiling an intermediate file takes the Objective-C code and turns it into machine code. This machine code is stored in an *object file*, one for each intermediate file.

The compiling phase – the transition to machine code – is where we see most of our errors as programmers. When the compiler doesn't understand our code, it generates an error. We call errors generated during this phase *compile-time errors* or *syntax errors*. Compile-time errors are typically misplaced semicolons, unbalanced brackets ([]) or braces ({}), spelling or capitalization errors.

These types of errors also occur when you use a class that hasn't been declared. To see an example of a compile-time error, comment out the following line in `WhereamiAppDelegate.h`:

```
// #import <CoreLocation/CoreLocation.h>
```

Build the application again, and the compile phase will fail. To see the problem up close, click the ▲ icon to open the issue navigator or hit Command-4. This navigator shows you any errors or warnings in your code (Figure 4.11). You can click on an individual error to see the line of code that generated the error.

Figure 4.11   Build results with compile-time error

Before you removed the import statement, the intermediate file created from `WhereamiAppDelegate.m` contained the code from `CoreLocation.h`, which contained the interface declaration for **CLLocationManager** and the protocol declaration for `CLLocationManagerDelegate`. Without the import statement, these files do not become part of the generated intermediate file, and the compiler has no idea what to do with these lines of code. Note that the compiler can only read one intermediate file at a time, so even though the class and protocol are in other intermediate files, the compiler still generates an error when they are not declared for WhereamiAppDelegate.m.

Uncomment the import statement. You should be able to build again with no errors.

Linking

An object file contains the machine code for the methods implemented in the implementation file. However, within an implementation file, you use code from other implementation files. For example, WhereamiAppDelegate.m uses the **startUpdatingLocation** method, and the machine code for that method is in the object file generated from CLLocationManager.m.

Instead of copying the code for this method into the object file for WhereamiAppDelegate.m, the compiler leaves a link to the object file for CLLocationManager.m. The Link Binary With Libraries phase is where these links are resolved. For short, we just call it the "linking phase."

Recall earlier in the chapter that you "linked" the Core Location framework to your target. A framework is a collection of classes, and a class is defined by two files: a header file and an implementation file. A framework, however, has pre-compiled its implementation files and shoved the resulting object files into one or more *library* files. (That's why in Objective-C you can't see the implementation files in a framework – they are already machine code.) Where you used code from the classes in the Core Location framework in your classes, the compiler put a link in your object files to the Core Location library (Figure 4.12).

Figure 4.12   Compiler creates object files; linker resolves links

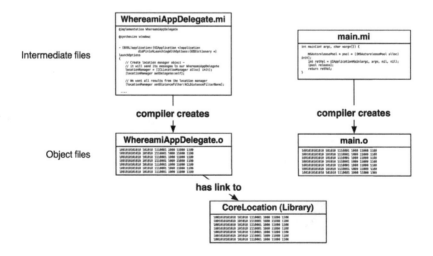

If a link cannot be resolved (because the object file that contains the code cannot be found or because the object file doesn't contain the referenced code), you get a linker error. Linker errors are more difficult for new developers to understand because they use unfamiliar terms and because there isn't one line of code that generated the error. So let's cause a linker error just for practice. Select CoreLocation.framework from the project navigator and hit the Delete key. On the window that appears, choose Remove Reference Only. Build the application again, and you will see new errors (Figure 4.13).

Figure 4.13   Build results with linker error

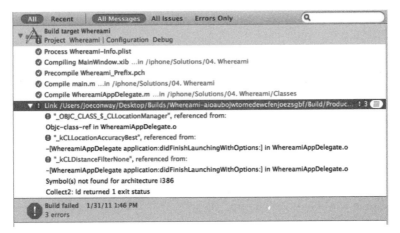

You can select an error in the issue navigator to see a more detailed description of what is going on. (You can also go to the log navigator and select the most recent Build Whereami item and see the same information.) Notice that the errors generated are underneath the item named Link. When you see linker errors, it is typically because you did not add the appropriate framework to your target. Add the CoreLocation.framework file back to the target in the Link Binary With Libraries build phase and build again to confirm that you have fixed the error.

5

MapKit and Text Input

In this chapter, you will finish the Whereami application using the MapKit framework, the **UITextField** class, and more delegation. We will also dive into the Apple documentation.

Right now, your Whereami application finds the location and prints it to the console. At the end of this chapter, the application will show a map of the current location instead. In addition, the user will have the option to tag and name the current location with a MapKit *annotation* The default MapKit annotation appears as a red pin on the map (Figure 5.1).

Figure 5.1   Completed Whereami application

Object Diagrams

iOS applications can get very large and use many classes and methods. One way to keep your head wrapped around a large and complex project is to draw an *object diagram*. Object diagrams show the major objects in an application and any objects they have as instance variables. (At Big Nerd Ranch, we use a program called OmniGraffle to draw our object diagrams.) Most exercises in this book will show you an object diagram to give you the big picture of the application you are developing. Figure 5.2 shows the object diagram for the complete Whereami application.

Figure 5.2   Whereami object diagram

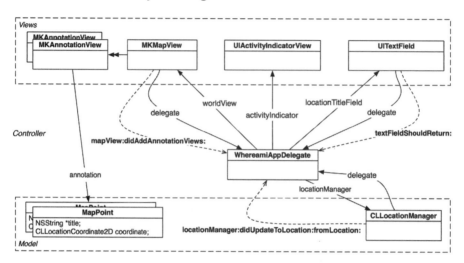

Let's go through this diagram. At the top are the view objects:

- Several instances of **MKAnnotationView** appear as icons on the **MKMapView**.

- An **MKMapView** displays the map and the labels for the recorded locations.

- A **UIActivityIndicatorView** indicates that the device is working and not stalled.

- A **UITextField** allows the user to input text to label the current location on the map.

The model objects are on the bottom. One is an instance of **CLLocationManager**, which interacts with the device's hardware to determine the user's location. The other model objects are instances of a class called **MapPoint**, which you will create later in this chapter.

In the middle of everything is the controller object, **WhereamiAppDelegate**. **WhereamiAppDelegate** is responsible for processing updates and requests from objects and for updating the user interface. It is the delegate for the **MKMapView**, **UITextField**, and **CLLocationManager**.

Take a look at the messages sent to **WhereamiAppDelegate** by these objects. **MKMapView** sends **mapView:didAddAnnotationViews:** when a view (or views) is added. **UITextField** sends **textFieldShouldReturn:** when the user has finished entering text. **CLLocationManager** sends **locationManager:didUpdateToLocation:fromLocation:** to inform **WhereamiAppDelegate** of a location update.

MapKit Framework

The Core Location framework tells us where we are in the world; the MapKit framework shows us that world. Most of MapKit's work is done by the class **MKMapView**. Instances of this type display a map, track touches, and display annotations. (They can do more, but that's all you'll need for this application.)

Add the MapKit framework to your project. (If you've forgotten how, flip back to the beginning of Chapter 4 and refresh your memory.) You must also import the MapKit header file into files that will use MapKit classes.

At the top of WhereamiAppDelegate.h, import the MapKit header.

```
#import <CoreLocation/CoreLocation.h>
#import <MapKit/MapKit.h>
```

To determine the necessary instance variables for the Whereami project, review the object diagram in Figure 5.2. You'll need an **MKMapView**, a **UITextField**, and a **UIActivityIndicatorView**. (We'll handle the **MKAnnotationView**s in a later section.) Declare these instance variables in WhereamiAppDelegate.h.

```
@interface WhereamiAppDelegate : NSObject
    <UIApplicationDelegate, CLLocationManagerDelegate>
{
    CLLocationManager *locationManager;

    IBOutlet MKMapView *worldView;
    IBOutlet UIActivityIndicatorView *activityIndicator;
    IBOutlet UITextField *locationTitleField;
}
@property (nonatomic, retain) IBOutlet UIWindow *window;

@end
```

Because you've used IBOutlet in these declarations, you're going to configure the objects in a XIB file. Open MainWindow.xib and select the Window object in the outline view. This will open the **UIWindow** instance, and we can begin building the user interface.

Interface Properties

In the object library, use the search box at the bottom of the library pane to find an **MKMapView** (Figure 5.3). Then drag the map view onto the **UIWindow**. (Remember – the object library is at the bottom of the utilities area. To show the utilities area, click the right button in the View segmented control in the top right corner of the workspace. The keyboard shortcut is Command-Option-0. Then, select the 🎁 icon from the library selector.)

Figure 5.3   Dropping MKMapView

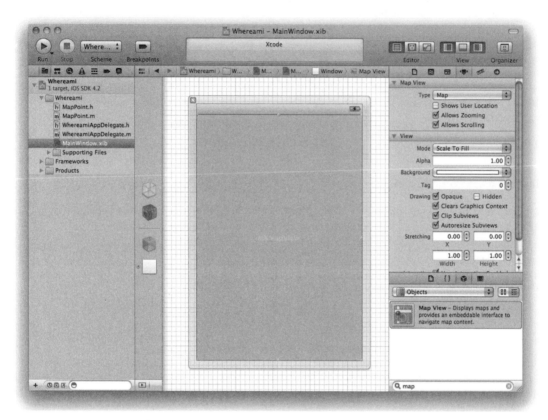

Now drag a **UITextField** and a **UIActivityIndicatorView** onto the **MKMapView**. Resize, position, and set their connections, as shown in Figure 5.4. To make a connection, first right click (or Control-click) on the object with the instance variable to bring up its connection panel. Then drag from the circle by the instance variable to the object you want it to point to. The arrows in Figure 5.4 show the direction to drag when making connections.

Figure 5.4   Whereami XIB layout

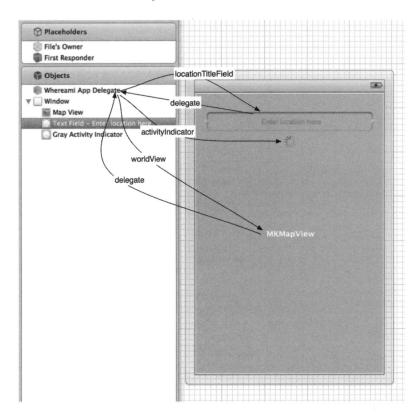

Now let's adjust the properties of the **UITextField**. First, we want the **UITextField** to have helpful placeholder text, like Enter Location Name. Next, consider the keyboard. When a **UITextField** is activated, a keyboard appears on the screen. (We'll see why this happens later in this chapter.) The keyboard's appearance is determined by a set of the **UITextField**'s properties called UITextInputTraits. One of these properties is the type of the keyboard's return key. For this application, we want the return key to read Done.

You can make these changes in the attributes inspector of the utilities area. Select the **UITextField** and from the inspector selector, select the ·⬇· icon to reveal the attributes inspector. Change the values for Placeholder and Return Key to match what is shown in Figure 5.5.

Figure 5.5   UITextField attributes

While we're here, wouldn't it be nice if the **UIActivityIndicatorView** hid itself when it's not spinning? Select the **UIActivityIndicatorView** and check the box labeled Hides When Stopped in the attributes inspector, as shown in Figure 5.6.

Figure 5.6   UIActivityIndicator attributes

Save MainWindow.xib. You won't have to return to it again in this project.

Being a MapView Delegate

When Whereami launches, we want it to find the current location and display it on a map. In the last chapter, you worked directly with Core Location to find the user's location. Now this won't be necessary because an instance of **MKMapView** knows how to use Core Location to find the user's location. All you have to do is set the showsUserLocation property of an **MKMapView** to YES, and it will show the user's location on the map.

At the end of **application:didFinishLaunchingWithOptions:**, replace the message that tells the locationManager to update its location with one that tells the **MKMapView** to show the current location.

```
- (BOOL)application:(UIApplication *)application
    didFinishLaunchingWithOptions:(NSDictionary *)launchOptions
{
    locationManager = [[CLLocationManager alloc] init];
    [locationManager setDelegate:self];

    [locationManager setDistanceFilter:kCLDistanceFilterNone];
    [locationManager setDesiredAccuracy:kCLLocationAccuracyBest];

    // [locationManager startUpdatingLocation];
    [worldView setShowsUserLocation:YES];

    // This line may say self.window, don't worry about that
    [[self window] makeKeyAndVisible];

    return YES;
}
```

Build and run the application. A few moments after the application launches, the map will display a blue annotation dot on your current location. Unfortunately, because you are looking at a map of the entire world, the blue dot is the size of Brazil and not exactly useful for figuring out where you are. Clearly, the application needs to zoom in on the current location. Let's figure out when and how we can do this.

For now, assume there is a "zoom-in-on-location" message you can send to an instance of **MKMapView**. The question is *when* would you send that message? When the application starts, it takes time for the device to determine the location. So you can't send it in **application:didFinishLaunchingWithOptions:** because you don't yet know the location to zoom in on. Nor do you want to continually tell the **MKMapView** to zoom its map; that would be inefficient.

Instead, how about delegation? **MKMapView** has a delegate property that you set to be the instance of **WhereamiAppDelegate**. In WhereamiAppDelegate.h, declare that **WhereamiAppDelegate** conforms to the MKMapViewDelegate protocol.

```
@interface WhereamiAppDelegate : NSObject
    <UIApplicationDelegate, CLLocationManagerDelegate, MKMapViewDelegate>
{
```

(While you do not have to declare that a class conforms to a delegate protocol, it is helpful to do so. First, a quick glance at the header file tells you that the class serves as a delegate for a particular type of object. Second, and perhaps more important, Xcode will see this declaration and offer code completion in the implementation file for the methods in that protocol.)

The map view will send messages to its delegate when interesting events happen. Perhaps there is a message in the MKMapViewDelegate protocol for when the map view finds the user's location. That would be the perfect time to "do the zoom." We can find out if the protocol declares such a message in the Apple documentation.

Using the documentation

There's nothing more important we can teach you than how to use the Apple documentation. So hang on as we tackle – step-by-step – the questions of when and how to display a zoomed-in map of the current location.

Overall, the documentation has four parts: API Reference, System Guides, Tools Guides, and Sample Code. The API Reference shows you every class, protocol, function, structure, method, and anything else you may use from Cocoa Touch. The System Guides give you high-level overviews and discussion about concepts in Cocoa Touch. The Tools Guide is the manual for Xcode and the rest of the developer tools suite.

While all four parts are useful, the API Reference is absolutely essential to everyday programming. There are so many classes and methods built into Cocoa Touch that it is impossible for a developer to remember them all. At no point in your iOS developer career will you outgrow the API Reference.

From the Help menu, choose Documentation and API Reference. The organizer window will appear with the Documentation item selected (Figure 5.7). Click the magnifying glass icon and choose Show Find Options to show the Find Options panel, which allows you to tailor your search. In the search box, enter MKMapViewDelegate.

Figure 5.7   Documentation Window

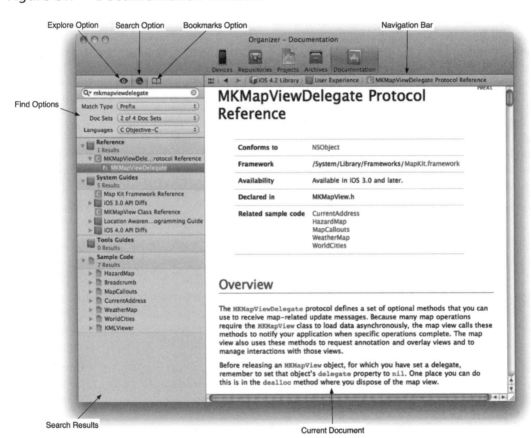

When you search for a term, the results from each part of the documentation are listed in the table on the left side of the window. The top section titled Reference is the API Reference.

Search results from the API Reference are contained in a number of nested categories. Each result has an icon that indicates whether it is a class, a method, a protocol or something else. Collectively, we call these items *symbols*, and their mappings are shown in Figure 5.8.

Figure 5.8 Documentation symbol guide

In your search results, look under the Reference heading for an item titled MKMapViewDelegate and labeled with a Pr icon. Select that item to see the reference page for the MKMapViewDelegate protocol (Figure 5.9). Then scroll down to the Tasks section, which groups the protocol's methods by what they used are for.

Figure 5.9 MKMapViewDelegate Protocol Reference

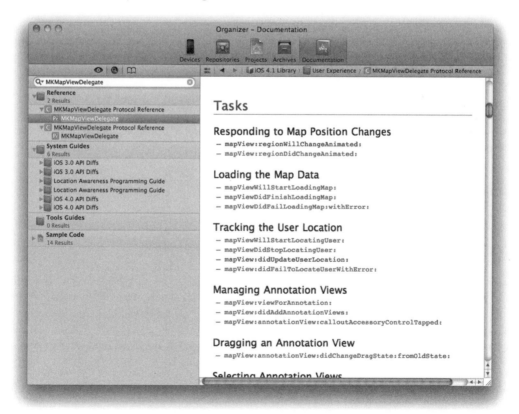

Recall that we're looking for a method that the **MKMapView** will send its delegate when it has found the user's location. See anything interesting? How about **mapView:didUpdateUserLocation:**? Blue text in the documentation indicates hyperlinks, so you can click on this method name to get more details (Figure 5.10).

Figure 5.10 A method in the API Reference

mapView:didUpdateUserLocation:

Tells the delegate that the location of the user was updated.

`- (void)mapView:(MKMapView *)`*mapView* `didUpdateUserLocation:(MKUserLocation *)`*userLocation*

Parameters

mapView
The map view that is tracking the user's location.

userLocation
The location object representing the user's latest location.

Discussion

While the `showsUserLocation` property is set to `YES`, this method is called whenever a new location update is received by the map view.

This method is not called if the application is currently running in the background. If you want to receive location updates while running in the background, you must use the Core Location framework.

Availability

Available in iOS 4.0 and later.

Declared In

`MKMapView.h`

The documentation confirms that this is the method we need, so go ahead and implement a stub for it in `WhereamiAppDelegate.m`. (If possible, copy and paste the method signature from the documentation; this is best for delegate methods where typos and capitalization errors are especially difficult to diagnose.)

```
- (void)mapView:(MKMapView *)mv didUpdateUserLocation:(MKUserLocation *)u
{

// Here we are...  but how do we actually zoom?

}
```

Now we know when to zoom, and we can turn our attention to the problem of how. To problem-solve in programming, it's best to start with the goal and what we already know. The goal is to display a map that is zoomed in on the user's current location. We know that when the **MKMapView** finds the user's location, it sends the message **mapView:didUpdateUserLocation:** to its delegate. We also know that, in the **mapView:didUpdateUserLocation:** method, a pointer to an **MKUserLocation** instance will be available.

In addition, we know from experience that the **MKMapView** does not automatically zoom in when it finds the user's location, so it must be told to do so. This, of course, means that **MKMapView** must implement a method that zooms in on a location. Let's track this method down in the API Reference.

Search for the **MKMapView** class. In the class reference page, look for Manipulating the Visible Portion of the Map in the Tasks section. There are a handful of methods and properties in this section; we'll start at the top with the region property. The details for region tell us that this property is of type MKCoordinateRegion and that it provides an implicit zoom. Sounds perfect. But to set this property, we need to know more about MKCoordinateRegion.

Search for MKCoordinateRegion. Its details are in the Map Kit Data Types Reference. MKCoordinateRegion has two members of types CLLocationCoordinate2D and MKCoordinateSpan. The CLLocationCoordinate2D is the center of the map and the MKCoordinateSpan determines the level of zoom (Figure 5.11).

Figure 5.11   Parts of an MKCoordinateRegion

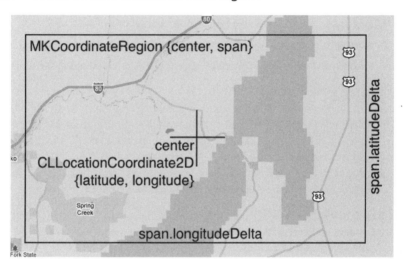

To set the region property of the map view, we'll need to package up one of these instances, so let's find out how we can do this. Search again for MKCoordinateRegion and this time select the Map Kit Functions Reference. One of these functions, **MKCoordinateRegionMakeWithDistance**, allows you to specify a region with a CLLocationCoordinate2D and the north-south and east-west limits of the zoom in meters. For the limits, we'll use 250 by 250 meters. For the coordinate, we need the user's location. Where can we get that?

How about the **MKUserLocation** object that the **MKMapView** sends its delegate in the **mapView:didUpdateUserLocation:** message? Search the documentation for **MKUserLocation**, and you'll find it has a property called location that holds the current location of the device. Keep drilling down, and you'll find that location is a **CLLocation** object, which has a coordinate property of type CLLocationCoordinate2D. Success! We can use information in the **MKUserLocation** to prepare an MKCoordinateRegion, which we then can use to set the region property of the map view.

Right now, getting the information from the **MKUserLocation** takes two steps: we send **MKUserLocation** the message **location** and then send the returned **CLLocation** object the message **coordinate**. The data returned from **coordinate** then becomes the MKCoordinateRegion's center.

But nosing around the API Reference has its rewards. Before we add this code to WhereamiAppDelegate.m, take another look at the **MKUserLocation** reference. At the top, it tells us that **MKUserLocation** conforms to the protocol MKAnnotation. Click on the link for that protocol, and you'll see that classes conforming to it are required to have a property named coordinate of type CLLocationCoordinate2D. So we can simplify the process and send the message **coordinate** directly to the **MKUserLocation**.

Now, in WhereamiAppDelegate.m, add the new code to **mapView:didUpdateUserLocation:**.

```
- (void)mapView:(MKMapView *)mv didUpdateUserLocation:(MKUserLocation *)u
{
    CLLocationCoordinate2D loc = [u coordinate];
    MKCoordinateRegion region = MKCoordinateRegionMakeWithDistance(loc, 250, 250);
    [worldView setRegion:region animated:YES];
}
```

Notice that the **MKMapView** is sent the message **setRegion:animated:** instead of simply **setRegion:**. What's the difference? Check the documentation.

Build and run the application again. When the map figures out where you are in the world, it zooms in on that location.

This is pretty standard workflow for iOS programming: you want an object to do something and you follow the bread crumbs in the API Reference. There will be dead ends and wild goose chases, but eventually you'll find what you need. As you go through this book, don't hesitate to look up the classes, protocols, and methods we use to see what else they can do. You want to become as comfortable as possible with the API Reference. The more you use it, the easier it will be to progress as an iOS developer. *You cannot be an iOS developer without using the API Reference.*

Apple will continue to update the iOS SDK and introduce iOS devices with new features and capabilities. If you understand and are comfortable using the Apple documentation, you will be ready to use whatever Apple dreams up in the future.

Your own MKAnnotation

Now that Whereami displays a nicely-zoomed map of the current location, we can turn to adding annotations. Let's start with an introduction to the MKAnnotation protocol.

MKAnnotation is not a delegate protocol. Instead, it declares a set of methods that are useful to any class that wants to put itself on the map. Imagine an application that maps everything in a neighborhood, including restaurants, factories, and train stations. These objects could be very different and hierarchically unrelated in your application, but they all can be added to a map view if they conform to MKAnnotation.

When an object conforming to MKAnnotation is added to an **MKMapView**, an instance of **MKAnnotationView** (or one of its subclasses) is created and added to the map view. The **MKAnnotationView** keeps a pointer to the MKAnnotation-conforming object that it represents so it can ask it for data as needed. The relationships between these objects are shown in Figure 5.12.

Figure 5.12 MKMapView and its annotations

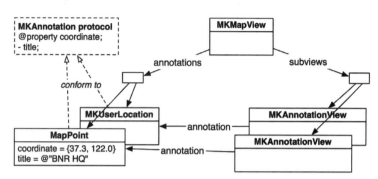

Now you're going to write a new class called **MapPoint** that will conform to MKAnnotation. When the user tags a location, an instance of **MapPoint** will be created and represented on the map.

From the File menu, select New and then New File.... Then choose Cocoa Touch from the iOS section, select Objective-C class, and click Next (Figure 5.13).

Figure 5.13 Creating an NSObject subclass

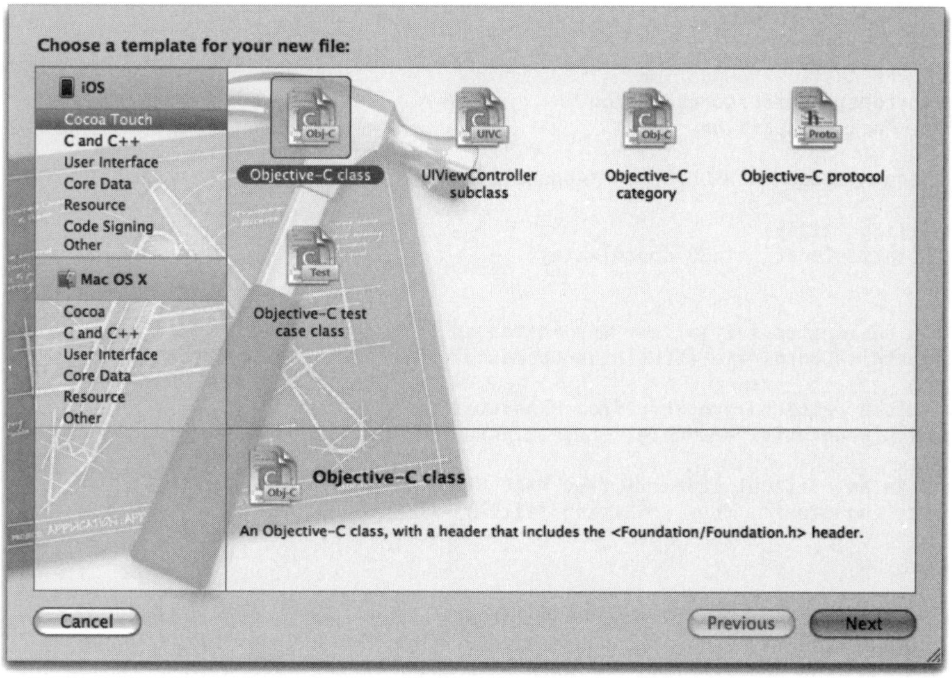

On the next pane, select **NSObject** from the superclass list and hit Next.

A sheet will drop down for you to save the files for this class. Name the class MapPoint and click Save (Figure 5.14). This creates the files MapPoint.h and MapPoint.m and adds them to your project.

Figure 5.14   Naming the subclass

In MapPoint.h, declare that **MapPoint** conforms to MKAnnotation. Also declare two properties and an initializer.

```
#import <Foundation/Foundation.h>
#import <CoreLocation/CoreLocation.h>
#import <MapKit/MapKit.h>

@interface MapPoint : NSObject <MKAnnotation>
{
    NSString *title;
    CLLocationCoordinate2D coordinate;
}

// A new designated initializer for instances of MapPoint
- (id)initWithCoordinate:(CLLocationCoordinate2D)c title:(NSString *)t;

// This is a required property from MKAnnotation
@property (nonatomic, readonly) CLLocationCoordinate2D coordinate;

// This is an optional property from MKAnnotation
@property (nonatomic, copy) NSString *title;

@end
```

The protocol defines **coordinate** as a read-only property, which means there is a method named **coordinate** that returns a CLLocationCoordinate2D. While most methods declared in the MKAnnotation protocol are optional, the **coordinate** method is required – if **MapPoint** is to conform to the MKAnnotation protocol, it must implement **coordinate**.

Switch to MapPoint.m. (The keyboard shortcut for switching between the header file and the implementation file is Command-Control-Up arrow.) Synthesize the properties and add the implementations for the initializer and **dealloc**.

```
#import "MapPoint.h"

@implementation MapPoint

@synthesize coordinate, title;

- (id)initWithCoordinate:(CLLocationCoordinate2D)c title:(NSString *)t
{
    self = [super init];
    if (self) {
        coordinate = c;
        [self setTitle:t];
    }
    return self;
}

- (void)dealloc
{
    [title release];
    [super dealloc];
}
@end
```

Note that you don't release `coordinate` in the **dealloc** method because it is not an Objective-C object and can't receive messages. The `CLLocationCoordinate2D` structure's memory will live inside each instance of **MapPoint**, and it will be created and destroyed automatically along with the object.

The protocol defines the required **coordinate** as a read-only property, which means there must be a method named **coordinate** that returns a `CLLocationCoordinate2D`, but it doesn't have to be a property in the class declaration. In fact, we don't have to create the matching instance variables, either. The `MKAnnotation` protocol, like all protocols, only dictates method signatures. As long as the signatures match exactly, the conforming class can implement them however it wants with whatever instance variables it chooses. For example, the **title** method could perform some logic with information is has available to it and then return a value:

```
- (NSString *)title
{
    if ([self isEastOfTheMississippi])
        return @"Buying supplies"

    return @"On the Oregon Trail, uncharted territory";
}
```

Therefore, we can think of a protocol as a contract, whereby the conforming class says, "I promise to give you my interpretation of this contract when asked." The objects that speak to the conforming class through the protocol honor this contract by saying, "I promise to only ask you things in this contract." For example, **MKAnnotationView** has a annotation property declared as

```
@property (nonatomic, retain) id <MKAnnotation> annotation;
```

This declaration says that the annotation can be of any type (id), as long as it conforms to the `MKAnnotation` protocol (<MKAnnotation>). Therefore, the **MKAnnotationView** will only send messages from the `MKAnnotation` protocol to its annotation; it won't make any assumptions about the other messages that object might respond to.

You've added a lot of code, so you may want to build the application to check for syntax errors before you continue. There's no need to run it, however, because the application's behavior has not changed.

Tagging locations

Now that you have your own class that conforms to MKAnnotation, you can tag locations on the map. The user will enter the location's name in the **UITextField** and then tap the Done button on the keyboard. The tapping of the Done button is the signal to add an annotation. How will we know this event has occurred? Delegation, of course.

In the XIB file, you set the text field's delegate to be the instance of **WhereamiAppDelegate**. This means **WhereamiAppDelegate** can implement methods from the UITextFieldDelegate protocol. One of these methods is **textFieldShouldReturn:**. When the keyboard's return key is tapped, the **UITextField** sends this message to its delegate and asks if it really should return. At the same time, the delegate has the opportunity to perform tasks that should coincide with the returning of the text field.

In WhereamiAppDelegate.h, declare that **WhereamiAppDelegate** conforms to the UITextFieldDelegate protocol.

```
@interface WhereamiAppDelegate : NSObject
    <UIApplicationDelegate, CLLocationManagerDelegate, MKMapViewDelegate,
    UITextFieldDelegate>
{
```

In WhereamiAppDelegate.m, implement **textFieldShouldReturn:**.

```
- (BOOL)textFieldShouldReturn:(UITextField *)tf
{
    // This method isn't implemented yet - but will be soon.
    [self findLocation];

    [tf resignFirstResponder];

    return YES;
}
```

For now, ignore **findLocation**. You will write the implementation for that in a moment. First, let's talk about text editing and the *first responder*.

UIResponder is a class in the UIKit framework. A responder is responsible for receiving and handling events that are associated with it. For example, a button is a responder that handles touch events, like a tap. In addition, one of the responders is the *first responder* of the window. Only one responder can be the first responder at a time. The first responder handles events that aren't associated with another responder. For instance, a tap is sent to the responder object that was tapped, but a shake has no associated responder and is sent to the first responder instead. We'll talk more about the first responder and event-handling in Chapter 8 and Chapter 20.

For now, let's focus on **UITextField**. A **UITextField** is also a responder: it is a direct subclass of **UIControl**, which is a subclass of **UIView**, which is a subclass of **UIResponder**. When a **UITextField** is tapped, it handles this event by becoming the first responder.

When a **UITextField** becomes the first responder, a keyboard appears on the screen. To remove the keyboard from the screen, you tell the **UITextField** to give up its first responder status by sending it the message **resignFirstResponder**. Once the first responder of the window is no longer a **UITextField**, the keyboard will disappear.

(Everything about **UITextField** holds true for the class **UITextView**, too. The difference between **UITextView** and **UITextField** is that **UITextView** allows for multi-line editing: a text view's return key enters the newline character whereas a text field's return key dispatches the delegate method `textFieldShouldReturn:`.)

Putting the pieces together

To finish your Whereami application, you just need to add two final methods: `findLocation`, which is sent in `textFieldShouldReturn:`, and `foundLocation:`, which will be sent in `locationManager:didUpdateToLocation:fromLocation:`. In WhereamiAppDelegate.h, declare these two methods.

```
@interface WhereamiAppDelegate : NSObject
    <UIApplicationDelegate, CLLocationManagerDelegate, MKMapViewDelegate,
     UITextFieldDelegate>
{
    CLLocationManager *locationManager;

    IBOutlet MKMapView *worldView;
    IBOutlet UIActivityIndicatorView *activityIndicator;
    IBOutlet UITextField *locationTitleField;
}

@property (nonatomic, retain) IBOutlet UIWindow *window;

- (void)findLocation;
- (void)foundLocation:(CLLocation *)loc;

@end
```

The **findLocation** method will tell the locationManager to start looking for the current location. It will also update the user interface so that the user can't re-enter text into the text field and will start the activity indicator spinning. The **foundLocation:** method will create an instance of **MapPoint** and add it to the worldView. It will also handle the map's zoom and reset the states of the UI elements and the locationManager.

In WhereamiAppDelegate.m, import MapPoint.h and implement the two methods.

```
#import "WhereamiAppDelegate.h"
#import "MapPoint.h"

@implementation WhereamiAppDelegate

- (void)findLocation
{
    [locationManager startUpdatingLocation];
    [activityIndicator startAnimating];
    [locationTitleField setHidden:YES];
}

- (void)foundLocation:(CLLocation *)loc
{
    CLLocationCoordinate2D coord = [loc coordinate];

    // Create an instance of MapPoint with the current data
    MapPoint *mp = [[MapPoint alloc] initWithCoordinate:coord
                                                  title:[locationTitleField text]];
    // Add it to the map view
    [worldView addAnnotation:mp];
```

```
    // MKMapView retains its annotations, we can release
    [mp release];

    // Zoom the region to this location
    MKCoordinateRegion region = MKCoordinateRegionMakeWithDistance(coord, 250, 250);
    [worldView setRegion:region animated:YES];

    [locationTitleField setText:@""];
    [activityIndicator stopAnimating];
    [locationTitleField setHidden:NO];
    [locationManager stopUpdatingLocation];
}
```

Note that when importing files, you put quotation marks around header files you create and angled brackets around header files from frameworks. Angled brackets tell the compiler, "Only look in your system libraries for this file." Quotation marks say, "Look in the directory for this project first, and if you don't find something, then look in the system libraries."

Finally, send the message **foundLocation:** when a new location is found by the **CLLocationManager**. Update the delegate method **locationManager:didUpdateToLocation:fromLocation:** in WhereamiAppDelegate.m:

```
- (void)locationManager:(CLLocationManager *)manager
    didUpdateToLocation:(CLLocation *)newLocation
           fromLocation:(CLLocation *)oldLocation
{
    NSLog(@"%@", newLocation);

    // How many seconds ago was this new location created?
    NSTimeInterval t = [[newLocation timestamp] timeIntervalSinceNow];

    // CLLocationManagers will return the last found location of the
    // device first, you don't want that data in this case.
    // If this location was made more than 3 minutes ago, ignore it.
    if (t < -180) {
        // This is cached data, you don't want it, keep looking
        return;
    }

    [self foundLocation:newLocation];
}
```

Build and run the application. Enter a title into the text field, and an annotation with that title will appear on the map at your current location.

Challenge: Annotation Extras

Using the **NSDate** and **NSDateFormatter** classes, have your tagged annotations show the dates they were tagged.

Challenge: Reverse Geocoding

Use delegation and the class **MKReverseGeocoder** to display the city and state of a **MapPoint** on the map.

6

Subclassing UIView

In previous chapters, you've created several views: a **UIButton**, a **UILabel**, etc. But what exactly is a view?

- A view is an instance of a **UIView** or one of its subclasses.

- A view knows how to draw itself on the application's window.

- A view exists within a hierarchy. The window (an instance of **UIWindow**) is a view and the root of the hierarchy. It has subviews (that appear on the window). Those views can also have subviews.

- A view handles touch events.

In this chapter, you are going to create your own **UIView** subclass that fills the screen with concentric circles, as shown in Figure 6.1. You will also learn how to draw text and enable scrolling and zooming.

Figure 6.1 View that draws concentric circles

Creating a Custom View

In Xcode, create a new iOS Window-based Application for iPhone. Name it Hypnosister.

Create a new iOS Objective-C class named **HypnosisView**. On the second pane of the assistant, you'll be asked to choose a superclass; select **NSObject**, even though **UIView** is listed as an option. Choosing **NSObject** here tells Xcode to use the most basic template to create your class files. Almost every class and project in this book uses the simplest template available in Xcode.

Why do we do this? Templates are great for speeding up development, but they get in the way when you're learning. Typing in every line of code instead of relying on the "magic" of a template will make you more comfortable when you're writing your own iOS applications in the future. After you become more experienced and understand what the templates are doing, you can use them to speed things up.

Open HypnosisView.h in the editor area. Now that Xcode has created your class files, change the superclass from **NSObject** to **UIView**.

```
@interface HypnosisView : UIView
```

The drawRect: method

Every **UIView** subclass implements the method **drawRect:**, which contains the drawing code for the view. For example, a **UIButton**'s **drawRect:** method draws a rounded rectangle with a title string in the center.

Each time an instance of **UIView** needs to be drawn (or redrawn), the system prepares a *graphics context* specifically for that view. Then the context is activated, and the message **drawRect:** is sent to the instance of **UIView** that is being drawn. The graphics context's type is **CGContextRef** (*Core Graphics Context Ref*erence), and it is responsible for aggregating drawing commands and producing an image as a result. This image is the appearance of the view instance. A graphics context also stores its drawing state, which includes things like the current drawing color, coordinate system, and the current line width.

Sometimes when drawing a view, you will use Objective-C to make calls defined in the UIKit framework that implicitly use the active graphics context. Other times, you will get hold of the graphics context explicitly and draw using the C functions of the Core Graphics framework. In this chapter, you will do both.

In HypnosisView.m, override the **drawRect:** method:

```
- (void)drawRect:(CGRect)rect
{
    // What rectangle am I filling?
    CGRect bounds = [self bounds];

    // Where is its center?
    CGPoint center;
    center.x = bounds.origin.x + bounds.size.width / 2.0;
    center.y = bounds.origin.y + bounds.size.height / 2.0;

    // From the center how far out to a corner?
    float maxRadius = hypot(bounds.size.width, bounds.size.height) / 2.0;

    // Get the context being drawn upon
    CGContextRef context = UIGraphicsGetCurrentContext();
```

```
    // All lines will be drawn 10 points wide
    CGContextSetLineWidth(context, 10);

    // Set the stroke color to light gray
    [[UIColor lightGrayColor] setStroke];

    // Draw concentric circles from the outside in
    for (float currentRadius = maxRadius; currentRadius > 0; currentRadius -= 20)
    {
        CGContextAddArc(context, center.x, center.y,
                        currentRadius, 0.0, M_PI * 2.0, YES);
        CGContextStrokePath(context);
    }
}
```

Notice that you are passed a CGRect structure. This is the rectangle that needs to be redrawn, sometimes called the *dirty rectangle*. Typically, you ignore the dirty rectangle and issue the drawing instructions as though the entire view needs to be redrawn. However, if your drawing code is intricate, you might only redraw the parts in the dirty rectangle to speed up drawing.

A CGRect structure contains the members origin and size (Figure 6.2). These two members are also structures. The origin is of type CGPoint and contains two float members: x and y. The size is of type CGSize and also has two float members: width and height. These structures are the basic building blocks of Core Graphics routines. (Remember that a structure is not an Objective-C object, so you can't send it messages.)

Figure 6.2   CGRect

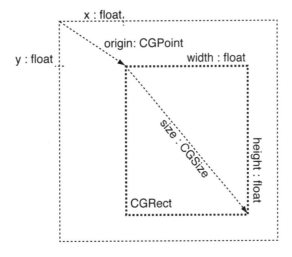

Instantiating a UIView

Recall that there are two ways to create an instance of your view:

- visually choose and position the view while editing the XIB file

- create it programmatically with **alloc** and **initWithFrame:** and make it a subview
  of the window

In Quiz and Whereami, you visually created views in the XIB file. In this chapter, you are going to
create views programmatically.

Open HypnosisterAppDelegate.h and add an instance variable for the new view:

```
#import <UIKit/UIKit.h>

// This is a "forward declaration"
@class HypnosisView;

@interface HypnosisterAppDelegate : NSObject <UIApplicationDelegate>
{
    HypnosisView *view;
}
@property (nonatomic, retain) IBOutlet UIWindow *window;

@end
```

Notice the @class directive after the import statement. This is a forward declaration for the class
HypnosisView. When you forward declare a class, you aren't going as far as importing the header file;
you are just informing HypnosisterAppDelegate.h of the class **HypnosisView** so the compiler can
validate it. Forward declaring a class saves time when compiling – especially with large projects.

HypnosisterAppDelegate.m, on the other hand, needs to know more about **HypnosisView**, so you
will import the header file. In HypnosisterAppDelegate.m, import HypnosisView.h, create the new
instance, and place it on the window.

```
#import "HypnosisterAppDelegate.h"

#import "HypnosisView.h"

@implementation HypnosisterAppDelegate

@synthesize window;

- (BOOL)application:(UIApplication *)application
    didFinishLaunchingWithOptions:(NSDictionary *)launchOptions
{
    // Make a CGRect that is the size of the window
    CGRect wholeWindow = [[self window] bounds];

    // Create an instance of HypnosisView that is the same size as the window
    view = [[HypnosisView alloc] initWithFrame:wholeWindow];

    // Set the background color of that view to "clear"
    [view setBackgroundColor:[UIColor clearColor]];

    // Add the view to the view hierarchy so that it appears on the window
```

```
    [[self window] addSubview:view];

    // This line may say self.window, don't worry about that
    [[self window] makeKeyAndVisible];
    return YES;
}

// A dealloc method that will never get called because
// HypnosisterAppDelegate will exist for the life of the application
- (void)dealloc
{
    [view release];
    [_window release];
    [super dealloc];
}

@end
```

Notice that you are calling **initWithFrame:**, the designated initializer for **UIView**. This gives the view a size and position. When the view is added to a view hierarchy (**addSubview:**), its position will be in the bounds of its superview (window).

(Retain count trivia: Because you created the view with **alloc** in HypnosisterAppDelegate.m and then added it to the window, the view is being retained by **HypnosisterAppDelegate** and the window, and so has a retain count of two. Also note that neither **HypnosisterAppDelegate** nor the window will ever get deallocated because they exist the entire time the application is running.)

Build and run your application.

Drawing Text and Shadows

While we are talking about drawing, let's add some text with a shadow to the view, as shown in Figure 6.3.

Figure 6.3   View that draws text

Open HypnosisView.m and add the following code to the end of your **drawRect:** method:

```
for (float currentRadius = maxRadius; currentRadius > 0; currentRadius -= 20)
{
    CGContextAddArc(context, center.x, center.y,
                    currentRadius, 0, M_PI * 2.0, YES);
    CGContextStrokePath(context);
}

// Create a string
NSString *text = @"You are getting sleepy.";

// Get a font to draw it in
UIFont *font = [UIFont boldSystemFontOfSize:28];

// Where am I going to draw it?
CGRect textRect;
textRect.size = [text sizeWithFont:font];
textRect.origin.x = center.x - textRect.size.width / 2.0;
textRect.origin.y = center.y - textRect.size.height / 2.0;

// Set the fill color of the current context to black
[[UIColor blackColor] setFill];
```

```
    // Set the shadow to be offset 4 points right, 3 points down,
    // dark gray and with a blur radius of 2 points
    CGSize offset = CGSizeMake(4, 3);
    CGColorRef color = [[UIColor darkGrayColor] CGColor];
    CGContextSetShadowWithColor(context, offset, 2.0, color);

    // Draw the string
    [text drawInRect:textRect
            withFont:font];
}
```

Build and run the application. You will see the text with a shadow appear on the view.

Notice that you only call drawing routines inside **drawRect:**. Outside of a **drawRect:** method, there is no active **CGContextRef**, and drawing routines will fail. (In Chapter 16, you will manage your own **CGContextRef** for offscreen drawing. Only then can you draw outside of **drawRect:**.)

Using UIScrollView

When you want to let the user scroll around your view, you typically make your view the subview of a **UIScrollView**, as shown in Figure 6.4.

Figure 6.4   Object diagram

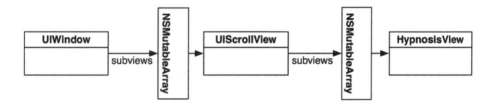

In HypnosisterAppDelegate.m, put your view inside a scroll view and add that scroll view to the window:

```
- (BOOL)application:(UIApplication *)application
    didFinishLaunchingWithOptions:(NSDictionary *)launchOptions
{
    CGRect wholeWindow = [[self window] bounds];

    UIScrollView *scrollView = [[UIScrollView alloc] initWithFrame:wholeWindow];
    [[self window] addSubview:scrollView];

    // Make your view twice as large as the window
    CGRect reallyBigRect;
    reallyBigRect.origin = CGPointZero;
    reallyBigRect.size.width = wholeWindow.size.width * 2.0;
    reallyBigRect.size.height = wholeWindow.size.height * 2.0;
    [scrollView setContentSize:reallyBigRect.size];

    // Center it in the scroll view
```

```
    CGPoint offset;
    offset.x = wholeWindow.size.width * 0.5;
    offset.y = wholeWindow.size.height * 0.5;
    [scrollView setContentOffset:offset];

    // Create the view
    view = [[HypnosisView alloc] initWithFrame:reallyBigRect];
    [view setBackgroundColor:[UIColor clearColor]];
    [scrollView addSubview:view];

    [scrollView release];


    [[self window] makeKeyAndVisible];
    return YES;
}
```

Build and run your application. You can to push your view up and down, left and right. However, zooming doesn't work. Yet.

Zooming

To add zooming, you need to give the scroll view a delegate. In HypnosisterAppDelegate.h, declare that **HypnosisterAppDelegate** conforms to the UIScrollViewDelegate protocol:

```
@interface HypnosisterAppDelegate : NSObject
    <UIApplicationDelegate, UIScrollViewDelegate>
```

Figure 6.5   HypnosisView in UIScrollView

Open HypnosisterAppDelegate.m. In **application:didFinishLaunchingWithOptions:**, set the delegate and the limits of the zoom:

```
- (BOOL)application:(UIApplication *)application
    didFinishLaunchingWithOptions:(NSDictionary *)launchOptions
{
    CGRect wholeWindow = [[self window] bounds];

    UIScrollView *scrollView = [[UIScrollView alloc] initWithFrame:wholeWindow];
    [[self window] addSubview:scrollView];

    // Make your view twice as large as the window
    CGRect reallyBigRect;
    reallyBigRect.origin = CGPointZero;
    reallyBigRect.size.width = wholeWindow.size.width * 2.0;
    reallyBigRect.size.height = wholeWindow.size.height * 2.0;
    [scrollView setContentSize:reallyBigRect.size];

    // Center it in the scroll view
    CGPoint offset;
    offset.x = wholeWindow.size.width * 0.5;
    offset.y = wholeWindow.size.height * 0.5;
    [scrollView setContentOffset:offset];

    // Enable zooming
    [scrollView setMinimumZoomScale:0.5];
    [scrollView setMaximumZoomScale:5];
    [scrollView setDelegate:self];

    // Create the view
    view = [[HypnosisView alloc] initWithFrame:reallyBigRect];
    [view setBackgroundColor:[UIColor clearColor]];
    [scrollView addSubview:view];

    [scrollView release];

    [[self window] makeKeyAndVisible];
    return YES;
}
```

In that same file, implement the delegate method **viewForZoomingInScrollView:** that tells the scroll view which view to transform.

```
- (UIView *)viewForZoomingInScrollView:(UIScrollView *)scrollView
{
    return view;
}
```

Build and run the application and zoom away! (In the simulator, use the Option key to simulate two finger touches.)

Hiding the Status Bar

When you're being hypnotized, you probably don't want to see the time or your remaining battery charge – these things cause anxiety. So, you're going to hide the status bar before you make the window visible. In HypnosisterAppDelegate.m, add a line near the end of **application:didFinishLaunchingWithOptions:**.

```
[scrollView addSubview:view];

[scrollView release];


[[UIApplication sharedApplication] setStatusBarHidden:YES
                             withAnimation:UIStatusBarAnimationFade];


[[self window] makeKeyAndVisible];
return YES;
}
```

Build and run the application again. Notice the status bar fading out after the application launches. You can also hide the status bar before your application appears on the screen by adding a new key-value pair to the application's info property list. To do this, select the project from the project navigator. Then select the Hypnosister target and the Info pane in the editor area (Figure 6.6). This pane is an editor for the Info.plist file that is a part of every iOS application. (You could select the Hypnosister-Info.plist file from the project navigator, but this interface shows the key-value pairs more clearly.)

Figure 6.6 Info property list with hidden status bar

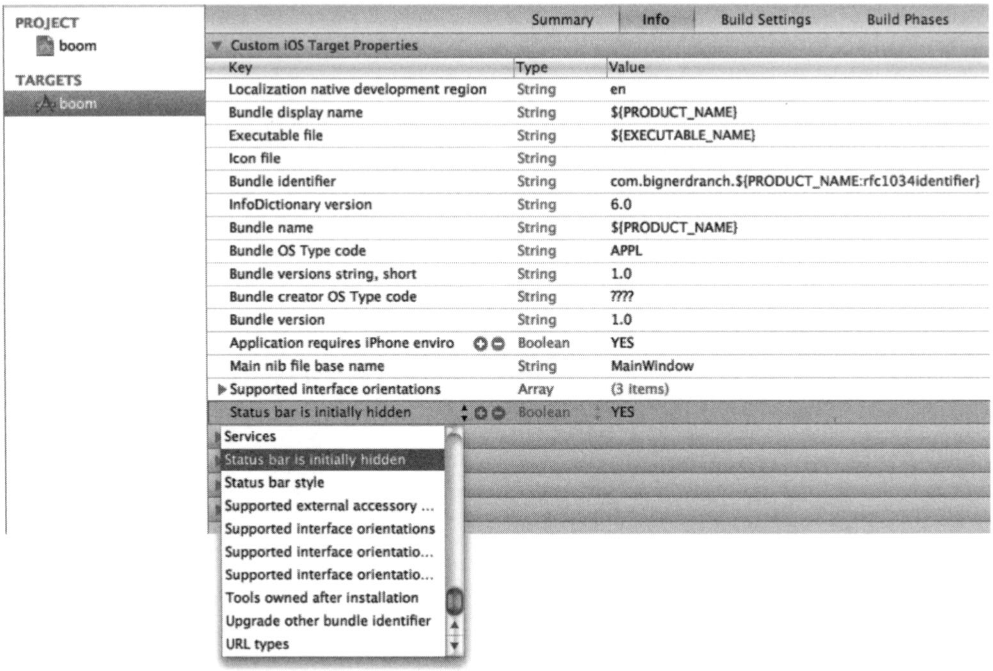

Select the last row and click the + icon next to the key name. A new row will appear, and a pop-up menu will open in the Key column. Choose Status bar is initially hidden from this list and hit return. In the Value column, change the value to YES. Now the status bar will be hidden as soon as you launch the application.

Challenge: Colors

Make the circles appear in assorted colors.

For the More Curious: Retain Cycles

A view hierarchy is made up of many parent-child relationships. When we talk about view hierarchies, we call parents *superviews* and their children *subviews*. When a view is added to a view hierarchy, it is retained by its superview, as shown in Figure 6.7.

Figure 6.7   View hierarchy ownership

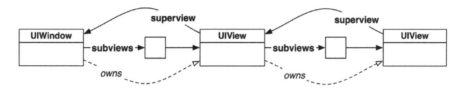

Every subview has a pointer back to its superview so that it can send its superview messages. The `superview` property of a **UIView** is set to its superview when the view is added to a view hierarchy. (When a view is not part of a view hierarchy, `superview` is `nil`.)

Superviews are *not* retained by their subviews. Why not? Well, imagine what would happen if they were. Every time a subview was added to a view (let's call it **BigView**), **BigView**'s retain count would be incremented. For example, if **BigView** had six subviews, it would have a retain count of seven – one for each subview and one for its superview.

What would happen if **BigView**'s superview wanted to get rid of **BigView**? The superview would send **BigView** the message **release**. However, **BigView** would still be retained by each of its subviews and would not be deallocated. As a result, **BigView**'s subviews would never be sent the message **release**. **BigView** and all of its subviews would be cut off from the rest of the application and exist in their own little cycle of independent objects where no other object could reach them.

We call this problem a *retain cycle*, and it can arise in any parent-child relationship, not just with view objects. The solution is simple: *children should never retain their parents*. Moreover, a child should never retain its parent's parent, or its parent's parent's parent, and so on. When you adhere to this rule, deallocating a parent object appropriately releases its child objects. If the parent is the only owner of its children, then these child objects are deallocated.

For the More Curious: Redrawing Views

When a **UIView** instance is sent the message **setNeedsDisplay**, that view is marked for re-display. View subclasses send themselves **setNeedsDisplay** when their drawable content changes. For example, **UITextField** will mark itself for re-display if it is sent the message **setText:**. (It has to redraw if the text it displays changes.)

When a view has marked itself for re-display, it is not immediately redrawn; instead, it is added to a list of views that need updating. Your application is a giant infinite loop called the *run loop*. The run loop's job is to check for input (a touch, Core Location updates, data coming in through a network interface, etc.) and then find the appropriate handlers for that event (like an action or delegate method for an object). Those handler methods call other methods, which call more methods, and so on. Views are not redrawn until *after* the methods have completed and control returns to the run loop, as shown in Figure 6.8.

Figure 6.8   Redrawing views with the run loop

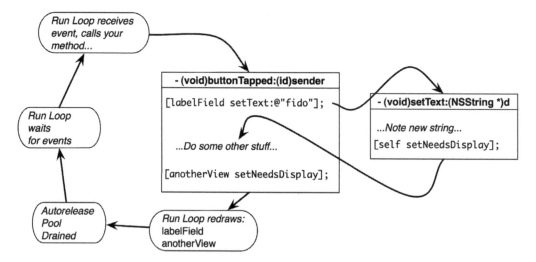

When control returns to the run loop, it says, "Well, a bunch of code was just executed. I'm going to check if any views need to be redrawn." Then the run loop prepares the necessary drawing contexts and sends the message **drawRect:** to all of the views that have been sent **setNeedsDisplay** in this iteration of the loop. After a view has redrawn itself, its subviews are automatically asked to redraw themselves as well.

7

View Controllers

View Controllers and XIB Files

In the Quiz application, you had one "screen," one controller, and one XIB file:

Figure 7.1   Quiz, a single screen application

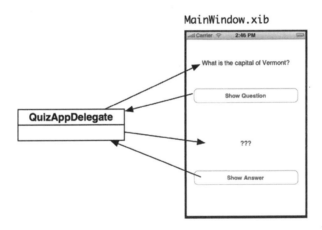

But what about applications with multiple "screens"? Typically, each screen gets its own controller and XIB file. Figure 7.2 shows an example application with two screens and the resulting controllers and XIB files.

Figure 7.2   Example of an application with two screens

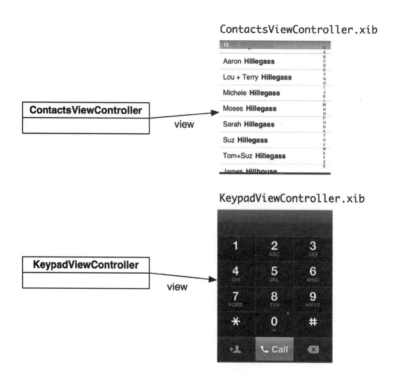

Each controller has a view that gets placed on the window. (The view often has subviews like buttons and labels.) Thus, we call these controllers *view controllers*. A view controller is a subclass of **UIViewController** and has an instance variable called view. The view controller acts as the controller for its view. And, we typically need an object to take care of the view swapping for us. In the example application below, the swapping is done by a **UITabBarController**. The object diagram for this application is shown in Figure 7.3.

Figure 7.3   Object diagram for the Phone application

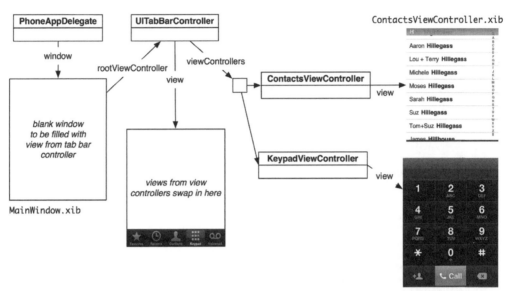

Note that this approach means that when you write an application with seven screens, you will typically write seven subclasses of **UIViewController**. Therefore, you may have up to eight XIB files (one for the window and one for each view controller).

However, sometimes there are fewer XIB files. When a view controller has just one view, it is usually easier to create a single view programmatically as you did in the last chapter.

Using View Controllers

In this chapter, you are going to write an application with two view controllers. One will display the **HypnosisView** you created in the last chapter, and the other will let the user get the current time by tapping a button (Figure 7.4). We will swap in the views using a **UITabBarController**.

Figure 7.4   HypnoTime screens

In Xcode, create a new Window-based Application iPhone project named HypnoTime. (Yes, there is a Tab Bar Application project template, but using that template makes things seem more complicated and magical than they are. Do not use it for this application.)

You will re-use **HypnosisView** in this application. Use Finder to locate HypnosisView.h and HypnosisView.m and drag them into the project navigator of this project. When the sheet appears, check the box labeled Copy items into destination group's folder and click Finish. Also, add the icons Hypno.png and Time.png (available at http://www.bignerdranch.com/solutions/iOSProgramming.zip) to the project navigator in the same way.

Creating the UITabBarController

In HypnoTimeAppDelegate.m, create the tab bar controller and set it as the rootViewController of the window:

```
- (BOOL)application:(UIApplication *)application
    didFinishLaunchingWithOptions:(NSDictionary *)launchOptions
{
    // Create the tabBarController
    UITabBarController *tabBarController = [[UITabBarController alloc] init];

    // Set tabBarController as rootViewController of window
    [[self window] setRootViewController:tabBarController];

    // The window retains tabBarController, we can release our reference
    [tabBarController release];
```

```
    // Show the window
    [[self window] makeKeyAndVisible];

    return YES;
}
```

Build and run the application. The big white space is where your views will get swapped in. Also notice the black tab bar at the bottom of the window. This is the **UITabBar**, a subview of the **UITabBarController**'s view. Right now, there aren't any tab bar items in it, but we'll fix that in the next section.

In previous applications, you manipulated the view hierarchy directly. For example, in Chapter 5, you added subviews to the window dragging them onto the window in a XIB file. In Chapter 6, you added subviews to the window using the method **addSubview:**.

When using view controllers, you don't have to manipulate the view hierarchy directly. **UIWindow** implements a method named **setRootViewController:**. Passing an instance of **UIViewController** as the argument to this method automatically adds the view of that view controller as a subview of the window and resizes it to fit. The window also retains its root view controller.

Figure 7.5   View hierarchy with UITabBarController

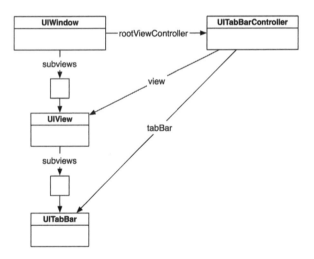

Creating view controllers and tab bar items

To create the first view controller for HypnoTime, select New File... from the New menu item in the File menu. While there is a UIViewController subclass template option, you won't use it here. Choose Objective-C class and select NSObject as the superclass on the next pane. Name this class **CurrentTimeViewController**.

Open CurrentTimeViewController.h and change the superclass to **UIViewController**.

```
@interface CurrentTimeViewController : UIViewController
```

Now create another class in the same way, but name it HypnosisViewController. In HypnosisViewController.h, change the superclass to **UIViewController**.

@interface HypnosisViewController : **UIViewController**

Now you need to create instances of the view controllers and add them to the tab bar controller. At the top of HypnoTimeAppDelegate.m, import the header files for these classes.

```
#import "HypnoTimeAppDelegate.h"
#import "HypnosisViewController.h"
#import "CurrentTimeViewController.h"
```

Then, also in HypnoTimeAppDelegate.m, modify the **application:didFinishLaunchingWithOptions:** method to create instances of these view controllers and add them to the tab bar controller.

```
- (BOOL)application:(UIApplication *)application
    didFinishLaunchingWithOptions:(NSDictionary *)launchOptions
{
    // Create the tabBarController
    UITabBarController *tabBarController = [[UITabBarController alloc] init];

    // Create two view controllers
    UIViewController *vc1 = [[HypnosisViewController alloc] init];
    UIViewController *vc2 = [[CurrentTimeViewController alloc] init];

    // Make an array containing the two view controllers
    NSArray *viewControllers = [NSArray arrayWithObjects:vc1, vc2, nil];

    // The viewControllers array retains vc1 and vc2, we can release
    // our ownership of them in this method
    [vc1 release];
    [vc2 release];

    // Attach them to the tab bar controller
    [tabBarController setViewControllers:viewControllers];

    // Put the tabBarController's view on the window
    [[self window] setRootViewController:tabBarController];
    [tabBarController release];

    // Show the window
    [[self window] makeKeyAndVisible];

    return YES;
}
```

Build and run the application. The tab bar now has two tabs that you can select, but there isn't anything interesting about the tabs. Every view controller has a tab bar item that controls the text or icon that appears in the tab bar as shown in Figure 7.6.

Figure 7.6 UITabBarItem example

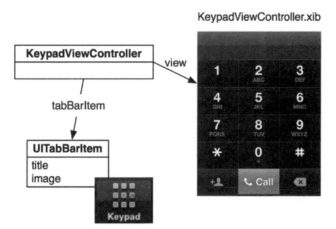

Let's start by putting a title on the tab bar items. Open HypnosisViewController.m. Create a new **init** method, override the designated initializer for the superclass (**UIViewController**), and edit the **viewDidLoad** method to match the code below:

```
- (id)init
{
    // Call the superclass's designated initializer
    self = [super initWithNibName:nil
                           bundle:nil];
    if (self) {
        // Get the tab bar item
        UITabBarItem *tbi = [self tabBarItem];

        // Give it a label
        [tbi setTitle:@"Hypnosis"];
    }

    return self;
}

- (id)initWithNibName:(NSString *)nibName bundle:(NSBundle *)bundle
{
    // Disregard parameters - nib name is an implementation detail
    return [self init];
}

// This method gets called automatically when the view is created
- (void)viewDidLoad
{
    [super viewDidLoad];

    NSLog(@"Loaded the view for HypnosisViewController");

    // Set the background color of the view so we can see it
    [[self view] setBackgroundColor:[UIColor orangeColor]];
}
```

133

Open `CurrentTimeViewController.m` and do all the same things, but use a different background color for the view:

```
- (id)init
{
    // Call the superclass's designated initializer
    self = [super initWithNibName:nil
                           bundle:nil];
    if (self) {
        // Get the tab bar item
        UITabBarItem *tbi = [self tabBarItem];

        // Give it a label
        [tbi setTitle:@"Time"];
    }

    return self;
}

- (id)initWithNibName:(NSString *)nibName bundle:(NSBundle *)bundle
{
    // Disregard parameters - implementation detail
    return [self init];
}

- (void)viewDidLoad
{
    [super viewDidLoad];

    NSLog(@"Loaded the view for CurrentTimeViewController");

    // Set the background color of the view so we can see it
    [[self view] setBackgroundColor:[UIColor greenColor]];
}
```

Build and run the application. Two labeled tab bar items will appear on the tab bar (Figure 7.7). Tap one and then the other, and you will see that the views for the view controllers are getting swapped in.

Figure 7.7   Tab bar items with labels

(If you are wondering why we made a new designated initializer for the **UIViewController** subclasses, hang on until Chapter 10 – we'll explain it then.)

Now let's add icons. Open `HypnosisViewController.m` and edit the **init** method:

```
- (id)init
{
    self = [super initWithNibName:nil
                           bundle:nil];

    if (self) {
        UITabBarItem *tbi = [self tabBarItem];
```

```
        [tbi setTitle:@"Hypnosis"];

        // Create a UIImage from a file
        UIImage *i = [UIImage imageNamed:@"Hypno.png"];

        // Put that image on the tab bar item
        [tbi setImage:i];
    }

    return self;
}
```

Next, open `CurrentTimeViewController.m` and edit its **init** method:

```
- (id)init
{
    self = [super initWithNibName:nil
                           bundle:nil];

    if (self) {
        UITabBarItem *tbi = [self tabBarItem];
        [tbi setTitle:@"Time"];
        UIImage *i = [UIImage imageNamed:@"Time.png"];
        [tbi setImage:i];
    }

    return self;
}
```

Now when you build and run the application, you will also see icons in the tab bar (Figure 7.8).

Figure 7.8   Tab bar items with labels and icons

Creating views for the view controllers

Now that you have a perfectly nice tab bar with two view controllers (and the two corresponding tab bar items), it's time to give your view controllers views. (Technically, they already have views, but they are default, blank views.) There are two ways to do this:

- create the view programmatically

- create a XIB file

How do you know when to do one versus the other? Here's a good rule-of-thumb: if the view has no subviews, create it programmatically; if it has subviews, create a XIB file.

When the view needs to be created, the view controller is sent the message **loadView**. In **HypnosisViewController**, you are going to override this method so that it creates an instance of **HypnosisView** programmatically. When an instance of a **UIViewController** is instantiated, its view is not created right away. A **UIViewController**'s view is created when it is placed in a view hierarchy (also known as "the first time it appears on screen" Add the following import statement and method to HypnosisViewController.m:

```
#import "HypnosisViewController.h"
#import "HypnosisView.h"

@implementation HypnosisViewController

- (void)loadView
{
    HypnosisView *hv = [[HypnosisView alloc] initWithFrame:CGRectZero];
    [hv setBackgroundColor:[UIColor whiteColor]];
    [self setView:hv];
    [hv release];
}
```

We no longer want the background of the view to be orange, so delete the following line from the **viewDidLoad** method in HypnosisViewController.m:

```
[[self view] setBackgroundColor:[UIColor orangeColor]];
```

Also delete the similar line of code from the **viewDidLoad** method in CurrentTimeViewController.m.

```
[[self view] setBackgroundColor:[UIColor greenColor]];
```

Build and run the application. You should see a **HypnosisView** like the one in Figure 7.9.

Figure 7.9   HypnosisViewController

The **CurrentTimeViewController**'s view will have subviews (a **UIButton** and a **UILabel**). Therefore, you will use a XIB file to load its view. Create a new XIB file by selecting New File... from the

New item in the File menu. From the iOS section, choose User Interface. Then, select the Empty XIB template. On the next pane, select iPhone from the pop-up menu.

Figure 7.10 Creating an empty XIB

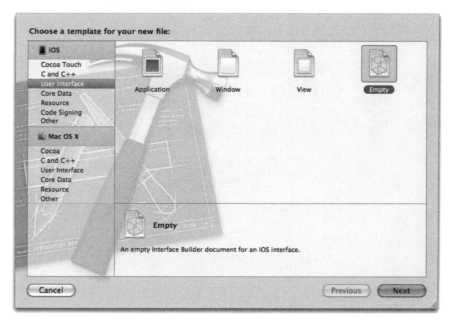

Name this file `CurrentTimeViewController.xib` and save it. Then, select it in the project navigator to show it in Xcode.

Demystifying the XIB: File's Owner

This is an empty XIB file, there are only two "objects" in it: File's Owner and First Responder. The goal of this XIB file is to create the view for the **CurrentTimeViewController**.

Open the utilities area and drag a **UIView** onto the canvas. Notice that this view was added to the gutter on the left edge of the XIB editor pane.

We would like this view to be *the* view of the **CurrentTimeViewController**. In other words, the instance variable view of **CurrentTimeViewController** should point at the view. Therefore, we must have an outlet connection from an instance of **CurrentTimeViewController** to the view. In previous exercises, this was simple: there was a AppDelegate object, and we'd set up connections between the view objects in the XIB file and that AppDelegate. However, there is not a **CurrentTimeViewController** object in this XIB file that you can make connections to and from.

Your first intuition may be to add a **CurrentTimeViewController** to the XIB file. But, if there was a **CurrentTimeViewController** object in the XIB file, whenever that XIB file was loaded it would create an instance of **CurrentTimeViewController**. This application already has an instance of **CurrentTimeViewController**, the one you created in `application:didFinishLaunchingWithOptions:`. If you were to add an instance of this class to the XIB file, you would have two `CurrentTimeViewController` instances.

Figure 7.11   File's Owner

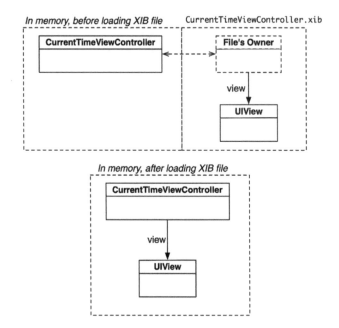

Instead, we need some way to connect objects loaded from the XIB file to objects that exist in memory before the XIB file is loaded. This way, the already existing `CurrentTimeViewController` could set its `view` instance variable to point at the view loaded from this XIB file. This is where the File's Owner comes in. The File's Owner is a *placeholder object*. When a XIB file is loaded, placeholder objects are *not* instantiated. You can think of a placeholder object as a hole in which existing objects can be placed so that connections can be made between them and the objects in the XIB file.

Take a peek at the available connections for the File's Owner by Control-clicking on it. There aren't any. That is because the type of the File's Owner defaults to `NSObject`, which has no `IBOutlets`. Because a `CurrentTimeViewController` will be the placeholder object, we must change the type of the File's Owner in this XIB file to be that class.

Select the File's Owner placeholder object on the outline view and click the ▣ icon to show the identity inspector. Change the Class field to `CurrentTimeViewController` and hit return.

Figure 7.12   Changing the type of an object in a XIB file

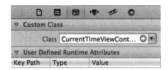

Now, Control-click on the File's Owner to see the available outlets. There is now a view outlet available because **UIViewController**'s view is an IBOutlet and **CurrentTimeViewController** is a subclass of **UIViewController**. Connect this outlet to the view in this XIB file.

Select the view and open the attributes inspector. Change its background color to something obnoxious, like bright purple.

Figure 7.13 Changing the background color of a view

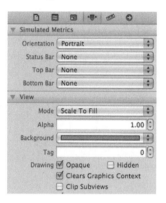

Build and run the application. While running, select the Time tab. Notice that you are looking at the exact same view you created in CurrentTimeViewController.xib.

So, how does this work? When you create an instance of a **UIViewController** subclass, you pass it the name of a XIB file through its designated initializer, **initWithNibName:bundle:**. When the view controller is asked for its view, it checks to see if a XIB file with that name exists in your application bundle. (If you specify nil as the name, it will search for a XIB file whose name matches the name of the view controller subclass.) It then loads that XIB file. You can be more explicit about the XIB file loaded in CurrentTimeViewController.m.

```
- (id)init
{
    self = [super initWithNibName:@"CurrentTimeViewController"
                           bundle:nil];

    if (self) {
        UITabBarItem *tbi = [self tabBarItem];
        [tbi setTitle:@"Time"];
        UIImage *i = [UIImage imageNamed:@"Time.png"];
        [tbi setImage:i];
    }

    return self;
}
```

The **loadView** method is responsible for this XIB loading behavior. The default implementation of this method does the checking for and loading of a XIB file. Therefore, when a view controller is loading its view from a XIB file, you do not override **loadView**. If instead you want to create a view for a view controller programmatically, you must override **loadView** so it does not load a XIB file.

The instance of **CurrentTimeViewController** that is loading the XIB file places itself in the File's Owner hole of that XIB file. Any connections to or from the File's Owner are made on that instance of **CurrentTimeViewController**. This concept allows placeholder objects to get pointers to objects loaded from a XIB file. If you did not set pointers from objects in memory to objects loaded from a XIB file, the loaded objects would be alive but nothing would have a pointer to it. This would be a leak.

Take a look at MainWindow.xib and check out the File's Owner in the identity inspector: its class is **UIApplication**. When your application first launches, an instance of **UIApplication** is created and it loads MainWindow.xib. The **UIApplication** is the File's Owner. The File's Owner of this file has a outlet connection for its delegate that has been connected to **HypnoTimeAppDelegate**. Therefore, after the XIB file loads, the delegate of the **UIApplication** is set to point at the **HypnoTimeAppDelegate** object – the reason why **HypnoTimeAppDelegate** gets sent the message **application:didFinishLaunchingWithOptions:**.

Understanding the File's Owner is an integral part of demystifying the magic of a XIB file. In Chapter 15, we will talk about how objects are archived into the XIB file.

Now that your XIB file is set up to work properly, you can continue creating the interface for **CurrentTimeViewController**. In CurrentTimeViewController.h, add an outlet and an action.

```
#import <UIKit/UIKit.h>

@interface CurrentTimeViewController : UIViewController
{
    IBOutlet UILabel *timeLabel;
}
- (IBAction)showCurrentTime:(id)sender;

@end
```

Save this file.

In CurrentTimeViewController.xib, drag a **UILabel** and **UIButton** object onto the view that is already there. Configure these objects and make connections, as shown in Figure 7.14.

Figure 7.14   Button and Label

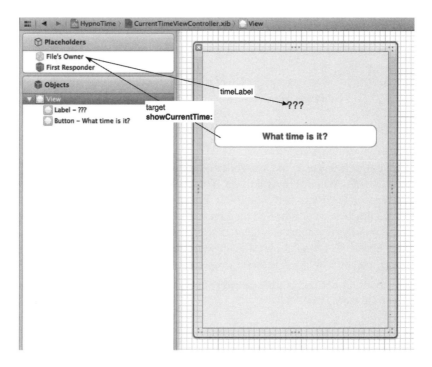

Implement the action method in CurrentTimeViewController.m:

```
- (IBAction)showCurrentTime:(id)sender
{
    NSDate *now = [NSDate date];

    // Static here means "only once." The *variable* formatter
    // is created when the program is first loaded into memory.
    // The first time this method runs, formatter will
    // be nil and the if-block will execute, creating
    // an NSDateFormatter object that formatter will point to.
    // Subsequent entry into this method will reuse the same
    // NSDateFormatter object.

    static NSDateFormatter *formatter = nil;

    if (!formatter) {
        formatter = [[NSDateFormatter alloc] init];
        [formatter setTimeStyle:NSDateFormatterShortStyle];
    }
    [timeLabel setText:[formatter stringFromDate:now]];
}
```

Build and run the application. You will be able to switch back and forth between the two views.
Clicking the button on the time view will display the current time.

Appearing and Disappearing Views

UIViewController has several methods that get called at certain times:

viewWillAppear:	when its view is about to be added to the window
viewDidAppear:	when its view has been added to the window
viewWillDisappear:	when its view is about to be dismissed, covered, or otherwise hidden from view
viewDidDisappear:	when its view has been dismissed, covered, or otherwise hidden from view

These methods are useful because a view controller is only created once, but its view usually gets displayed (and dismissed or hidden) several times. You often need a way to override the default behavior at these times in the life of view controller. For example, you may want to do some sort of initialization each time the view is moved on screen. Here you would use **viewWillAppear:** or **viewDidAppear:**. Similarly, if you had a large data structure that you only need while the view controller is being displayed, you might want to do some clean-up each time the view controller is moved off screen. Then you would use **viewWillDisappear:** or **viewDidDisappear:**.

Note that these methods, as defined in **UIViewController**, do nothing. They are there so that your subclasses can override them.

```
- (void)viewWillAppear:(BOOL)animated;
- (void)viewDidAppear:(BOOL)animated;
- (void)viewWillDisappear:(BOOL)animated;
- (void)viewDidDisappear:(BOOL)animated;
```

Now let's override **viewWillAppear:** to initialize the time label of the **CurrentTimeViewController** to the current time each time it is displayed and **viewWillDisappear:** to log to the console. In CurrentTimeViewController.m, make the following changes:

```
- (void)viewWillAppear:(BOOL)animated
{
    NSLog(@"CurrentTimeViewController will appear");
    [super viewWillAppear:animated];
    [self showCurrentTime:nil];
}
- (void)viewWillDisappear:(BOOL)animated
{
    NSLog(@"CurrentTimeViewController will DISappear");
    [super viewWillDisappear:animated];
}
```

Build and run the application. Note that each time you return to the Time screen, the time label is updated. And each time you leave that screen, you will see the log statement in the console.

The View Controller Lifecycle and Low-Memory Warnings

A view controller, like any other object, is created through **alloc** and **init**. It does not, however, create its view at that time. Instead, it waits until the view is really needed before it calls **loadView**. This lazy creation of the view is good: for example, if you have a tab view with a dozen view controllers, the view for any particular view controller will only be created if that particular tab is selected. You can see this behavior in the console when you build and run HypnoTime – you will only see the log message indicating that the **CurrentTimeViewController**'s view is loaded after you switch to the Time tab for the first time.

How does a view controller know when to load its view? When it is sent the message **view**. The implementation of this method in **UIViewController** looks something like this:

```
- (UIView *)view
{
    if ([self isViewLoaded] == NO)
    {
        // If I don't currently have a view, then create it
        [self loadView];
        [self viewDidLoad];
    }

    // The view is definitely going to exist here, so return it
    return view;
}
```

This code says that anytime an object asks a view controller for its view, it will create it if it doesn't already exist. This is exactly what happens when the user selects a tab from the tab bar: the **UITabBarController** sends the message **view** to the associated view controller and then places the returned view in the view hierarchy. Imagine what would happen if you were to send the message **view** to **CurrentTimeViewController** in its **init** method. In CurrentTimeViewController.m, access the view in **init** and change its background color to yellow:

```
- (id)init
{
    self = [super initWithNibName:@"CurrentTimeViewController"
                           bundle:nil];

    if (self) {
        UITabBarItem *tbi = [self tabBarItem];
        [tbi setTitle:@"Time"];
        UIImage *i = [UIImage imageNamed:@"Time.png"];
        [tbi setImage:i];

        [[self view] setBackgroundColor:[UIColor yellowColor]];
    }

    return self;
}
```

Build and run the application. Switch to the Time screen and notice that it is yellow. More importantly, notice that the console says the **CurrentTimeViewController**'s view is loaded as soon as you start the application. By accessing the view in a view controller's initialization method, the view is no longer loaded lazily. This doesn't seem like that big of an issue; that is, until you factor in *low memory warnings*.

When the system is running low on RAM, it issues a low memory warning to the running application. The application responds by freeing up any resources that it doesn't need at the moment and can easily recreate. View controllers, during a low memory warning, are sent the message **didReceiveMemoryWarning**. The default implementation of this method will check to see if the view is currently on screen; if it is not, it is released. (If the view is on screen, nothing happens.)

Run the application on the simulator. Switch to the Time tab, notice the view is yellow, and then switch back to the Hypno tab. From the Hardware menu in the simulator, select Simulate Memory Warning. This will issue a low memory warning to your application. Then, switch back to the Time tab: the view is no longer yellow.

Why isn't the view yellow anymore? When a low memory warning occurs, `CurrentTimeViewController`'s view is destroyed – but the instance of `CurrentTimeViewController` is not. When you switch back to the Time tab, the view is recreated, but the `CurrentTimeViewController` itself is not recreated. Thus, the message `init`, which sets the background color of the view to yellow, is never sent to the instance of `CurrentTimeViewController` again.

We can make a rule out of this: never access a view controller's view in that view controller's initialization method. If you have extra work you want to perform on the view, do so in `viewDidLoad`. This message is sent to a view controller each time it loads its view. Delete the line of code that sets the background color of the view to yellow from the `init` method and add it to `viewDidLoad` in `CurrentTimeViewController.m`.

```
- (void)viewDidLoad
{
    [super viewDidLoad];

    NSLog(@"Loaded the view for CurrentTimeViewController");

    [[self view] setBackgroundColor:[UIColor yellowColor]];
}
```

Build and run the application. You can simulate as many memory warnings as you want and the view will always be yellow. This is the desired behavior for handling low memory warnings – the user should never know that one occurred.

Figure 7.15   Retain count of views

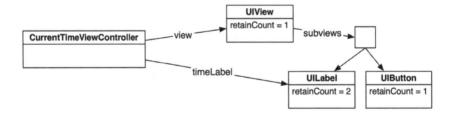

In addition to `viewDidLoad`, you may also have to implement its counterpart, `viewDidUnload`. A view controller's view can have subviews and some of these subviews will be connected as outlets from the view controller. When an object is connected via an outlet, it is retained by the object that has the outlet to it. For example, the `timeLabel` is an outlet of `CurrentTimeViewController`. Therefore, `CurrentTimeViewController` retains its `timeLabel`. A view is also retained by its superview, so `timeLabel` has a retain count of two.

When a low memory warning occurs, the `view` of the `CurrentTimeViewController` will be deallocated (its retain count will only be one, since `CurrentTimeViewController` is the only thing that retains it when it is not on the screen). When this view is deallocated, it will send **release** to its subviews. The timeLabel then has a retain count of one (from the **CurrentTimeViewController**), but it doesn't have a superview any longer. When **CurrentTimeViewController** reloads its view, a new **UILabel** instance is created from the XIB file.

Therefore, as soon as a view controller's view is unloaded, you should release all outlets since they will eventually be replaced by a new object. Do so by implementing **viewDidUnload** in CurrentTimeViewController.m.

```
- (void)viewDidUnload
{
    NSLog(@"CurrentTimeViewController's view was unloaded due to memory warning");
    [super viewDidUnload];
    [timeLabel release];
    timeLabel = nil;
}
```

Notice that we did not release the button, which is also a subview of the **CurrentTimeViewController**'s view. This is because we did not have an outlet to this object.

When a view controller is deallocated, it is not sent the message **viewDidUnload**. (Its view is still released, though.) Therefore, a view controller that will get deallocated must release its outlets in **dealloc**. Even though **CurrentTimeViewController** will not be released in this application, implement its **dealloc** in CurrentTimeViewController.m.

```
- (void)dealloc
{
    [timeLabel release];
    [super dealloc];
}
```

The biggest thing to keep in mind is that the view and its view controller are separate objects. A view controller will see its view created, moved on screen, moved off screen, destroyed and created again – perhaps many times over. You can think of the view as a renewable resource that the view controller uses to communicate with the user. Figure 7.16 shows the life cycle of a view controller's view in full.

Figure 7.16   Lifecycle of a view controller

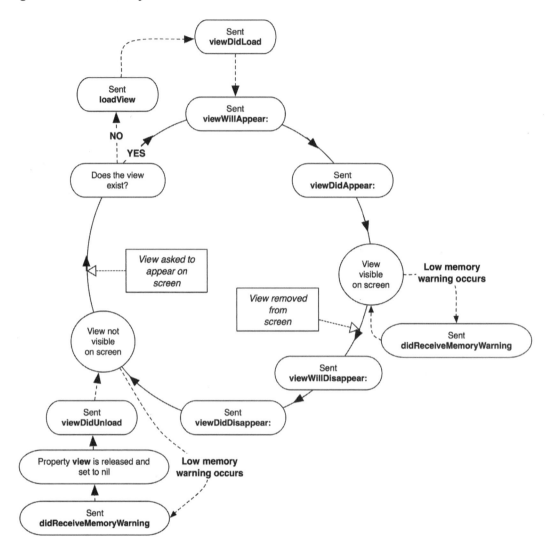

View Controller Subclasses and Templates

In this exercise, you were asked to create a **UIViewController** subclass by using the **NSObject** template and an empty XIB file that you configured for the view controller. This is useful for learning how the XIB file works. However, in practice, you typically let Xcode do the grunt work and use the **UIViewController** subclass template.

Throughout the rest of this book, you will create a lot of view controllers. To save on time and potential errors, we will instruct you to use the **UIViewController** template when that view controller will have a XIB file. When you create a view controller subclass with a XIB template, the XIB's File's

Owner is already set to the class of that view controller. It also has an instance of **UIView** that has been hooked up to the File's Owner's `view` outlet.

There is a drawback to using the view controller templates: there is a lot of code written in the implementation file. It becomes difficult to explain where to type the code with all of this extra junk in the file. Therefore, when you create a view controller using these templates, we will instruct you to delete all of the code in the implementation file between the `@implementation` and `@end` directives. We'll tell you this each time you create a file, so you don't have to remember this, but consider this a heads-up.

Challenge: Map Tab

Add another view controller to the tab bar controller. This new view controller should display an **MKMapView** that shows the user's location.

8

The Accelerometer

One of the flashiest features of iOS is the *accelerometer*. The accelerometer detects the device's real-world orientation by tracking the force of the earth's gravity on its X, Y, and Z axes. You can also use accelerometer data to detect changes in the device's velocity.

In this chapter, you are going to use the accelerometer to skew the center of the **HypnosisView** according to the device's orientation: when the user tilts the phone, the center will slide in the direction of the tilt, as shown in Figure 8.1.

Figure 8.1   HypnoTime, tilted

Setting Up the Accelerometer

To receive accelerometer data, your application needs to get hold of the application's shared instance of **UIAccelerometer** and give it an updateInterval and a delegate. The delegate needs to implement the method **accelerometer:didAccelerate:**. This method reports changes in the accelerometer data every updateInterval seconds in the form of a **UIAcceleration** object.

Open the HypnoTime project. Before you add any code, you need to decide which object will be the **UIAccelerometer** delegate. There are two options:

- Make the **HypnosisView** the delegate. It will receive the updates directly and use them to change the center of drawing internally.

- Make the **HypnosisViewController** the delegate. It will receive the updates and forward the necessary bits in messages to its view, the **HypnosisView**.

If the **HypnosisView** is the accelerometer delegate, it becomes a self-contained object, which makes reusing it simpler. The problem is there can only be one accelerometer delegate. What if other objects need input from the accelerometer? **HypnosisView** can't forward information on to other objects – it's not a controller. Therefore, the better option is to let **HypnosisViewController** be the delegate and receive the accelerometer updates, as shown in Figure 8.2. **HypnosisViewController** can easily inform the **HypnosisView** of a change in orientation, and it can inform other objects, too, if necessary.

Figure 8.2   Object diagram for HypnoTime

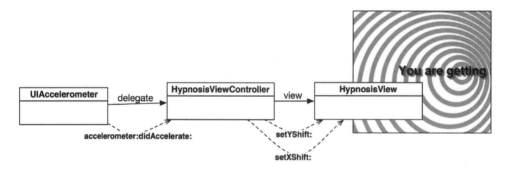

In HypnosisViewController.h, let the **HypnosisViewController** know it conforms to the UIAccelerometerDelegate protocol.

```
@interface HypnosisViewController : UIViewController <UIAccelerometerDelegate>
```

In HypnosisViewController.m, override the method **viewWillAppear:** to get a pointer to the accelerometer and set its update interval and delegate.

```
- (void)viewWillAppear:(BOOL)animated
{
    [super viewWillAppear:animated];

    NSLog(@"Monitoring accelerometer");
    UIAccelerometer *a = [UIAccelerometer sharedAccelerometer];

    // Receive updates every 1/10th of a second.
    [a setUpdateInterval:0.1];
    [a setDelegate:self];
}
```

When the **HypnosisViewController**'s view is moved off screen, the accelerometer updates become unnecessary, and you should set the accelerometer's delegate to nil. Setting the **UIAccelerometer** delegate to `nil` stops the updates to the controller and powers down the accelerometer hardware to conserve battery life. Make this change in `HypnosisViewController.m`:

```
- (void)viewWillDisappear:(BOOL)animated
{
    [super viewWillDisappear:animated];
    [[UIAccelerometer sharedAccelerometer] setDelegate:nil];
}
```

Getting Accelerometer Data

In `HypnosisViewController.m`, add the following implementation of the **UIAccelerometer** delegate method, **accelerometer:didAccelerate:**. This method will log accelerometer updates to the console. Notice that the types of the two parameters are different even though they look similar:

```
- (void)accelerometer:(UIAccelerometer *)meter
        didAccelerate:(UIAcceleration *)accel
{
    NSLog(@"%f, %f, %f", [accel x], [accel y], [accel z]);
}
```

Build and run the application on your device. Watch the console as you rotate and shake the phone to get a feel for the data that the accelerometer produces.

Orientation and Scale of Acceleration

The device's acceleration is measured in Gs. 1G is the force due to the earth's gravity. (When the device is still, the accelerometer doesn't know if it is moving at a constant velocity in the earth's gravity well or if it is far out in space and accelerating upwards at 9.8 meters per second every second.)

While the application is running, hold the device vertically in front of your face as if you were using it. Check the console: the y-component of the acceleration is approximately -1, and the x- and z-components are approximately 0. If you lay the device on its back, the z-component of the acceleration is approximately -1, and the others are approximately 0. If you balance the device on the edge with the volume switch down, the x-component of the acceleration is approximately -1, and the others are approximately 0. If you drop your device, all three components are 0 – until it hits the floor.

Using Accelerometer Data

This application will use the accelerometer data to offset the center of drawing in the **HypnosisView**. So, **HypnosisView** needs two properties to define the offset. In `HypnosisView.h`, add these properties.

```
@interface HypnosisView : UIView
{
    float xShift, yShift;
}
@property (nonatomic, assign) float xShift;
@property (nonatomic, assign) float yShift;
@end
```

Now synthesize these properties in `HypnosisView.m`:

```
@implementation HypnosisView
@synthesize xShift, yShift;
```

HypnosisView needs to know how to use these properties when it draws. In HypnosisView.m, add code to **drawRect:** to offset the center using the xShift and yShift instance variables:

```
// Draw concentric circles
for (float currentRadius = maxRadius; currentRadius > 0; currentRadius -= 20)
{
    center.x += xShift;
    center.y += yShift;
    CGContextAddArc(context, center.x, center.y,
                    currentRadius, 0, M_PI * 2.0, YES);
    CGContextStrokePath(context);
}
```

Using the **UIAcceleration** object the accelerometer sends its delegate, set xShift and yShift and redraw the view. In HypnosisViewController.m, replace the following method:

```
- (void)accelerometer:(UIAccelerometer *)meter
        didAccelerate:(UIAcceleration *)accel
{
    HypnosisView *hv = (HypnosisView *)[self view];
    [hv setXShift:10.0 * [accel x]];
    [hv setYShift:-10.0 * [accel y]];

    // Redraw the view
    [hv setNeedsDisplay];
}
```

Build and run your application. The center of the view will move as you tilt the device. But the movement of the **HypnosisView** has a jerky feel that is not so conducive to hypnosis. We'll fix that next.

Smoothing Accelerometer Data

Each time the accelerometer sends an update, the center of the view changes to reflect the orientation of the device. However, because the accelerometer's updateInterval is constant and the device's movement is variable, the center of the view jumps around instead of moving in calm, peaceful, smooth manner. To get smooth movement, you need "smoothed" data. To smooth accelerometer data, you apply a low-pass filter.

In HypnosisViewController.m, add the following lines of code to filter the accelerometer data:

```
- (void)accelerometer:(UIAccelerometer *)meter
        didAccelerate:(UIAcceleration *)accel
{
    HypnosisView *hv = (HypnosisView *)[self view];
    float xShift = [hv xShift] * 0.8 + [accel x] * 2.0;
    float yShift = [hv yShift] * 0.8 - [accel y] * 2.0;
    [hv setXShift:xShift];
    [hv setYShift:yShift];

    // Redraw the view
    [hv setNeedsDisplay];
}
```

Build and run your application. The application will have a smoother response and a nicer feel.

Detecting Shakes

To detect when the user is shaking the device, you could perform some intricate math on the signal that comes from the accelerometer. However, the class **UIResponder** has been kind enough to implement methods that do the math for you.

```
// Triggered when a shake is detected
- (void)motionBegan:(UIEventSubtype)motion
         withEvent:(UIEvent *)event;

// Triggered when the shake is complete
- (void)motionEnded:(UIEventSubtype)motion
         withEvent:(UIEvent *)event;

// Triggered when a shake is interrupted (by a call for example)
// Or if a shake lasts for more than a second
- (void)motionCancelled:(UIEventSubtype)motion
            withEvent:(UIEvent *)event;
```

Now in HypnoTime, let's override **motionBegan:withEvent:** to change the stripe color when the phone is shaken. First, add an instance variable to HypnosisView.h to hold the new color:

```
@interface HypnosisView : UIView {
    UIColor *stripeColor;
    float xShift, yShift;
}
@property (nonatomic, assign) float xShift;
@property (nonatomic, assign) float yShift;
@end
```

The designated initializer for **UIView** is **initWithFrame:**. In HypnosisView.m, initialize the stripeColor in **initWithFrame:**.

```
- (id)initWithFrame:(CGRect)r
{
    self = [super initWithFrame:r];

    if (self) {
        // Notice we explicitly retain the UIColor instance
        // returned by the convenience method lightGrayColor,
        // because it is autoreleased and we need to keep it around
        // so we can use it in drawRect:.
        stripeColor = [[UIColor lightGrayColor] retain];
    }

    return self;
}
```

Finally, use the stripeColor in your **drawRect:** method of HypnosisView.m.

```
    CGContextSetLineWidth(context, 10);

    // Set the stroke color to the current stripeColor
    [stripeColor setStroke];

    // Draw concentric circles
    for (float currentRadius = maxRadius; currentRadius > 0; currentRadius -= 20)
    {
```

Build and run the application just to make sure you haven't broken anything. It should work exactly as before.

Because stripeColor is owned by **HypnosisView**, it must be released in the view's **dealloc** method. Override **dealloc** in HypnosisView.m.

```
- (void)dealloc
{
    [stripeColor release];
    [super dealloc];
}
```

Now override **motionBegan:withEvent:** to change the color and redraw the view in HypnosisView.m.

```
- (void)motionBegan:(UIEventSubtype)motion withEvent:(UIEvent *)event
{
    // Shake is the only kind of motion for now,
    // but we should (for future compatibility)
    // check the motion type.
    if (motion == UIEventSubtypeMotionShake) {
        NSLog(@"shake started");
        float r, g, b;

        // Notice the trailing .0 on the dividends... this is necessary
        // to tell the compiler the result is a floating point number.. otherwise,
        // you will always get 0
        r = random() % 256 / 256.0;
        g = random() % 256 / 256.0;
        b = random() % 256 / 256.0;
        [stripeColor release];
        stripeColor = [UIColor colorWithRed:r
                                      green:g
                                       blue:b
                                      alpha:1];
        [stripeColor retain];
        [self setNeedsDisplay];
    }
}
```

There's one more important detail: the window's firstResponder is the object that gets sent all of the motion events. Right now, the first responder is not **HypnosisView**, but you can change that in two steps. First, you need to override **canBecomeFirstResponder** in HypnosisView.m:

```
- (BOOL)canBecomeFirstResponder
{
    return YES;
}
```

Then, when your view appears on the screen, you need to make it the first responder. In HypnosisViewController.m, add the following line of code to **viewWillAppear:animated**.

```
- (void)viewWillAppear:(BOOL)animated
{
    [super viewWillAppear:animated];
    NSLog(@"Monitoring accelerometer");
    UIAccelerometer *a = [UIAccelerometer sharedAccelerometer];
    [a setUpdateInterval:0.1];
    [a setDelegate:self];
```

```
    [[self view] becomeFirstResponder];
}
```

Build and run the application. Shake the device and watch the color of the stripes change. Notice that the color does not continue to change if you continue shaking. This is because there isn't a "while motion continues" method. To change the color, you have to shake the device, stop shaking it, and then shake it again. (If you wanted the color to continue to change, you could use an **NSTimer** to send periodic "change the color now" messages. You would create the timer in **motionBegan:withEvent:** and destroy it in **motionEnded:withEvent:** and **motionCancelled:withEvent:**.)

Also, it's important to note that motion events have nothing to do with the **UIAccelerometer** delegate. The system determines there is a shake by querying the accelerometer hardware and then sends the appropriate messages to the firstResponder.

Challenge: Changing Colors

Change the colors of the stripes based on the orientation of the device. There are three color channels (Red, Green, Blue) and three axes of movement (X, Y, Z). Assign a color to each axis. When the G force on an axis is closer to -1, set its color channel to 0 and when it is closer to 1 set its color channel to 1. Use the documentation!

For the More Curious: Filtering and Frequency

In general, there are two ways of altering the accelerometer data to suit your needs: change the frequency of accelerometer data updates and apply a filter to the data. When you're writing an application that relies on accelerometer data, you should determine the update interval and filtering algorithm that gives the user the best experience.

In terms of update intervals, here are some recommendations:

Orientation Applications	If your application relies on the current orientation of the device (for example, to rotate an arrow to point in a certain direction), the accelerometer can update infrequently. A value of 1/20 to 1/10 seconds for the updateInterval is sufficient.
Game Applications	An application that uses accelerometer data as input for controlling a visual object in real-time needs a slightly faster update interval. For applications like this, the updateInterval should be between 1/30 to 1/60 seconds.
High-Frequency Applications	Applications that need to squeeze every little update out of the accelerometer should set the updateInterval between 1/70 and 1/100 seconds (the smallest possible interval). An application that detects shakes is updating at a high frequency.

Once you have chosen the right update interval, you need to choose what type of filter is best. Typically, you'll choose either a low-pass filter or a high-pass filter.

Using a *low-pass filter*, as you did in the exercise, isolates the gravity component of the acceleration data and reduces the effect of sudden changes in the device's orientation. In most situations, it gives you just the orientation of the device. A basic low-pass filter equation looks like this:

```
float filteringFactor = 0.1;
lowPassed = newValue * filteringFactor + lowPassed * (1.0 - filteringFactor);
```

where `lowPassed` is the output. Notice that the previous output is used the next time the equation is solved and that the new value produced by the accelerometer is blended with all of the previous values. The output of a low-pass filter is essentially a weighted average of previous inputs, and sudden movements will not affect the output as much as they would with unfiltered data.

On the other hand, sometimes you want to ignore orientation and focus on sudden movements, like a shake. For this, you would use a *high-pass filter*. Now that you know the low-pass filter, the high-pass signal is what's left if you subtract out the low-pass signal:

```
float filteringFactor = 0.1;
lowPassed = newValue * filteringFactor + lowPassed * (1.0 - filteringFactor);
highPassed = newValue - lowPassed;
```

There are other algorithms for high-pass filtering, but this one is especially easy to understand.

Figure 8.3 is a graph over time of low-pass and high-pass filtering on a device that is being shaken.

Figure 8.3   Low- and high-pass filter graphs

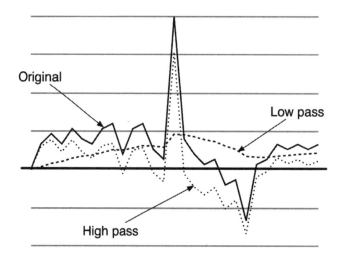

For the More Curious: Retina Display

With the release of iPhone 4, Apple introduced the Retina display for the iPhone and iPod touch. The Retina display has much higher resolution – 640x960 pixels compared to 320x480 pixels on earlier devices. Let's look at what you should do to make graphics look their best on both displays.

For vector graphics, like **HypnosisView**'s **drawRect:** method and drawn text, you don't need to do anything; the same code will render as crisply as the device allows. However, if you draw using Core

Graphics functions, these graphics will appear differently on different devices. In Core Graphics, also called Quartz, we describe lines, curves, text, etc. in terms of *points*. On a non-Retina display, a point is 1x1 pixel. On a Retina display, a point is 2x2 pixels (Figure 8.4).

Figure 8.4   Rendering to different resolutions

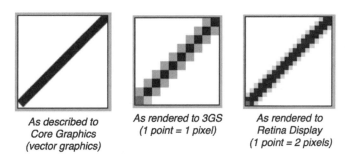

As described to
Core Graphics
(vector graphics)

As rendered to 3GS
(1 point = 1 pixel)

As rendered to
Retina Display
(1 point = 2 pixels)

What about printers? When you print, 72 points is equal to one inch.

Given these differences, bitmap images (like JPEG or PNG files) will be unattractive if the image isn't tailored to the device's screen type. Say your application includes a small image of 25x25 pixels. If this image is displayed on a Retina display, then the image must be stretched to cover an area of 50x50 pixels. At this point, the system does a type of averaging called anti-aliasing to keep the image from looking jagged. The result is an image that isn't jagged – but it is fuzzy (Figure 8.5).

Figure 8.5   Fuzziness from stretching an image

You could use a larger file instead, but the averaging would then cause problems in the other direction when the image is shrunk for a non-Retina display. The only solution is to bundle two image files with your application: one at a pixel resolution equal to the number of points on the screen for non-Retina displays and one twice that size in pixels for Retina displays.

Fortunately, you do not have to write any extra code to handle which image gets loaded on which device. All you have to do is suffix the higher-resolution image with @2x. Then, when you use

UIImage's **imageNamed:** method to load the image, this method looks in the bundle and gets the file that is appropriate for the particular device.

Let's see this in action with HypnoTime. In the last chapter, you added two image files (Hypno.png and Time.png) to your project from the iOSProgramming.zip file. In the same directory as those files, find Hypno@2x.png and Time@2x.png and add them to the HypnoTime project. Then build and run on the simulator.

Once the simulator application is running, you can change which display is being simulated. To see HypnoTime in a Retina display, go to the Hardware menu, select Device, and then choose iPhone (Retina). Notice that the tab bar items are crisp on both types of displays. (If you're even more curious, you can remove the @2x files from your project and build and run again to see the difference.)

9

Notification and Rotation

Objective-C code is all about objects sending messages to other objects. This communication usually occurs between two objects, but sometimes a bunch of objects are concerned with one object. They all want to know when this object does something interesting. But it's just not feasible for that object to send messages to every interested object.

Instead, an object can post notifications about what it is doing to a centralized notification center. Interested objects register to receive a message when a particular notification is posted or when a particular object posts. In this chapter, you will learn how to use a notification center to handle notifications. You'll also learn about the autorotation behavior of **UIViewController**.

Notification Center

Every application has an instance of **NSNotificationCenter**, which works like a smart bulletin board. An object can register as an observer ("Send me 'lost dog' notifications."). When another object posts a notification ("I lost my dog."), the notification center forwards the notification to the registered observers.

Notifications are instances of **NSNotification**. Every **NSNotification** object has a name and a pointer back to the object that posted it. When you register as an observer, you can specify a notification name, a posting object, and the message you want to be sent.

This snippet of code registers you for notifications named LostDog that have been posted by any object. When an object posts a LostDog notification, you'll be sent the message **retrieveDog:**.

```
NSNotificationCenter *nc = [NSNotificationCenter defaultCenter];
[nc addObserver:self                    // The object self will be sent
     selector:@selector(retrieveDog:)   // retrieveDog:
         name:@"LostDog"                // when @"LostDog" is posted
       object:nil];                     // by any object.
```

Note that nil works as a wildcard in the notification center world. You can pass nil as the name argument, which will give you every notification regardless of its name. If you pass nil for the notification name and the posting object, you will get every notification.

The method that is triggered when the notification arrives takes an **NSNotification** object as the argument:

```
- (void)retrieveDog:(NSNotification *)note
{
    id poster = [note object];
```

```
    NSString *name = [note name];
    NSDictionary *extraInformation = [note userInfo];
    ....
}
```

Notice that the notification object may also have a `userInfo` dictionary attached to it. This dictionary is used to pass additional information, like a description of the dog that was found. Here's an example of an object posting a notification with a `userInfo` dictionary attached:

```
NSDictionary *extraInfo = ...;
NSNotification *note = [NSNotification notificationWithName:@"LostDog"
                                                    object:self
                                                  userInfo:extraInfo];
[[NSNotificationCenter defaultCenter] postNotification:note];
```

For a (real-world) example, when a keyboard is coming onto the screen, it posts a `UIKeyboardDidShowNotification` that has a `userInfo` dictionary. This dictionary contains the on-screen region that the newly visible keyboard occupies.

This is important: the notification center does not retain observers. If an object registers with the notification center, that object must unregister before it is deallocated. If it doesn't, the next time a notification it registered for is posted, the center will try to send the object a message. Since that object has been deallocated, your application will crash.

```
- (void)dealloc
{
    [[NSNotificationCenter defaultCenter] removeObserver:self];
    [super dealloc];
}
```

UIDevice Notifications

One object that regularly posts notifications is **UIDevice**. Here are the constants that serve as the names of the notifications that a **UIDevice** posts:

```
UIDeviceOrientationDidChangeNotification
UIDeviceBatteryStateDidChangeNotification
UIDeviceBatteryLevelDidChangeNotification
UIDeviceProximityStateDidChangeNotification
```

Wouldn't it be cool to get a message when the device rotates? Or when the phone is placed next to the user's face? These notifications do just that.

Create a new Window-based Application iPhone project and name it HeavyRotation. In HeavyRotationAppDelegate.m, register to receive notifications when the orientation of the device changes:

```
- (BOOL)application:(UIApplication *)application
    didFinishLaunchingWithOptions:(NSDictionary *)launchOptions
{
    // Get the device object
    UIDevice *device = [UIDevice currentDevice];

    // Tell it to start monitoring the accelerometer for orientation
    [device beginGeneratingDeviceOrientationNotifications];
```

```
    // Get the notification center for the app
    NSNotificationCenter *nc = [NSNotificationCenter defaultCenter];

    // Add yourself as an observer
    [nc addObserver:self
           selector:@selector(orientationChanged:)
               name:UIDeviceOrientationDidChangeNotification
             object:device];

    [[self window] makeKeyAndVisible];

    return YES;
}
```

Now, whenever the device's orientation changes, the message **orientationChanged:** will be sent to the instance of **HeavyRotationAppDelegate**. In the same file, add an **orientationChanged:** method:

```
- (void)orientationChanged:(NSNotification *)note
{
    // Log the constant that represents the current orientation
    NSLog(@"orientationChanged: %d", [[note object] orientation]);
}
```

Build and run the application. (This is best run on the device because the simulator won't let you achieve some orientations. If you must use the simulator, you can change the orientation by choosing Rotate Left or Rotate Right from the Hardware menu.)

Many classes post notifications including **UIApplication**, **NSManagedObjectContext**, **MPMoviePlayerController**, **NSFileHandle**, **UIWindow**, **UITextField**, and **UITextView**. See their class reference pages in the documentation for details.

Autorotation

Many applications rotate and resize all of their views when the user rotates the device. You could implement this using notifications, but it would be a lot of work. Thankfully, you can use *autorotation* to simplify the process.

If the view on screen is controlled by a view controller, when the device is rotated, the view controller is asked if it is okay to rotate the view. If the view controller agrees, the view is resized and rotated. Its subviews are also resized and rotated.

To implement autorotation in HeavyRotation, you need to do two things:

- Override **shouldAutorotateToInterfaceOrientation:** in **HeavyViewController** to allow autorotation.

- Carefully set the autoresize mask on each subview so that it acts reasonably when the superview is resized to fill the rotated window.

Create a new class by selecting File → New → New File.... Choose the UIViewController subclass template from the Cocoa Touch item under iOS and click Next.

Figure 9.1   UIViewController template

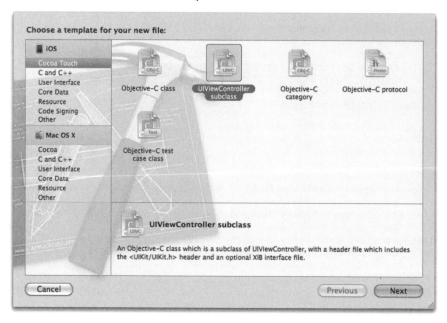

On the next pane, select UIViewController as the superclass, uncheck Targeted for iPad, and check With XIB for user interface.

Figure 9.2   UIViewController template options

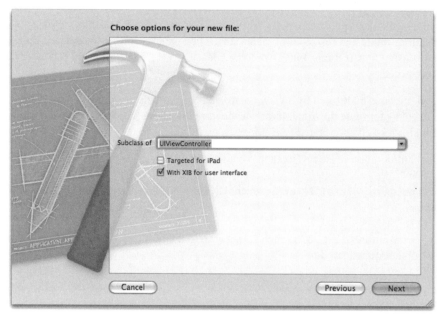

Name this class **HeavyViewController** and save it. Then, open HeavyViewController.m and delete everything between @implementation and @end. The file should look like this:

```
#import "HeavyViewController.h"

@implementation HeavyViewController

@end
```

Using this template, you get a subclass of **UIViewController** named **HeavyViewController**. You also get a XIB file named HeavyViewController.xib. This XIB file has a file's owner of type **HeavyViewController**, whose view outlet is connected to a 320x460 point sized view object.

At this point, you could create an **init** method that specifies the NIB to load and override the designated initializer of the superclass to call that **init** method:

```
- (id)init
{
    self = [super initWithNibName:@"HeavyViewController"
                           bundle:nil];
    return self;
}

- (id)initWithNibName:(NSString *)nibName bundle:(NSBundle *)bundle
{
    return [self init];
}
```

However, your **HeavyViewController** class can get by with the default implementation of the **init** method of its superclass, **UIViewController**. The **init** method of **UIViewController** calls **initWithNibName:bundle:**, passing nil as the nibName. When the nibName is nil, the view controller looks for a NIB file with the same name as the class of the object being initialized. In this case, that's HeavyViewController. In addition, **HeavyViewController** doesn't have any instance variables of its own to initialize. So this class doesn't need an initializer at all; the default behavior is perfect.

When the device rotates, view controllers whose views are currently on the screen will be sent the message **shouldAutorotateToInterfaceOrientation:**. This method returns a BOOL that indicates whether it is okay to autorotate the view controller's view.

For iPhone applications, you typically allow right-side up, landscape left, and landscape right. On the iPad, you typically allow all orientations, including upside-down. In HeavyViewController.m, implement this method to return YES for the three typical iPhone orientations.

```
- (BOOL)shouldAutorotateToInterfaceOrientation:(UIInterfaceOrientation)x
{
    // Return YES if incoming orientation is Portrait
    // or either of the Landscapes, otherwise, return NO
    return (x == UIInterfaceOrientationPortrait)
        || UIInterfaceOrientationIsLandscape(x);
}
```

Now let's find something to rotate. Drag any image (smaller than 1024x1024) from Finder into the project navigator. (Alternatively, you can use the file joeeye.jpg in the solutions at http://www.bignerdranch.com/solutions/iOSProgramming.zip.)

Open HeavyViewController.xib. Drop a slider, an image view, and two buttons onto the window. Then select the **UIImageView** and show the attributes inspector. Set the Image property to your image file, set the Mode to Aspect Fit, and set the background color to gray, as shown in Figure 9.3.

Figure 9.3   UIImageView

When the device rotates, two things happen. First, the view is rotated to be aligned with the device orientation. Second, the view is resized to fit the screen. For example, a view that is 320 points wide and 480 points tall in portrait mode will be 480 points wide and 320 points tall in landscape mode. When a view is resized, it will *autoresize* all of its subviews. Each subview is resized according to its *autoresizing mask* property. You can modify the autoresizing mask of a view by selecting it in the XIB file and then clicking the 📏 icon to reveal the *size inspector* (Figure 9.4).

Figure 9.4   Autosizing in size inspector

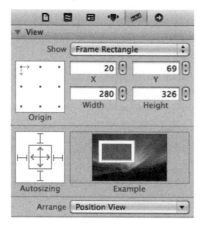

Check out the box labeled Autosizing in Figure 9.4. You can click this control in six different places: on the four sides outside the inner box and along the vertical and horizontal axes inside the inner box. We call the outside four *struts*, and the inside two *springs*. Clicking on one of these areas toggles an autoresizing mask option. A solid red line means the option is on, and a dim red dotted line means the option is off.

A spring that is turned on tells the view to change size when its superview changes size. For example, if you turn on the horizontal spring, the view will change its width at the same rate its superview changes its width.

A strut tells the view to keep the margin between the view and its superview constant. For example, if you turn on the left strut, the view will maintain the distance from the left side of its superview when the superview changes its width.

You can toggle the springs and struts and watch the animated example next to the Autosizing area to see what happens.

In your HeavyRotation application, you have four views. Here's how you want them to handle autorotation:

- The image view should stay centered and resize with its superview.

- The slider should get wider but not taller. It should stay fixed at the top of the superview and keep the same distance from the left and right edges.

- The two buttons should stay with their respective corners and *not* resize.

Now select each view and set the autoresize mask appropriately, as shown in Figure 9.5.

Figure 9.5   Autoresizing mask for views

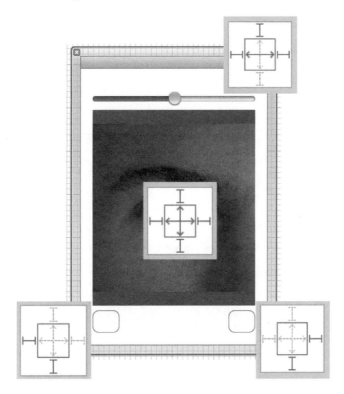

Finally, to finish this application, you need to create an instance of **HeavyViewController** and set it as the rootViewController of the window. Add the following lines of code to **application:didFinishLaunchingWithOptions:** in HeavyRotationAppDelegate.m. Make sure to include the import statement at the top of the file.

```
#import "HeavyViewController.h"

@implementation HeavyRotationAppDelegate
- (BOOL)application:(UIApplication *)application
    didFinishLaunchingWithOptions:(NSDictionary *)launchOptions
{
    // Get the device object
    UIDevice *device = [UIDevice currentDevice];

    // Tell it to start monitoring the accelerometer for orientation
    [device beginGeneratingDeviceOrientationNotifications];

    // Get the notification center for the app
    NSNotificationCenter *nc = [NSNotificationCenter defaultCenter];

    // Add yourself as an observer
    [nc addObserver:self
          selector:@selector(orientationChanged:)
              name:UIDeviceOrientationDidChangeNotification
            object:device];


    HeavyViewController *hvc = [[[HeavyViewController alloc] init] autorelease];
    [[self window] setRootViewController:hvc];

    [[self window] makeKeyAndVisible];

    return YES;
}
```

Build and run the application. It should autorotate when you rotate the device, as shown in Figure 9.6. (You can also run the application in the simulator and rotate it from the Hardware menu or use the keyboard shortcuts Command-Right Arrow and Command-Left Arrow.)

Figure 9.6   Running rotated

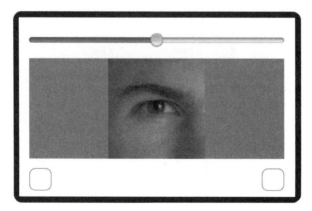

When a view is autorotated, it must change size (the width becomes the height and vice versa). This is why the mask is called an auto*resizing* mask. Another time a view's size must change is when the size of the device does. For instance, if HeavyRotation was a *universal application* (that runs on both the iPad and iPhone device families), then the interface for the iPad version would have to fit the larger screen size.

One approach to universalizing the interface is to create two separate XIB files – one for each device family. However, for HeavyRotation, you do not need to do this, thanks to the autoresizing masks. The view of **HeavyViewController** has its autoresizing mask set to resize when its superview is resized. Its superview is the **UIWindow** instance, which will automatically be resized to fit the screen when the application is launched. The subviews of the view will also be repositioned and resized according to their autoresizing masks.

Let's make HeavyRotation a universal application to see this happen. Select the project from the project navigator. Then, select the HeavyRotation target from the editor area. Select Universal from the Device Family pop-up menu as shown in Figure 9.7. A sheet will drop down asking if you wish to create a copy of your XIB files for, choose No.

Figure 9.7   Universalizing HeavyRotation

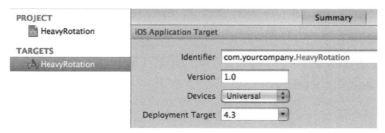

From the Scheme menu next to the Run button, choose either the iPad simulator or an iPad device if you've got one plugged in. Then build and run. Notice that the interface automatically resizes itself appropriately for the larger window.

Setting autoresizing masks programmatically and bitwise operations

The autoresizing mask can also be set programmatically by sending the message **setAutoresisingMask:** to a view.

```
[view setAutoresizingMask:UIViewAutoresizingFlexibleLeftMargin |
                UIViewAutoresizingFlexibleHeight];
```

This says that the view will resize its height when its superview's height changes; this is the same as checking the vertical spring in a XIB file. It also says that the left margin is flexible – which is the same as *un*-checking the left strut. In a XIB file, this autoresizing mask would match the one shown in Figure 9.8.

Figure 9.8   Autoresizing mask with flexible left margin and flexible height

See the | operator? That's a bitwise-OR operator. Each autoresizing constant is equal to a power of two. (You can find all the UIViewAutoresizing constants in the **UIView** class reference page in the documentation.) For example, the flexible left margin constant is 1 (2^0), and the flexible height constant is 16 (2^4). The property autoresizingMask is just an int and, like all values on a computer, is represented in binary. Binary numbers are a string of 1s and 0s. Here are a few examples of numbers in base 10 (decimal; the way we think about numbers) and base 2 (binary; the way a computer thinks about numbers):

```
 1₁₀ = 00000001₂
 2₁₀ = 00000010₂
16₁₀ = 00010000₂
27₁₀ = 00011011₂
34₁₀ = 00100010₂
```

In decimal representation, we have 10 different digits: 0 - 9. When we count past 9, we run out of symbols to represent the number, so we add a new digit column. A digit in the second column is worth 10 times more than a digit in the first column; a digit in the third column is worth 10 times more than the second column and so on. The same general idea is true for binary numbers, except we only have two digits (0 and 1), so we must add a new digit column each time we would normally use a 2. Because of this, each digit in binary is only worth two times more than the digit to the right of it. The rightmost digit is multiplied by 1, the one to the left of that is multiplied by 2, then 4, 8, and so on.

When talking about binary numbers, we call each digit a *bit*. We can think of each bit as an on-off switch, where 1 is "on" and 0 is "off." When thinking in these terms, we can use an int (which has space for at least 32 bits) as a set of on-off switches. Each position in the number represents one switch – a value of 1 means true, 0 means false. Essentially, we are shoving a ton of BOOLs into a single value. We call numbers used in this way *bitmasks*, and that's why the autoresize settings of a view are called the autoresizing *mask*.

A number that only has one bit set to 1 (the rest are 0) is a power of two. Therefore, we can use numbers that are powers of two to represent a single switch in a bitmask – each autoresizing constant is a single switch. We can turn on a switch in a bitmask using the bitwise-OR operation. This operation takes two numbers and produces a number where a bit is set to 1 if either of the original numbers had a 1 in the same position. When you bitwise-OR a number with 2^n, it flips on the switch at the nth position. For example, if you bitwise-OR 1 and 16, you get the following:

```
  00000001 ( 1₁₀, UIViewAutoresizingFlexibleLeftMargin)
| 00010000 (16₁₀, UIViewAutoresizingFlexibleHeight)
----------
  00010001 (17₁₀, both UIViewAutoresizingFlexibleHeight
                  and UIViewAutoresizingFlexibleLeftMargin)
```

The complement to the bitwise-OR operator is the bitwise-AND (&) operator. When you bitwise-AND two numbers, the result is a number that has a 1 in each bit where there is a 1 in the same position as *both* of the original numbers.

```
  00010001 (17₁₀, FlexibleHeight and FlexibleLeftMargin)
& 00010000 (16₁₀, FlexibleHeight)
----------
  00010000 (16₁₀, YES)

  00010001 (17₁₀, FlexibleHeight and FlexibleLeftMargin)
& 00000010 ( 2₁₀, FlexibleWidth)
----------
```

```
00000000 ( 0₁₀, NO)
```

Since any non-zero number means YES (and zero is NO), we use the bitwise-AND operator to check whether a switch is on or not. Thus, when a view's autoresizing mask is checked, the code looks like this:

```
if ([self autoresizingMask] & UIViewAutoresizingFlexibleHeight)
{
    // Resize the height
}
```

Forcing Landscape Mode

If your application only makes sense in landscape mode, you can force it to run that way. First, in your view controller implement **shouldAutorotateToInterfaceOrientation:** to only return YES for landscape orientations.

```
- (BOOL)shouldAutorotateToInterfaceOrientation:(UIInterfaceOrientation)x
{
    return UIInterfaceOrientationIsLandscape(x);
}
```

An application's Info.plist contains a key-value pair that specifies the valid initial orientations of the application. There is also an easy-to-use interface for changing this value: select the project from the project navigator, then the HeavyRotation target from the editor area, and finally the Summary pane.

Figure 9.9   Choosing the initial orientations

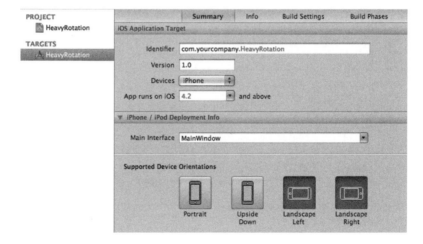

Find a section in the target's summary called Supported Device Orientations. This section contains four toggle buttons that specify which orientations are allowed. Buttons that are pushed in are valid.

Note that selecting orientations here only applies to orientation when the application launches; it does not control orientation once the application is running. You still have to tell your view controller to allow autorotation only to landscape orientations in **shouldAutorotateToInterfaceOrientation:**.

Challenge: Proximity Notifications

Register for proximity notifications. Proximity refers to the nearness of the device to the user. It is typically used to tell whether the iPhone is next to the user's face (as in talking on the phone). When this notification is posted, change the background color of **HeavyViewController**'s view to dark gray. You will need to turn on proximity monitoring, which is only available on the iPhone:

```
[device setProximityMonitoringEnabled:YES];
```

For the More Curious: Overriding Autorotation

In most cases, autorotation does the right thing if the autoresizing masks are properly set. However, you might want to take additional action on an autorotation or override the autorotation process altogether to change the way the view looks when it rotates. You can do this by overriding **willAnimateRotationToInterfaceOrientation:duration:** in a view controller subclass.

When a view controller is about to autorotate its view, it checks to see if you have implemented this method. If you have, then this method is invoked during the animation block of the rotation code. Therefore, all changes to subviews in this method will be animated as well. You can also perform some custom code within this method. Here is an example that will reposition a button and change the background color on autorotation:

```
- (void)willAnimateRotationToInterfaceOrientation:(UIInterfaceOrientation)x
                                        duration:(NSTimeInterval)duration
{
    // Assume "button" is a subview of this view controller's view

    UIColor *color = nil;
    CGRect bounds = [[self view] bounds];
    // If the orientation is rotating to Portrait mode...
    if (UIInterfaceOrientationIsPortrait(x)) {

        // Put the button in the top right corner
        [button setCenter:CGPointMake(bounds.size.width - 30,
                                      20)];

        // the background color of the view will be red
        color = [UIColor redColor];
    } else {  // If the orientation is rotating to Landscape mode

        // Put the button in the bottom right corner
        [button setCenter:CGPointMake(bounds.size.width - 30,
                                      bounds.size.height - 20)];

        // the background color of the view will be blue
        color = [UIColor blueColor];
    }
    [[self view] setBackgroundColor:color];
}
```

Overriding this method is useful when you want to update your user interface for a different orientation. For example, you could change the zoom or position of a scroll view or even swap in an entirely different view. Make sure, however, that you do not replace the view of the view controller in this method. If you wish to swap in another view, you must swap a subview of the view controller's view.

10

UITableView and UITableViewController

Many iOS applications show the user a list of items and allow the user to select, delete, or reorder items on the list. Whether it's a list of people in the user's address book or a list of items on the App Store, it's a **UITableView** doing the work. A **UITableView** displays a single column of data with a variable number of rows. Figure 10.1 shows some examples of **UITableView**.

Figure 10.1   Examples of UITableView

Beginning the Homepwner Application

In this chapter, you are going to start an application called Homepwner that keeps an inventory of all your possessions. In the case of a fire or other catastrophe, you'll have a record for your insurance company. ("Homepwner," by the way, is not a typo. If you need a definition for the word "pwn," please visit www.urbandictionary.com.)

So far, your iOS projects have been small, but Homepwner will grow into a realistically complex application over the course of nine chapters. By the end of this chapter, Homepwner will present a list of **Possession** objects in a **UITableView**, as shown in Figure 10.2.

Figure 10.2   Homepwner: phase 1

Create a new iPhone Window-based Application project and name it Homepwner.

UITableViewController

UITableView is a view object, so, according to Model-View-Controller, it knows how to draw itself, but that's it. It doesn't handle application logic or data. Thus, when using a **UITableView**, you must consider what else is necessary to get the table working in your application

- First, a **UITableView** needs a *data source*. A **UITableView** asks its data source for the number of rows to display, the data to be shown in those rows, and other tidbits that make a **UITableView** a useful user interface. Without a data source, a table view is just an empty container. The dataSource for a **UITableView** can be any type of Objective-C object as long as it conforms to the UITableViewDataSource protocol.

- A **UITableView** also typically needs a *delegate* that can inform other objects of events involving the **UITableView**. The delegate can be any object as long as it (you guessed it!) conforms to the UITableViewDelegate protocol.

- Finally, there is typically a view controller that creates and destroys the instance of **UITableView**.

Meet **UITableViewController**, a subclass of **UIViewController**. An instance of **UITableViewController** can fill all three roles: data source, view controller, and delegate. A **UITableViewController**'s view is always an instance of **UITableView**, and the **UITableViewController** handles the preparation and presentation of the **UITableView**. When a **UITableViewController** creates its view, the dataSource and delegate instance variables of the **UITableView** are automatically set to point at the **UITableViewController** (Figure 10.3).

Figure 10.3 UITableViewController-UITableView relationship

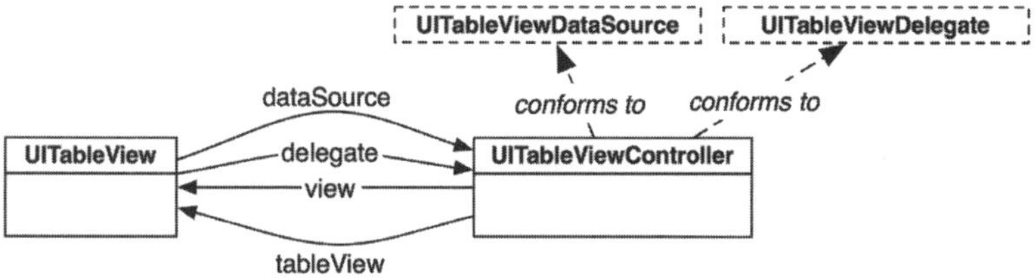

Subclassing UITableViewController

Now you're going to write a subclass of **UITableViewController** for Homepwner. From the File menu, select New and then New File.... Then, select Cocoa Touch from the iOS section. Before we go further, let's discuss file templates in a bit more detail.

Templates exist to speed up the process of creating new classes. Every class has a .h and .m file; using a template creates these two files and adds them to your project. With every set of class files, a new class and its superclass are declared in the .h file and an implementation block is declared in the .m file. Therefore, every template automatically adds this code for you.

The various templates differ in two ways: the superclass specified for the new class and the method stubs added to the implementation file. (A method stub is a method with no code between its curly braces.) There are two categories of class templates: Objective-C class and UIViewController subclass. Each of these categories has a number of templates. For example, there is a **UIView** template in the Objective-C class category. Using this template will create a .h file that has the superclass specified as **UIView** and an implementation file with method stubs for **initWithFrame:**, **drawRect:** and **dealloc**.

This additional code is useful when you know what you are doing and want to save time typing. However, these oh-so-helpful templates can get in the way when you're learning. Therefore, when creating new classes, we will use the **NSObject** template (available in the Objective-C class category). This template enters **NSObject** as the superclass of the new class and does not add any code to the implementation file. You are forced to type in and understand every line of code you are writing.

Once the files have been added to your project, you can change their contents as you please # you are not stuck with the superclass the template entered for you. You can create all of your classes using the **NSObject** template and simply change the superclass in the generated .h file. Do this for your new **UITableViewController** subclass.

Select Objective-C class and hit Next. Then, select NSObject from the pop-up menu and click Next again. Save this class as **ItemsViewController**.

As promised, you now have two files in your project: ItemsViewController.h and ItemsViewController.m. This class needs to be a subclass of **UITableViewController**, so open ItemsViewController.h and change its superclass:

```
@interface ItemsViewController : UITableViewController
```

Now, **ItemsViewController** is a subclass of **UITableViewController**, even though we used the **NSObject** template to create it.

In `ItemsViewController.m`, implement the following initializers.

```
#import "ItemsViewController.h"

@implementation ItemsViewController

- (id)init
{
    // Call the superclass's designated initializer
    self = [super initWithStyle:UITableViewStyleGrouped];

    return self;
}
- (id)initWithStyle:(UITableViewStyle)style
{
    return [self init];
}
```

The **initWithStyle:** method is the designated initializer of **UITableViewController**. In the code above, you override it to call a new designated initializer for your subclass – **init**. Overriding the designated initializer is a style choice that we use at Big Nerd Ranch for all view controller subclasses. When we subclass a view controller (or a table view controller), we will make **init** the designated initializer and, according to the initializer rules in Chapter 2, override the designated initializer of the superclass to call our new designated initializer.

Note that you've done this with view controllers in previous chapters. For instance, in the HypnoTime application in Chapter 7, you overrode the designated initializer of **HypnosisViewController**'s superclass. The superclass is **UIViewController**, its designated initializer is **initWithNibName:bundle:**, and the new designated initializer for **HypnosisViewController** is **init**.

```
- (id)init
{
    // Call the superclass's designated initializer
    self = [super initWithNibName:nil
                           bundle:nil];

    // Code specific to a HypnosisViewController
    ...

    return self;
}
- (id)initWithNibName:(NSString *)nibName bundle:(NSBundle *)bundle
{
    return [self init];
}
```

The reason we initialize our view controller subclasses this way is that the arguments passed to the superclass designated initializers are details that are specific to each view controller instance. (The details for the two examples here are the name of the view controller's NIB file for **UIViewController** and the style of the table view for **UITableViewController**.) Because these details are the same for each instance, the object responsible for creating the instance shouldn't be supplying them. Better that the creating object only send the message **init** to a view controller instance. The view controller can figure out its own details.

You'll see this pattern for the rest of the book every time you create a view controller, so we wanted to spell it out here. Now back to our regularly scheduled program.

Open HomepwnerAppDelegate.m. In **application:didFinishLaunchingWithOptions:**, create an instance of **ItemsViewController** and set it as the rootViewController of the window. Make sure to import the header file for **ItemsViewController** at the top of this file.

```
#import "ItemsViewController.h"

@implementation HomepwnerAppDelegate

- (BOOL)application:(UIApplication *)application
    didFinishLaunchingWithOptions:(NSDictionary *)launchOptions
{
    // Create a ItemsViewController
    ItemsViewController *itemsViewController = [[ItemsViewController alloc] init];

    // Place ItemsViewController's table view in the window hierarchy
    [[self window] setRootViewController:itemsViewController];

    [itemsViewController release];

    [[self window] makeKeyAndVisible];
    return YES;
}
```

(Does releasing itemsViewController here worry you? Remember that the window retains the object that is passed in **setRootViewController:**. Your table view controller is safe.)

Build and run your application. You will see the default appearance of a plain **UITableView** with no content, as shown in Figure 10.4. How did you get a table view? As a subclass of **UIViewController**, a **UITableViewController** inherits the **view** method. This method calls **loadView**, which creates and loads an empty view object if none exists. A **UITableViewController**'s view is always an instance of **UITableView**, so sending **view** to the **UITableViewController** gets you a bright, shiny, and empty table view.

Figure 10.4   Empty UITableView

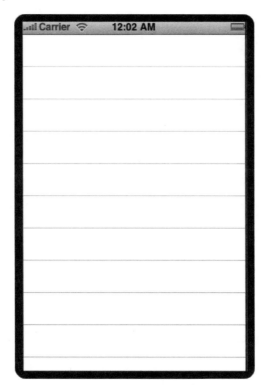

Poor empty table view! You should give it some rows to display. Remember the **Possession** class you wrote in Chapter 2? Now you're going to use that class again: each row of the table view will display an instance of **Possession**. Locate the header and implementation files for **Possession** (Possession.h and Possession.m) in Finder and drag them onto Homepwner's project navigator.

When dragging these files onto your project window, make sure to select the checkbox labeled Copy items into destination group's folder when prompted. This will copy the files from their current directory to your project's directory on the filesystem and add them to your project.

UITableView's Data Source

The process of providing a **UITableView** with rows in Cocoa Touch is different from the typical procedural programming task. In a procedural design, you tell the table view what it should display. In Cocoa Touch, the table view asks another object – its dataSource – what it should display. In our case, the **ItemsViewController** is the data source, so it needs a way to store possession data.

In Chapter 2, you used an **NSMutableArray** to store **Possession** instances. You will do the same thing in this exercise, but with a little twist. The **NSMutableArray** that holds the **Possession** instances will be abstracted into a **PossessionStore** (Figure 10.5).

Figure 10.5   Homepwner object diagram

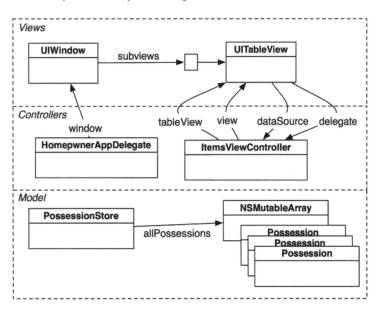

PossessionStore: a singleton

If an object wants to see all of the possessions, it will ask the **PossessionStore** for the array that contains them. In future chapters, you'll make the store responsible for performing operations on the array, like reordering, adding, and removing **Possession**s. It will also be responsible for saving and loading the **Possession**s from disk.

From the File menu, select New and then New File.... Create a new **NSObject** subclass and name it **PossessionStore**.

PossessionStore will be a singleton, just like **UIAccelerometer**. This means there will only be one instance of this type in the application; if you try and create another instance, the class will quietly return the existing instance instead.

To get the **PossessionStore**, you will send the class the message **defaultStore**. Declare this class method in PossessionStore.h.

```
#import <Foundation/Foundation.h>

@interface PossessionStore : NSObject
{

}
// Notice that this is a class method, and is prefixed with a + instead of a -
+ (PossessionStore *)defaultStore;

@end
```

When this message is sent to the **PossessionStore** class, the class will check to see if the instance of **PossessionStore** has already been created. If the store exists, the class will return the instance. If not, it will create the instance and return it. To do this, you'll use a global static variable. At the top of PossessionStore.m, create a global static variable to hold the instance of **PossessionStore** where the class can access it.

```
#import "PossessionStore.h"
#import "Possession.h"

static PossessionStore *defaultStore = nil;

@implementation PossessionStore
```

Also in PossessionStore.m, implement **+defaultStore, +allocWithZone:** and **-init** so that only one instance of the class can be created.

```
+ (PossessionStore *)defaultStore
{
    if (!defaultStore) {
        // Create the singleton
        defaultStore = [[super allocWithZone:NULL] init];
    }
    return defaultStore;
}

// Prevent creation of additional instances
+ (id)allocWithZone:(NSZone *)zone
{
    return [self defaultStore];
}

- (id)init
{
    // If we already have an instance of PossessionStore...
    if (defaultStore) {

        // Return the old one
        return defaultStore;
    }

    self = [super init];

    return self;
}
```

This code is a bit tricky; let's walk through it. Whenever the message **defaultStore** is sent to the class **PossessionStore**, it checks if the defaultStore variable is nil. The first time this message is sent, defaultStore will be nil, and an instance of **PossessionStore** will be created by calling **allocWithZone:** and **init**.

You have overridden **allocWithZone:** to return the existing defaultStore to protect the **PossessionStore**'s singleton status. That's why **defaultStore** must call [super allocWithZone:nil] instead of [self allocWithZone:nil].

Now, override the retain count methods so that no one can release the defaultStore

```
- (id)retain
{
    // Do nothing
    return self;
}

- (void)release
{
    // Do nothing
}

- (NSUInteger)retainCount
{
    return NSUIntegerMax;
}
```

Now you have a singleton.

In PossessionStore.h, give **PossessionStore** an instance variable to hold an array of **Possession** instances and declare two more methods:

```
#import <Foundation/Foundation.h>

@class Possession;

@interface PossessionStore : NSObject
{
    NSMutableArray *allPossessions;
}
+ (PossessionStore *)defaultStore;

- (NSArray *)allPossessions;
- (Possession *)createPossession;

@end
```

In PossessionStore.m, create an instance of **NSMutableArray** and assign it to the instance variable in the **init** method.

```
- (id)init
{
    if (defaultStore) {
        return defaultStore;
    }

    self = [super init];
    if (self) {
        allPossessions = [[NSMutableArray alloc] init];
    }

    return self;
}
```

Now implement the two methods in PossessionStore.m.

```
- (NSArray *)allPossessions
{
    return allPossessions;
}

- (Possession *)createPossession
{
    Possession *p = [Possession randomPossession];

    [allPossessions addObject:p];

    return p;
}
```

Implementing data source methods

In ItemsViewController.m, import PossessionStore.h and Possession.h and update the designated initializer to add 10 random possessions to the **PossessionStore**.

```
#import "ItemsViewController.h"
#import "PossessionStore.h"
#import "Possession.h"

@implementation ItemsViewController

- (id)init
{
    // Call the superclass's designated initializer
    self = [super initWithStyle:UITableViewStyleGrouped];

    if (self) {
        for (int i = 0; i < 10; i++) {
            [[PossessionStore defaultStore] createPossession];
        }
    }

    return self;
}

- (id)initWithStyle:(UITableViewStyle)style
{
    return [self init];
}
```

Now that there are some possessions in the store, you need to teach **ItemsViewController** how to turn those possessions into rows that its **UITableView** can display. When a **UITableView** wants to know what to display, it uses a set of messages declared in the UITableViewDataSource protocol.

From the Help menu, choose Documentation and API Reference to open the iOS SDK documentation. Find the UITableViewDataSource protocol documentation (Figure 10.6).

Figure 10.6   UITableViewDataSource protocol documentation

There are many methods here, but notice the two marked *required method*. For **ItemsViewController** to conform to UITableViewDataSource, it must implement **tableView:numberOfRowsInSection:** and **tableView:cellForRowAtIndexPath:**. These methods tell the table view how many rows it should display and what content to display in each row.

Whenever a **UITableView** needs to display itself, it sends a series of messages (the required methods plus any optional ones that have been implemented) to its dataSource. The required method **tableView:numberOfRowsInSection:** returns an integer value for the number of rows that the **UITableView** should display. In the table view for Homepwner, there should be a row for each entry in the store (Figure 10.7).

Figure 10.7   Obtaining the number of rows

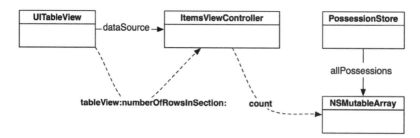

Implement **tableView:numberOfRowsInSection:** in ItemsViewController.m.

```
- (NSInteger)tableView:(UITableView *)tableView
  numberOfRowsInSection:(NSInteger)section
{
    return [[[PossessionStore defaultStore] allPossessions] count];
}
```

Wondering about the section that this method refers to? Table views can be broken up into sections, and each section has its own set of rows. For example, in the address book, all names beginning with "D" are grouped together in a section. By default, a table view has one section, and for this exercise, we will work with only one. Once you understand how a table view works, it's not hard to use multiple sections. In fact, it's one of the challenges at the end of this chapter.

The second required method in the UITableViewDataSource protocol is **tableView:cellForRowAtIndexPath:**. To implement this method, we'll need to learn about another class – **UITableViewCell**.

UITableViewCells

A **UITableViewCell** is a subclass of **UIView**, and each row in a **UITableView** is a **UITableViewCell**. (Recall that a table in iOS can only have one column, so a row only has one cell.) The **UITableViewCell**s are subviews of the **UITableView**.

A cell itself has one subview # its contentView (Figure 10.8). The contentView is the superview for the content of the cell. It also can draw an accessory indicator. The accessory indicator shows an action-oriented icon, such as a checkmark, a disclosure icon, or a fancy blue dot with a chevron inside. These icons are accessed through pre-defined constants for the appearance of the accessory indicator. The default is UITableViewCellAccessoryNone, and that's what we'll use in this chapter. But you'll see the accessory indicator again in Chapter 16. (Curious now? See the reference page for **UITableViewCell** for more details.)

Figure 10.8   UITableViewCell layout

The real meat of a **UITableViewCell** is the other three subviews of the contentView. Two of those subviews are **UILabel** instances that are properties of **UITableViewCell** named textLabel and detailTextLabel. The third subview is a **UIImageView** called imageView (Figure 10.9). For this chapter, we'll only use textLabel.

Figure 10.9   UITableViewCell hierarchy

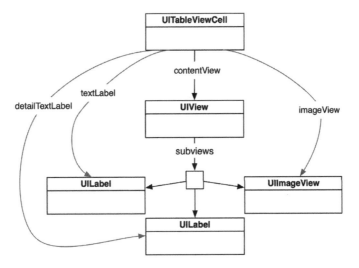

In addition to its subviews, each cell has a UITableViewCellStyle that determines which subviews are used and their position within the contentView. Examples of these styles and their constants are shown in Figure 10.10.

Figure 10.10   UITableViewCellStyles

Creating and retrieving UITableViewCells

In this chapter, each cell will display the **description** of a **Possession** as its textLabel. To make this happen, you need to implement the second required method from the UITableViewDataSource protocol, **tableView:cellForRowAtIndexPath:**. This method will create a cell, set its `textLabel` to the **description** of the corresponding **Possession**, and return it to the **UITableView** (Figure 10.11).

Figure 10.11   UITableViewCell retrieval

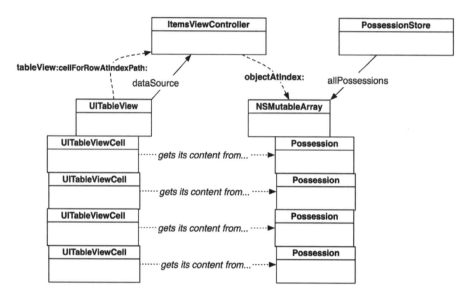

How do you decide which cell a **Possession** corresponds to? One of the parameters sent to **tableView:cellForRowAtIndexPath:** is an **NSIndexPath**, which has two properties: `section` and `row`. When this message is sent to a data source, the table view is asking, "Can I have a cell to display in section X, row Y?" Because there is only one section in this exercise, the table view only needs to know the row. In `ItemsViewController.m`, implement **tableView:cellForRowAtIndexPath:** so that the *n*th row displays the *n*th entry in the `allPossessions` array.

```
- (UITableViewCell *)tableView:(UITableView *)tableView
        cellForRowAtIndexPath:(NSIndexPath *)indexPath
{
    // Create an instance of UITableViewCell, with default appearance
    UITableViewCell *cell =
        [[[UITableViewCell alloc] initWithStyle:UITableViewCellStyleDefault
                                reuseIdentifier:@"UITableViewCell"] autorelease];

    // Set the text on the cell with the description of the possession
    // that is at the nth index of possessions, where n = row this cell
    // will appear in on the tableview
    Possession *p = [[[PossessionStore defaultStore] allPossessions]
                                        objectAtIndex:[indexPath row]];

    [[cell textLabel] setText:[p description]];


    return cell;
}
```

A **UITableView** retains any **UITableViewCell** returned to it by **tableView:cellForRowAtIndexPath:**, which is why you can autorelease it here.

Build and run the application now, and you'll see a **UITableView** populated with a list of random **Possession**s. Yep, it was that easy. You didn't have to change anything about **Possession** – you simply changed the controller object and let the controller interface with a different view. This is why Model-View-Controller is such a powerful concept. With a minimal amount of code, you were able to show the same data in an entirely different way.

Reusing UITableViewCells

iOS devices have a limited amount of memory. If we were displaying a list with thousands of entries in a **UITableView**, we would have thousands of instances of **UITableViewCell**. And your long-suffering iPhone would sputter and die. In its dying breath, it would say "You only needed enough cells to fill the screen... arrrghhh!" It would be right.

To preserve the lives of iOS devices everywhere, you can reuse table view cells. When the user scrolls the table, some cells move offscreen. Offscreen cells are put into a pool of cells available for reuse. Then, instead of creating a brand new cell for every request, the data source first checks the pool. If there is an unused cell, the data source configures it with new data and returns it to the table view.

Figure 10.12   Reusable UITableViewCells

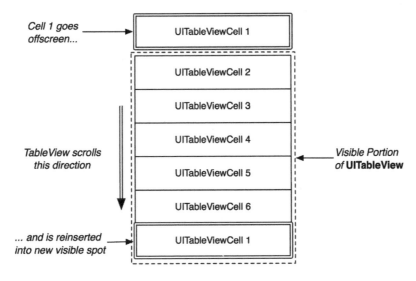

There is one problem: sometimes a **UITableView** has different types of cells. Occasionally, you have to subclass **UITableViewCell** to create a special look or behavior. However, different subclasses floating around the pool of reusable cells create the possibility of getting back a cell of the wrong type. You must be sure of the type of the cell returned to you so that you can be sure of what properties and methods it has.

Note that you don't care about getting any specific cell out of the pool because you're going to change the cell content anyway. What you want is a cell of a specific type. The good news is every cell has a reuseIdentifier property of type **NSString**. When a data source asks the table view for a reusable cell, it passes a string and says, "I need a cell with this reuse identifier." By convention, the reuse identifier is simply the name of the cell class.

In ItemsViewController.m, update **tableView:cellForRowAtIndexPath:** to reuse cells:

```objc
- (UITableViewCell *)tableView:(UITableView *)tableView
        cellForRowAtIndexPath:(NSIndexPath *)indexPath
{
    // Check for a reusable cell first, use that if it exists
    UITableViewCell *cell =
        [tableView dequeueReusableCellWithIdentifier:@"UITableViewCell"];

    // If there is no reusable cell of this type, create a new one
    if (!cell) {
        cell = [[[UITableViewCell alloc]
                    initWithStyle:UITableViewCellStyleDefault
                 reuseIdentifier:@"UITableViewCell"] autorelease];
    }

    Possession *p = [[[PossessionStore defaultStore] allPossessions]
                                        objectAtIndex:[indexPath row]];

    [[cell textLabel] setText:[p description]];

    return cell;
}
```

(If you have a table view that uses multiple styles of the same type of cell, you can suffix the reuse identifier with the name of that style, e.g. UITableViewCell-Default.)

Reusing cells means that you only have to create a handful of cells, which puts fewer demands on memory. Your application's users (and iOS devices everywhere) will thank you. Build and run the application. The behavior of the application should remain the same.

Code Snippet Library

You may have noticed that when you start typing the word init, Xcode will automatically add an **init** implementation in your source file. If you haven't noticed this, go ahead and type init in an implementation file and wait for the code-completion to kick in.

The freebie code comes from the *code snippet library*. You can see the code snippet library by opening the utilities area and selecting the {} icon in the library selector (Figure 10.13). Alternatively, you can use the shortcut Command-Control-Option-2, which reveals the utilities area and the Code Snippet Library. Substituting another number in the shortcut selects the corresponding library.

Figure 10.13   Code Snippet Library

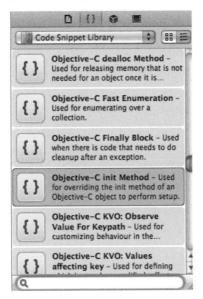

Notice that there are a number of code snippets available (Figure 10.13). Click on one, and in a moment, a window will appear with the details for that snippet. Click the Edit button on the code snippet detail window (Figure 10.14).

Figure 10.14   Snippet editing window

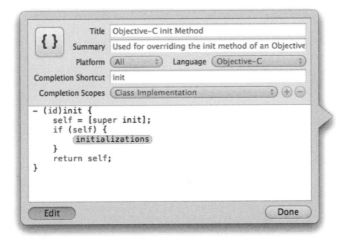

The Completion Shortcut field in the edit window shows you what to type in a source file to have Xcode add the snippet. This window also tells you that this snippet can be used in an Objective-C file as long as you are in the scope of a class implementation.

You can't edit any of the pre-defined code snippets, but you can create your own. In `ItemsViewController.m`, locate the implementation of **tableView:numberOfRowsInSection:**. Highlight the entire method:

```
- (NSInteger)tableView:(UITableView *)tableView
 numberOfRowsInSection:(NSInteger)section
{
    return [[[PossessionStore defaultStore] allPossessions] count];
}
```

Drag this highlighted code into the code snippet library. The edit window will appear again, allowing you to fill out the details for this snippet.

One issue with this snippet is that the return statement is really specific to this application – it would be much more useful if the value returned was a code completion placeholder that you could fill in easily. In the edit window, modify the code snippet so it looks like this:

```
- (NSInteger)tableView:(UITableView *)tableView
 numberOfRowsInSection:(NSInteger)section
{
    return <#number of rows#>;
}
```

Then, fill out the rest of the fields in the edit window as shown in Figure 10.15 and click Done.

Figure 10.15   Creating a new snippet

Back in `ItemsViewController.m`, start typing `tablerows`. Xcode will recommend this code snippet and pressing the return key will automatically complete it for you – and the `number of rows` placeholder will be selected. You'll have to type in that bit of code to get the number of rows yourself. Snippets aren't magical – just handy.

Make sure to remove the code entered by the snippet, since you have already defined **tableView:numberOfRowsInSection:** in `ItemsViewController.m`.

188

Challenge: Sections

Have the **UITableView** display two sections – one for possessions worth more than $50 and one for the rest. Before you start this challenge, copy the folder containing the project and all of its source files in Finder. Then tackle the challenge in the copied project; you'll need the original to build on in the coming chapters.

11
Editing UITableView

In the last chapter, you created an application that displays a list of **Possession** instances in a **UITableView**. The next step for Homepwner is allowing the user to interact with that table – to move, delete, and insert rows. Figure 11.1 shows what Homepwner will look like by the end of this chapter.

Figure 11.1   Homepwner in editing mode

Editing Mode

UITableView has an editing property, and when this property is set to YES, the **UITableView** enters editing mode. Once the table view is in editing mode, the rows of the table can be manipulated by the user. The user can change the order of the rows, add rows, or remove rows. Editing mode does not allow the user to edit the *content* of a row.

But first, the user needs a way to put the **UITableView** in editing mode. For now, you're going to include a button that toggles editing mode in the *header view* of the table. A header view appears at the top of a section of a table and is useful for adding section-wide or table-wide titles and controls. It can be any **UIView** instance. There's also a footer view for the bottom of a section that works the same way. Figure 11.2 shows a table with two sections. Each section has a **UISlider** for a header view and a **UILabel** for a footer view.

Figure 11.2   UITableView header and footer views

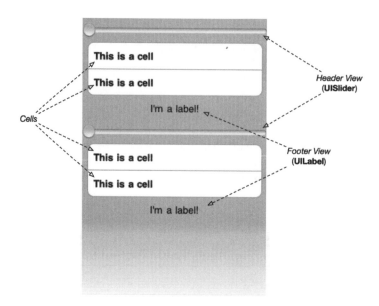

Reopen Homepwner.xcodeproj. In ItemsViewController.h, declare an instance variable of type **UIView** for your header view and three new methods.

```
@interface ItemsViewController : UITableViewController
{
    IBOutlet UIView *headerView;
}
- (UIView *)headerView;
- (IBAction)addNewPossession:(id)sender;
- (IBAction)toggleEditingMode:(id)sender;

@end
```

The headerView will appear at the top of the list of **Possession**s. It will have two subviews that are instances of **UIButton**: one to toggle editing mode and the other to add a new **Possession** to the table. You will create this view and its subviews in a XIB file, and **ItemsViewController** will unarchive that XIB file when it needs to display the headerView.

From the File menu, select New and then New File.... Then choose the Empty template from the User Interface section under iOS (Figure 11.3). On the next pane, select iPhone. Save this file as HeaderView.

Figure 11.3   Creating a new XIB file

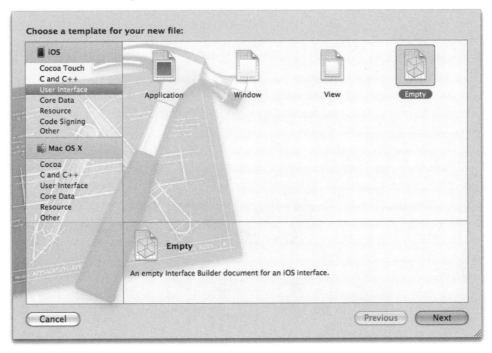

In `HeaderView.xib`, change the Class of the File's Owner to **ItemsViewController** (Figure 11.4).

Figure 11.4   Changing the File's Owner

Drag a **UIView** onto the canvas. Drag two instances of **UIButton** onto that view. Then, make connections, as shown in Figure 11.5.

Figure 11.5   HeaderView XIB Layout

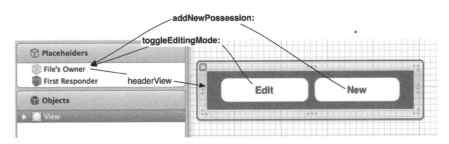

Also, change the background color of the **UIView** instance to be completely transparent. To do this, select the view and show the attributes inspector. Click the color picker labeled Background to show the color wheel and then drag the Opacity slider to 0 (Figure 11.6).

Figure 11.6   Setting background color to clear

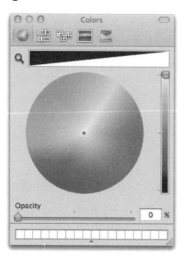

So far, your XIB files have been loaded automatically by the implementation of classes like **UIApplication** and **UIViewController**. For HeaderView.xib, you're going to write the code to load this XIB file manually.

To load a XIB file manually, you use **NSBundle**. This class is the interface between an application and the application bundle it lives in. When you want to access a file in the application bundle, you ask **NSBundle** for it. An instance of **NSBundle** is created when your application launches, and you can get a pointer to this instance by sending the message **mainBundle** to **NSBundle**.

Once you have a pointer to the main bundle object, you can ask it to load a XIB file. In ItemsViewController.m, implement **headerView**.

```
- (UIView *)headerView
{
    // If we haven't loaded the headerView yet...
    if (!headerView) {
        // Load HeaderView.xib
        [[NSBundle mainBundle] loadNibNamed:@"HeaderView" owner:self options:nil];
    }

    return headerView;
}
```

You don't have to specify the suffix of the file name; **NSBundle** will figure it out. Also, you passed self as the owner of the XIB file. This places the instance of **ItemsViewController** as the File's Owner of the XIB file.

XIB files are typically used to create the window and application delegate (MainWindow.xib) and to create the view for a view controller (for example, CurrentTimeViewController.xib).

The code to load these XIB files is already written in the implementations of **UIApplication** and **UIViewController**.

However, as you can see, a XIB file can be used any time you wish to archive view objects, and any object can load a XIB file. **UIViewController**'s default XIB loading behavior uses the same code as you have just written. The only difference is that it connects its view outlet to the view object in the XIB file. Imagine what the default implementation of **loadView** for **UIViewController** probably looks like:

```
- (void)loadView
{
    // If a nibName was passed to initWithNibName:bundle:...
    if ([self nibName]) {
        // Load that nib file, with ourselves as the file's owner, thus connecting
        // the view outlet to the view in the nib
        [[NSBundle mainBundle] loadNibNamed:[self nibName] owner:self options:nil];
    }
    else {
        // What is the name of this class?
        NSString *className = NSStringFromClass([self class]);

        // What's the full path of the nib file?
        NSString *nibPath = [[NSBundle mainBundle] pathForResource:className
                                                            ofType:@"nib"];

        // If there really is a nib file at that path, load it
        if ([[NSFileManager defaultManager] fileExistsAtPath:nibPath]) {
            [[NSBundle mainBundle] loadNibNamed:className owner:self options:nil];
        }
        else {
            // If there is no nib, just create a blank UIView and set it as the view
            UIView *view = [[UIView alloc] initWithFrame:CGRectZero];
            [self setView:view];
            [view release];
        }
    }
}
```

The first time the **headerView** message is sent to **ItemsViewController**, it loads HeaderView.xib and keeps a pointer to the view object in the instance variable headerView. The buttons in this view send messages to **ItemsViewController** when tapped.

Now that you've created headerView, you need to make it the header view of the table. This requires implementing two methods from the UITableViewDelegate protocol in ItemsViewController.m.

```
- (UIView *)tableView:(UITableView *)tv viewForHeaderInSection:(NSInteger)sec
{
    return [self headerView];
}

- (CGFloat)tableView:(UITableView *)tv heightForHeaderInSection:(NSInteger)sec
{
    return [[self headerView] bounds].size.height;
}
```

These two methods are optional, but if you implement one, you must implement both.

The first time **tableView:heightForHeaderInSection:** is sent to **ItemsViewController**, it sends itself the message **headerView**. At this time, headerView will be nil, which causes **headerView** to be loaded from the XIB file.

(You should really release headerView in **dealloc** and **viewDidUnload**, but in the next chapter you are going to eliminate the header view and put these buttons on a navigation bar. So, ignore the leak for now.)

Build and run the application. The two buttons appear at the top of the table, but tapping them will generate an exception because you haven't implemented their action methods yet.

In the **toggleEditingMode:** method, you could toggle the editing property of **UITableView** directly. However, **UITableViewController** also has an editing property. A **UITableViewController** instance automatically sets the editing property of its table view to match its own editing property. Which one should you set? Follow the Model-View-Controller pattern: talk to the controller and let the controller talk to the view.

To set the editing property for a view controller, you send it the message **setEditing:animated:**. In ItemsViewController.m, implement **toggleEditingMode:**.

```
- (void)toggleEditingMode:(id)sender
{
    // If we are currently in editing mode...
    if ([self isEditing]) {
        // Change text of button to inform user of state
        [sender setTitle:@"Edit" forState:UIControlStateNormal];
        // Turn off editing mode
        [self setEditing:NO animated:YES];
    } else {
        // Change text of button to inform user of state
        [sender setTitle:@"Done" forState:UIControlStateNormal];
        // Enter editing mode
        [self setEditing:YES animated:YES];
    }
}
```

Build and run your application, tap the Edit button, and the **UITableView** will enter editing mode (Figure 11.7).

Figure 11.7   UITableView in editing mode

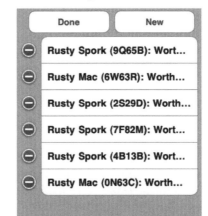

Adding Rows

There are a number of ways to add rows to a table view at runtime. The built-in behavior for adding a row is to display a new row with a green plus sign icon. However, this technique has fallen out of favor in iOS applications because it's cumbersome to enter editing mode and then find the row with the plus sign icon – especially in larger tables.

So we're going to put a New button in the header view instead. Recall that when a table view first appears on screen, it asks its data source for the data it needs to display, and the data source provides it. You can force this process to run again by sending the message **reloadData** to the table view. That way, if you add a **Possession** to the **PossessionStore**, you can reload the table, and the new **Possession** will be included in the data sent to the table for display.

In ItemsViewController.m, implement the action method for the New button so that a new random **Possession** is added to the store and the table is reloaded.

```
- (IBAction)addNewPossession:(id)sender
{
    [[PossessionStore defaultStore] createPossession];

    // tableView returns the controller's view
    [[self tableView] reloadData];
}
```

Notice the **tableView** message that the **ItemsViewController** sends itself. Every **UITableViewController** implements **tableView**, which returns the table controller's view. Because we know this method returns an instance of **UITableView**, we can send it **UITableView**-specific messages, like **reloadData**.

Build and run the application and tap your New button. A new random possession will appear at the bottom of the table.

Now that you have the ability to add rows, remove the code in the **init** method in
ItemsViewController.m that immediately puts 10 random possessions into the store. The **init**
method should now look like this:

```
- (id)init
{
    // Call the superclass's designated initializer
    self = [super initWithStyle:UITableViewStyleGrouped];

    return self;
}
```

Deleting Rows

In editing mode, the red circles with the dash (shown in Figure 11.7) are deletion controls, and
touching one should delete that row. However, at this point, touching a deletion control doesn't delete
anything. (Try it and see.) Before the table view will delete a row, it sends its data source a message
about the deletion and waits for confirmation before pulling the trigger.

A **UITableView** asks its data source for the cells it should display when it is first loaded and at least
three other times:

- when the user scrolls the table view

- when the table view is removed from the view hierarchy and then added back to the view hierarchy

- when an object sends it the message **reloadData**

Now consider what would happen if deleting a row only removed the row from the table view and
not from the data source. The **PossessionStore** would still have the **Possession** instance displayed
by that row, and the next time the **UITableView** asked for its rows, the data source would create a cell
for the supposedly deleted **Possession**. The unwanted row would rise from the dead and return to the
table.

To prevent zombie cells from roaming your table, you must update your data source to remove objects
that should no longer be displayed in the table. First, we need a way to remove objects from the
PossessionStore. In PossessionStore.h, add a new method that deletes a **Possession**.

```
@interface PossessionStore : NSObject
{
    NSMutableArray *allPossessions;
}
+ (PossessionStore *)defaultStore;

- (void)removePossession:(Possession *)p;
```

In PossessionStore.m, implement **removePossession:**.

```
- (void)removePossession:(Possession *)p
{
    [allPossessions removeObjectIdenticalTo:p];
}
```

Now you will implement **tableView:commitEditingStyle:forRowAtIndexPath:**, a method from the
UITableViewDataSource protocol. (This message is sent to the **ItemsViewController**. Keep in mind

that while the **PossessionStore** is the where the data is kept, the **ItemsViewController** is the table view's "data source.")

When **tableView:commitEditingStyle:forRowAtIndexPath:** is sent to the data source, two extra arguments are passed along with it. The first is the **UITableViewCellEditingStyle**, which, in this case, is UITableViewCellEditingStyleDelete. The other argument is the **NSIndexPath** of the row in the table. In ItemsViewController.m, implement this method to have the **PossessionStore** remove the right object and to confirm the row deletion by sending the message **deleteRowsAtIndexPaths:withRowAnimation:** back to the table view.

```
- (void)tableView:(UITableView *)tableView
    commitEditingStyle:(UITableViewCellEditingStyle)editingStyle
     forRowAtIndexPath:(NSIndexPath *)indexPath
{
    // If the table view is asking to commit a delete command...
    if (editingStyle == UITableViewCellEditingStyleDelete)
    {
        PossessionStore *ps = [PossessionStore defaultStore];
        NSArray *possessions = [ps allPossessions];
        Possession *p = [possessions objectAtIndex:[indexPath row]];
        [ps removePossession:p];

        // We also remove that row from the table view with an animation
        [tableView deleteRowsAtIndexPaths:[NSArray arrayWithObject:indexPath]
                        withRowAnimation:YES];
    }
}
```

Build and run your application and then delete a row. It will disappear. Now scroll the list to force the table view to reload. Then return to where the deleted row was and confirm that your data source was updated.

Moving Rows

To change the order of rows in a **UITableView**, you will use another method from the UITableViewDataSource protocol – **tableView:moveRowAtIndexPath:toIndexPath:**.

To delete a row, you had to send the message **deleteRowsAtIndexPaths:withRowAnimation:** to the **UITableView** to confirm the deletion. Moving a row, however, doesn't require confirmation; the table view moves the row on its own authority and sends the data source the message **tableView:moveRowAtIndexPath:toIndexPath:** to report the move. You just have to catch this message to update your data source to match the new order.

But before we can implement the data source method, we need to give the **PossessionStore** a method to change the order of **Possession**s in its allPossessions array. In PossessionStore.h, declare this method.

```
- (void)movePossessionAtIndex:(int)from
                    toIndex:(int)to;
```

Implement this method in PossessionStore.m.

```
- (void)movePossessionAtIndex:(int)from
                    toIndex:(int)to
```

```
{
    if (from == to) {
        return;
    }
    // Get pointer to object being moved
    Possession *p = [allPossessions objectAtIndex:from];

    // Retain it... (retain count of p = 2)
    [p retain];

    // Remove p from array, it is automatically sent release (retain count of p = 1)
    [allPossessions removeObjectAtIndex:from];

    // Insert p in array at new location, retained by array (retain count of p = 2)
    [allPossessions insertObject:p atIndex:to];

    // Release p (retain count = 1, only owner is now array)
    [p release];
}
```

Now in ItemsViewController.m, implement **tableView:moveRowAtIndexPath:toIndexPath:** to update the store.

```
- (void)tableView:(UITableView *)tableView
    moveRowAtIndexPath:(NSIndexPath *)fromIndexPath
        toIndexPath:(NSIndexPath *)toIndexPath
{
    [[PossessionStore defaultStore] movePossessionAtIndex:[fromIndexPath row]
                                                  toIndex:[toIndexPath row]];
}
```

Build and run your application. Check out the new reordering controls (the three horizontal lines) on the side of each row. Touch and hold a reordering control and move the row to a new position (Figure 11.8).

Figure 11.8   Moving a row

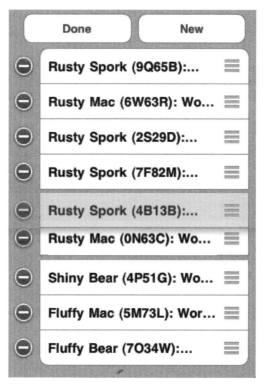

Note that simply implementing **tableView:moveRowAtIndexPath:toIndexPath:** caused the reordering controls to appear. This is because Objective-C is a very smart language. The **UITableView** can ask its data source at runtime whether it implements **tableView:moveRowAtIndexPath:toIndexPath:**. If it does, the table view says, "Good, you can handle moving rows. I'll add the re-ordering controls." If not, it says, "You bum. If you are too lazy to implement that method, I'm not putting controls there."

12

UINavigationController

In Chapter 7, you learned about **UITabBarController** and how it allows a user to access different screens. A tab bar controller is great when you have screens that don't rely on each other, but what if you want to move between related screens?

For example, the Settings application has multiple related screens of information: a list of settings (like Sounds), a detailed page for each setting, and a selection page for each detail. This type of interface is called a *drill-down interface*.

In this chapter, you will use a **UINavigationController** to add a drill-down interface to Homepwner that lets the user view and edit the details of a **Possession**. (Figure 12.1).

Figure 12.1   Homepwner with UINavigationController

UINavigationController

When your application presents multiple screens of information, **UINavigationController** maintains a stack of those screens. The stack is an **NSArray** of view controllers, and each screen is the view of a **UIViewController**. When a **UIViewController** is on top of the stack, its view is visible.

When you initialize an instance of **UINavigationController**, you give it one **UIViewController**. This **UIViewController** is called the *root view controller*. The root view controller is always on the bottom of the stack (which is also the top if there is only one item). Figure 12.2 shows a navigation controller with two view controllers: a root view controller and an additional view controller above it at the top of the stack. The additional view controller is the one the user sees. When the **UIViewController** is pushed onto the stack, its view slides onto the screen from the right. When the stack is popped, the top view controller is removed from the stack, and the view of the one below it slides onto the screen from the left.

Figure 12.2   UINavigationController's stack

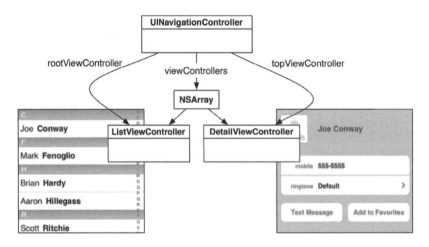

More view controllers can be pushed on top of the **UINavigationController**'s stack during execution. This ability to add to the stack during execution is missing in **UITabBarController**, which gets all of its view controllers when it is initialized. With a navigation controller, only the root view controller is guaranteed to always be in the stack.

The **UIViewController** that is currently on top of the stack is accessed by sending the message **topViewController** to the **UINavigationController** instance. You can also get the entire stack as an **NSArray** by sending the navigation controller the message **viewControllers**. The viewControllers array is ordered so that the root view controller is the first entry and the top view controller is the last entry.

UINavigationController is a also subclass of **UIViewController**, so it has a view of its own. Its view always has at least two subviews: a **UINavigationBar** and the view of its topViewController (Figure 12.3).

Figure 12.3 A UINavigationController's view

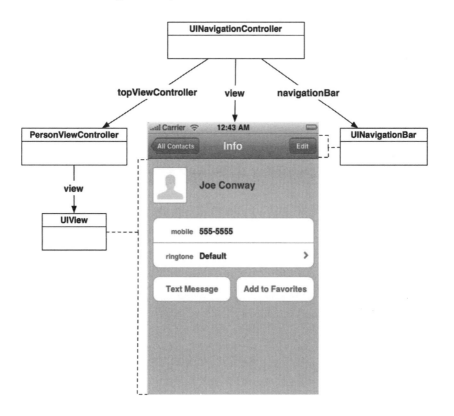

In this chapter, you will add a **UINavigationController** to the Homepwner application and make the **ItemsViewController** the **UINavigationController**'s rootViewController. Then, you will create another subclass of **UIViewController** that can be pushed onto the **UINavigationController**'s stack. When a user selects one of the possession rows, the new **UIViewController**'s view will slide onto the screen. This view controller will allow the user to view and edit the properties of the selected **Possession**. The object diagram for the updated Homepwner application is shown in Figure 12.4.

Figure 12.4   Homepwner object diagram

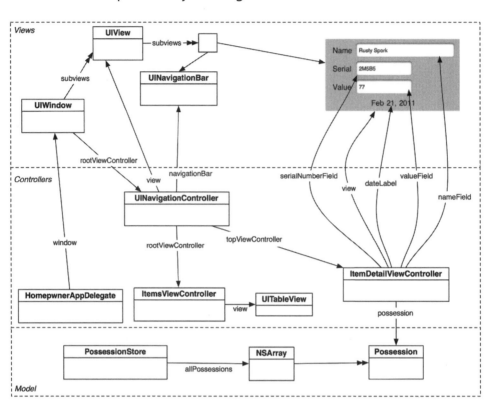

This application is getting fairly large, as you can see in the massive object diagram. Fortunately, view controllers and **UINavigationController** know how to deal with this type of complicated object diagram. When writing iOS applications, it is important to treat each **UIViewController** as its own little world. The stuff that has already been implemented in Cocoa Touch will do the heavy lifting.

Now let's give Homepwner a navigation controller. Reopen the Homepwner project and then open HomepwnerAppDelegate.m. The only requirements for using a **UINavigationController** are that you give it a root view controller and add its view to the visible view hierarchy. In **application:didFinishLaunchingWithOptions:**, create the **UINavigationController**, give it a root view controller of its own, and set the **UINavigationController** as the root view controller of the window.

```
- (BOOL)application:(UIApplication *)application
    didFinishLaunchingWithOptions:(NSDictionary *)launchOptions
{
    ItemsViewController *itemsViewController = [[ItemsViewController alloc] init];

    // Create an instance of a UINavigationController
    // its stack contains only itemsViewController
    UINavigationController *navController = [[UINavigationController alloc]
```

```
        initWithRootViewController:itemsViewController];

    // You can now release the itemsViewController here,
    // UINavigationController will retain it
    [itemsViewController release];

    // Place navigation controller's view in the window hierarchy
    [[self window] setRootViewController:navController];

    [navController release];


    [[self window] makeKeyAndVisible];
    return YES;
}
```

This code initializes the **UINavigationController** instance with **ItemsViewController** as its root
view controller and makes the **UINavigationController** the rootViewController of the window.
Becoming the window's rootViewController places the navigation controller's view in the view
hierarchy.

Build and run the application. Homepwner will look the same as it did before – except now it has a
UINavigationBar at the top of the screen (Figure 12.5). Notice how **ItemsViewController**'s view was
resized to fit the screen with a navigation bar. **UINavigationController** did this for you.

Figure 12.5   Homepwner with an empty navigation bar

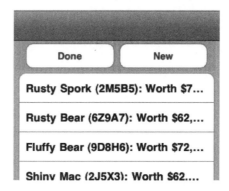

UINavigationBar

The **UINavigationBar** isn't very interesting right now. At a minimum, a **UINavigationBar**
should display a descriptive title for the **UIViewController** that is currently on top of the
UINavigationController's stack.

Every **UIViewController** has a navigationItem property of type **UINavigationItem**. However,
unlike **UINavigationBar**, **UINavigationItem** is not a subclass of **UIView**, so it cannot appear on the
screen. Instead, the navigation item supplies the navigation bar with the content it needs to draw. When
a **UIViewController** comes to the top of a **UINavigationController**'s stack, the **UINavigationBar**
uses the **UIViewController**'s navigationItem to configure itself, as shown in Figure 12.6.

Figure 12.6   UINavigationItem

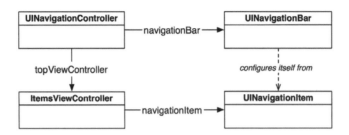

That's not the easiest thing to understand at first glance. So, consider the following analogy. Think of a **UIViewController** as an NFL football team, and moving to the top of the stack as going to the Super Bowl. The **UINavigationItem** is the team logo design, which is the property of the team and, no matter what happens, remains unchanged. The **UINavigationController** is the stadium, and the **UINavigationBar** is an end zone. In a similar manner, when a **UIViewController** is moved to the top of the stack, its **UINavigationItem** is painted on the **UINavigationBar** of the **UINavigationController**.

By default, a **UINavigationItem** is empty. At the most basic level, a **UINavigationItem** has a simple title string. When a **UIViewController** is moved to the top of the navigation stack and its navigationItem has a valid string for its title property, the navigation bar will display that string (Figure 12.7).

Figure 12.7   UINavigationItem with title

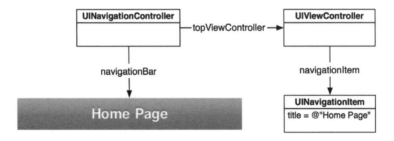

A navigation item can hold more than just a title string, as shown in Figure 12.8. There are three customizable areas for each **UINavigationItem**: a leftBarButtonItem, a rightBarButtonItem, and a titleView. The left and right bar button items are pointers to instances of **UIBarButtonItem**, which contains the information for a button that can only be displayed on a **UINavigationBar** or a **UIToolbar**.

Figure 12.8 UINavigationItem with everything

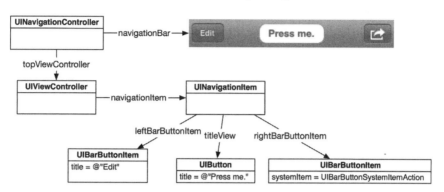

Like **UINavigationItem**, **UIBarButtonItem** is not a subclass of **UIView** but supplies the content that a **UINavigationBar** needs to draw. Consider the **UINavigationItem** and its **UIBarButtonItem**s to be containers for strings, images, and other content. A **UINavigationBar** knows how to look in those containers and draw the content it finds.

The third customizable area of a **UINavigationItem** is its `titleView`. You can either use a basic string as the title or have a subclass of **UIView** sit in the center of the navigation item. You cannot have both. If it suits the context of a specific view controller to have a custom view (like a button, a slider, an image, or even a map), you would set the `titleView` of the navigation item to that custom view. Figure 12.8 shows an example of a **UINavigationItem** with a custom view as its `titleView`. Typically, however, a title string is sufficient, and that's what we'll do in this chapter.

Now let's give Homepwner a **UINavigationBar** it can be proud of. In `ItemsViewController.m`, create a **UIBarButtonItem** instance. This button will sit on the right side of the navigation bar when the **ItemsViewController** is on top of the stack. When tapped, it will add a new **Possession** to the list. Also, set the navigation item's title. This string will be displayed in the center of the navigation bar.

```
- (id)init
{
    self = [super initWithStyle:UITableViewStyleGrouped];

    if (self) {
        // Create a new bar button item that will send
        // addNewPossession: to ItemsViewController
        UIBarButtonItem *bbi = [[UIBarButtonItem alloc]
                        initWithBarButtonSystemItem:UIBarButtonSystemItemAdd
                                             target:self
                                             action:@selector(addNewPossession:)];

        // Set this bar button item as the right item in the navigationItem
        [[self navigationItem] setRightBarButtonItem:bbi];

        // The navigationItem retains its buttons, so bbi can be released
        [bbi release];

        // Set the title of the navigation item
        [[self navigationItem] setTitle:@"Homepwner"];
    }
```

```
        return self;
}
```

Build and run the application. Tap the + button, and a new row will appear in the table. (Note that this is not the only way to set up a bar button item; check the documentation for other initialization messages you can send an instance of **UIBarButtonItem**.)

A bar button item has a target-action pair that works like **UIControl**'s target-action mechanism: when tapped, it sends the action message to the target. When you set a target-action pair in a XIB file, you Control-drag from a button to its target and then select a method from the list of IBActions. To programmatically set up a target-action pair, you pass the target and the action to the button. The action is passed as a value of type SEL.

The SEL data type is a pointer to a *selector*. A selector is a unique ID for a method. Wrapping a method name in the @selector() directive returns the SEL that points at that method. Remember that a selector is the entire method name including any colons. Here are some examples of method declarations and how you would wrap them in @selector():

```
- (void)method;
- (int)methodWithArg:(id)arg1;
- (BOOL)methodWithArg:(id)arg1 andAnotherArg:(id)arg2;

SEL m1 = @selector(method);
SEL m2 = @selector(methodWithArg:);
SEL m3 = @selector(methodWithArg:andAnotherArg:);
```

Notice that @selector() doesn't care about the return type, argument types, or names of arguments – only the selector itself. Also, know that @selector() doesn't check to see if the method actually exists. If you give a SEL to a button, that button will send the corresponding message regardless of whether the method is implemented by the target.

Now you're going to replace the Edit button in the table view header with a **UIBarButtonItem**. In ItemsViewController.m, edit the **init** method.

```
- (id)init
{
    self = [super initWithStyle:UITableViewStyleGrouped];

    if (self) {
        UIBarButtonItem *bbi = [[UIBarButtonItem alloc]
                        initWithBarButtonSystemItem:UIBarButtonSystemItemAdd
                                             target:self
                                             action:@selector(addNewPossession:)];

        [[self navigationItem] setRightBarButtonItem:bbi];

        [bbi release];

        [[self navigationItem] setTitle:@"Homepwner"];

        [[self navigationItem] setLeftBarButtonItem:[self editButtonItem]];
    }
    return self;
}
```

Surprisingly, that's all the code you need to get an edit button on the navigation bar. Build and run, tap the Edit button, and watch the **UITableView** enter editing mode! Where does **editButtonItem** come from? **UIViewController** has an editButtonItem property, and when sent **editButtonItem**, the view controller creates a **UIBarButtonItem** with the title Edit. Even better, this button comes with a target-action pair: it sends the message **setEditing:animated:** to its **UIViewController** when tapped.

Now that Homepwner has a fully functional navigation bar, you can get rid of the header view. In ItemsViewController.m, delete the following two methods.

```
// Delete these!
- (UIView *)tableView:(UITableView *)aTableView
    viewForHeaderInSection:(NSInteger)section
{
    return [self headerView];
}

- (CGFloat)tableView:(UITableView *)tableView
    heightForHeaderInSection:(NSInteger)section
{
    return [[self headerView] frame].size.height;
}
```

Also remove the instance variable headerView along with the implementation of the methods **headerView** and **toggleEditingMode:**.

Now you can build and run again. The old Edit and New buttons are gone, leaving you with a lovely **UINavigationBar** (Figure 12.9).

Figure 12.9   Homepwner with navigation bar

An Additional UIViewController

To see the real power of **UINavigationController**, you need another **UIViewController** to put on the navigation controller's stack. Create a new **UIViewController** subclass (File → New → New File...).

Choose the UIViewController subclass template. When prompted, check the box With XIB for user interface (Figure 12.10). Save this class as `ItemDetailViewController`.

Figure 12.10   View controller with XIB subclass

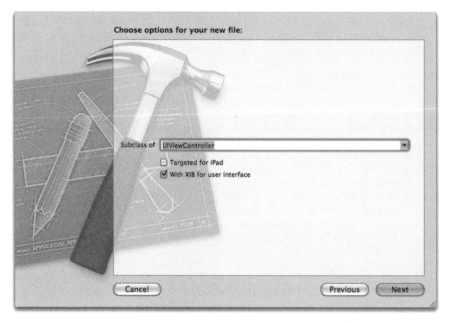

In `ItemDetailViewController.m`, delete all of the code between the `@implementation` and `@end` directives.

In Homepwner, we want the user to be able to tap a possession to get another screen with editable text fields for each property of that **Possession**. This view will be controlled by an instance of **ItemDetailViewController**.

The detail view needs four subviews – one for each instance variable of a **Possession** instance. And because you need to be able to access these subviews during runtime, **ItemDetailViewController** needs outlets for these subviews. Therefore, you must add four new outlets to **ItemDetailViewController**, drag the subviews onto the view in the XIB file, and then make the connections.

In previous exercises, these were three distinct steps: you added the outlets, then you configured the interface, and then you made connections. We can combine these steps using a shortcut in Xcode. First, open `ItemDetailViewController.xib` by clicking on it in the project navigator.

Now, Option-click on `ItemDetailViewController.h` in the project navigator. This shortcut opens the file in the *assistant editor*, right next to `ItemDetailViewController.xib`. (You can toggle the assistant editor by clicking the middle button from the Editor control at the top of the workspace; the shortcut to display the assistant editor is Command-Option-Return; to return to the standard editor, use Command-Return.)

212

You will also need the object library available so that you can drag the subviews onto the view. Show the utilities area by clicking the right button in the View control at the top of the workspace (or Command-Option-0).

Your window is now sufficiently cluttered. Let's make some temporary space. Hide the navigator area by clicking the left button in the View control at the top of the workspace (the shortcut for this is Command-0). Then, change the outline view in the XIB file to the dock view by clicking the toggle button in the lower left corner of the outline view. Your workspace should now look like Figure 12.11.

Figure 12.11 Laying out the workspace

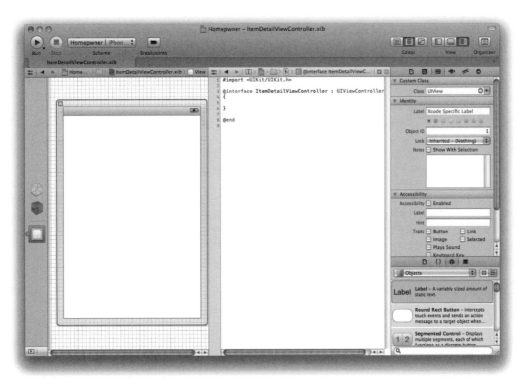

Now, drag four **UILabel**s and three **UITextField**s onto the view in the canvas area and configure them to look like Figure 12.12. For each of the **UITextField**s, uncheck the Clear when editing begins box in the attribute inspector.

Figure 12.12   Configured ItemDetailViewController XIB

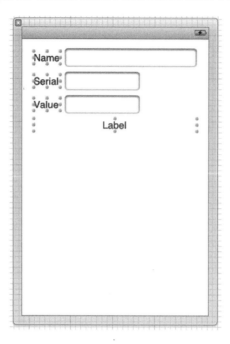

The three **UITextField**s and bottom **UILabel** will be outlets in **ItemDetailViewController**. Here comes the exciting part. Control-drag from the **UITextField** underneath the Name label to the instance variable area in ItemDetailViewController.h, as shown in Figure 12.13.

Figure 12.13 Dragging from XIB to source file

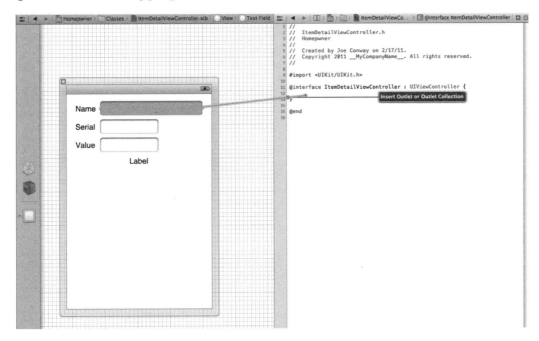

Let go while still inside the instance variable area, and a pop-up window will appear. Enter nameField into this field and click Connect.

Figure 12.14 Auto-generating an outlet and making a connection

This will create an IBOutlet instance variable of type **UITextField** named nameField in **ItemDetailViewController**. It will also connect this **UITextField** to the nameField outlet of the File's Owner in the XIB file. You can verify this by Control-clicking on the File's Owner to see the connections – notice that hovering your mouse above the nameField connection in the panel that appears will reveal the **UITextField** that you connected. Two birds, one stone. Create the other three outlets in the same way and name them as shown in Figure 12.15.

215

Figure 12.15   Connection diagram

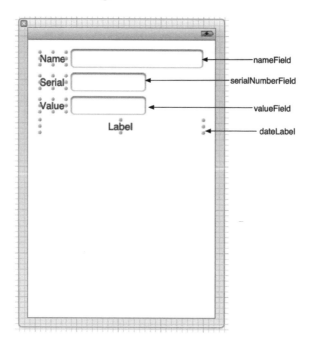

For each of the **UITextField**s in the XIB file, connect their delegate property to the File's Owner. (Remember, Control-drag from the **UITextField** to the File's Owner and select delegate from the list.)

Next, let's consider the **ItemDetailViewController**'s view. Right now, it has a plain white background. Let's give it the same background as the **UITableView**. Recall that a view controller's view is not created until the view controller loads it the first time, so when should you make this change to the view? After a **UIViewController** loads its view, it is immediately sent the message **viewDidLoad**. This message is sent whether that view is loaded from a XIB file or programmatically. If you need to do any extra initialization to a **UIViewController** that requires its view to already exist, you must override **viewDidLoad**. Override **viewDidLoad** in ItemDetailViewController.m.

```
- (void)viewDidLoad
{
    [super viewDidLoad];
    [[self view] setBackgroundColor:[UIColor groupTableViewBackgroundColor]];
}
```

When **ItemDetailViewController**'s view gets unloaded, its subviews will still be retained by **ItemDetailViewController**. They need to be released and set to nil in **viewDidUnload**. (When you add outlets to a class by Control-dragging into a source file, code is automatically added to **viewDidUnload** that will release the instance variables that you created; however, they may not be set to nil.) Override this method in ItemDetailViewController.m.

```
- (void)viewDidUnload
{
    [super viewDidUnload];

    [nameField release];
    nameField = nil;

    [serialNumberField release];
    serialNumberField = nil;

    [valueField release];
    valueField = nil;

    [dateLabel release];
    dateLabel = nil;
}
```

And, finally, you need a **dealloc** method because this view controller will be instantiated and destroyed multiple times while the application is running:

```
- (void)dealloc
{
    [nameField release];
    [serialNumberField release];
    [valueField release];
    [dateLabel release];
    [super dealloc];
}
```

Now that this project has a good number of source files, you will be switching between them fairly regularly. One way to speed up switching between commonly accessed files is to use Xcode tabs. If you double-click on a file in the project navigator, the file will open in a new tab. You can also open up a blank tab with the shortcut Command-T. The keyboard shortcuts for cycling through tabs are Command-Shift-} and Command-Shift-{. (You can see the other shortcuts for project organization by selecting the General tab from Xcode's preferences.)

Navigating with UINavigationController

Now you have a navigation controller, a navigation bar, and two view controllers. Time to put all the pieces together. The user should be able to tap a row in **ItemsViewController**'s table view and have the **ItemDetailViewController**'s view slide onto the screen and display the properties of the selected **Possession** instance.

Pushing view controllers

Of course, you need to create an instance of **ItemDetailViewController**. Where should this object be created? Think back to previous exercises where you instantiated all of your controllers in the method **application:didFinishLaunchingWithOptions:**. For example, in the Chapter 7 chapter, you created both view controllers and immediately added them to tab bar controller's viewControllers array.

However, when using a **UINavigationController**, you cannot simply store all of the possible view controllers in its stack. The viewControllers array of a navigation controller is dynamic – you start with a root view controller and add view controllers depending on user input. Therefore, some object other than the navigation controller needs to create the instance of **ItemDetailViewController** and be responsible for adding it to the stack.

This object must meet two requirements: it needs to know when to push **ItemDetailViewController** onto the stack, and it needs a pointer to the navigation controller. Why must this object have a pointer to the navigation controller? If it is to dynamically add view controllers to the navigation controller's stack, it must be able to send the navigation controller messages, namely, **pushViewController:animated:**.

ItemsViewController fills both requirements. First, it knows when a row is tapped in a table view because, as the table view's delegate, it receives the message **tableView:didSelectRowAtIndexPath:**. Second, any view controller in a navigation controller's stack can get a pointer to the navigation controller by sending itself the message **navigationController**. As the root view controller, **ItemsViewController** is always in the navigation controller's stack and thus can always access it. Therefore, **ItemsViewController** will be responsible for creating the instance of **ItemDetailViewController** and adding it to the stack.

At the top of ItemsViewController.h, import the interface file for **ItemDetailViewController**.

```
#import "ItemDetailViewController.h"

@interface ItemsViewController : UITableViewController
```

When a row is tapped, its delegate is sent **tableView:didSelectRowAtIndexPath:**, which contains the index path of the selected row. In ItemsViewController.m, implement this method to allocate a **ItemDetailViewController** and then push it on top of the navigation controller's stack.

```
@implementation ItemsViewController

- (void)tableView:(UITableView *)aTableView
    didSelectRowAtIndexPath:(NSIndexPath *)indexPath
{
    ItemDetailViewController *detailViewController =
        [[[ItemDetailViewController alloc] init] autorelease];

    // Push it onto the top of the navigation controller's stack
    [[self navigationController] pushViewController:detailViewController
                                          animated:YES];
}
```

Build and run the application. Select a row from the **UITableView**. Not only will you be taken to **ItemDetailViewController**'s view, but you will get a free animation *and* a button in the **UINavigationBar** titled Homepwner. Tapping this button will take you back to **ItemsViewController**.

Also, notice that the instance of **ItemDetailViewController** is autoreleased after it is instantiated. The **UINavigationController** will retain it and then release it when it is popped from the stack. Therefore, when the user taps the back button, the **ItemDetailViewController** will be deallocated. This is why you implemented the **dealloc** method for **ItemDetailViewController** – instances of this class definitely get destroyed while this application is running.

Having a view controller push the next view controller is a common pattern. In any application with a **UINavigationController**, the navigation controller has one root view controller. The root view controller typically creates the next view controller, and the next view controller creates the one after that, and so on. Some applications may have view controllers that can push different view controllers depending on user input. For example, the Photos will push a video view controller or an image view controller onto the navigation stack depending on what type of media was selected.

(The iPad-only class **UISplitViewController** calls for a different pattern. The iPad's larger screen size allows two view controllers in a drill-down interface to appear on screen simultaneously instead of being pushed onto the same stack. You'll learn more about **UISplitViewController** in Chapter 26.)

Passing data between view controllers

Of course, the **UITextField**s on the screen are currently empty. To fill these fields, you need a way to pass data between the **ItemsViewController** and the **ItemDetailViewController**. How do you pass data between **UIViewController**s?

What you're going to do is implement a method in **ItemDetailViewController** that accepts a **Possession** instance and fills the contents of its **UITextField**s. **ItemsViewController** will select the appropriate possession from its array and pass it through that method to the **ItemDetailViewController**.

In ItemDetailViewController.h, add an instance variable to hold the **Possession** that is being edited and declare a method to set that instance variable. The class declaration should now look like this:

```
#import <UIKit/UIKit.h>

@class Possession;

@interface ItemDetailViewController : UIViewController
{
    IBOutlet UITextField *nameField;
    IBOutlet UITextField *serialNumberField;
    IBOutlet UITextField *valueField;
    IBOutlet UILabel *dateLabel;

    Possession *possession;
}
@property (nonatomic, retain) Possession *possession;
@end
```

In ItemDetailViewController.m, synthesize the accessors for possession and import **Possession**'s header file.

```
#import "Possession.h"

@implementation ItemDetailViewController

@synthesize possession;
```

Since an instance of **ItemDetailViewController** will retain its possession, this instance variable must be released when the view controller is deallocated. An instance of **ItemDetailViewController** will be deallocated when the user goes back to the **ItemsViewController**. That user action removes the **ItemDetailViewController** from the stack, which causes the navigation controller, its only owner, to release it. In ItemDetailViewController.m, add this to the **dealloc** method.

```
- (void)dealloc
{
    [possession release];
```

```
    [nameField release];
    [serialNumberField release];
    [valueField release];
    [dateLabel release];
    [super dealloc];
}
```

When the **ItemDetailViewController**'s view appears on the screen, it needs to set the values of its subviews to match the properties of the possession. Override **viewWillAppear:** in ItemDetailViewController.m to transfer the possession's properties to the various **UITextField**s.

```
- (void)viewWillAppear:(BOOL)animated
{
    [super viewWillAppear:animated];

    [nameField setText:[possession possessionName]];
    [serialNumberField setText:[possession serialNumber]];
    [valueField setText:[NSString stringWithFormat:@"%d",
                            [possession valueInDollars]]];

    // Create a NSDateFormatter that will turn a date into a simple date string
    NSDateFormatter *dateFormatter = [[[NSDateFormatter alloc] init]
                                            autorelease];
    [dateFormatter setDateStyle:NSDateFormatterMediumStyle];
    [dateFormatter setTimeStyle:NSDateFormatterNoStyle];

    // Use filtered NSDate object to set dateLabel contents
    [dateLabel setText:
        [dateFormatter stringFromDate:[possession dateCreated]]];

    // Change the navigation item to display name of possession
    [[self navigationItem] setTitle:[possession possessionName]];
}
```

Now you must invoke this method when the **ItemDetailViewController** is being pushed onto the navigation stack. In ItemsViewController.m, add the following line of code to **tableView:didSelectRowAtIndexPath:**.

```
- (void)tableView:(UITableView *)aTableView
    didSelectRowAtIndexPath:(NSIndexPath *)indexPath
{
    ItemDetailViewController *detailViewController =
        [[[ItemDetailViewController alloc] init] autorelease];

    NSArray *possessions = [[PossessionStore defaultStore] allPossessions];

    // Give detail view controller a pointer to the possession object in row
    [detailViewController setPossession:
                [possessions objectAtIndex:[indexPath row]]];

    [[self navigationController] pushViewController:detailViewController
                                        animated:YES];
}
```

Many programmers new to iOS struggle with how data is passed between **UIViewController**s. The technique you just implemented, having all of the data in the root view controller and passing subsets of that data to the next **UIViewController**, is a clean and efficient way of performing this task.

Build and run your application. Select one of the rows in the **UITableView**, and the view that appears will contain the information for the **Possession** in that row. While you can edit this data, the **UITableView** won't have changed when you return to it. To fix this problem, you need to implement code to update the properties of the **Possession** being edited. Next, we'll look at when to do this.

Appearing and disappearing views

Whenever a **UINavigationController** is about to swap views, it sends out two messages: **viewWillDisappear:** and **viewWillAppear:**. The **UIViewController** that is about to be popped off the stack is sent the message **viewWillDisappear:**. The **UIViewController** that will then be on top of the stack is sent **viewWillAppear:**.

When **ItemDetailViewController** is popped off the stack, you will set the properties of the possession to the values in the **UITextField**s. When implementing these methods for views appearing and disappearing, it is important to call the superclass's implementation – it has some work to do as well. In ItemDetailViewController.m, implement **viewWillDisappear:**.

```
- (void)viewWillDisappear:(BOOL)animated
{
    [super viewWillDisappear:animated];

    // Clear first responder
    [[self view] endEditing:YES];

    // "Save" changes to possession
    [possession setPossessionName:[nameField text]];
    [possession setSerialNumber:[serialNumberField text]];
    [possession setValueInDollars:[[valueField text] intValue]];
}
```

Notice the use of **endEditing:**. When the message **endEditing:** is sent to a view, if it or any of its subviews are currently the first responder, it will resign its first responder status, and the keyboard will be dismissed. (The argument passed determines whether the first responder is forced into retirement. Some first responders might refuse to resign, and passing YES ignores that refusal.)

Now the values of the **Possession** will be updated when the user taps the Homepwner back button on the **UINavigationBar**. When **ItemsViewController** appears back on the screen, it is sent the message **viewWillAppear:**. Take this opportunity to reload its **UITableView** so the user can immediately see the changes. In ItemsViewController.m, override **viewWillAppear:**.

```
- (void)viewWillAppear:(BOOL)animated
{
    [super viewWillAppear:animated];
    [[self tableView] reloadData];
}
```

Build and run your application now. Now you can move back and forth between the **UIViewController**s you created and change the data with ease.

Challenge: Number Pad

The keyboard for the **UITextField** that displays a **Possession**'s valueInDollars is a QWERTY keyboard. It would be better if it was a number pad. Change the Keyboard Type of that **UITextField** to the Number Pad. (Hint: You can do this in the XIB file using the attributes inspector.)

13

Camera

In this chapter, you're going to add photos to the Homepwner application. You will present a **UIImagePickerController** so that the user can take and save a picture of each possession. The image will then be associated with a **Possession** instance, stored in an image store, and viewable in the possession's detail view. Then, when the insurance company demands proof, the user has a visual record of owning that 70" HDTV.

Figure 13.1   Homepwner with camera addition

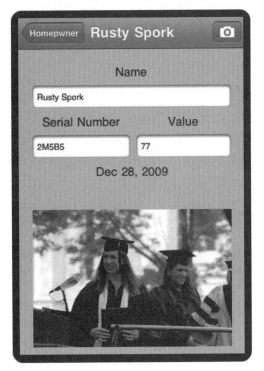

Displaying Images and UIImageView

Because we want the image to appear in the possession's detail view, your first step is to have the **ItemDetailViewController** get and display an image. An easy way to display an image

is to put an instance of **UIImageView** on the screen. Open Homepwner.xcodeproj and click
ItemDetailViewController.xib in the project navigator to open the interface in the canvas area.
Then drag an instance of **UIImageView** onto the view, as shown in Figure 13.2.

Figure 13.2   UIImageView on ItemDetailViewController's view

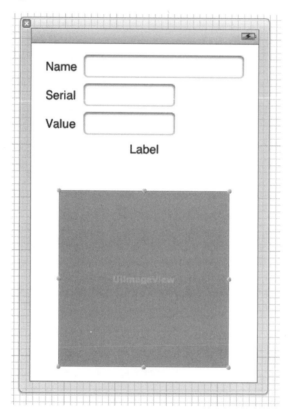

A **UIImageView** displays an image according to its contentMode property. This property determines
where to position and how to resize the content within its frame. The default value for contentMode
is UIViewContentModeCenter, which centers but does not resize the content to fit within the bounds
of the view. If you keep the default, the large image produced by the camera will take up most of the
screen. You have to change the contentMode of the image view so that it resizes the image.

Select the **UIImageView** and open the attributes inspector. Find the Mode attribute and change it
to Aspect Fit, as shown in Figure 13.3. This will resize the image to fit within the bounds of the
UIImageView.

Figure 13.3 Image view attributes

Now, Option-click ItemDetailViewController.h in the project navigator to open it in the assistant editor. Control-drag from the **UIImageView** to the instance variable area in ItemDetailViewController.h. Name the outlet imageView and click Connect.

Because imageView is a new subview of **ItemDetailViewController**'s view that is instantiated when the XIB file is loaded, it needs to be released and its pointer cleared in **viewDidUnload**. In ItemDetailViewController.m, make the following changes.

```
- (void)viewDidUnload
{
    [super viewDidUnload];

    [nameField release];
    nameField = nil;

    [serialNumberField release];
    serialNumberField = nil;

    [valueField release];
    valueField = nil;

    [dateLabel release];
    dateLabel = nil;

    [imageView release];
    imageView = nil;
}
```

Also release the image view in **dealloc**:

```
- (void)dealloc
{
    [nameField release];
    [serialNumberField release];
    [valueField release];
    [dateLabel release];

    [imageView release];
```

```
    [super dealloc];
}
```

Taking pictures and UIImagePickerController

Now you need a button to initiate the photo-taking process. It would be nice to put this button on the navigation bar, but we will need the navigation bar for another button later. Instead, we will create an instance of **UIToolbar** and place it at the bottom of **ItemDetailViewController**'s view. In ItemDetailViewController.xib, drag a **UIToolbar** onto the bottom of the view.

A **UIToolbar** works a lot like a **UINavigationBar** in that you can add **UIBarButtonItem**s to it. However, where a navigation bar has two bar button items, a toolbar has an array of items. You can place as many **UIBarButtonItem**s in a toolbar as can fit on the screen.

By default, a new instance of **UIToolbar** created in a XIB file comes with one **UIBarButtonItem**. Select this bar button item and open the attribute inspector. Change the Identifier to Camera, and the item will show a camera icon (Figure 13.4).

Figure 13.4   UIToolbar with bar button item

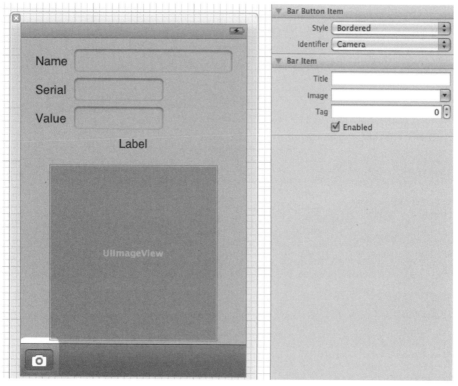

The camera button needs to send a message to the instance of **ItemDetailViewController** when it is tapped. In previous exercises, you connected action methods in two steps: declaring them in the header file and then hooking them up in the XIB file. Just like you did with outlets, you can do both steps at once by opening a source file in the assistant editor and Control-dragging from a XIB file to the file. Option-click ItemDetailViewController.h in the project navigator to open it in the assistant editor.

Select the camera button and Control-drag from the button to the method declaration area in ItemDetailViewController.h (Figure 13.5).

Figure 13.5 Creating and connecting an action method from a XIB

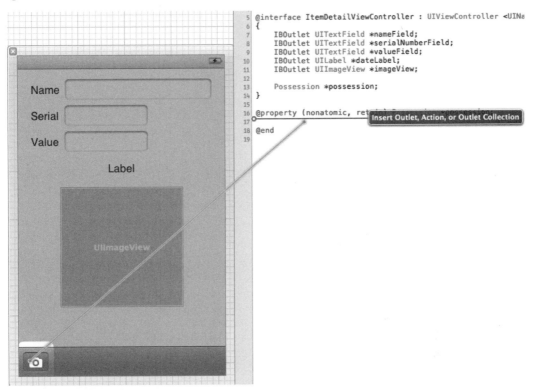

Let go of the mouse, and a window will appear that allows you to specify the type of connection you are creating. From the Connection pop-up menu, choose Action. Then, name this method **takePicture:** and click Connect (Figure 13.6).

Figure 13.6 Creating the action

Now the action method is declared in the header file, and the **UIBarButtonItem** instance in the XIB is hooked up to send this message to the **ItemDetailViewController** when tapped. There is also a stub for the method in ItemDetailViewController.m.

```
- (IBAction)takePicture:(id)sender
{
}
```

In the **takePicture:** method, you will instantiate a **UIImagePickerController** and present it on the screen. When creating an instance of **UIImagePickerController**, you must set its sourceType property and assign it a delegate.

The sourceType is a constant that tells the image picker where to get images. It has three possible values:

- UIImagePickerControllerSourceTypeCamera – The user will take a new picture.

- UIImagePickerControllerSourceTypePhotoLibrary – The user will be prompted to select an album and then a photo from that album.

- UIImagePickerControllerSourceTypeSavedPhotosAlbum – The user picks from the most recently taken photos.

Figure 13.7 shows the results of using each constant.

Figure 13.7   UIImagePickerControllerTypes

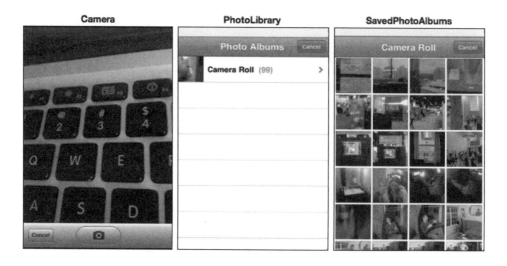

The first source type, UIImagePickerControllerSourceTypeCamera, won't work on a device that doesn't have a camera. So before using this type, you have to check for a camera by sending the

UIImagePickerController class the message **isSourceTypeAvailable:**. Sending this message to **UIImagePickerController** with one of the source type constants returns a boolean value for whether the device supports that source type.

In addition to a source type, the **UIImagePickerController** instance needs a delegate to handle requests from its view. When the user taps the Use Photo button on the **UIImagePickerController**'s interface, the delegate is sent the message **imagePickerController:didFinishPickingMediaWithInfo:**. (The delegate receives another message – **imagePickerControllerDidCancel:** – if the process was cancelled.)

Once the **UIImagePickerController** has a source type and a delegate, it's time to put its view on the screen. Unlike other **UIViewController** subclasses you've used, an instance of **UIImagePickerController** is presented *modally*. When a view controller is *modal*, it takes over the entire screen until it has finished its work. To present a view modally, **presentModalViewController:animated:** is sent to the **UIViewController** whose view is on the screen. The view controller to be presented is passed to it, and its view slides up from the bottom of the screen.

In ItemDetailViewController.m, implement the method **takePicture:** to create, configure, and present the **UIImagePickerController**. (Remember – there's already a stub for this method, so locate the stub in ItemDetailViewController.m and add the following code there.)

```
- (void)takePicture:(id)sender
{
    UIImagePickerController *imagePicker =
            [[UIImagePickerController alloc] init];

    // If our device has a camera, we want to take a picture, otherwise, we
    // just pick from photo library
    if ([UIImagePickerController
            isSourceTypeAvailable:UIImagePickerControllerSourceTypeCamera]) {
        [imagePicker setSourceType:UIImagePickerControllerSourceTypeCamera];
    } else {
        [imagePicker setSourceType:UIImagePickerControllerSourceTypePhotoLibrary];
    }

    // This line of code will generate 2 warnings right now, ignore them
    [imagePicker setDelegate:self];

    // Place image picker on the screen
    [self presentModalViewController:imagePicker animated:YES];

    // The image picker will be retained by ItemDetailViewController
    // until it has been dismissed
    [imagePicker release];
}
```

You can build and run the application now. Select a **Possession** to see its details and then tap the camera button on the **UIToolbar**. **UIImagePickerController**'s interface will appear on the screen (Figure 13.8), and you can take a picture (or choose an existing image if you don't have a camera). Tapping the Use Photo button dismisses the **UIImagePickerController**.

Figure 13.8   UIImagePickerController preview interface

But, oops – you don't have a reference to the image anywhere in the code. You need to implement the delegate method **imagePickerController:didFinishPickingMediaWithInfo:** in **ItemDetailViewController** to hold on to the selected image. But before you implement this method, let's take care of the two warnings that appeared during the last build telling you that **ItemDetailViewController** does not conform to the UIImagePickerControllerDelegate or the UINavigationControllerDelegate protocol. In ItemDetailViewController.h, add the protocols to the class declaration. (Why UINavigationControllerDelegate? **UIImagePickerController** is a subclass of **UINavigationController**.)

```
@interface ItemDetailViewController : UIViewController
    <UINavigationControllerDelegate, UIImagePickerControllerDelegate>
{
```

That's better. Now we're all up to code.

When a photo is selected, the **imagePickerController:didFinishPickingMediaWithInfo:** message will be sent to the image picker's delegate. In ItemDetailViewController.m, implement this method to put the image into the **UIImageView** that you created earlier.

```
- (void)imagePickerController:(UIImagePickerController *)picker
didFinishPickingMediaWithInfo:(NSDictionary *)info
```

```
{
    // Get picked image from info dictionary
    UIImage *image = [info objectForKey:UIImagePickerControllerOriginalImage];

    // Put that image onto the screen in our image view
    [imageView setImage:image];

    // Take image picker off the screen -
    // you must call this dismiss method
    [self dismissModalViewControllerAnimated:YES];
}
```

Build and run the application again. Take a photo, and the image picker is dismissed and you are returned to the **ItemDetailViewController**'s view. Do you see your image? Oddly enough, you might see it or you might not. Let's figure out what's going on and fix the problem.

When a photo is taken, that image is loaded into memory. However, the image file is so large that it causes a low-memory warning. Recall that a low-memory warning gives the system the option of requiring view controllers to release their views if they are not currently visible. When a modal view controller is on the screen, its view is visible – and the view of the view controller that presented it is not. In our case, the low-memory warning destroys **ItemDetailViewController**'s view, and the imageView is no longer available when we try to set it.

To get around this problem, we must create a separate store for images. Instead of putting the image directly into the imageView, we will put it into this store. Then when the **ItemDetailViewController**'s view next appears on screen, we'll have the **ItemDetailViewController** grab the image from the image store and put it into its own imageView. In general, this is a best practice: a view controller should re-populate its view's subviews with data whenever it is sent the message **viewWillAppear:**, eliminating the possibility that a low-memory warning could wipe out its content.

ImageStore

The image store will hold all the pictures the user will take. In Chapter 15, you will have the **Possession** objects write out their instance variables to a file, which will then be read in when the application starts. However, as we've found out, images tend to be very large, so it's a good idea to keep them separate from the other possession data. The image store will fetch and cache the images as they are needed. It will also be able to flush the cache if the device runs low on memory.

All of that nifty saving/fetching/loading stuff comes later; in this chapter, the image store is little more than a dictionary of key-value pairs in which the keys are unique strings and the values are images. Create a new **NSObject** subclass called **ImageStore**. Open ImageStore.h and create its interface:

```
#import <UIKit/UIKit.h>

@interface ImageStore : NSObject
{
    NSMutableDictionary *dictionary;
}
+ (ImageStore *)defaultImageStore;

- (void)setImage:(UIImage *)i forKey:(NSString *)s;
- (UIImage *)imageForKey:(NSString *)s;
- (void)deleteImageForKey:(NSString *)s;

@end
```

NSDictionary

Notice that the `dictionary` is an instance of **NSMutableDictionary**. A dictionary is a collection object similar to an array. However, an array is an ordered list of pointers to objects that is accessed by an index. When you have an array, you can ask it for the object at the *n*th index:

```
// Put some object at the beginning of an array
[someArray insertObject:someObject atIndex:0];

// Get that same object out
someObject = [someArray objectAtIndex:0];
```

A dictionary's objects are not ordered within the collection. So instead of accessing entries with an index, you use a *key*. The key is usually an instance of **NSString**.

```
// Add some object to a dictionary for the key "MyKey"
[someDictionary setObject:someObject forKey:@"MyKey"];

// Get that same object out
someObject = [someDictionary objectForKey:@"MyKey"];
```

An **NSDictionary** is useful when you want to access entries within a collection by name. In other development environments, this is called a *hash map* or *hash table* (Figure 13.9).

Figure 13.9   NSDictionary diagram

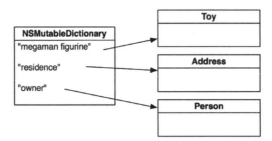

There can only be one object for each key. If you add an object to a dictionary with a key that matches the key of an object already present in the dictionary, the earlier object is removed. If you need to store multiple objects under one key, you can put them in an array and add the array to the dictionary.

Finally, note that a dictionary's memory management is like that of an array. Whenever you add an object to a dictionary, the dictionary retains it, and whenever you remove an object from a dictionary, the dictionary releases it.

Like the **PossessionStore**, the **ImageStore** needs to be a singleton. In ImageStore.m, write the following code to ensure **ImageStore**'s singleton status.

```
static ImageStore *defaultImageStore = nil;

@implementation ImageStore

+ (id)allocWithZone:(NSZone *)zone
```

```
{
    return [self defaultImageStore];
}

+ (ImageStore *)defaultImageStore
{
    if (!defaultImageStore) {
        // Create the singleton
        defaultImageStore = [[super allocWithZone:NULL] init];
    }
    return defaultImageStore;
}

- (id)init
{
    if (defaultImageStore) {
        return defaultImageStore;
    }

    self = [super init];
    if (self) {
        dictionary = [[NSMutableDictionary alloc] init];
    }

    return self;
}

- (void)release
{
    // no op
}

- (id)retain
{
    return self;
}

- (NSUInteger)retainCount
{
    return NSUIntegerMax;
}
```

Then, implement the three methods declared in the header file.

```
- (void)setImage:(UIImage *)i forKey:(NSString *)s
{
    [dictionary setObject:i forKey:s];
}

- (UIImage *)imageForKey:(NSString *)s
{
    return [dictionary objectForKey:s];
}

- (void)deleteImageForKey:(NSString *)s
{
    if(!s)
        return;
    [dictionary removeObjectForKey:s];
}
```

Note that there is no **dealloc** method because once created, the store will exist for the life of the application.

Creating and using keys

When an image is added to the store, it will be put into a dictionary under a unique key, and the associated **Possession** object will be given that key. When the **ItemDetailViewController** wants an image from the store, it will ask its possession for the key and search the dictionary for the image. Add an instance variable to Possession.h to store the key.

```
    NSDate *dateCreated;
    NSString *imageKey;
}
@property (nonatomic, copy) NSString *imageKey;
```

Synthesize this new property in the implementation file.

```
@implementation Possession
@synthesize possessionName, serialNumber, valueInDollars, dateCreated;
@synthesize imageKey;
```

You also need to release this object when a **Possession** is deallocated. Add this code to the **dealloc** method in Possession.m.

```
- (void)dealloc
{
    [possessionName release];
    [serialNumber release];
    [dateCreated release];
    [imageKey release];

    [super dealloc];
}
```

The image keys need to be unique in order for your dictionary to work. While there are many ways to hack together a unique string, we're going to use the Cocoa Touch mechanism for creating universally unique identifiers (UUIDs), also known as globally unique identifiers (GUIDs). Objects of type **CFUUIDRef** represent a UUID and are generated using the time, a counter, and a hardware identifier, which is usually the MAC address of the ethernet card.

However, **CFUUIDRef** is not an Objective-C object; it is a C structure and part of the Core Foundation API. Core Foundation is a C API that is included in template projects and contains the building blocks for applications, such as strings, arrays, and dictionaries. Core Foundation "classes" are prefixed with CF and suffixed with Ref. Other examples include **CFArrayRef** and **CFStringRef**.

Like Objective-C objects, Core Foundation structures have a retain count mechanism.

Many objects in Core Foundation have an Objective-C counterpart; for example, **NSString** * is the Objective-C counterpart of **CFStringRef**. However, **CFUUIDRef** does not have an Objective-C counterpart and, in fact, knows nothing at all about Objective-C. Thus, when it produces a UUID as a string, that string cannot be an **NSString** – it must be a **CFStringRef**.

Recall that your instance variable for the image key is of type **NSString** *. Do you have to change it to **CFStringRef** in order to work with **CFUUIDRef**? Nope. Many Core Foundation objects can simply be *typecast* as their Objective-C counterparts. Here's an example:

```
// Create an instance of a CFStringRef
CFStringRef someString = CFSTR("String");
// Turn it in to an NSString
NSString *coolerString = (NSString *)someString;
```

We call this *toll-free bridging*. (And it works because the structures in memory are equivalent. How smart is that?)

At the top of ItemDetailViewController.m, import the header for **ImageStore**.

#import "ImageStore.h"

@implementation ItemDetailViewController

Now, in ItemDetailViewController.m, make changes to **imagePickerController:didFinishPickingMediaWithInfo:** to create and use a key for a possession image.

```
- (void)imagePickerController:(UIImagePickerController *)picker
        didFinishPickingMediaWithInfo:(NSDictionary *)info
{
    NSString *oldKey = [possession imageKey];

    // Did the possession already have an image?
    if (oldKey) {

        // Delete the old image
        [[ImageStore defaultImageStore] deleteImageForKey:oldKey];
    }

    UIImage *image = [info objectForKey:UIImagePickerControllerOriginalImage];

    // Create a CFUUID object - it knows how to create unique identifier strings
    CFUUIDRef newUniqueID = CFUUIDCreate (kCFAllocatorDefault);

    // Create a string from unique identifier
    CFStringRef newUniqueIDString =
            CFUUIDCreateString (kCFAllocatorDefault, newUniqueID);

    // Use that unique ID to set our possessions imageKey
    [possession setImageKey:(NSString *)newUniqueIDString];

    // We used "Create" in the functions to make objects, we need to release them
    CFRelease(newUniqueIDString);
    CFRelease(newUniqueID);

    // Store image in the ImageStore with this key
    [[ImageStore defaultImageStore] setImage:image
                                      forKey:[possession imageKey]];

    // Put that image onto the screen in our image view
    [imageView setImage:image];

    // Take image picker off the screen
    [self dismissModalViewControllerAnimated:YES];
}
```

In this method, we call the C functions **CFUUIDCreate** and **CFUUIDCreateString**. When the name of a C function contains the word Create, you are responsible for releasing its memory just as if you

235

had sent the message **alloc** to a class. So you released these Core Foundation objects by calling the function **CFRelease** with the object as a parameter.

Figure 13.10   Cache

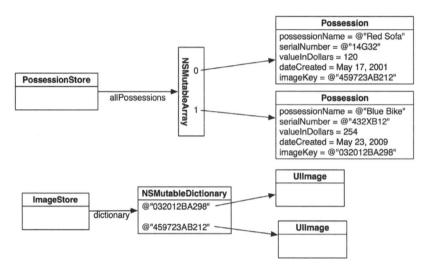

Now, when **ItemDetailViewController**'s view appears on the screen, it should grab an image from the **ImageStore** using the imageKey of the **Possession**. Then, it should place the image in the **UIImageView**. Add the following code to **viewWillAppear:** in ItemDetailViewController.m.

```
- (void)viewWillAppear:(BOOL)animated
{
    [super viewWillAppear:animated];

    [nameField setText:[possession possessionName]];
    [serialNumberField setText:[possession serialNumber]];
    [valueField setText:[NSString stringWithFormat:@"%d",
                            [possession valueInDollars]]];

    NSDateFormatter *dateFormatter = [[[NSDateFormatter alloc] init]
                                        autorelease];
    [dateFormatter setDateStyle:NSDateFormatterMediumStyle];
    [dateFormatter setTimeStyle:NSDateFormatterNoStyle];

    [dateLabel setText:
            [dateFormatter stringFromDate:[possession dateCreated]]];

    [[self navigationItem] setTitle:[possession possessionName]];

    NSString *imageKey = [possession imageKey];

    if (imageKey) {
        // Get image for image key from image store
        UIImage *imageToDisplay =
                [[ImageStore defaultImageStore] imageForKey:imageKey];
```

```
        // Use that image to put on the screen in imageView
        [imageView setImage:imageToDisplay];
    } else {
        // Clear the imageView
        [imageView setImage:nil];
    }
}
```

Notice that if no image exists in the image store for that key (or there is no key for that possession), the pointer to the image will be nil. When the image is nil, the **UIImageView** just won't display an image.

Build and run the application. Create a **Possession** and select it from the **UITableView**. Then, tap the camera button and take a picture. The image will appear as it should.

Dismissing the keyboard

When the keyboard appears on the screen in the possession detail view, it obscures **ItemDetailViewController**'s imageView. This is annoying when you're trying to see an image, so you're going to implement the delegate method **textFieldShouldReturn:** to have the text field resign its first responder status to dismiss the keyboard. (This is why you hooked up the delegate outlets earlier.) But first, in ItemDetailViewController.h, have **ItemDetailViewController** conform to the UITextFieldDelegate protocol.

```
@interface ItemDetailViewController : UIViewController
    <UINavigationControllerDelegate, UIImagePickerControllerDelegate,
        UITextFieldDelegate>
```

In ItemDetailViewController.m, implement **textFieldShouldReturn:**.

```
- (BOOL)textFieldShouldReturn:(UITextField *)textField
{
    [textField resignFirstResponder];
    return YES;
}
```

It would be stylish to also dismiss the keyboard if the user taps anywhere on **ItemDetailViewController**'s view. We can dismiss the keyboard by sending the view the message **endEditing:**. This message causes the text field (as a subview of the view) to resign as first responder. Now let's figure out how to get the view to send a message when tapped.

We have seen how classes like **UIButton** can send an action message to a target when tapped. Buttons inherit this target-action behavior from their superclass, **UIControl**. You're going to change the view of **ItemDetailViewController** from an instance of **UIView** to an instance of **UIControl** so that it can handle touch events.

In ItemDetailViewController.xib, select the main view instance. Open the identity inspector and change the view's class to **UIControl** (Figure 13.11).

Figure 13.11   Changing the class of ItemDetailViewController's view

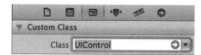

Then, open ItemDetailViewController.h in the assistant editor. Control-drag from the view (now a **UIControl**) to the method declaration area of **ItemDetailViewController**. When the pop-up window appears, select Action from the Connection pop-up menu. Notice that the interface of this pop-up window is slightly different than one you saw when creating and connecting the **UIBarButtonItem**. A **UIBarButtonItem** is a simplified version of **UIControl** – it only sends its target an action message when it is tapped. A **UIControl**, on the other hand, can send action messages on a variety of events.

Therefore, you must choose the appropriate event type to trigger the action message being sent. In this case, you want the action message to be sent when the user taps on the view. Configure this pop-up window to appear as it does in Figure 13.12 and click Connect.

Figure 13.12   Configuring a UIControl action

This will create a stub method in ItemDetailViewController.m. Enter the following code into that method.

```
- (IBAction)backgroundTapped:(id)sender
{
    [[self view] endEditing:YES];
}
```

Build and run your application and test both ways of dismissing the keyboard.

Challenge: Removing an Image

Add a button that clears the image for a possession.

For the More Curious: Recording Video

Once you understand how to use **UIImagePickerController** to take pictures, making the transition to recording video is trivial. Recall that an image picker controller has a sourceType property that determines whether an image comes from the camera, photo library, or saved photos album. Image picker controllers also have a mediaTypes property, which is an array of strings that contains identifiers for what types of media can be selected from the three source types.

There are two types of media a **UIImagePickerController** can select: still images and video. By default, the mediaTypes array only contains the constant string kUTTypeImage. Thus, if you do not change the mediaTypes property of an image picker controller, the camera will only allow the user to take still photos, and the photo library and saved photos album will only display images.

Adding the ability to record video or choose a video from the disk is as simple as adding the constant string kUTTypeMovie to the mediaTypes array. However, not all devices support video through the **UIImagePickerController**. Just like the class method **isSourceTypeAvailable:** allows you to determine if the device has a camera, the **availableMediaTypesForSourceType:** method checks to see if that camera can capture video. To set up an image picker controller that can record video or take still images, you would write the following code:

```
UIImagePickerController *ipc = [[UIImagePickerController alloc] init];
NSArray *availableTypes = [UIImagePickerController
    availableMediaTypesForSourceType:UIImagePickerControllerSourceTypeCamera];
[ipc setMediaTypes:availableTypes];
[ipc setSourceType:UIImagePickerControllerSourceTypeCamera];
[ipc setDelegate:self];
```

Now when this image picker controller interface is presented to the user, there will be a switch that allows them to choose between the still image camera or the video recorder. If the user chooses to record a video, you need to handle that in the **UIImagePickerController** delegate method **imagePickerController:didFinishPickingMediaWithInfo:**.

When dealing with still images, the info dictionary that is passed as an argument contains the full image as a **UIImage** object. However, there is no "UIVideo" class. (Loading an entire video into memory at once would be tough to do with device memory constraints.) Therefore, recorded video is written to disk in a temporary directory. When the user finalizes the video recording, **imagePickerController:didFinishPickingMediaWithInfo:** is sent to the image picker controller's delegate, and the path of the video on the disk is in the info dictionary. You can get the path like so:

```
- (void)imagePickerController:(UIImagePickerController *)picker
didFinishPickingMediaWithInfo:(NSDictionary *)info
{
    NSURL *mediaURL = [info objectForKey:UIImagePickerControllerMediaURL];
}
```

We will talk about the filesystem in Chapter 15, but what you should know now is that the temporary directory is not a safe place to store the video. It needs to be moved to another location.

```
- (void)imagePickerController:(UIImagePickerController *)picker
didFinishPickingMediaWithInfo:(NSDictionary *)info
{
    NSURL *mediaURL = [info objectForKey:UIImagePickerControllerMediaURL];
    if (mediaURL) {

        // Make sure this device supports videos in its photo album
        if (UIVideoAtPathIsCompatibleWithSavedPhotosAlbum([mediaURL path])) {

            // Save the video to the photos album
            UISaveVideoAtPathToSavedPhotosAlbum([mediaURL path], nil, nil, nil);

            // Remove the video from the temporary directory it was saved at
            [[NSFileManager defaultManager] removeItemAtPath:[mediaURL path]
                                                       error:nil];
        }
    }
}
```

That is really all there is to it. There is just one situation that requires some additional information: suppose you want to restrict the user to choosing *only videos*. Restricting the user to images is simple (leave mediaTypes as the default). Allowing the user to choose between images and videos is just as simple (pass the return value from **availableMediaTypesForSourceType:**). However, to allow video only, you have to jump through a few hoops. First, you must make sure the device supports video and then set the mediaTypes property to an array containing the identifier for video only.

```
NSArray *availableTypes = [UIImagePickerController
    availableMediaTypesForSourceType:UIImagePickerControllerSourceTypeCamera];

if ([availableTypes containsObject:(NSString *)kUTTypeMovie])
    [ipc setMediaTypes:[NSArray arrayWithObject:(NSString *)kUTTypeMovie]];
```

Wondering why kUTTypeMovie is cast to an **NSString**? This constant is declared as:

```
const CFStringRef kUTTypeVideo;
```

If you build this code, it will fail, and the compiler will complain that it's never heard of kUTTypeMovie. Oddly enough, both kUTTypeMovie and kUTTypeImage are declared and defined in another framework – MobileCoreServices. You have to explicitly add this framework and import its header file into your project to use these two constants.

14

UIPopoverController and Modal View Controllers

So far, you have seen four ways to show a view controller's view: setting it as the root view controller of the window, pushing it onto a **UINavigationController**'s stack, adding it to a **UITabBarController** and presenting it modally.

In this chapter, we will look at **UIPopoverController** and more options for presenting modal view controllers. Some of these options are only available on the iPad, so we'll start by making Homepwner a *universal application* – an application that runs natively on the iPad as well as the iPhone and iPod touch.

Figure 14.1   Homepwner on the iPad

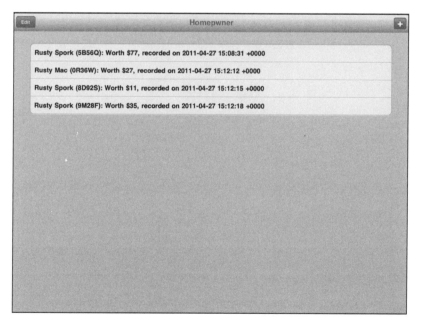

Universalizing Homepwner

Open Homepwner.xcodeproj and select the Homepwner project from the project navigator. Then select the Homepwner target in the editor area. In the Summary pane, change the Devices pop-up to Universal (Figure 14.2). A sheet will drop down and ask if you want to copy and convert MainWindow.xib: choose No. (We'll talk more about the option in a moment.)

Figure 14.2   Universalizing Homepwner

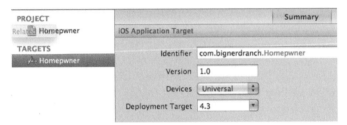

A universal application needs to size its window to fit the screen dimensions of the device. Open MainWindow.xib and select the Window object. Then reveal the utilities area and select the attributes inspector. Check the box for Full Screen at Launch (Figure 14.3).

Figure 14.3   Making the window fit the screen

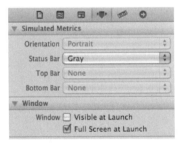

Click on the Scheme pop-up button next to the Run button. You'll see that there is now an iPad Simulator option. Select this option and build and run the application.

The **ItemsViewController** view looks great on the iPad, but if you select a row, you'll see that the **ItemDetailViewController** and its subviews could use some work.

One way to improve the looks of the **ItemDetailViewController**'s interface on the iPad is to change the autoresizing masks of the subviews in ItemDetailViewController.xib so that when its view is resized to fit the iPad, all of the subviews are organized nicely. This is what you did when you universalized your HeavyRotation application.

Another way is to create two completely independent XIB files: one for the iPhone device family and the other for the iPad. This is most useful when you want to have a different interface on the iPad that takes advantage of the additional screen space. Just remember that you will have to recreate the entire view hierarchy and re-establish connections in the iPad version of the XIB file.

When you create separate XIB files for the two device families, you do not need to write any extra code to load the appropriate XIB file. Every **UIViewController** has a nibName that you pass in the initializer message. (If you pass nil, the nibName is effectively the name of the class.) When a view controller goes to load its view, it loads the XIB file that matches its nibName. However, if the application is running on an iPad, it first checks for a matching XIB file suffixed with ~ipad. If there is one, it loads that XIB file instead.

At this point, we're not really concerned about the appearance of the **ItemDetailViewController**'s view, so we have another option: leave it as it is. But let's do something about the painfully white background. In **ItemDetailViewController**'s **viewDidLoad** method, the background color of the view is set to be the **groupTableViewBackgroundColor** color. This color is not available on the iPad, which is why you get the all-white background instead. So when the application is running on an iPad, let's set the color to closely match the background color of **ItemsViewController**'s view.

First, we need to check what type of device the application is running on. The object to ask is the **UIDevice** singleton. You access the object by sending the class method **currentDevice** to the **UIDevice** class. Then you can check the value of its userInterfaceIdiom property. At this time, there are only two possible values: UIUserInterfaceIdiomPad (for an iPad) and UIUserInterfaceIdiomPhone (for an iPhone or an iPod touch).

In ItemDetailViewController.m, modify **viewDidLoad**.

```
- (void)viewDidLoad
{
    [super viewDidLoad];

    UIColor *clr = nil;
    if([[UIDevice currentDevice] userInterfaceIdiom] == UIUserInterfaceIdiomPad) {
        clr = [UIColor colorWithRed:0.875 green:0.88 blue:0.91 alpha:1];
    } else {
        clr = [UIColor groupTableViewBackgroundColor];
    }
    [[self view] setBackgroundColor:clr];
}
```

Notice that the existing code for the iPhone is now in the else clause of the new if-else block. (Be sure to include that last closing brace!) Build and run the application on the iPad simulator or on an iPad. Navigate to the **ItemDetailViewController** and sigh in relief at the much nicer color.

iPad users expect applications to work in all orientations, so add the following method to both ItemsViewController.m and ItemDetailViewController.m:

```
- (BOOL)shouldAutorotateToInterfaceOrientation:(UIInterfaceOrientation)io
{
    if ([[UIDevice currentDevice] userInterfaceIdiom] == UIUserInterfaceIdiomPad) {
        return YES;
    } else {
        return (io == UIInterfaceOrientationPortrait);
    }
}
```

Now that Homepwner can run on the iPad, let's take advantage of some iPad-only ways to present view controllers, starting with **UIPopoverController**.

UIPopoverController

iOS applications sometimes present a view controller so that the user can make a choice. For example, the **UIImagePickerController** shows the user a table of images to choose from. On the iPhone and iPod touch, view controllers like this are presented modally and take up the entire screen. However, the iPad has more screen real estate and offers another option: **UIPopoverController**.

A popover controller displays another view controller's view in a bordered window that floats above the rest of the application's interface. When you create a **UIPopoverController**, you set this other view controller as the popover controller's contentViewController. (You can only instantiate **UIPopoverController**s on the iPad family of devices; trying to create one on an iPhone will throw an exception.)

In this exercise, you will present the **UIImagePickerController** in a **UIPopoverController** when the user taps the camera bar button item in the **ItemDetailViewController**'s view. Now that Homepwner runs on the iPad, this modification is actually required – when using **UIImagePickerController** on the iPad, it must be presented in a popover controller.

Figure 14.4   UIPopoverController

In ItemDetailViewController.h, add an instance variable to hold the popover controller. Also, declare that **ItemDetailViewController** conforms to the UIPopoverControllerDelegate protocol.

```
@interface ItemDetailViewController : UIViewController
    <UINavigationControllerDelegate, UIImagePickerControllerDelegate,
    UIPopoverControllerDelegate>
```

```
{
    IBOutlet UITextField *nameField;
    IBOutlet UITextField *serialNumberField;
    IBOutlet UITextField *valueField;
    IBOutlet UILabel *dateLabel;
    IBOutlet UIImageView *imageView;

    Possession *possession;

    UIPopoverController *imagePickerPopover;
}
```

In ItemDetailViewController.m, add the following code to the **takePicture:** method.

```
- (void)takePicture:(id)sender
{
    UIImagePickerController *imagePicker =
                [[UIImagePickerController alloc] init];

    if ([UIImagePickerController
            isSourceTypeAvailable:UIImagePickerControllerSourceTypeCamera])
    {
        [imagePicker setSourceType:UIImagePickerControllerSourceTypeCamera];
    } else {
        [imagePicker setSourceType:UIImagePickerControllerSourceTypePhotoLibrary];
    }
    [imagePicker setDelegate:self];


    // Place image picker on the screen
    if ([[UIDevice currentDevice] userInterfaceIdiom] == UIUserInterfaceIdiomPad) {
        // Create a new popover controller that will display the imagePicker
        imagePickerPopover = [[UIPopoverController alloc]
                initWithContentViewController:imagePicker];

        [imagePickerPopover setDelegate:self];

        // Display the popover controller, sender
        // is the camera bar button item
        [imagePickerPopover presentPopoverFromBarButtonItem:sender
                                    permittedArrowDirections:UIPopoverArrowDirectionAny
                                                    animated:YES];
    } else {
        [self presentModalViewController:imagePicker animated:YES];
    }

    [imagePicker release];
}
```

Notice that the line of code that presents the image picker modally is now inside the else clause.

Build and run the application on the iPad simulator or on an iPad. Navigate to the **ItemDetailViewController** and tap the camera icon. The popover should appear and show the **UIImagePickerController**'s view. Select an image from the picker, and it will appear in **ItemDetailViewController**'s view.

You can dismiss the popover controller by tapping anywhere else on the screen. When a popover is dismissed in this way, it sends the message **popoverControllerDidDismissPopover:** to its delegate. Implement this method in ItemDetailViewController.m.

```
- (void)popoverControllerDidDismissPopover:(UIPopoverController *)popoverController
{
    NSLog(@"User dismissed popover");
    [imagePickerPopover autorelease];
    imagePickerPopover = nil;
}
```

Notice that you autorelease the **UIPopoverController** after it is dismissed. Why not just release it? In this case, the popover's dismissal is animated. By autoreleasing the popover, the animation code gets a chance to retain it before the autorelease pool drains. After the animation finishes, the popover is deallocated.

The popover should also be dismissed when you select an image from the image picker. In ItemDetailViewController.m, at the end of **imagePickerController:didFinishPickingMediaWithInfo:**, dismiss the popover when an image is selected.

```
[imageView setImage:image];

if([[UIDevice currentDevice] userInterfaceIdiom] == UIUserInterfaceIdiomPhone) {
    [self dismissModalViewControllerAnimated:YES];
} else {
    [imagePickerPopover dismissPopoverAnimated:YES];
    [imagePickerPopover autorelease];
    imagePickerPopover = nil;
}
}
```

Notice that here, we check for an iPhone (or iPod touch) interface instead of checking for an iPad one. The iPad-only code is inside the else clause.

When you explicitly send the message **dismissPopoverAnimated:** to dismiss the popover controller, it does not send **popoverControllerDidDismissPopover:** to its delegate.

Modal View Controllers

In this part of the exercise, you will update Homepwner to present the **ItemDetailViewController** modally – but only when the user creates a *new* **Possession**. When the user selects an existing **Possession**, the **ItemDetailViewController** will be pushed onto the **UINavigationController**'s stack as before.

Figure 14.5   New item

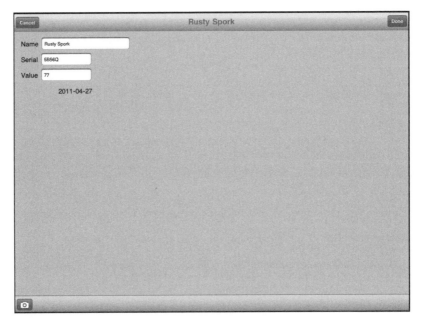

To implement this dual usage of **ItemDetailViewController**, you will give it a new designated initializer, **initForNewItem:isNew:**. This initializer will check whether the instance is being used for creating a new **Possession** or for showing an existing one and then configure the interface accordingly.

In ItemDetailViewController.h, declare this initializer.

```
}
- (id)initForNewItem:(BOOL)isNew;

@property (nonatomic, retain) Possession *possession;
```

If the **ItemDetailViewController** is being used to create a new **Possession**, it will show a Done button and a Cancel button on its navigation item. Implement this method in ItemDetailViewController.m.

```
- (id)initForNewItem:(BOOL)isNew
{
    self = [super initWithNibName:@"ItemDetailViewController" bundle:nil];

    if (self) {
        if (isNew) {
            UIBarButtonItem *doneItem = [[UIBarButtonItem alloc]
                    initWithBarButtonSystemItem:UIBarButtonSystemItemDone
                                         target:self
                                         action:@selector(save:)];
            [[self navigationItem] setRightBarButtonItem:doneItem];
            [doneItem release];
```

```
        UIBarButtonItem *cancelItem = [[UIBarButtonItem alloc]
              initWithBarButtonSystemItem:UIBarButtonSystemItemCancel
                                   target:self
                                   action:@selector(cancel:)];
        [[self navigationItem] setLeftBarButtonItem:cancelItem];
        [cancelItem release];
    }
  }

  return self;
}
```

In the past, when you've changed the designated initializer of a class from its superclass' designated initializer, you've overridden the superclass' initializer to call the new one. In this case, you're going to make it illegal to use the superclass' designated initializer by throwing an exception when anyone calls it.

In `ItemDetailViewController.m`, override **UIViewController**'s designated initializer.

```
- (id)initWithNibName:(NSString *)nibName bundle:(NSBundle *)bundle
{
    @throw [NSException exceptionWithName:@"Wrong initializer"
                                  reason:@"Use initForNewItem:"
                                userInfo:nil];
    return nil;
}
```

This code creates an autoreleased instance of **NSException** with a name and a reason and then throws an exception. This halts the application and shows the exception in the console.

To confirm that this exception will be thrown, let's return to where **initWithNibName:bundle:** is currently called – the **tableView:didSelectRowAtIndexPath:** method of **ItemsViewController**. In this method, **ItemsViewController** creates an instance of **ItemDetailViewController** and sends it the message **init**, which eventually calls **initWithNibName:bundle:**. Therefore, selecting a row in the table view will result in the "Wrong initializer" exception being thrown.

Build and run the application and tap a row. You will see an exception in the console, and your application will halt. Notice that the name and the reason are part of the console message. The debugger will show you that sending **init** to the **ItemDetailViewController** was the cause.

You don't want to see this exception again, so in `ItemsViewController.m`, update **tableView:didSelectRowAtIndexPath:** to use the new initializer.

```
- (void)tableView:(UITableView *)tableView
    didSelectRowAtIndexPath:(NSIndexPath *)indexPath
{
    ItemDetailViewController *detailViewController =
        [[[ItemDetailViewController alloc] initForNewItem:NO] autorelease];

    NSArray *possessions = [[PossessionStore defaultStore] allPossessions];
```

Build and run the application again. Nothing new and exciting will happen, but your application should no longer crash when you select a row in the table.

Now that we've got our new initializer in place, let's change what happens when the user adds a new possession.

In `ItemsViewController.m`, edit the **addNewPossession:** method to create an instance of **ItemDetailViewController** in a **UINavigationController** and present the navigation controller modally.

```
- (IBAction)addNewPossession:(id)sender
{
    Possession *newPossession = [[PossessionStore defaultStore] createPossession];
    ItemDetailViewController *detailViewController =
        [[ItemDetailViewController alloc] initForNewItem:YES];

    [detailViewController setPossession:newPossession];

    UINavigationController *navController = [[UINavigationController alloc]
                             initWithRootViewController:detailViewController];

    [detailViewController release];

    // navController is retained by self when presented
    [self presentModalViewController:navController animated:YES];

    [navController release];
}
```

Build and run the application and tap the New button to create a new possession. An instance of **ItemDetailViewController** will slide up from the bottom of the screen – but now it has a Done button and a Cancel button on its navigation item. (Tapping these buttons, of course, will throw an exception since you haven't implemented the action methods yet.)

Dismissing modal view controllers

Every view controller has a property named `modalViewController`. If a view controller presents another view controller modally, then this property holds a pointer to that view controller. Every modally-presented view controller has a pointer named `parentViewController` that it sets to the view controller that presented it (Figure 14.6). These relationships are useful when it comes time to dismiss modal view controllers.

Figure 14.6   Parent-Modal Relationship

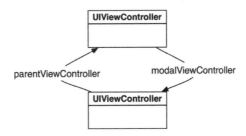

When a view controller is sent the message **dismissModalViewControllerAnimated:**, it removes its `modalViewController`'s view from the screen, releases that view controller, and sets its modalViewController property to nil. The modalViewController's parentViewController property is also set to nil. Therefore, when either of these two buttons is tapped, we need to tell the parentViewController of the **ItemDetailViewController** to **dismissModalViewControllerAnimated:**.

At the top of ItemDetailViewController.m, make the following import statement.

```
#import "PossessionStore.h"
```

Then, implement the action methods in ItemDetailViewController.m to dismiss the view controller.

```
- (IBAction)save:(id)sender
{
    // This message gets forwarded to the parentViewController
    [self dismissModalViewControllerAnimated:YES];
}

- (IBAction)cancel:(id)sender
{
    // If the user cancelled, then remove the Possession from the store
    [[PossessionStore defaultStore] removePossession:possession];

    // This message gets forwarded to the parentViewController
    [self dismissModalViewControllerAnimated:YES];
}
```

Notice that this code sends **dismissModalViewControllerAnimated:** to the **ItemDetailViewController**. This is odd because **ItemDetailViewController** is not the parentViewController. It turns out that view controllers are smarter than they look. If you send the message **dismissModalViewControllerAnimated:** to a modal view controller (like **ItemDetailViewController**), it thinks, "I don't have a modalViewController... I must *be* the modalViewController. I'll forward this message to my parent."

Build and run the application. Create a new possession and tap the Cancel button. The instance of **ItemDetailViewController** will slide off the screen, and nothing will be added to the table view. Then, create a new possession and tap the Done button. The **ItemDetailViewController** will slide off the screen, and your new **Possession** will appear in the table view.

Modal view controller styles

On the iPhone or iPod touch, a modal view controller takes over the entire screen. This is the default behavior and only possibility on these devices. On the iPad, you have two additional options: a form sheet style and a page sheet style. You change the presentation of the modal view controller by setting its modalPresentationStyle property to a pre-defined constant – UIModalPresentationFormSheet or UIModalPresentationPageSheet.

The form sheet style shows the modal view controller's view in a rectangle in the center of the iPad's screen and dims out the presenting view controller's view (Figure 14.7). The page sheet style is the same as the default full-screen style in portrait mode. In landscape mode, it keeps the same width as in portrait mode and dims the left and right edges of the presenting view controller's view that stick out behind it.

Figure 14.7 Form Sheet

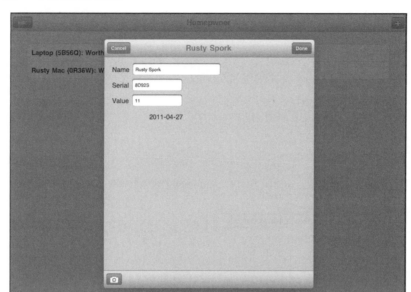

In ItemsViewController.m, modify the **addNewPossession:** method to change the presentation style of the **UINavigationController** that is being presented.

```
[navController setModalPresentationStyle:UIModalPresentationFormSheet];
```

```
[self presentModalViewController:navController animated:YES];
```

Build and run the application on the iPad simulator or on an iPad. Tap the button to add a new possession and watch the modal view controller slide onto the screen. Add some possession details and then tap the Done button. The table view reappears, but your new **Possession** isn't there. What happened?

Before you changed its presentation style, the modal view controller took up the entire screen, which caused the view of the **ItemsViewController** to disappear. When the modal view controller was dismissed, the **ItemsViewController** was sent the messages **viewWillAppear:** and **viewDidAppear:** and took this opportunity to reload its table to catch any updates to the **PossessionStore**.

With the new presentation style, the **ItemsViewController**'s view doesn't disappear when it presents the view controller. So it isn't sent the re-appearing messages when the modal view controller is dismissed, and it doesn't get the chance to reload its table view.

We have to find another opportunity for the **ItemsViewController** to reload its table view. We know that to dismiss the **ItemDetailViewController**, we send it the message **dismissModalViewControllerAnimated:** – a message it forwards to its parentViewController. One potential approach, then, is to override **dismissModalViewControllerAnimated:** in **ItemsViewController** and reload the table there.

But the **ItemDetailViewController**'s parentViewController is not the **ItemsViewController**; it's the navigation controller that holds the **ItemDetailViewController**. "No problem" you say, "I'll just get the parentViewController of the navigation controller... which is the **ItemsViewController**, right?"

Unfortunately, no. When a view controller presents a modal view controller, the parentViewController of the modal view controller is set to be the parent of the presenting view controller. Thus, the parentViewController of the **UINavigationController** that holds the **ItemDetailViewController** is set to the **UINavigationController** that holds the **ItemsViewController**. These relationships are shown in Figure 14.8.

Figure 14.8   Parent-Modal Relationships

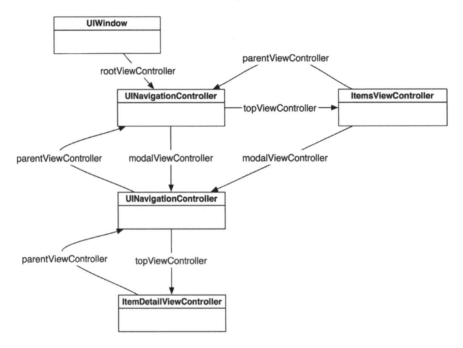

Writing a view controller delegate protocol

Instead of relying on the (somewhat complicated) relationships that the SDK has established, we're going to create a new relationship between these two view controllers so that they can send messages to each other directly. But how should we structure this relationship? Let's consider three options:

- For view controllers that are closely related, like a table view controller and its detail view controller, you can simply give them instance variables that point to each other. This is the easiest way to send messages between two view controllers, but it is also the least adaptable.

  ```
  // Send message to another view controller, kept as instance variable
  [myDetailViewController showItem:myItem];
  ```

- You can also create a delegate protocol that specifies the messages one view controller can send to the others. This technique allows multiple controllers to adopt the same protocol. It also means the view controller sending the message does not have to know what type of object it is sending the message to; it only needs to know that it conforms to the protocol.

```
// A protocol specified by the sending view controller
@protocol ItemShowingProtocol
- (void)showItem:(id)sender;
@end

// Send message to another view controller
id <ItemShowingProtocol> detail =
    [[[self navigationController] viewControllers] objectAtIndex:1];

[detail showItem:myItem];
```

- The third approach is to use the notification system. This solution is essential when the view controllers are not related. It is also useful when multiple view controllers are interested in a single controller. A view controller can post to the **NSNotificationCenter**, and interested objects can register for that notification.

In our case, you could choose to give the **ItemDetailViewController** a pointer to the **ItemsViewController** that effectively presented it. Then, when the **ItemDetailViewController** is dismissed, it would send a message to the **ItemsViewController** to say, "I'm being removed from the screen – do what you need to do."

However, it is possible that a different view controller might one day be responsible for presenting the **ItemDetailViewController**. To prepare for this possibility, you're going to create a delegate protocol for **ItemDetailViewController** and give it a delegate property. Although the **ItemsViewController** will serve as the delegate, using the delegate pattern will allow any object to present the **ItemDetailViewController** and be informed when it is dismissed.

In ItemDetailViewController.h, create a new protocol at the top of the file.

@class ItemDetailViewController;

@protocol ItemDetailViewControllerDelegate <NSObject>

@optional
- (void)itemDetailViewControllerWillDismiss:(ItemDetailViewController *)vc;

@end

@interface ItemDetailViewController : UIViewController

In ItemDetailViewController.h, add a new property to **ItemDetailViewController**.

- (id)initForNewItem:(BOOL)isNew;

@property (nonatomic, assign)
**   id <ItemDetailViewControllerDelegate> delegate;**

@property (nonatomic, retain) Possession *possession;

In ItemDetailViewController.m, synthesize this property.

@synthesize delegate;

(Notice that we did not create an instance variable for the delegate. Remember that when you synthesize a property that does not have a matching instance variable, the instance variable is automatically created for you.)

Now, in `ItemDetailViewController.m`, update the two action methods to inform its delegate that it is being dismissed. Because the delegate method is optional, use **respondsToSelector:** to make sure the delegate implements the method before you call it.

```
- (IBAction)save:(id)sender
{
    [self dismissModalViewControllerAnimated:YES];

    if([delegate respondsToSelector:@selector(itemDetailViewControllerWillDismiss:)])
        [delegate itemDetailViewControllerWillDismiss:self];
}
- (IBAction)cancel:(id)sender
{
    [[PossessionStore defaultStore] removePossession:possession];

    [self dismissModalViewControllerAnimated:YES];

    if([delegate respondsToSelector:@selector(itemDetailViewControllerWillDismiss:)])
        [delegate itemDetailViewControllerWillDismiss:self];
}
```

In `ItemsViewController.h`, declare that **ItemsViewController** conforms to this new protocol and import the header file for **ItemDetailViewController**.

```
#import "ItemDetailViewController.h"

@interface ItemsViewController : UITableViewController
    <ItemDetailViewControllerDelegate>
```

In `ItemsViewController.m`, implement the method from the delegate protocol to reload the table.

```
- (void)itemDetailViewControllerWillDismiss:(ItemDetailViewController *)vc
{
    [[self tableView] reloadData];
}
```

Then, update **addNewPossession:** in `ItemsViewController.m` to set the delegate of the presented **ItemDetailViewController**.

```
- (IBAction)addNewPossession:(id)sender
{
    Possession *newPossession = [[PossessionStore defaultStore] createPossession];
    ItemDetailViewController *detailViewController =
            [[ItemDetailViewController alloc] initForNewItem:YES];

    [detailViewController setDelegate:self];
```

Build and run the application. Create a new **Possession** and then return to the table view. The table view will update appropriately.

Modal view controller transitions

In addition to the presentation style of a modal view controller, you can change the animation that places it on screen. Just like with the presentation styles, there is a view controller property (`modalTransitionStyle`) that you can set with a pre-defined constant. By default, the animation will slide the modal view controller up from the bottom of the screen. You can also have the view controller fade in, flip in, or appear underneath a page curl (like in the Maps application).

In `ItemsViewController.m`, update the **addNewPossession:** method to use a different transition.

```
[navController setModalPresentationStyle:UIModalPresentationFormSheet];
[navController setModalTransitionStyle:UIModalTransitionStyleFlipHorizontal];

[self presentModalViewController:navController animated:YES];
```

Build and run the application and notice the change in animation. Try out some of the other options, but make sure to read the fine print in the documentation. For instance, you can't use the page curl transition unless the presentation style is full screen. Also, note that these transitions will still work if you switch back to deploying on an iPhone. The presentation style, however, will always be full screen.

15

Saving, Loading, and Multitasking

Every iOS application has its own *application sandbox*. An application sandbox is a directory on the filesystem that is barricaded from the rest of the filesystem. Your application must stay in its sandbox, and no other application can access your sandbox.

Application Sandbox

Figure 15.1   Application sandbox

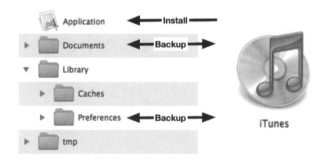

The application sandbox contains a number of directories:

application bundle	This directory contains all the resources and the executable. It is read-only.
Library/Preferences/	This directory is where any preferences are stored and where the Settings application looks for application preferences. Library/Preferences is handled automatically by the class **NSUserDefaults** (which you will learn about in Chapter 19) and is backed up when the device is synchronized with iTunes.
tmp/	This directory is where you write data that you will use temporarily during an application's runtime. You should

remove files from this directory when done with them, and the operating system may purge them while your application is not running. It does not get backed up when the device is synchronized with iTunes. To get the path to the tmp directory in the application sandbox, you can use the convenience function **NSTemporaryDirectory**.

Documents/

This directory is where you write data that the application generates during runtime and that you want to persist between runs of the application. It is backed up when the device is synchronized with iTunes. If something goes wrong with the device, files in this directory can be restored from iTunes. For example, in a game application, the saved game files would be stored here.

Library/Caches/

This directory is where you write data that the application generates during runtime and that you want to persist between runs of the application. However, unlike the Documents directory, it does not get backed up when the device is synchronized with iTunes. A major reason for not backing up cached data is that the data can be very large and extend the time it takes to synchronize your device. Data stored somewhere else – like a web server – can be placed in this directory. If the user needs to restore the device, this data can be downloaded from the web server again.

Constructing a file path

We want **Possession**s to persist in Homepwner. (It's not much fun if you have to enter all your possessions every time you start the application.) The data for the **Possession**s will be saved and loaded into a single file in the Documents directory of Homepwner's sandbox. The **PossessionStore** will handle writing to and reading from the filesystem. To do this, the **PossessionStore** needs a path to the file in Documents containing the **Possession** data.

To get the full path for a directory in the sandbox, you use the C function **NSSearchPathForDirectoriesInDomains**. This function takes three parameters: the type of directory, the domain mask, and a boolean value that decides if it should expand a tilde (~) if one exists in the path. The first parameter is an **NSSearchPathDirectory** constant. The last two parameters are always the same on iOS: NSUserDomainMask and YES. For instance, to get the Documents directory for an application, you would call the function as follows:

```
NSArray *documentPaths =
    NSSearchPathForDirectoriesInDomains(NSDocumentDirectory,
                                        NSUserDomainMask,
                                        YES);
NSString *ourDocumentPath = [documentPaths objectAtIndex:0];
```

Notice that **NSSearchPathForDirectoriesInDomains** returns an **NSArray**. This is because this function comes from Mac OS X where there could be multiple directories for the parameters. In iOS, however, there is only one directory for the possible constants, and it is safe to grab the first **NSString** from the array.

You can also get the path for the sandbox itself using the function **NSHomeDirectory**. Note that you cannot write files or create directories at the root-level of the sandbox. Any new directories or files must be created within one of the writeable directories in the sandbox: `Documents`, `Library`, or `tmp`. You can append the names of the directories to the string returned from this function.

```
NSString *sandboxPath = NSHomeDirectory();
// Once you have the full sandbox path, you can create a path from it
NSString *documentPath = [sandboxPath
          stringByAppendingPathComponent:@"Documents"];
```

However, it is safer to use **NSSearchPathForDirectoriesInDomains** than **NSHomeDirectory** with an appended directory name. The name of a directory could change in future releases of the operating system or you could mistype the string you are appending.

Open the Homepwner project. In `PossessionStore.h`, declare a new method that specifies the name of the file on the filesystem that contains the data for all of the **Possession**s.

```
- (NSString *)possessionArchivePath;
```

In `PossessionStore.m`, implement this method so that it returns the full path to where the **Possession**s will be stored.

```
- (NSString *)possessionArchivePath
{
    // The returned path will be Sandbox/Documents/possessions.data
    // Both the saving and loading methods will call this method to get the same path,
    // preventing a typo in the path name of either method

    return pathInDocumentDirectory(@"possessions.data");
}
```

Notice the **pathInDocumentDirectory** function. That's what you'll create next. This function will return the full path of a file in the `Documents` directory when given the name of that file. It is not a part of an Objective-C class but a stand-alone C function. You'll use this function many different places, so create a separate file for it. Use the **NSObject** template like before (File → New → New File...) and name your subclass **FileHelpers**.

Now you're going to remove the class interface and implementation from the two files. (The **NSObject** template is just a quick and easy way to create two new files with .h and .m suffixes.) Open `FileHelpers.h`, delete the interface declaration, and declare the new function. The file should look just like this:

```
#import <Foundation/Foundation.h>

NSString *pathInDocumentDirectory(NSString *fileName);
```

In `FileHelpers.m`, delete the implementation block and define the **pathInDocumentDirectory** function. `FileHelpers.m` should look exactly like this:

```
#import "FileHelpers.h"

// To use this function, you pass it a file name, and it will construct
// the full path for that file in the Documents directory.
NSString *pathInDocumentDirectory(NSString *fileName)
{
    // Get list of document directories in sandbox
```

```
    NSArray *documentDirectories =
            NSSearchPathForDirectoriesInDomains(NSDocumentDirectory,
                                        NSUserDomainMask, YES);

    // Get one and only document directory from that list
    NSString *documentDirectory = [documentDirectories objectAtIndex:0];

    // Append passed in file name to that directory, return it
    return [documentDirectory stringByAppendingPathComponent:fileName];
}
```

This function will eventually be called from a number of different files and will have to be imported into each file that uses it, which is a bit of a nuisance. We can avoid this nuisance by importing FileHelpers.h into Homepwner's precompiled header file. Every project has a precompiled header file (.pch), and this file is imported into every file in the project. Open Homepwner-Prefix.pch from the project navigator and import FileHelpers.h.

```
#ifdef __OBJC__
    #import <Foundation/Foundation.h>
    #import <UIKit/UIKit.h>
    #import "FileHelpers.h"
#endif
```

Now every file in the Homepwner project will effectively import FileHelpers.h. Note that if you modify a file that is imported in the precompiled header file, it forces your entire project to be recompiled. Thus, you should only import files into the precompiled header file that rarely or never change.

Archiving

There are many ways to write data to the filesystem on iOS, and one of the most important is called *archiving*. Archiving is the process of taking one or more objects from memory and writing them to the filesystem. Unarchiving reads these objects back from the filesystem into memory.

Archiving works by creating an instance of **NSCoder**, which is essentially just a container for data, and placing objects and their data inside it. Once the **NSCoder** has all of the data you have instructed it to collect, it will be written to a specific file in the filesystem.

Not all objects can be archived – only those whose class conforms to the NSCoding protocol. The NSCoding protocol has two methods, and both are required: **encodeWithCoder:** (for archiving) and **initWithCoder:** (for unarchiving).

In Possession.h, declare that **Possession** conforms to the NSCoding protocol.

```
@interface Possession : NSObject <NSCoding>
```

Archiving objects

To write objects that conform to NSCoding to the filesystem, you use the class method **archiveRootObject:toFile:** of **NSKeyedArchiver**, which is a subclass of **NSCoder**. The first argument of this method is the *root object*, and the second argument is the path of the file to be written to.

The root object must be an instance of a class that conforms to NSCoding. So what's our root object in Homepwner? While you could archive each **Possession** separately, it is far simpler to begin with the allPossessions array of **PossessionStore**. The array can be the root object because **NSMutableArray** also conforms to NSCoding.

In PossessionStore.h, declare a new method that will archive allPossessions to the result of **possessionArchivePath**.

```
- (BOOL)saveChanges;
```

Implement this method in PossessionStore.m.

```
- (BOOL)saveChanges
{
    // returns success or failure
    return [NSKeyedArchiver archiveRootObject:allPossessions
                                       toFile:[self possessionArchivePath]];
}
```

The **archiveRootObject:toFile:** method creates an instance of **NSKeyedArchiver** and then sends **encodeWithCoder:** to allPossessions. The **NSKeyedArchiver** is passed as the argument. When an array is archived, all of its contents are archived along with it (as long as those contents conform to NSCoding), so passing an array full of **Possession** instances to **archiveRootObject:toFile:** kicks off a chain reaction of encoding. This process is shown in Figure 15.2.

Figure 15.2   Archiving an array

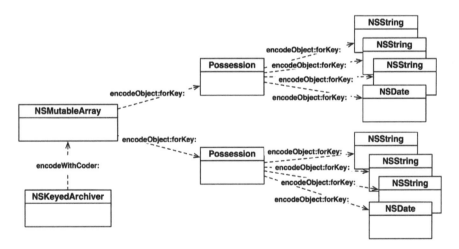

Within its implementation of **encodeWithCoder:**, an object can send messages to the **NSCoder** (in our case, the **NSKeyedArchiver**) to encode its instance variables.

In Possession.m, add the following implementation of **encodeWithCoder:**.

```
- (void)encodeWithCoder:(NSCoder *)encoder
{
    // For each instance variable, archive it under its variable name
    // These objects will also be sent encodeWithCoder:
    [encoder encodeObject:possessionName forKey:@"possessionName"];
    [encoder encodeObject:serialNumber forKey:@"serialNumber"];
```

```
[encoder encodeObject:dateCreated forKey:@"dateCreated"];
[encoder encodeObject:imageKey forKey:@"imageKey"];

// For the primitive valueInDollars, make sure to use encodeInt:forKey:
// the value in valueInDollars will be placed in the coder object
[encoder encodeInt:valueInDollars forKey:@"valueInDollars"];
}
```

Notice the two different messages sent (**encodeObject:forKey:** and **encodeInt:forKey:**) for the **Possession**'s two different types of instance variables. Also, what's with all the keys?

This type of archiving is called *keyed archiving*. Keyed archives work a lot like an **NSMutableDictionary** – you add an object to it with a key, and the key is used to retrieve that object later. The key is always an instance of **NSString** and is typically the name of the instance variable that it is being encoded.

If any of the instance variables encoded into the **NSCoder** are objects, then those objects are also sent **encodeWithCoder:** (Figure 15.3). So archiving is a recursive process that starts at the root object, who encodes his friends, who encode their friends, and so on.

Figure 15.3   Encoding an object

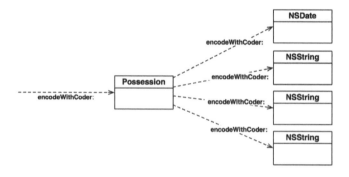

(By the way, another class you are familiar with conforms to NSCoding: **UIView**. This is how XIB files are created. Instances of **UIView** are created when you drag them onto the canvas area. When the XIB file is saved, these views are archived into the XIB file. When your application launches, it unarchives the views from the XIB file. There are some minor differences between a XIB file and a standard archive, but overall, it's the same process.)

Unarchiving objects

When an application wants to load archived objects, it unarchives them. First, an instance of **NSCoder** is created, and data from the filesystem is read into it. Then, the archived objects are decoded.

To bring a set of objects back from the filesystem, you use the class method **unarchiveObjectWithFile:** of **NSKeyedUnarchiver**, another subclass of **NSCoder**. This method takes the path of an archive on the filesystem as its one argument. The contents at the path are then read into memory, and a chain reaction of unarchiving begins.

In `PossessionStore.h`, declare a new method that will kick off the unarchiving.

```
- (void)fetchPossessionsIfNecessary;
```

Implement this method in `PossessionStore.m`.

```
- (void)fetchPossessionsIfNecessary
{
    // If we don't currently have an allPossessions array, try to read one from disk
    if (!allPossessions) {
        NSString *path = [self possessionArchivePath];
        allPossessions = [[NSKeyedUnarchiver unarchiveObjectWithFile:path] retain];
    }

    // If we tried to read one from disk but does not exist, then create a new one
    if (!allPossessions) {
        allPossessions = [[NSMutableArray alloc] init];
    }
}
```

(Note that the return value of **unarchiveObjectWithFile:** is of type id and can therefore be any object. It is the programmer's responsibility to know the type of the root object that is being unarchived. Also, notice that the object returned from **unarchiveObjectWithFile:** is retained because the method returns an autoreleased object.)

This method attempts to load the archive from the filesystem into the `allPossessions` array. If the archive doesn't exist, it creates an empty `allPossessions` array. If the archive does exist, an instance of **NSKeyedUnarchiver** is created. The class of the root object is also determined and then sent **alloc**. Once an uninitialized instance of that class has been created, the instance is sent **initWithCoder:** with the instance of **NSKeyedUnarchiver** passed as the argument.

Our root object is `allPossesions` – an **NSMutableArray**. **NSMutableArray**'s implementation of **initWithCoder:** decodes the contents of the archived array by sending each archived object the message **decodeObjectForKey:**. For each object being decoded, the class of the object is found, sent **alloc**, and then sent **initWithCoder:**.

In our case, the objects are **Possession**s, so in `Possession.m`, add the following implementation of **initWithCoder:**.

```
- (id)initWithCoder:(NSCoder *)decoder
{
    self = [super init];

    if (self) {
        // For each instance variable that is archived, we decode it,
        // and pass it to our setters. (Where it is retained)
        [self setPossessionName:[decoder decodeObjectForKey:@"possessionName"]];
        [self setSerialNumber:[decoder decodeObjectForKey:@"serialNumber"]];
        [self setImageKey:[decoder decodeObjectForKey:@"imageKey"]];

        // Make sure to use decodeIntForKey:, since valueInDollars is not an object
        [self setValueInDollars:[decoder decodeIntForKey:@"valueInDollars"]];

        // dateCreated is read only, we have no setter. We explicitly
        // retain it and set our instance variable pointer to it
        dateCreated = [[decoder decodeObjectForKey:@"dateCreated"] retain];
    }
```

```
        return self;
}
```

Notice that you make use of the setter methods in **Possession** where they are available. This ensures proper memory management. When you decode an object from an instance of **NSCoder**, that object has a retain count of 1 and is autoreleased. (You can tell because it doesn't say alloc or copy anywhere.) Your setter methods are all set up to copy or retain the objects they receive. The dateCreated instance variable is read-only and doesn't have a setter. So, instead, you set your instance variable here and explicitly retain it. The primitive valueInDollars doesn't need any memory management because it is not an object.

When the decoding process finishes, you will be left with an **NSMutableArray** full of **Possession**s that exactly matches the originally archived array (Figure 15.4).

Figure 15.4   Archived object

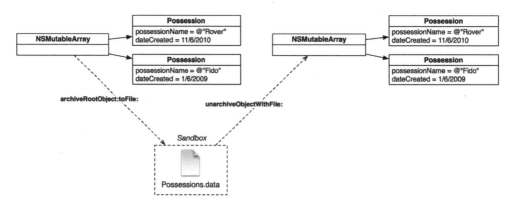

Build your application to check for any syntax errors. Note that **initWithCoder:** does not replace the other initialization methods. If you wish to create a **Possession** programmatically, you use the other initialization methods. The method **initWithCoder:** is only used during unarchiving.

Now that **fetchPossessionsIfNecessary** is responsible for creating allPossessions, we need to remove some code from the **init** method of **PossessionStore**. In PossessionStore.m, remove the line of code in **init** that instantiates allPossessions. The method should now look like this:

```
- (id)init
{
    if (defaultStore) {
        return defaultStore;
    }
    self = [super init];
    return self;
}
```

While you're in PossessionStore.m, modify the following methods:

```objc
- (NSArray *)allPossessions
{
    // This ensures allPossessions is created
    [self fetchPossessionsIfNecessary];

    return allPossessions;
}

- (Possession *)createPossession
{
    // This ensures allPossessions is created
    [self fetchPossessionsIfNecessary];

    Possession *p = [Possession randomPossession];

    [allPossessions addObject:p];

    return p;
}
```

These changes set up lazy loading for the **PossessionStore**. When the **PossessionStore** is first instantiated, there will be no allPossessions array. When another object asks for the **Possession**s (like **ItemsViewController** does when populating the table) or when a new **Possession** is created, the store checks to see if the array exists. If it does not, it tries to unarchive one. If there is no archive, it creates an empty array.

You can build the application to check for syntax errors, but before you run it, we need to fill one last hole: the **PossessionStore** is never sent **saveChanges**. We have to figure out when we can send this message to the **PossessionStore** so that the application data will be saved.

Application States, Transitions, and Multitasking

To know when an application should save its data to filesystem, it helps to understand the states that an application can be in as well as the transitions between them.(Figure 15.5).

Figure 15.5   States of typical application

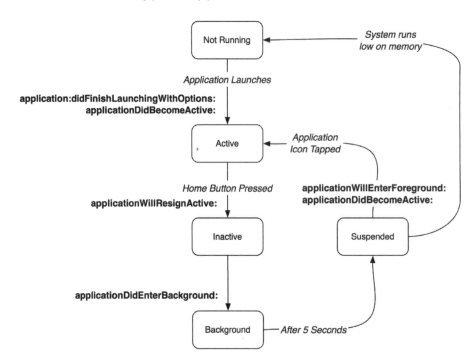

When an application is not running, it is in the *not running* state, and it does not execute any code or have any memory reserved in RAM.

After the user launches an application, it enters the *active state*. Its interface is on the screen, it is accepting events, and your code is handling those events. There is also an *inactive state* that is similar to the active state, except that the application is not currently receiving events. An application is in the inactive state when it is first being launched (before the run loop is created) or when a SMS message or other system-event (like an alarm) occurs. Applications typically spend very little time in the inactive state.

When the user presses the Home button while an application is running, it goes from active, briefly to inactive, and then to the *background state*. While an application is in the background state, it can still execute code, but it is no longer visible. Its icon appears in the dock, which is accessible by double-clicking the Home button. By default, an application that enters the background state has five seconds before it enters the *suspended state*. (An application can request to stay in the background state for longer, though. We'll cover this in Chapter 27.)

An application in the suspended state cannot execute code, and any resources it doesn't need while suspended are released. A suspended application is essentially freeze-dried and can be quickly thawed when the user relaunches it. The resources that are released are ones that can be reloaded, like cached images, system-managed caches, and other graphics data. (You don't have to worry about releasing and reloading these resources; your application handles the destruction and renewal of them automatically.)

You can see the background and suspended applications by double-clicking the home button on your device.

Figure 15.6 Background and suspended applications in the dock

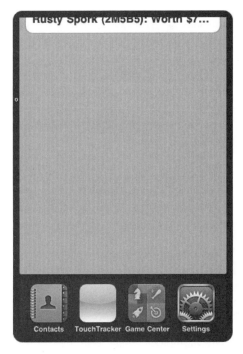

An application in the suspended state also will remain in the dock as long as there is adequate system memory. When the operating system decides memory is getting low, it terminates suspended applications as needed. And it will do so without warning. A suspended application gets no notification that it is about to be terminated; it is simply removed from memory. (An application may remain in the dock after it has been terminated, but it will be relaunched when tapped.)

When an application changes its state, the application delegate is sent a message. Here are some of the messages from the `UIApplicationDelegate` protocol that announce application state transitions.

- `application:didFinishLaunchingWithOptions:`
- `applicationDidBecomeActive:`
- `applicationWillResignActive:`
- `applicationDidEnterBackground:`
- `applicationWillEnterForeground:`

So, when should we save application data? Clearly, the not running and suspended states are out of the question; no code can be executed in those states. You could periodically "autosave" your data while in the active state, but that may slow down the user experience. (By the way, if you need to write a lot of data at once, you will be better served using Core Data, which you will learn about in Chapter 17.)

We could save in the transition to the inactive state. Then data would be saved either when a system-event occurs or when the application is on its way to the background state. However, saving data here is a waste of time because the application will either become active again shortly or it will enter the background.

Saving in the transition to the background state is our best option. At this point, the application is likely on its way to being suspended, and at that point, it will be subject to being terminated by the operating system. We definitely need to save before then.

The message sent to the application delegate when the application enters the background state is **applicationDidEnterBackground:**. We'll implement that method and save changes there.

Open HomepwnerAppDelegate.m and import the header file for **PossessionStore**.

```
#import "HomepwnerAppDelegate.h"
#import "PossessionStore.h"
```

In HomepwnerAppDelegate.m, implement **applicationDidEnterBackground:** so that it tells the **PossessionStore** to save its data to the filesystem.

```
- (void)applicationDidEnterBackground:(UIApplication *)application
{
    [[PossessionStore defaultStore] saveChanges];
}
```

Now all of the **Possession** instances will be archived to the filesystem when the user presses the Home button.

Not all iOS devices support these different application states. Before iOS 4, there was no background state, and only one application could be running at a time. When you pressed the Home button, the current application terminated so that you could launch another. Pressing the Home button sent the application delegate the message **applicationWillTerminate:**.

To support pre-iOS 4 devices, you can implement **applicationWillTerminate:** and save changes there, too. This method will happily coexist with the others.

In HomepwnerAppDelegate.m, implement **applicationWillTerminate:** to perform the same task as its multitasking counterpart.

```
- (void)applicationWillTerminate:(UIApplication *)application
{
    [[PossessionStore defaultStore] saveChanges];
}
```

Build and run the application. Create a few **Possession**s and hit the Home button. Next, double-click the Home button and touch and hold the Homepwner icon. Tap the delete control in the top left corner of the icon to terminate the application. Then, re-launch the application, and your **Possession**s will appear in the table view. (Alternatively, you can kill the task from Xcode by clicking the Stop button, but make sure you press the Home button first.) Your **Possession** images, however, are not being saved. We'll get to that next.

Writing to filesystem with NSData

The images for **Possession** instances are created by user interaction and are only stored within the application. Therefore, the Documents directory is the best place to store them. Let's extend the image store to save images as they are added and fetch them as they are needed. You can use the image key generated when the user takes a picture to name the image in the filesystem.

In this section, you are going to copy the JPEG representation of an image into a buffer in memory. Instead of just malloc'ing a buffer, Objective-C programmers have a handy class to create, maintain, and destroy these sorts of buffers – **NSData**. An **NSData** instance holds some number of bytes of binary data, and you're going to use **NSData** store image data.

Open ImageStore.m and extend the **setImage:forKey:** method to write a JPEG of the image to the Documents directory.

```
- (void)setImage:(UIImage *)i forKey:(NSString *)s
{
    // Put it in the dictionary
    [dictionary setObject:i forKey:s];

    // Create full path for image
    NSString *imagePath = pathInDocumentDirectory(s);

    // Turn image into JPEG data,
    NSData *d = UIImageJPEGRepresentation(i, 0.5);

    // Write it to full path
    [d writeToFile:imagePath atomically:YES];
}
```

Let's examine this code more closely. The function **UIImageJPEGRepresentation** takes two parameters: a **UIImage** and a compression quality. The compression quality is a float from 0 to 1, where 1 is the highest quality. The function returns an instance of **NSData**.

This **NSData** instance can be written to the filesystem by sending it the message **writeToFile:atomically:**. The bytes held in this **NSData** are then written to the path specified by the first parameter. The second parameter, **atomically**, is a boolean value. If it is YES, the file is written to a temporary place on the filesystem, and, once the writing operation is complete, that file is renamed to the path of the first parameter, replacing any previously existing file. This prevents data corruption should your application crash during the write procedure.

It is worth noting that this way of writing data to the filesystem is *not* archiving. While **NSData** instances can be archived, using the method **writeToFile:atomically:** is a binary write to the filesystem.

In ImageStore.m, make sure that when an image is deleted from the store, it is also deleted from the filesystem:

```
- (void)deleteImageForKey:(NSString *)s
{
    if(!s)
        return;
    [dictionary removeObjectForKey:s];
    NSString *path = pathInDocumentDirectory(s);
    [[NSFileManager defaultManager] removeItemAtPath:path
                                        error:NULL];
}
```

Now that the image is stored in the filesystem, the **ImageStore** will need to load that image when it is requested. The class method **imageWithContentsOfFile:** of **UIImage** will read in an image from a file, given a path.

In ImageStore, replace the method **imageForKey:** so that the **ImageStore** will load the image from the filesystem if it doesn't already have it.

```
- (UIImage *)imageForKey:(NSString *)s
{
    // If possible, get it from the dictionary
    UIImage *result = [dictionary objectForKey:s];

    if (!result) {
        // Create UIImage object from file
        result = [UIImage imageWithContentsOfFile:pathInDocumentDirectory(s)];

        // If we found an image on the file system, place it into the cache
        if (result)
            [dictionary setObject:result forKey:s];
        else
            NSLog(@"Error: unable to find %@", pathInDocumentDirectory(s));
    }
    return result;
}
```

When a **Possession** is removed from the store, its image should also be removed from the filesystem. At the top of PossessionStore.m, import the header for the **ImageStore** and add the following code to **removePossession:**.

```
#import "ImageStore.h"

@implementation PossessionStore

- (void)removePossession:(Possession *)p
{
    NSString *key = [p imageKey];
    [[ImageStore defaultImageStore] deleteImageForKey:key];

    [allPossessions removeObjectIdenticalTo:p];
}
```

Build and run the application again. Take a photo for a possession, exit the application, and then kill it from the dock. Launch the application again. Selecting that same possession will show all its saved details – including the photo you just took.

More on Low-Memory Warnings

You have seen how view controllers handle low-memory warnings – they are sent the message **didReceiveMemoryWarning** and release their view if it is not on the screen. This is an appropriate solution to handling a low-memory warning: an object gets rid of anything it isn't currently using and can recreate later. Objects other than view controllers may have data that they aren't using and can recreate later. The **ImageStore** is such an object – when its images aren't on the screen, it is okay to destroy them because they can be loaded from the filesystem when they're needed again.

Whenever a low-memory warning occurs, UIApplicationDidReceiveMemoryWarningNotification is posted to the notification center. Objects that want to implement their own low-memory warning handlers can register for this notification. In ImageStore.m, edit the **init** method to register the image store as an observer of this notification.

```
- (id)init
{
    if(defaultImageStore)
    {
        [self dealloc];
        return defaultImageStore;
    }

    defaultImageStore = self;
    dictionary = [[NSMutableDictionary alloc] init];

    NSNotificationCenter *nc = [NSNotificationCenter defaultCenter];
    [nc addObserver:self
            selector:@selector(clearCache:)
                name:UIApplicationDidReceiveMemoryWarningNotification
              object:nil];

    return self;
}
```

Now, a low-memory warning will send the message **clearCache:** to the **ImageStore** instance. In ImageStore.m, implement **clearCache:** to remove all the **UIImage** objects from the **ImageStore**'s dictionary.

```
- (void)clearCache:(NSNotification *)note
{
    NSLog(@"flushing %d images out of the cache", [dictionary count]);
    [dictionary removeAllObjects];
}
```

Removing an object from a dictionary releases it, so flushing the cache releases all of the images. Images that aren't being used by other objects are deallocated, and when they are needed again, they will be reloaded from the filesystem. If an image is currently displayed in the **ItemDetailViewController**'s imageView, then it will not be deallocated. An image that is being used during a memory warning remains in memory until the object using it releases it. At that point, it is deallocated and will be reloaded from the filesystem when it is needed again.

Model-View-Controller-Store Design Pattern

In this exercise, we expanded on the **PossessionStore** to allow it to save and load **Possession** instances from the filesystem. The controller object asks the **PossessionStore** for the model objects it needs, but it doesn't have to worry about where those objects actually came from. As far as the controller is concerned, if it wants an object, it will get one; the **PossessionStore** is responsible for making sure that happens.

The standard Model-View-Controller design pattern calls for the controller to be bear the burden of saving and loading model objects. However, in practice, this can become overwhelming – the controller is simply "too busy" handling the interactions between model and view objects to deal with the details of how objects are fetched and saved. Therefore, it is useful to move the logic that deals with where model objects come from and where they are saved to into another type of object: a *store*.

A store simply exposes a number of methods that allow a controller object to fetch and save model objects. Where these model objects come from is up to the store: in this exercise, the store worked with a simple file. However, the store could also access a database, talk to a web service, or use some other method to produce the model objects for the controller. The controller doesn't care – it will get the model objects it wants, and the details are abstracted into the store.

One benefit of this approach, besides simplified controller classes, is that you can swap out *how* the store works without modifying the controller or the rest of your application. This can be a simple change, like the directory structure of the data, or a much larger change, like the format of the data. Thus, if an application has more than one controller object that needs to save and load data, you only have to change the store object.

You can also apply the idea of a store to objects like **CLLocationManager**. The location manager is a store that returns model objects of type **CLLocation**. The basic idea still stands: a model object is returned to the controller; the controller doesn't care where it came from.

Thus, we introduce a new design pattern called *Model-View-Controller-Store*, or simply MVCS. It's the hip, new design pattern that programmers are talking about everywhere.

Challenge: Archiving Whereami

Another application you wrote could benefit from archiving: Whereami. In Whereami, archive the **MapPoint** objects so they can be reused. (Hint: you cannot archive structures. However, you can break up structures into their primitive types....)

For The More Curious: Application State Transitions

Let's write some quick code to get a better understanding of the different application state transitions.

You already know about self, an implicit variable that points to the instance that is executing the current method. There is another implicit variable called _cmd, which is the selector for the current method. You can get the **NSString** representation of a selector with the function **NSStringFromSelector**.

In HomepwnerAppDelegate.m, implement the application state transition delegate methods so that they print out the name of the method. You'll need to add three more methods:

```
- (void)applicationWillResignActive:(UIApplication *)application
{
    NSLog(@"%@", NSStringFromSelector(_cmd));
}

- (void)applicationWillEnterForeground:(UIApplication *)application
{
    NSLog(@"%@", NSStringFromSelector(_cmd));
}

- (void)applicationDidBecomeActive:(UIApplication *)application
{
    NSLog(@"%@", NSStringFromSelector(_cmd));
}
```

Now, add the following **NSLog** statements to the top of
application:didFinishLaunchingWithOptions:, **applicationWillTerminate:**, and
applicationDidEnterBackground:.

```
- (BOOL)application:(UIApplication *)application
  didFinishLaunchingWithOptions:(NSDictionary *)launchOptions
{
    NSLog(@"%@", NSStringFromSelector(_cmd));
    ...
}

- (void)applicationDidEnterBackground:(UIApplication *)application
{
    NSLog(@"%@", NSStringFromSelector(_cmd));
    [[PossessionStore defaultStore] saveChanges];
}

- (void)applicationWillTerminate:(UIApplication *)application
{
    NSLog(@"%@", NSStringFromSelector(_cmd));
    [[PossessionStore defaultStore] saveChanges];
}
```

Build and run the application. You will see that the application gets sent
application:didFinishLaunchingWithOptions: and then **applicationDidBecomeActive:**. Click
the Home button, and the console will report that the application briefly inactivated and then went to
the background state. Relaunch the application by tapping its icon on the Home screen or in the dock.
The console will report that the application entered the foreground and then became active. Double-
click the Home button to launch the dock and then touch and hold the Homepwner icon until it begins
to jiggle. Tap the red terminate button in the icon's upper left corner and note that no message is sent to
your application delegate – it is simply terminated immediately.

For the More Curious: Reading and Writing to the filesystem

In addition to archiving and **NSData**'s binary read and write methods, there are a few more methods for
transferring data to and from the filesystem. One of them, Core Data, is coming up in Chapter 17. A
couple of the others are worth mentioning here.

You have access to the standard file I/O functions from the C library. These functions look like this:

```
FILE *inFile = fopen("textfile", "rt");
char *buffer = malloc(someSize);
fread(buffer, byteCount, 1, inFile);

FILE *outFile = fopen("binaryfile", "w");
fwrite(buffer, byteCount, 1, outFile);
```

However, you won't see these functions used much because there are more convenient ways of reading and writing binary and text data. Using **NSData** works well for binary data. For text data, **NSString** has two instance methods **writeToFile:atomically:encoding:error:** and **initWithContentsOfFile:**. They are used as follows:

```
// A local variable to store an error object if one comes back
NSError *err;

NSString *someString = @"Text Data";
BOOL success = [someString writeToFile:@"/some/path/"
                           atomically:YES
                             encoding:NSUTF8StringEncoding
                                error:&err];
if (!success) {
    NSLog(@"Error writing file: %@", [err localizedDescription]);
}

NSString *x = [[NSString alloc] initWithContentsOfFile:@"/some/path/"
                                          encoding:NSUTF8StringEncoding
                                             error:&err];
if (!x) {
    NSLog(@"Error reading file: %@", [err localizedDescription]);
}
```

What's that **NSError** object? Some methods might fail for a variety of reasons – for example, writing to the filesystem might fail because the path is invalid or the user doesn't have permission to write to the specified path. **NSError** objects contain the reasons for failure. You can send the message **localizedDescription** to an instance of **NSError** for a human-readable description of the error. This is something you can show to the user or print out to a debug console.

Error objects also have code and domain properties. The code is an integer representing the error. The domain represents the error domain. For example, not having permission to write to a directory results in error code 513 in error domain NSCocoaErrorDomain. Each domain has its own set of error codes, and codes within different domains can have the same integer value; therefore, an error is uniquely specified by its code and error domain. You can check out the error codes for the NSCocoaErrorDomain in the file Foundation/FoundationErrors.h.

The syntax for getting back an **NSError** instance is a little strange. An error object is only created if an error occurred; otherwise, there is no need for the object. When a method can return an error through one of its arguments, you create a local variable that is a pointer to an **NSError** object. Notice that you don't instantiate the error object – that is the job of the method you are calling. Instead, you pass the *address* of your pointer variable (&err) to the method that might generate an error. If an error occurs in the implementation of that method, an **NSError** instance is created, and your pointer is set to point at that new object. If you don't care about the error object, you can always pass nil.

Sometimes you want to show the error to the user. This is typically done with an **UIAlertView**:

```
NSString *x = [[NSString alloc] initWithContentsOfFile:@"/some/path/"
                                          encoding:NSUTF8StringEncoding
```

```
                                                error:&err];
if (!x) {
    UIAlertView *a = [[[UIAlertView alloc] initWithTitle:@"Read Failed"
                                          message:[err localizedDescription]
                                          delegate:nil
                               cancelButtonTitle:@"OK"
                               otherButtonTitles:nil] autorelease];
    [a show];
}
```

Figure 15.7   UIAlertView

Like **NSString**, the classes **NSDictionary** and **NSArray** have **writeToFile:** and
initWithContentsOfFile: methods. In order to write objects of these types to the filesystem in this
fashion, they must contain only *property list serializable* objects. The only objects that are *property list
serializable* are **NSString**, **NSNumber**, **NSDate**, **NSData**, **NSArray**, and **NSDictionary**. When an **NSArray**
or **NSDictionary** is written to the filesystem with these methods, an *XML property list* is created. An
XML property list is a collection of tagged values:

```
<?xml version="1.0" encoding="UTF-8"?>
<!DOCTYPE plist PUBLIC "-//Apple//DTD PLIST 1.0//EN"
      "http://www.apple.com/DTDs/PropertyList-1.0.dtd">
<plist version="1.0">
<array>
    <dict>
        <key>firstName</key>
        <string>Joe</string>
        <key>lastName</key>
        <string>Conway</string>
    </dict>
    <dict>
        <key>firstName</key>
        <string>Aaron</string>
        <key>lastName</key>
        <string>Hillegass</string>
    </dict>
</array>
</plist>
```

XML property lists are a convenient way to store data because they can be read on nearly any system.
Many web service applications use property lists as input and output. The code for writing and reading
a property list looks like this:

```
NSMutableDictionary *d = [NSMutableDictionary dictionary];
[d setObject:@"A string" forKey:@"String"];
[d writeToFile:@"/some/path" atomically:YES];
```

```
NSMutableDictionary *anotherD = [[NSMutableDictionary alloc]
                     initWithContentsOfFile:@"/some/path"];
```

For the More Curious: The Application Bundle

When you build an iOS application project in Xcode, you create an *application bundle*. The application bundle contains the application executable and any resources you have bundled with your application. Resources are things like XIB files, images, audio files – any files that will be used at runtime. When you add a resource file to a project, Xcode is smart enough to realize that it should be bundled with your application and categorizes it accordingly.

How can you tell which files are being bundled with your application? Select the Homepwner project from the project navigator. Check out the Build Phases pane in the Homepwner target. Everything under Copy Bundle Resources will be added to the application bundle when it is built.

Each item in the Homepwner target group is one of the phases that occurs when you build a project. The Copy Bundle Resources phase is where all of the resources in your project get copied into the application bundle.

You can check out what an application bundle looks like on the filesystem after you install an application on the simulator. Navigate to ~/Library/Application Support/iPhone Simulator/ (version number)/Applications. The directories within this directory are the application sandboxes for applications installed on your computer's iOS Simulator. Opening one of these directories will show you what you expect in an application sandbox: an application bundle and the Documents, tmp, and Library directories. Right or Command-click the application bundle and choose Show Package Contents from the contextual menu.

Figure 15.8 Viewing an Application Bundle

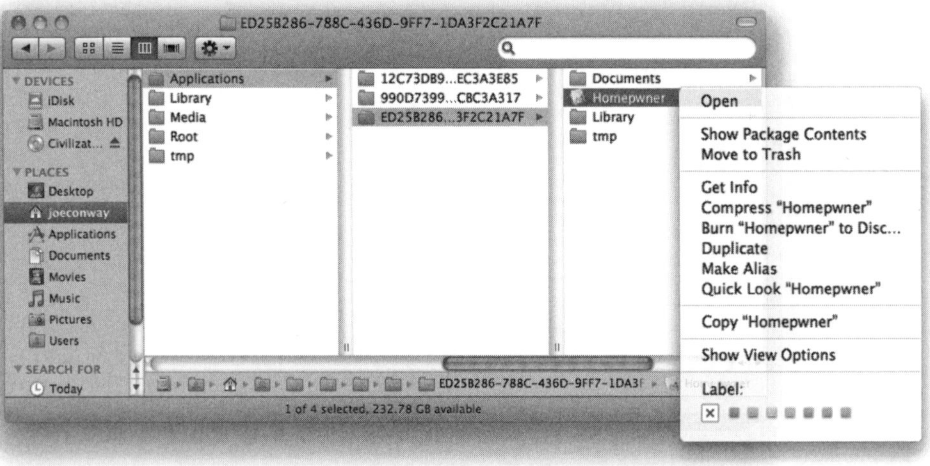

A Finder window will appear showing you the contents of the application bundle. When a user downloads your application from the App Store, these files are copied to their device.

Figure 15.9 The Application Bundle

You can load files from the application's bundle at runtime. To get the full path for files in the application bundle, you need to get a pointer to the application bundle and then ask it for the path of a resource.

```
// Get a pointer to the application bundle
NSBundle *applicationBundle = [NSBundle mainBundle];

// Ask for the path to a resource named myImage.png in the bundle
NSString *path = [applicationBundle pathForResource:@"myImage"
                                             ofType:@"png"];
```

If you ask for the path to a file that is not in the application's bundle, this method will return nil. If the file does exist, then the full path is returned, and you can use this path to load the file with the appropriate class.

Also, files within the application bundle are read-only. You cannot modify them nor can you dynamically add files to the application bundle at runtime. Files in the application bundle are typically things like button images, interface sound effects, or the initial state of a database you ship with your application. You will use this method in later chapters to load these types of resources at runtime.

16

Subclassing UITableViewCell

A **UITableView** displays a list of **UITableViewCell**s. For many applications, the basic cell with its textLabel, detailTextLabel, and imageView is sufficient. However, when you need a cell with more detail or a different layout, you subclass **UITableViewCell**.

In this chapter, you will create a custom subclass of **UITableViewCell** to display **Possession** instances more eloquently. Each of these cells will show a **Possession**'s name, its value in dollars, and a thumbnail of its image (Figure 16.1).

Figure 16.1   Homepwner with subclassed UITableViewCells

Open Homepwner.xcodeproj. Create a new **NSObject** subclass and name it **HomepwnerItemCell**. In HomepwnerItemCell.h, change the superclass to **UITableViewCell** and import the header file from UIKit.

```
#import <Foundation/Foundation.h>

#import <UIKit/UIKit.h>

@interface HomepwnerItemCell : UITableViewCell
```

Creating HomepwnerItemCell

UITableViewCell is a **UIView** subclass. When subclassing **UIView** (or any of its subclasses), you typically override its **drawRect:** method to customize the view's appearance. However, when subclassing **UITableViewCell**, you don't change the cell's appearance directly. Each cell has a subview named contentView, which is a container for the view objects that make up the layout of a cell subclass (Figure 16.2). You subclass **UITableViewCell** by changing the view objects in a cell's contentView. For instance, you could create instances of the classes **UITextField**, **UILabel**, and **UIButton** and add them to the contentView. (If you wanted something even more daring, you could create a **UIView** subclass, override its **drawRect:**, and add an instance of it to the contentView.)

Figure 16.2   HomepwnerItemCell hierarchy

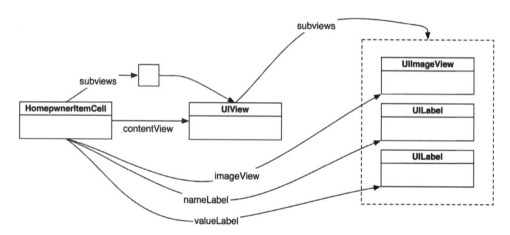

Adding subviews to the contentView instead of directly to the **UITableViewCell** subclass is important because the cell will resize the contentView at certain times. For example, when a table view enters editing mode, the contentView redraws itself to make room for the editing controls (Figure 16.3). If you were to add subviews directly to the **UITableViewCell**, these editing controls would obscure the subviews. The cell doesn't know to adjust its size when entering edit mode, but the contentView does.

Figure 16.3   Table view cell layout in standard and editing mode

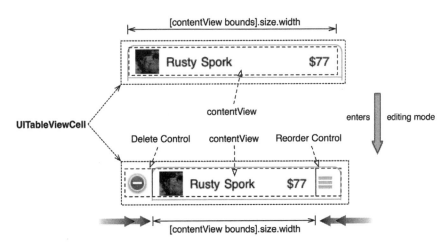

Creating subviews

In your cell subclass, you need an instance variable for each subview so that you can set its content as it is displayed in a table view. In HomepwnerItemCell.h, create instance variables for the necessary subviews.

```
#import <UIKit/UIKit.h>

@interface HomepwnerItemCell : UITableViewCell
{
    UILabel *valueLabel;
    UILabel *nameLabel;
    UIImageView *imageView;
}
@end
```

When an instance of **HomepwnerItemCell** is created, it will instantiate its valueLabel, nameLabel, and imageView. Then, these subviews will be added to the cell's contentView. Override the designated initializer in HomepwnerItemCell.m to do this. HomepwnerItemCell.m should now look like this:

```
#import "HomepwnerItemCell.h"

#import "Possession.h"

@implementation HomepwnerItemCell
- (id)initWithStyle:(UITableViewCellStyle)style
    reuseIdentifier:(NSString *)reuseIdentifier
{
    self = [super initWithStyle:style reuseIdentifier:reuseIdentifier];

    if (self) {
        // Create a subview - don't need to specify its position/size
        valueLabel = [[UILabel alloc] initWithFrame:CGRectZero];

        // Put it on the content view of the cell
```

```
    [[self contentView] addSubview:valueLabel];

    // It is being retained by its superview
    [valueLabel release];

    // Same thing with the name
    nameLabel = [[UILabel alloc] initWithFrame:CGRectZero];
    [[self contentView] addSubview:nameLabel];
    [nameLabel release];

    // Same thing with the image view
    imageView = [[UIImageView alloc] initWithFrame:CGRectZero];
    [[self contentView] addSubview:imageView];

    // Tell the imageview to center its image inside its frame
    [imageView setContentMode:UIViewContentModeCenter];
    [imageView release];
  }

  return self;
}
@end
```

Laying out subviews

When a table view's data source is asked for a cell, it creates a cell, configures its content, and returns it to the table view. The table view then adds the cell as a subview of itself and positions and sizes the cell. Therefore, when you first create a cell, it doesn't know its size quite yet. For this reason, you do not set the frames of a cell's content view at initialization time. Instead, you wait until the cell knows how big it is.

When a view changes size, it is sent the message **layoutSubviews**. Because **UITableViewCell** (and therefore **HomepwnerItemCell**) is a subclass of **UIView**, it also is sent **layoutSubviews** when its size changes.

In HomepwnerItemCell.m, override **layoutSubviews** to give each of the subviews a frame. (If you have a hard time picturing the sizes of frame rectangles in your head, draw them out on a piece of paper first.)

```
- (void)layoutSubviews
{
    // We always call this, the table view cell needs to do its own work first
    [super layoutSubviews];

    // We'll use this to add spacing between borders
    float inset = 5.0;

    // How much space do we have to work with?
    CGRect bounds = [[self contentView] bounds];

    // Let's pull out.of the height and width
    // into easier-to-type variable names
    float h = bounds.size.height;
    float w = bounds.size.width;

    // This will be a constant value for the valueField's width
    float valueWidth = 40.0;
```

```
    // Create a rectangle on the left hand side of the cell for the imageView
    CGRect imageFrame = CGRectMake(inset, inset, 40, 40);
    [imageView setFrame:imageFrame];

    // Create a rectangle in the middle for the name
    CGRect nameFrame = CGRectMake(imageFrame.size.width + imageFrame.origin.x + inset,
                                  inset,
                                  w - (h + valueWidth + inset * 4.0),
                                  h - inset * 2.0);
    [nameLabel setFrame:nameFrame];

    // Create a rectangle on the right side of the cell for the value
    CGRect valueFrame = CGRectMake(nameFrame.size.width + nameFrame.origin.x + inset,
                                   inset,
                                   valueWidth,
                                   h - inset * 2.0);
    [valueLabel setFrame:valueFrame];
}
```

This method is fairly ugly, but let's look at it more closely. First, you always invoke the superclass' implementation of **layoutSubviews**. Invoking this method allows the **UITableViewCell** to layout its subview, the contentView. Then, you get the bounds of the contentView to find out how much area you have to work with when sizing and positioning all of the subviews. (If you don't invoke the superclass' implementation of **layoutSubviews**, the bounds of the contentView may not be correct.) Finally, you set the frame of each subview relative to the contentView's bounds. This process ensures that instances of **HomepwnerItemCell** will have an appropriate layout regardless of the size of the **UITableViewCell**.

Using the custom cell

Now let's look at the two options for setting the content of the subviews (imageView, nameLabel, and valueLabel). The first option is to create a property for each subview to use when you set the cell content in **tableView:cellForRowAtIndexPath:** (like you are currently accessing the textLabel property of each cell). The second option is to pass the cell an instance of **Possession** and have it fill its own subviews. In this chapter, you will use the second option. Either way is perfectly reasonable; however, in the second option, the **HomepwnerItemCell** is made specifically to represent a **Possession** instance, so the code is written in a way that's easier to follow. (The drawback is that **HomepwnerItemCell** will only be able to represent **Possession** instances.)

In HomepwnerItemCell.m, implement the method **setPossession:** to extract values from a **Possession** instance and display them in the cell.

```
- (void)setPossession:(Possession *)possession
{
    // Using a Possession instance, we can set the values of the subviews
    [valueLabel setText:
        [NSString stringWithFormat:@"$%d", [possession valueInDollars]]];
    [nameLabel setText:[possession possessionName]];
}
```

Note that we're not setting the imageView yet. We'll get to that in the next section.

Also, declare **setPossession:** in HomepwnerItemCell.h:

```
@class Possession;

@interface HomepwnerItemCell : UITableViewCell
{
    UILabel *valueLabel;
    UILabel *nameLabel;
    UIImageView *imageView;
}
- (void)setPossession:(Possession *)possession;
@end
```

You can build the application to make sure there are no compile errors. Running it won't show anything new because you aren't yet returning **HomepwnerItemCell**s from the **UITableView** data source method implemented by **ItemsViewController**. In ItemsViewController.m, import the header file for **HomepwnerItemCell**.

```
#import "HomepwnerItemCell.h"

@implementation ItemsViewController
```

In ItemsViewController.m, update the method **tableView:cellForRowAtIndexPath:** to return instances of your new cell subclass.

```
- (UITableViewCell *)tableView:(UITableView *)tableView
        cellForRowAtIndexPath:(NSIndexPath *)indexPath
{
    // Get instance of a HomepwnerItemCell - either an unused one or a new one.
    // The method returns a UITableViewCell; we typecast it as a HomepwnerItemCell.
    HomepwnerItemCell *cell = (HomepwnerItemCell *)[tableView
                        dequeueReusableCellWithIdentifier:@"HomepwnerItemCell"];

    if (!cell) {
        cell = [[[HomepwnerItemCell alloc]
                    initWithStyle:UITableViewCellStyleDefault
                    reuseIdentifier:@"HomepwnerItemCell"] autorelease];
    }

    NSArray *possessions = [[PossessionStore defaultStore] allPossessions];
    Possession *p = [possessions objectAtIndex:[indexPath row]];

    // Instead of setting each label directly, we pass it a possession object
    // it knows how to configure its own subviews
    [cell setPossession:p];

    return cell;
}
```

Notice that the **dequeueReusableCellWithIdentifier:** method returns a **UITableViewCell** that we typecast as a **HomepwnerItemCell** because we know that's what we're getting back. Remember that typecasting does not change anything about the object; it only helps the compiler know what messages are valid.

Image Manipulation

To display an image within a cell, you could just resize the large image of the possession from the image store. However, doing so would incur a performance penalty because a large number of bytes would need to be read, filtered, and resized to fit within the cell. A better idea is to create and use a thumbnail of the image instead.

To create a thumbnail of a **Possession** image, you are going to draw a scaled-down version of the full image to an offscreen context and keep a pointer to that new image inside a **Possession** instance. You'll create this thumbnail when you take a photo and save the image for a **Possession**. However, this application will only create a thumbnail when an image is taken, and, if the user exits the application, the thumbnails will be lost. Therefore, you need a place to store this thumbnail image so that it can be reloaded when the application launches again.

In Chapter 13, we put the full-sized images in the **ImageStore** so that they can be flushed if necessary. However, the thumbnail images will be small enough that we can archive them with the other **Possession** instance variables.

Big problem, though: the thumbnail will be an instance of **UIImage**. **UIImage** doesn't conform to the NSCoding protocol, so you can't encode the thumbnail directly in an **NSCoder**. What you can do is encode the thumbnail as data (JPEG format) and wrap it in an **NSData** object, which does conform to NSCoding.

Open Possession.h. Declare two instance variables: a **UIImage** and an **NSData**. You will also want methods to turn a full-sized image into a thumbnail and another to return the desired thumbnail size.

```
@interface Possession : NSObject <NSCoding> {
    NSString *possessionName;
    NSString *serialNumber;
    int valueInDollars;
    NSDate *dateCreated;
    NSString *imageKey;

    UIImage *thumbnail;
    NSData *thumbnailData;
}
+ (CGSize)thumbnailSize;

@property (readonly) UIImage *thumbnail;

- (void)setThumbnailDataFromImage:(UIImage *)image;
```

In Possession.m, create a getter method for thumbnail that will create it from the data if necessary:

```
- (UIImage *)thumbnail
{
    // Am I imageless?
    if (!thumbnailData) {
        return nil;
    }

    // Is there no cached thumbnail image?
    if (!thumbnail) {

        // Create the image from the data
        thumbnail = [[UIImage imageWithData:thumbnailData] retain];
    }
    return thumbnail;
}
```

Also in `Possession.m`, implement the class method that returns the size of a thumbnail.

```
+ (CGSize)thumbnailSize
{
    return CGSizeMake(40, 40);
}
```

Both objects (the **UIImage** and the **NSData**) will be retained, so you need to send them **release** messages when a **Possession** instance is deallocated.

```
- (void)dealloc
{
    [thumbnail release];
    [thumbnailData release];
    [possessionName release];
    [serialNumber release];
    [dateCreated release];
    [imageKey release];
    [super dealloc];
}
```

Now let's turn to the **setThumbnailDataFromImage:** method. This method will take a full-sized image, create a smaller representation of it in an offscreen context object, and set the `thumbnail` pointer to the image produced by the offscreen context.

iOS provides a convenient suite of functions to create offscreen contexts and produce images from them. To create an offscreen image context, you use the function **UIGraphicsBeginImageContextWithOptions**. This function accepts a CGSize structure that specifies the width and height of the image context, a scaling factor, and whether the image should be opaque. When this function is called, a new **CGContextRef** is created and becomes the current context.

To draw to a **CGContextRef**, you use Core Graphics, just as though you were implementing a **drawRect:** method for a **UIView** subclass. To get a **UIImage** from the context after it has been drawn, you call the function **UIGraphicsGetImageFromCurrentImageContext**.

Once you have produced an image from an image context, you must clean up the context with the function **UIGraphicsEndImageContext**.

In `Possession.m`, implement the following methods to create a thumbnail using an offscreen context.

```
// Private setter
- (void)setThumbnail:(UIImage *)image
{
    [image retain];
    [thumbnail release];
    thumbnail = image;
}

// Private setter
- (void)setThumbnailData:(NSData *)d
{
    [d retain];
    [thumbnailData release];
    thumbnailData = d;
}
```

```
- (void)setThumbnailDataFromImage:(UIImage *)image
{
    CGSize origImageSize = [image size];

    CGRect newRect;
    newRect.origin = CGPointZero;
    newRect.size = [[self class] thumbnailSize];

    // How do we scale the image?
    float ratio = MAX(newRect.size.width/origImageSize.width,
                      newRect.size.height/origImageSize.height);

    // Create a bitmap image context
    UIGraphicsBeginImageContext(newRect.size);

    // Round the corners
    UIBezierPath *path = [UIBezierPath bezierPathWithRoundedRect:newRect
                                                   cornerRadius:5.0];
    [path addClip];

    // Into what rectangle shall I composite the image?
    CGRect projectRect;
    projectRect.size.width = ratio * origImageSize.width;
    projectRect.size.height = ratio * origImageSize.height;
    projectRect.origin.x = (newRect.size.width - projectRect.size.width) / 2.0;
    projectRect.origin.y = (newRect.size.height - projectRect.size.height) / 2.0;

    // Draw the image on it
    [image drawInRect:projectRect];

    // Get the image from the image context, retain it as our thumbnail
    UIImage *small = UIGraphicsGetImageFromCurrentImageContext();
    [self setThumbnail:small];

    // Get the image as a PNG data
    NSData *data = UIImagePNGRepresentation(small);
    [self setThumbnailData:data];

    // Cleanup image contex resources, we're done
    UIGraphicsEndImageContext();
}
```

In ItemDetailViewController.m, add the following line of code to
imagePickerController:didFinishPickingMediaWithInfo: to create a thumbnail when the camera
takes the original image.

```
- (void)imagePickerController:(UIImagePickerController *)picker
didFinishPickingMediaWithInfo:(NSDictionary *)info
{
    NSString *oldKey = [possession imageKey];

    if (oldKey) {

        // Delete the old image
        [[ImageStore defaultImageStore] deleteImageForKey:oldKey];
    }
    UIImage *image = [info objectForKey:UIImagePickerControllerOriginalImage];
```

```
    CFUUIDRef newUniqueID = CFUUIDCreate (kCFAllocatorDefault);

    CFStringRef newUniqueIDString =
                CFUUIDCreateString (kCFAllocatorDefault, newUniqueID);

    [possession setImageKey:(NSString *)newUniqueIDString];

    CFRelease(newUniqueIDString);
    CFRelease(newUniqueID);

    [[ImageStore defaultImageStore] setImage:image
                                      forKey:[possession imageKey]];

    [imageView setImage:image];

    [possession setThumbnailDataFromImage:image];

    // Take image picker off the screen
    [self dismissModalViewControllerAnimated:YES];
}
```

In HomepwnerItemCell.m, add the following line of code to **setPossession:** to use this thumbnail to set the imageView of the cells when they are configured for the table view.

```
- (void)setPossession:(Possession *)possession
{
    [valueLabel setText:
            [NSString stringWithFormat:@"$%d", [possession valueInDollars]]];
    [nameLabel setText:[possession possessionName]];
    [imageView setImage:[possession thumbnail]];
}
```

In HomepwnerItemCell.m, edit the **layoutSubviews** method to set the imageView's frame according to the **Possession**'s desired thumbnail size.

```
    float valueWidth = 40.0;
    CGSize thumbnailSize = [Possession thumbnailSize];
    float imageSpace = h - thumbnailSize.height;
    CGRect imageFrame = CGRectMake(inset, imageSpace / 2.0,
                                   thumbnailSize.width,
                                   thumbnailSize.height);
    [imageView setFrame:imageFrame];
```

Now build and run the application. Take a picture for a **Possession** instance and return to the table view. That row will display a thumbnail image along with the name and value of the **Possession**.

Don't forget to add the thumbnail data to your archive! Open Possession.m:

```
- (id)initWithCoder:(NSCoder *)decoder
{
    self = [super init];

    if (self) {
        [self setPossessionName:[decoder decodeObjectForKey:@"possessionName"]];
        [self setSerialNumber:[decoder decodeObjectForKey:@"serialNumber"]];
        [self setValueInDollars:[decoder decodeIntForKey:@"valueInDollars"]];
        [self setImageKey:[decoder decodeObjectForKey:@"imageKey"]];
        dateCreated = [[decoder decodeObjectForKey:@"dateCreated"] retain];

        thumbnailData = [[decoder decodeObjectForKey:@"thumbnailData"] retain];
```

```
    }
    return self;
}
- (void)encodeWithCoder:(NSCoder *)encoder
{
    // For each instance variable, archive it under its variable name
    [encoder encodeObject:possessionName forKey:@"possessionName"];
    [encoder encodeObject:serialNumber forKey:@"serialNumber"];
    [encoder encodeInt:valueInDollars forKey:@"valueInDollars"];
    [encoder encodeObject:dateCreated forKey:@"dateCreated"];
    [encoder encodeObject:imageKey forKey:@"imageKey"];

    [encoder encodeObject:thumbnailData forKey:@"thumbnailData"];
}
```

Build and run the application. Take some photos of possessions and then exit and relaunch the application. The thumbnails will now appear for saved possession objects.

Challenge: Accessory Indicators

HomepwnerItemCell only displays three properties of a Possession instance. To show all of a Possession's properties, create two different display modes: one that shows the serial number and the creation date of a Possession and another that shows the name and value in dollars. Then give HomepwnerItemCell an accessory indicator that, when tapped, will toggle between the two different display modes.

Challenge: Shrinking the Main Image

When moving from the list of Possessions presented by the ItemsViewController to the detailed view of the ItemDetailViewController, you may notice a considerable stutter in the animation. This stutter is due to the large size of image that has to be loaded and drawn. To get rid of the stutter, when an image is added to the cache for the first time, shrink the image to a more manageable size.

17

Core Data

There are a few different approaches to saving and loading for iOS applications. When deciding between them, the first question is typically "Local or remote?" If you want to save data to a remote server, this is typically done with a web service. Web services are covered in Chapter 25, so let's assume that you want to store data locally. The next question is typically "Archiving or Core Data?"

At the moment, Homepwner uses keyed archiving to save possession data to the filesystem. The biggest drawback to archiving is its all-or-nothing nature: to access anything in the archive, you must unarchive the entire file; to save any changes, you must rewrite the entire file. Core Data, on the other hand, can fetch a small subset of the stored objects. And if you change any of those objects, you can update just that part of the file. This incremental fetching, updating, deleting, and inserting can radically improve the performance of your application when you have a lot of model objects being shuttled between the filesystem and RAM.

Object-Relational Mapping

Core Data is a framework that provides *object-relational mapping*. In other words, Core Data can turn Objective-C objects into data that is stored in a SQLite database file and vice-versa. SQLite is a relational database that is stored in a single file. (Technically, SQLite is the library that manages the database file, but we use the word to mean both the file and the library.) It is important to note that SQLite is not a full-fledged relational database server like Oracle, MySQL or SQLServer, which are their own applications that clients can connect to over a network.

Core Data gives us the ability to fetch and store data in a relational database without having to know SQL. However, you do have to understand a bit about how relational databases work. This chapter will give you that understanding while replacing keyed archiving with Core Data in Homepwner's `PossessionStore`. (If you'd like more help understanding relational data, we suggest reading Joe Celko's *SQL for Smarties*.)

Moving Homepwner to Core Data

Your Homepwner application currently uses archiving to save and reload its data. For a moderately sized object model (say, under 1000 objects), this is fine. As your object model gets larger, however, you will want to be able to do incremental fetches and updates, and Core Data can do this.

The very first step is to add the Core Data framework to your project. Select the Homepwner target and under Build Phases, open the Link Binary With Libraries build phase. Click the + button to add the Core Data framework.

Figure 17.1   Add Core Data framework

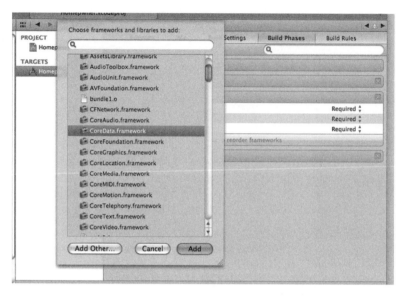

The model file

In a relational database, we have something called a *table*. A table represents some type; You can have a table of people, a table of a credit card purchases, or a table of real-estate listings. Each table has a number of columns to hold a piece of information about that thing. A table that represents people might have a column for the person's name, social security number, height, and age. Every row in the table represents a single person.

Figure 17.2   Role of Core Data

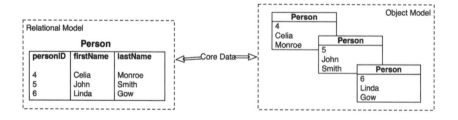

This organization translates well to Objective-C. Every table is like an Objective-C class. Every column is one of the class' instance variables. Every row is one of the instances of that class. Thus, Core Data's job is to move data to and from these two organizations (Figure 17.2).

Core Data uses different terminology to describe these ideas of table/class, column/instance variable and row/object. A table is called a *entity*. The instance variables are called *attributes*. A Core Data model file is the description of every entity and their attributes in your application. Therefore, you will describe a **Possession** entity in a model file and give it attributes like possessionName, serialNumber and valueInDollars.

From the File menu, create a new file. Select Core Data and create a new Data Model. Name it Homepwner.xcdatamodeld.

Figure 17.3 Create the model File

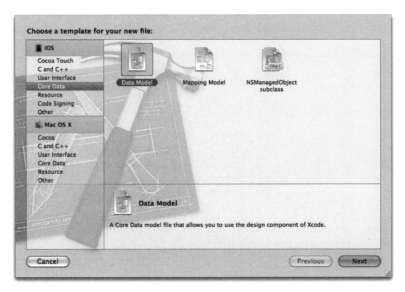

This will create a Homepwner.xcdatamodeld file and add it to your project. Open this file. The editor area will now show the user interface for manipulating a Core Data model file.

Click the Add Entity button near the bottom of the window. A new Entity will appear in the Entities list. Double-click this entity and change its name to **Possession** (Figure 17.4).

Figure 17.4   Create the Possession entity

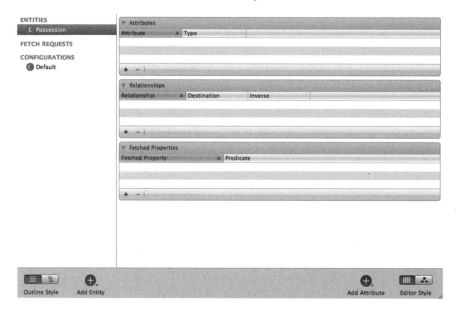

Now you will add attributes to the **Possession** entity, remembering that these will be the instance variables of the **Possession** class. For each attribute, click the + button in the Attributes section and edit the Attribute and Type values for each one:

- possessionName is a String

- serialNumber is a String

- valueInDollars is an Integer 32

- dateCreated is a Date

- imageKey is a String

- thumbnailData is a Binary Data

- thumbnail is an Undefined (It's a **UIImage**, but that isn't one of the possibilities.)

Select thumbnail from the Attributes list and show the data model inspector. Check the box for Transient (Figure 17.5). This means it will not be saved and loaded from the file. You will create it at runtime from the thumbnailData instead.

Figure 17.5   Add attributes to the Possession entity

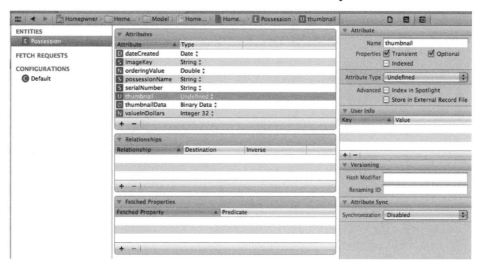

There is one more attribute to add. In Homepwner, users can order their possessions by moving them around in the table view. Archiving possessions in an array naturally respects this order. However, relational tables don't order their rows. Instead, when you fetch a set of rows, you specify their order using one of the attributes ("Fetch me all the **Employee** objects ordered by lastName."). To maintain the order of possessions, you need to create an attribute to record each possession's position in the table view. Then when you fetch possessions, you can ask for them to be ordered by this attribute. (You'll also need to update that attribute when the possessions are reordered.) Create this final attribute: name it orderingValue and make it a Double.

At this point, your model file is sufficient to save and load possessions. However, one of the benefits to using Core Data is that entities can be related to one another. In this exercise, you will add a new entity called **AssetType**, which describes a category for the possessions. For example, a painting might be of the Art asset type. Of course, **AssetType** will be an entity in the model file, and each row of that table will be mapped to an Objective-C object at runtime. Every **Possession** will have a pointer to its **AssetType** object, and every **AssetType** will have a list of the **Possession**s that fall into its category.

Figure 17.6   Entities

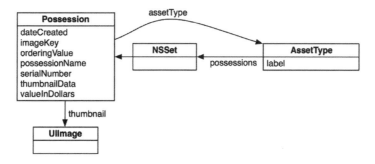

Create a new entity called **AssetType**.

Figure 17.7   Create the AssetType entity

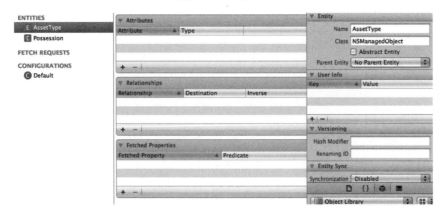

Add an attribute called label of type String to **AssetType**. This will be the name of the category the **AssetType** represents.

Now, you need to establish the relationship between **AssetType** and **Possession**. There are two kinds of relationships: *to-many* and *to-one*. When an entity has a to-one relationship, each instance of that entity will have a pointer to an instance in the entity it has a relationship to. For example, the **Possession** entity will have a to-one relationship to the **AssetType** entity. Thus, a **Possession** instance will have a pointer to its **AssetType** instance.

The **AssetType** entity, on the other hand, will have a to-many relationship to **Possession** since many **Possession**s can be of the same **AssetType** type. With these relationships, we can ask an **AssetType** object for a set of all of the **Possession**s that fall into its category, and we can ask a **Possession** which **AssetType** it falls under.

Let's add these relationships. Select the AssetType entity and then click the + button in the Relationships section. Name the relationship possessions in the Relationship column. Then, select Possession from the Destination column. In the data model inspector, check the box for To-Many Relationship (Figure 17.8).

Figure 17.8   Create the possessions relationship

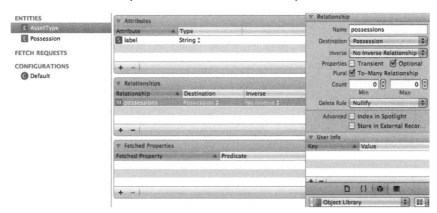

Now go back to the **Possession** entity. Add a relationship named assetType and pick AssetType as its destination. In the Inverse column, select possessions (Figure 17.9).

Figure 17.9   Create the assetType relationship

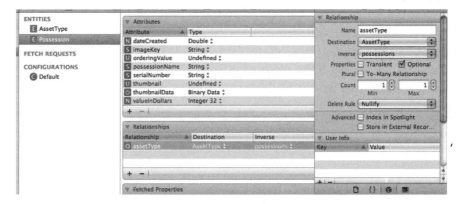

One final note on terminology: In the language of entity-relationship modeling, the attributes and relationships of an entity are collectively known as its *properties*.

NSManagedObject and subclasses

When an object is fetched with Core Data, its class is, by default, **NSManagedObject**. **NSManagedObject** is a subclass of **NSObject** that knows how to cooperate with the rest of Core Data. Therefore, when you fetch an **AssetType** or a **Possession** from Core Data, the object that you get back is an instance of **NSManagedObject**. This can be confusing, since these two entities have different attributes and therefore the classes that represent these entities should have different instance variables. However, **NSManagedObject** works a bit like a dictionary in that it holds arbitrary key-value pairs. Thus, an **NSManagedObject** holds a key-value pair for every property in the entity.

NSManagedObject is little more than a data container. Sometimes, you would like your model objects to *do* something in addition to holding data. For example, the **Possession** class knows how to create a thumbnail from an image. When an objects of a particular entity need to perform custom behavior, you must create a subclass of **NSManagedObject**. Then, in your model file, you must specify that this entity is represented by instances of this subclass, not the standard **NSManagedObject**.

Select the Possession entity. Show the data model inspector and change the Class field to **Possession**, as shown in Figure 17.10. Now, when a **Possession** entity is fetched with Core Data, the type of this object will be **Possession**. (**AssetType** instances will still be of type **NSManagedObject**.)

Figure 17.10   Changing the class of an entity

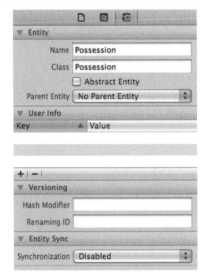

There is one problem: you already have a **Possession** class, and it does not inherit from **NSManagedObject**. Changing the superclass of **Possession** to **NSManagedObject** will require considerable changes. Thus, the easiest solution is to copy the behavior methods from your current **Possession** class, have Core Data generate a new **Possession** class, and then add your behavior methods back in to the new class files.

In Finder, drag both Possession.h and Possession.m to your desktop. Then, in Xcode, delete these two files from the project navigator.

Then, create a new file. Under Core Data, select the NSManagedObject subclass option and hit Next. On the next pane, select the Homepwner data model. On the following pane, select the Possession entity.

Xcode will generate two new files, Possession.h and Possession.m. In Possession.h, change the type of the thumbnail property to **UIImage** and add two method declarations that you had previously implemented in the earlier **Possession**.

```
#import <Foundation/Foundation.h>
#import <CoreData/CoreData.h>

@interface Possession : NSManagedObject {
```

```
@private
}
@property (nonatomic, retain) NSString *serialNumber;
@property (nonatomic, retain) NSNumber *valueInDollars;
@property (nonatomic, retain) UIImage *thumbnail;
@property (nonatomic, retain) NSString *imageKey;
@property (nonatomic, retain) NSDate *dateCreated;
@property (nonatomic, retain) NSString *possessionName;
@property (nonatomic, retain) NSData *thumbnailData;
@property (nonatomic, retain) NSNumber *orderingValue;
@property (nonatomic, retain) NSManagedObject *assetType;

- (void)setThumbnailDataFromImage:(UIImage *)image;
+ (CGSize)thumbnailSize;


@end
```

Next, in Possession.m, copy the **setThumbnailFromImage:** and **thumbnailSize** methods from your old Possession.m to the new one:

```
- (void)setThumbnailDataFromImage:(UIImage *)image
{
    CGSize origImageSize = [image size];

    CGRect newRect;
    newRect.origin = CGPointZero;
    newRect.size = [[self class] thumbnailSize];

    float ratio = MAX(newRect.size.width/origImageSize.width,
                        newRect.size.height/origImageSize.height);

    // Create a bitmap image context
    UIGraphicsBeginImageContext(newRect.size);

    // Round the corners
    UIBezierPath *path = [UIBezierPath bezierPathWithRoundedRect:newRect
                                                    cornerRadius:5.0];
    [path addClip];

    // Into what rectangle shall I composite the image?
    CGRect projectRect;
    projectRect.size.width = ratio * origImageSize.width;
    projectRect.size.height = ratio * origImageSize.height;
    projectRect.origin.x = (newRect.size.width - projectRect.size.width) / 2.0;
    projectRect.origin.y = (newRect.size.height - projectRect.size.height) / 2.0;

    // Draw the image on it
    [image drawInRect:projectRect];

    // Get the image from the image context, retain it as our thumbnail
    UIImage *small = UIGraphicsGetImageFromCurrentImageContext();
    [self setThumbnail:small];

    // Get the image as a PNG data
    NSData *data = UIImagePNGRepresentation(small);
    [self setThumbnailData:data];

    // Cleanup image contex resources, we're done
    UIGraphicsEndImageContext();
```

```
}

+ (CGSize)thumbnailSize
{
    return CGSizeMake(40, 40);
}
```

The thumbnail attribute is not going to be saved – it is a transient attribute. You'll need to update thumbnail from the thumbnailData when the object first emerges from the filesystem. When Homepwner used keyed archiving, we did this in **initWithCoder:**. Now that we're using Core Data, objects are initialized by another Core Data object that handles creating, updating, and deleting **NSManagedObject**s. (You will meet this object in a moment.) Thus, you do not implement **init** methods for **NSManagedObject** subclasses. Instead, if you want to configure an object after it has been created, you override the method **awakeFromFetch**. Implement this method in Possession.m to set the thumbnail from the thumbnailData (which is saved).

```
- (void)awakeFromFetch
{
    [super awakeFromFetch];

    UIImage *tn = [UIImage imageWithData:[self thumbnailData]];
    [self setPrimitiveValue:tn forKey:@"thumbnail"];
}
```

As mentioned earlier, an instance of **NSManagedObject** works like a dictionary – it can hold a large number of key-value pairs. The method **setPrimitiveValue:forKey:** works like **setObject:forKey:** of **NSMutableDictionary**. One of the amazing and delightful things about Core Data is that instances of **NSManagedObject** can dynamically create accessor methods as they are called. It will also automatically create methods for primitive access. For example, the following also would have worked:

```
- (void)awakeFromFetch
{
    [super awakeFromFetch];

    UIImage *tn = [UIImage imageWithData:[self thumbnailData]];

    // At runtime, setPrimitiveThumbnail: will be created when first called
    [self setPrimitiveThumbnail:tn];
}
```

However, we would have received a warning from the compiler because it has no declaration of this method.

Of course, when you first launch an application, there are no saved **Possession**s or **AssetType**s. When the user creates a new **Possession** instance, it will be added to the database. When objects are added to the database, they are sent the message **awakeFromInsert**. Here is where you will set the dateCreated instance variable of a **Possession**. Implement this method in Possession.m.

```
- (void)awakeFromInsert
{
    [super awakeFromInsert];
    [self setDateCreated:[NSDate date]];
}
```

Updating PossessionStore

The portal through which you talk to the database is the **NSManagedObjectContext**. The **NSManagedObjectContext** uses an **NSPersistentStoreCoordinator**. You ask the persistent store coordinator to open a SQLite database at a particular filename. The persistent store coordinator uses the model file in the form of an instance of **NSManagedObjectModel**.

Figure 17.11   PossessionStore and NSManagedObjectContext

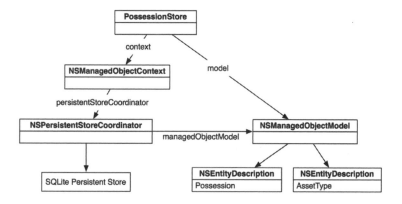

In PossessionStore.h, add instance variables and import Core Data. Also, create a method for getting all the **AssetType** objects:

```
#import <CoreData/CoreData.h>

@class Possession;

@interface PossessionStore : NSObject
{
    NSMutableArray *allPossessions;
    NSMutableArray *allAssetTypes;
    NSManagedObjectContext *context;
    NSManagedObjectModel *model;
}

+ (PossessionStore *)defaultStore;
- (BOOL)saveChanges;

#pragma mark Possessions
- (NSArray *)allPossessions;
- (Possession *)createPossession;
- (void)removePossession:(Possession *)p;
```

```
- (void)movePossessionAtIndex:(int)from toIndex:(int)to;

#pragma mark Asset types
- (NSArray *)allAssetTypes;

@end
```

This is the first time you've seen the #pragma mark construct. Objective-C programmers often use this to group methods. It isn't used by the compiler at all – rather, Xcode notes it when it creates the pop-up at the top of the editor (Figure 17.12).

Figure 17.12   #pragma mark in popup

When the **PossessionStore** is initialized, it needs to set up the **NSManagedObjectContext** and **NSPersistentStoreCoordinator**. The persistent store coordinator needs to know two things: "What are all of my entities and their attribute and relationships?" and "Where am I saving and loading data from?" Therefore, you will create an instance of **NSManagedObjectModel** to hold the entity information from Homepwner.xcdatamodeld and initialize the persistent store coordinator with this object. Then, you will create the instance of **NSManagedObjectContext** and specify that it use this persistent store coordinator to save and load objects. Update **init** in PossessionStore.m.

```
- (id)init
{
    if (defaultStore) {
        return defaultStore;
    }

    self = [super init];

    // Read in Homepwner.xcdatamodeld
    model = [[NSManagedObjectModel mergedModelFromBundles:nil] retain];
    // NSLog(@"model = %@", model);

    NSPersistentStoreCoordinator *psc =
        [[NSPersistentStoreCoordinator alloc] initWithManagedObjectModel:model];

    // Where does the SQLite file go?
    NSString *path = pathInDocumentDirectory(@"store.data");
    NSURL *storeURL = [NSURL fileURLWithPath:path];

    NSError *error = nil;
```

```
    if (![psc addPersistentStoreWithType:NSSQLiteStoreType
                           configuration:nil
                                     URL:storeURL
                                 options:nil
                                   error:&error]) {
        [NSException raise:@"Open failed"
                    format:@"Reason: %@", [error localizedDescription]];
    }

    // Create the managed object context
    context = [[NSManagedObjectContext alloc] init];
    [context setPersistentStoreCoordinator:psc];
    [psc release];

    // The managed object context can manage undo, but we don't need it
    [context setUndoManager:nil];

    return self;
}
```

Before, **PossessionStore** would write out the entire **NSMutableArray** of **Possession**s when you asked it to save using keyed archiving. Now, you will have it send the message **save:** to the **NSManagedObjectContext**. The context will update all of the records in store.data with any changes since the last time it was saved. Change this method in PossessionStore.m.

```
- (BOOL)saveChanges
{
    NSError *err = nil;
    BOOL successful = [context save:&err];
    if (!successful) {
        NSLog(@"Error saving: %@", [err localizedDescription]);
    }
    return successful;
}
```

Note that this method is already called when the application is moved to the background.

In this application, we will fetch all of the **Possession**s in store.data the first time we need to use them. In order to get objects back from the **NSManagedObjectContext**, you must prepare and execute an **NSFetchRequest**. After a fetch request is executed, you will get an array of all the objects that match the parameters of that request.

A fetch request needs an entity description that defines which entity you want to get objects from. In order to fetch **Possession** instances, you specify the **Possession** entity. You can also set the request's *sort descriptors*, which specify the order of the objects in the array. A sort descriptor has a key that maps to an attribute of the entity and a BOOL that indicates if the order should be ascending or descending. You will sort the returned **Possession**s by their orderingValue in ascending order. Replace the **fetchPossessionsIfNecessary** method in PossessionStore.m.

```
- (void)fetchPossessionsIfNecessary
{
    if (!allPossessions) {
        NSFetchRequest *request = [[[NSFetchRequest alloc] init] autorelease];

        NSEntityDescription *e = [[model entitiesByName] objectForKey:@"Possession"];
        [request setEntity:e];
```

```
    NSSortDescriptor *sd = [NSSortDescriptor
                            sortDescriptorWithKey:@"orderingValue"
                                        ascending:YES];
    [request setSortDescriptors:[NSArray arrayWithObject:sd]];

    NSError *error;
    NSArray *result = [context executeFetchRequest:request error:&error];
    if (!result) {
        [NSException raise:@"Fetch failed"
                    format:@"Reason: %@", [error localizedDescription]];
    }

    allPossessions = [[NSMutableArray alloc] initWithArray:result];
    }
}
```

In this application, you immediately fetched all the instances of the **Possession** entity. This is a relatively simple case. In an application with a much larger data set, you would carefully fetch just the instances you needed. You would add a *predicate* (an **NSPredicate**) to your fetch request, and only the objects that satisfied the predicate would be returned.

A predicate contains a condition which can be true or false. For example, if you only wanted the possessions worth more than $50, you would create a predicate and add it to the fetch request like this:

```
NSPredicate *p = [NSPredicate predicateWithFormat:@"valueInDollars > 50"];
[request setPredicate:p];
```

The format string for a predicate can be very long and complex. Apple's *Predicate Programming Guide* is a complete discussion of what is possible.

Predicates can also be used to filter the contents of an array. So, even if you had already fetched the allPossessions array, you could still use a predicate:

```
NSArray *expensiveStuff = [allPossessions filteredArrayUsingPredicate:p];
```

This handles saving and loading, but what about adding and deleting? When the user wants to create a new **Possession**, you will not allocate and initialize this new **Possession**. Instead, you will ask the **NSManagedObjectContext** to insert a new object from the **Possession** entity. It will then return an instance of **Possession**. In PossessionStore.m, edit the **createPossession** method.

```
- (Possession *)createPossession
{
    // Ensure the array is initialized
    [self fetchPossessionsIfNecessary];

    double order;
    if ([allPossessions count] == 0) {
        order = 1.0;
    } else {
        order = [[[allPossessions lastObject] orderingValue] doubleValue] + 1.0;
    }
    NSLog(@"Adding after %d items, order = %.2f",[allPossessions count], order);

    Possession *p = [NSEntityDescription insertNewObjectForEntityForName:@"Possession"
                                           inManagedObjectContext:context];
```

```
[p setOrderingValue:[NSNumber numberWithDouble:order]];

    [allPossessions addObject:p];

    return p;
}
```

When a user deletes a **Possession**, you must inform the context so that it is removed from the database when saved. Add the following code to PossessionStore.m's **removePossession:** method.

```
- (void)removePossession:(Possession *)p
{
    NSString *key = [p imageKey];
    [[ImageStore defaultImageStore] deleteImageForKey:key];
    [context deleteObject:p];
    [allPossessions removeObjectIdenticalTo:p];
}
```

The last bit of functionality you need to replace for **Possession** is the ability to re-order **Possession**s in the **PossessionStore**. Because Core Data will not handle ordering automatically, we must update a **Possession**'s orderingValue every time it is moved in the table view.

This would get rather complicated if the orderingValue was an integer: every time a **Possession** was placed in a new index, we would have to change the orderingValue's of other **Possession**s. Instead, orderingValue is a double. We can then take the orderingValues of the **Possession** that will be before and after the moving possession, add them together, and divide by two. Thus, the new orderingValue will fall directly in between the values of the **Possession**s that surround it. Modify **movePossessionAtIndex:toIndex:** in PossessionStore.m.

```
- (void)movePossessionAtIndex:(int)from
                      toIndex:(int)to
{
    if (from == to) {
        return;
    }
    // Get pointer to object being moved
    Possession *p = [allPossessions objectAtIndex:from];

    // Retain it so it doesn't get dealloced while out of array
    [p retain];

    // Remove p from our array
    [allPossessions removeObjectAtIndex:from];

    // Re-insert p into array at new location
    [allPossessions insertObject:p atIndex:to];

    // Computing a new orderValue for the object that was moved
    double lowerBound = 0.0;

    // Is there an object before it in the array?
    if (to > 0) {
        lowerBound = [[[allPossessions objectAtIndex:to - 1]
                                        orderingValue] doubleValue];
    } else {
        lowerBound = [[[allPossessions objectAtIndex:1]
                                        orderingValue] doubleValue] - 2.0;
    }
```

305

```
    double upperBound = 0.0;

    // Is there an object after it in the array?
    if (to < [allPossessions count] - 1) {
        upperBound = [[[allPossessions objectAtIndex:to + 1]
                                       orderingValue] doubleValue];
    } else {
        upperBound = [[[allPossessions objectAtIndex:to - 1]
                                       orderingValue] doubleValue] + 2.0;
    }

    // The order value will be the midpoint between the lower and upper bounds
    NSNumber *n = [NSNumber numberWithDouble:(lowerBound + upperBound)/2.0];

    NSLog(@"moving to order %@", newOrderValue);
    [p setOrderingValue:n];

    // Release p (retain count = 1, only owner is now array)
    [p release];

}
```

One last detail. When we moved **Possession** to a subclass of **NSManagedObject**, the valueInDollars property became an instance of **NSNumber** instead of an int. There are three places we still use this instance variable. Update the code in the **viewWillAppear:** method of ItemDetailViewController.m.

```
- (void)viewWillAppear:(BOOL)animated
{
    [super viewWillAppear:animated];

    [nameField setText:[possession possessionName]];
    [serialNumberField setText:[possession serialNumber]];

    if([possession valueInDollars]) {
        // Notice that the format string changed
        [valueField setText:[NSString stringWithFormat:@"%@",
                                        [possession valueInDollars]]];
    } else {
        [valueField setText:@"0"];
    }

    NSDateFormatter *dateFormatter = [[[NSDateFormatter alloc] init] autorelease];
```

In the same file, update **viewWillDisappear:**.

```
- (void)viewWillDisappear:(BOOL)animated
{
    [super viewWillDisappear:animated];

    // End any incomplete editing
    [[self view] endEditing:YES];

    // "Save" changes to possession
    [possession setPossessionName:[nameField text]];
    [possession setSerialNumber:[serialNumberField text]];
    NSNumber *valueNum = [NSNumber numberWithInt:[[valueField text] intValue]];
    [possession setValueInDollars:valueNum];
}
```

And the third and final spot, in `HomepwnerItemCell.m`:

```
- (void)setPossession:(Possession *)possession
{
    // The format string changes again
    [valueLabel setText:[NSString stringWithFormat:@"$%@",
                        [possession valueInDollars]]];
    [nameLabel setText:[possession possessionName]];
    [imageView setImage:[possession thumbnail]];
}
```

Finally, you can build and run your application. Of course, the behavior is the same as it always was, but it is now using Core Data. Now, you need to take care of the new asset type functionality.

Adding AssetTypes to Homepwner

In the model file, you described a new entity, **AssetType**, that every possession will have a to-one relationship to. You need a way for the user to set the **AssetType** of **Possession**s and create new **AssetType**s. Also, the **PossessionStore** will need a way to fetch the **AssetType**s. (Creating new **AssetType**s is left as a challenge.)

In `PossessionStore.h`, declare a new method.

```
- (NSArray *)allAssetTypes;
```

In `PossessionStore.m`, define this method. If this is the first time the application is being run – and therefore there are no **AssetType**s in the store – create three default types.

```
- (NSArray *)allAssetTypes
{
    if (!allAssetTypes) {
        NSFetchRequest *request = [[[NSFetchRequest alloc] init] autorelease];

        NSEntityDescription *e = [[model entitiesByName] objectForKey:@"AssetType"];

        [request setEntity:e];

        NSError *error;
        NSArray *result = [context executeFetchRequest:request error:&error];
        if (!result) {
            [NSException raise:@"Fetch failed"
                        format:@"Reason: %@", [error localizedDescription]];
        }
        allAssetTypes = [result mutableCopy];
    }

    // Is this the first time the program is being run?
    if ([allAssetTypes count] == 0) {
        NSManagedObject *type;

        type = [NSEntityDescription insertNewObjectForEntityForName:@"AssetType"
                                        inManagedObjectContext:context];
        [type setValue:@"Furniture" forKey:@"label"];
        [allAssetTypes addObject:type];

        type = [NSEntityDescription insertNewObjectForEntityForName:@"AssetType"
                                        inManagedObjectContext:context];
```

```
    [type setValue:@"Jewelry" forKey:@"label"];
    [allAssetTypes addObject:type];

    type = [NSEntityDescription insertNewObjectForEntityForName:@"AssetType"
                                    inManagedObjectContext:context];
    [type setValue:@"Electronics" forKey:@"label"];
    [allAssetTypes addObject:type];

    }
    return allAssetTypes;
}
```

Now, you need change the user interface so that the user can see the **AssetType** of the **Possession** in the **ItemDetailViewController** and change it.

Figure 17.13   Interface for AssetType

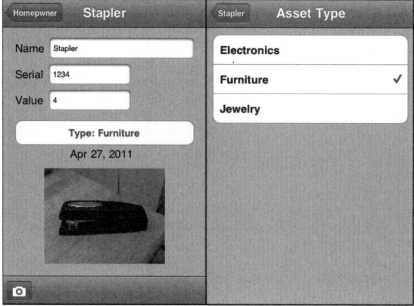

Create a new Objective-C class template file and choose NSObject as the superclass. Name this class **AssetTypePicker**.

In AssetTypePicker.h, change the superclass to **UITableViewController** and give it a **Possession** property.

```
#import <UIKit/UIKit.h>
@class Possession;

@interface AssetTypePicker : UITableViewController
{
    Possession *possession;
}
```

```
@property (nonatomic, retain) Possession *possession;
@end
```

This table view controller will show a list of the available **AssetType**s. Tapping a button on the **ItemDetailViewController**'s view will display it (in a popover on the iPad and in a navigation controller on the iPhone). Implement the data source methods and import the appropriate header files in AssetTypePicker.m.

```
#import "AssetTypePicker.h"
#import "PossessionStore.h"
#import "Possession.h"


@implementation AssetTypePicker

@synthesize possession;

- (id)init
{
    return [super initWithStyle:UITableViewStyleGrouped];
}
- (id)initWithStyle:(UITableViewStyle)style
{
    return [self init];
}
- (void)dealloc
{
    [possession release];
    [super dealloc];
}

- (NSInteger)tableView:(UITableView *)tableView
 numberOfRowsInSection:(NSInteger)section
{
    return [[[PossessionStore defaultStore] allAssetTypes] count];
}

- (UITableViewCell *)tableView:(UITableView *)tableView
        cellForRowAtIndexPath:(NSIndexPath *)ip
{
    UITableViewCell *cell =
        [tableView dequeueReusableCellWithIdentifier:@"UITableViewCell"];
    if (cell == nil) {
        cell = [[[UITableViewCell alloc] initWithStyle:UITableViewCellStyleDefault
                                       reuseIdentifier:@"UITableViewCell"]
                                       autorelease];
    }

    NSArray *allAssets = [[PossessionStore defaultStore] allAssetTypes];
    NSManagedObject *assetType = [allAssets objectAtIndex:[ip row]];

    // Use key-value coding to get the asset type's label
    NSString *assetLabel = [assetType valueForKey:@"label"];
    [[cell textLabel] setText:assetLabel];

    // Checkmark the one that is currently selected
    if (assetType == [possession assetType]) {
        [cell setAccessoryType:UITableViewCellAccessoryCheckmark];
    } else {
```

```
        [cell setAccessoryType:UITableViewCellAccessoryNone];
    }

    return cell;
}

- (void)tableView:(UITableView *)tableView
didSelectRowAtIndexPath:(NSIndexPath *)ip
{
    UITableViewCell *cell = [tableView cellForRowAtIndexPath:ip];

    [cell setAccessoryType:UITableViewCellAccessoryCheckmark];

    NSArray *allAssets = [[PossessionStore defaultStore] allAssetTypes];
    NSManagedObject *assetType = [allAssets objectAtIndex:[ip row]];
    [possession setAssetType:assetType];

    [[self navigationController] popViewControllerAnimated:YES];
}

@end
```

In `ItemDetailViewController.xib`, add a new **UIButton** to the view. Create and connect outlets as shown in Figure 17.14.

Figure 17.14   Add a UIButton

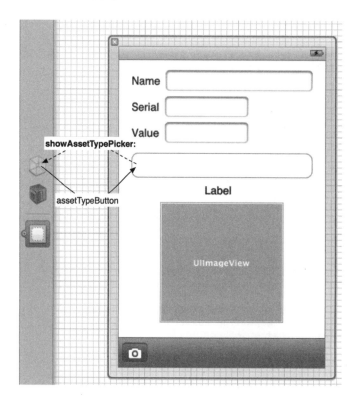

At the top of `ItemDetailViewController.m`, import the header for this new table view controller.

```
#import "ItemDetailViewController.h"

#import "AssetTypePicker.h"
```

Implement **showAssetTypePicker:** in `ItemDetailViewController.m`. (If you generated the action method by Control-dragging from the XIB to the source file, the method will already be entered with an empty body.)

```
- (IBAction)showAssetTypePicker:(id)sender
{
    [[self view] endEditing:YES];

    AssetTypePicker *assetTypePicker = [[[AssetTypePicker alloc] init] autorelease];
    [assetTypePicker setPossession:possession];

    [[self navigationController] pushViewController:assetTypePicker
                                          animated:YES];
}
```

And finally, update the title of the button to show the asset type of a **Possession**. Add the following code to **viewWillAppear:** in `ItemDetailViewController.m`.

```
    if (imageKey) {
        // Get image for image key from image cache
        UIImage *imageToDisplay = [[ImageStore defaultImageStore]
                                             imageForKey:imageKey];

        // Use that imge to put on the screen in imageView
        [imageView setImage:imageToDisplay];
    } else {
        // clear the imageView
        [imageView setImage:nil];
    }
    NSString *typeLabel = [[possession assetType] valueForKey:@"label"];
    if(!typeLabel)
        typeLabel = @"None";

    [assetTypeButton setTitle:[NSString stringWithFormat:@"Type: %@", typeLabel]
                    forState:UIControlStateNormal];
}
```

Build and run the application. Select a **Possession** and set its asset type.

More About SQL

In this chapter, you used SQLite via Core Data. If you're curious about what SQL commands Core Data is executing, you can use a command-line argument to log all communications with the SQLite database to the console. From the Product menu, choose Edit Scheme.... Select the Run Homepwner.app item and the Arguments tab. Add two arguments: -com.apple.CoreData.SQLDebug and 1.

Figure 17.15   Turning on Core Data logging

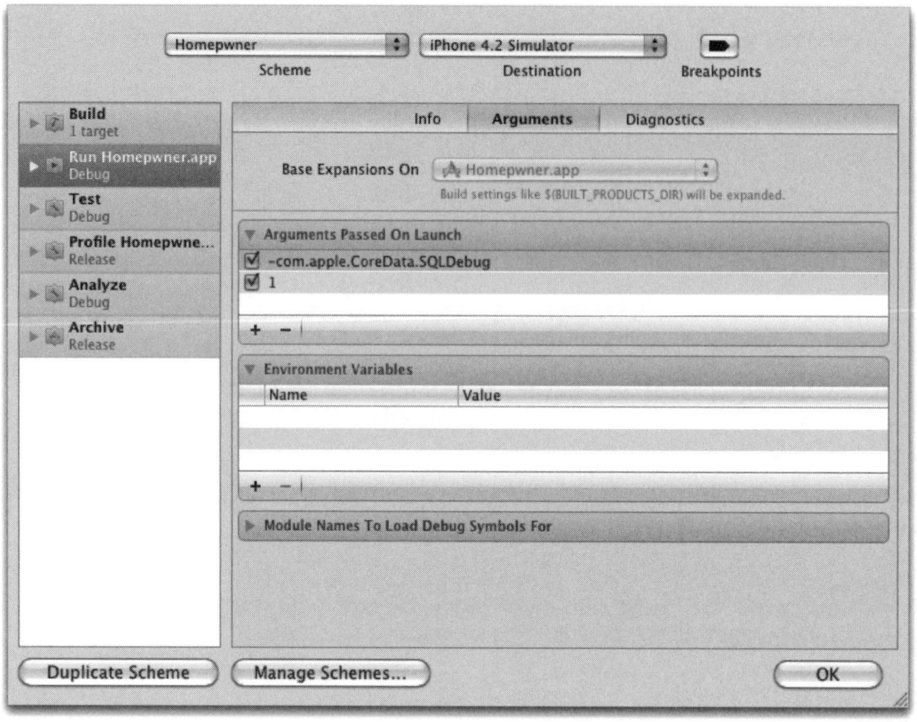

[Xcode scheme editor screenshot]

Build and run the application again. Make sure the debug area and console are visible so you can see the SQL logging. Add a few locations and inventory items; then navigate around the application looking at various items.

Relationships are fetched in a lazy manner. When you fetch a managed object with relationships, the objects at the other end of those relationship are *not* fetched. Instead, Core Data uses *faults*. There are to-many faults (which stand in for sets) and to-one faults (which stand in for managed objects). So, for example, when the instances of **Possession** are fetched into your application, the instances of **AssetType** are not. Instead, fault objects are created that stand in for the **AssetType** objects until they are really needed.

Figure 17.16   Object faults

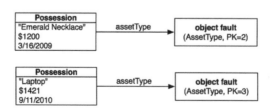

An object fault knows what entity it is from and what its primary key is. So, for example, when you ask a fault that represents an asset type what its label is, you'll see SQL executed that looks something like this:

```
SELECT t0.Z_PK, t0.Z_OPT, t0.ZLABEL FROM ZASSETTYPE t0 WHERE t0.Z_PK = 2
```

(Why is everything prefixed with Z_? I don't know. What is OPT? I don't know, but I would guess it is short for "optimistic locking". These details are not important.) The fault is replaced, in the exact same location in memory, with a managed object containing the real data.

Figure 17.17   After one fault is replaced

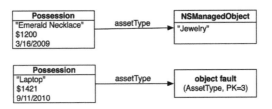

This lazy fetching makes Core Data not only easy to use, but also quite efficient.

What about to-many faults? Imagine that your application worked the other way: the user is presented with a list of **AssetType** objects to select from. Then, the possessions for that asset type are fetched and displayed. How would this work? When the assets are first fetched, each one has a set fault that is standing in for the **NSSet** of possession objects:

Figure 17.18   Set faults

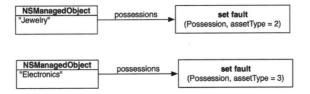

When the set fault is sent a message that requires the **Possession** objects, it fetches them and replaces itself with an **NSSet**:

Figure 17.19   Set faults

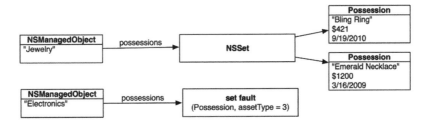

Core Data is a very powerful and flexible persistence framework, and this chapter has been just a quick introduction to its capabilities. For more details, we strongly suggest that you read Apple's *Core Data Programming Guide*. Here are some of the things we have not delved into:

- **NSFetchRequest** is a powerful mechanism for specifying data you want from the persistent store. We used it a little, but you will want to go deeper. You should also explore the following related classes: **NSPredicate**, **NSSortOrdering**, **NSExpressionDescription**, and **NSExpression**. Also, fetch request templates can be created as part of the model file.

- A *fetched property* is a little like a to-many relationship and a little like an **NSFetchRequest**. You typically specify them in the model file.

- As your app evolves from version to version, you'll need to change the data model over time. This can be tricky – in fact, Apple has an entire book about it: *Data Model Versioning and Data Migration Programming Guide*.

- There is good support for validating data as it goes into your instances of **NSManagedObject** and again as it moves from your managed object into the persistent store.

- You can have a single **NSManagedObjectContext** working with more than one persistent store. You partition your model into *configurations* and then assign each configuration to a particular persistent store. You are not allowed to have relationships between entities in different stores, but you can use fetched properties to achieve a similar result.

Trade-offs of Persistence Mechanisms

At this point, you can start thinking about the tradeoffs between the common ways that iOS applications can store their data Which is best for your application? Use Table 17.1 to help you decide.

Table 17.1. Data storage pros and cons

Technique	Pros	Cons
Archiving	Allows ordered relationships (arrays, not sets). Easy to deal with versioning.	Reads all the objects in (no faulting). No incremental updates.
Web Service	Makes it easy to share data with other devices and applications.	Requires a server and a connection to the internet.
Core Data	Lazy fetches by default. Incremental updates.	Versioning is awkward (but can certainly be done using an **NSModelMapping**). No real ordered relationships (at the time this is being written).

Challenge: New Asset Types

Make it possible for the user to add new asset types by adding a button to the **AssetTypePicker**'s `navigationItem`.

Challenge: Assets on the iPad

On the iPad, present the **AssetTypePicker** in a **UIPopoverController**.

18

Localization

The appeal of iOS is global – iOS users live in many different countries and speak many different languages. You can ensure that your application is ready for this global audience through the processes of internationalization and localization. *Internationalization* is making sure your native cultural information is not hard-coded into your application. (By cultural information, we mean language, currency, date formats, number formats, and more.) *Localization*, on the other hand, is providing the appropriate data in your application based on the user's Language and Region Format settings. You can find these settings in the Settings application. Select the General row and then the International row.

Figure 18.1 International Settings

Incredibly, Apple makes these processes simple. An application that takes advantage of the localization APIs does not even need to be recompiled to be distributed in other languages or regions. In this chapter, you're going to localize the possession detail view of Homepwner. (By the way, internationalization and localization are big words. Commonly, they are abbreviated to i18n and L10n, respectively. In order to prevent confusion, I will type out the full words. But you owe me a beer at the next WWDC.)

Internationalization using NSLocale

In this first section, you will use the class **NSLocale** to internationalize the currency symbol for a value of a possession.

NSLocale knows how different regions display symbols, dates, and decimals and whether they use the metric system. An instance of **NSLocale** represents one region's settings for these variables. In the Settings application, the user can choose a region like United States or United Kingdom. (Why does Apple use "region" instead of "country"? Some countries have more than one region with different settings. Scroll through the options in Region Format to see for yourself.)

When you send the message **currentLocale** to **NSLocale**, the instance of **NSLocale** that represents the user's region setting is returned. Once you have a pointer to that instance of **NSLocale**, you can ask it questions like, "What's the currency symbol for this region?" or "Does this region use the metric system?" To ask a question, you send the **NSLocale** instance the message **objectForKey:** with one of the **NSLocale** constants as an argument. (You can find all of these constants in the **NSLocale** documentation page.)

Let's internationalize the currency symbol displayed in each **HomepwnerItemCell**. Open Homepwner.xcodeproj and, in HomepwnerItemCell.m, locate the method **setPossession:**. When the text of the valueLabel is set in this method, the string "$%@" is used, which makes the currency symbol always a dollar sign. Replacing that code with the following will get and display the appropriate currency symbol for the user's region.

```
- (void)setPossession:(Possession *)possession
{
    NSString *currencySymbol = [[NSLocale currentLocale]
                            objectForKey:NSLocaleCurrencySymbol];
    [valueLabel setText:[NSString stringWithFormat:@"%@%@",
                    currencySymbol,
                    [possession valueInDollars]]];

    [nameLabel setText:[possession possessionName]];
    [imageView setImage:[possession thumbnail]];
}
```

Build and run the application. If the currency symbol is the dollar sign in your region, you'll need to change your region format in order to test this code. Exit the Homepwner application and kill it in the dock. Then, in the Settings application, change Region Format to United Kingdom.

Run your application again. This time, you will see values displayed in pounds (£). (Note that this is not a currency conversion from dollars to pounds; you're just replacing the symbol.)

While your region format is set to the UK, check out the date format of the date a possession was created. It's Day Month Year. Now exit and kill Homepwner and change your region to US. Relaunch Homepwner and navigate to a possession's details. The date is now formatted as Month Day, Year. The text for the date label has already been internationalized. When did this happen?

In Chapter 12, you used an instance of **NSDateFormatter** to set the text of the date label of **ItemDetailViewController**. **NSDateFormatter** has a **locale** property, which is set to the device's current locale. Whenever you use an **NSDateFormatter** to create a date, it checks its **locale** property and sets the format accordingly. So the text of the date label has been internationalized from the start.

Localizing Resources

When internationalizing, you ask the instance of **NSLocale** questions. But the **NSLocale** only has a few region-specific variables. This is where localization comes into play: Localization is the process by which application-specific substitutions given a region or a language setting are created. This usually means one of two things:

- generating multiple copies of resources like images, sounds, and interfaces for different regions and languages

- creating and accessing "strings tables" to translate text into different languages

Any resource, whether it's an image or a XIB file, can be localized with just a little work. In this section, you're going to localize one of Homepwner's interfaces: the `ItemDetailViewController.xib` file. Select `ItemDetailViewController.xib` in the project navigator. Then, show the utilities area.

Click the ▣ icon in the inspector selector to open the file inspector. Find the section in the inspector area named Localization and click the + button at the bottom of the section. This signifies to Xcode that this file can be localized and automatically creates an English version of it. Click the + button again and select Spanish. The inspector area should look like Figure 18.2.

Figure 18.2   Localizing ItemDetailViewController.xib

When you add a localization, two things happen: first, a copy of the resource file is made. Then, the copy is separated into an `lproj` directory named after the localization. In this case, look in

Finder where `ItemDetailViewController.xib` was, and you will see two directories: `en.lproj` and `es.lproj`. There is a copy of `ItemDetailViewController.xib` in each. (en is the Unicode form for English and es is the Unicode form of Spanish.)

Now, back in Xcode, look in the project navigator. Click the disclosure button next to `ItemDetailViewController.xib` (Figure 18.3) and then click the Spanish file. This is the `ItemDetailViewController.xib` that is in the `es.lproj` folder.

Figure 18.3 Localized XIB in the project navigator

When the Spanish XIB file opens, the text is unfortunately still in English. You do have to translate it yourself; that part isn't automatic. One option is to manually edit each string in the Spanish XIB file in Xcode. However, what happens when you add a new label or button to your localized XIB? You have to add this view to the XIB for every language. This is not fun.

Instead, you can use a command-line tool named ibtool to suck the strings from your native language XIB file into a file. Then, you can translate these strings and create a new XIB file for each language. To get started, open Terminal.app in the `Applications/Utilities` directory.

Once Terminal launches, you'll need to navigate to the location of `ItemDetailViewController.xib` in `en.lproj`. If you are familiar with Unix, have at it. If not, you're about to learn a cool trick. In Terminal, type the following:

```
cd
```

followed by a space.

Use Finder to find `en.lproj` in this project's directory. Drag this folder's icon from the Finder onto the Terminal window. Terminal will fill out the path for you. Hit return. The current working directory of Terminal is now this directory. For example, my terminal command looks like this:

```
cd /iphone/Homepwner/Homepwner/en.lproj
```

Next, you will use ibtool to suck the strings from this XIB file. Enter the following in the terminal (all terminal commands will be on the same line, we break them up onto multiple lines to fit the page):

```
ibtool --generate-strings-file ~/Desktop/ItemDetailViewController.strings
            ItemDetailViewController.xib
```

This will create a `ItemDetailViewController.strings` file on your desktop that contains all of the strings in your XIB file. Edit this file:

```
/* Class = "IBUILabel"; text = "Name"; ObjectID = "4"; */
"4.text" = "Nombre";

/* Class = "IBUILabel"; text = "Serial"; ObjectID = "5"; */
"5.text" = "Numéro de serie";

/* Class = "IBUILabel"; text = "Value"; ObjectID = "6"; */
"6.text" = "Valor";

/* Class = "IBUILabel"; text = "Label"; ObjectID = "7"; */
"7.text" = "Label";
```

Save this file.

Now you will use ibtool to create a new XIB file, based on the English version of
`ItemDetailViewController.xib`, that will replace all of the strings with the values from
`ItemDetailViewController.strings`. To pull this off, you will need to know the path of your English
XIB file and the path of your Spanish directory in this project's directory. In Finder, navigate to your
project's root directory (where all of your source files are).

In Terminal.app, enter the following command, followed by a space after `write`:

```
ibtool --strings-file ~/Desktop/ItemDetailViewController.strings --write
```

Next, find `ItemDetailViewController.xib` in `es.lproj` and drag it onto the terminal window. Then,
find `ItemDetailViewController.xib` in the `en.lproj` folder and drag it onto the terminal window.
Your command should look similar to this:

```
ibtool --strings-file ~/Desktop/ItemDetailViewController.strings --write
    /iphone/Homepwner/Homepwner/es.lproj/Homepwner.xib
    /iphone/Homepwner/Homepwner/en.lproj/Homepwner.xib
```

Hit return.

This command says, "Create `ItemDetailViewController.xib` in `es.lproj` from the
`ItemDetailViewController.xib` in `en.lproj`, and then replace all of the strings with the values from
`ItemDetailViewController.strings`." Open `ItemDetailViewController.xib` (Spanish) in Xcode.
This XIB file will now be localized to Spanish. (You will have to resize the label and text field for the
serial number, as shown in Figure 18.4.)

Figure 18.4   Spanish ItemDetailViewController.xib

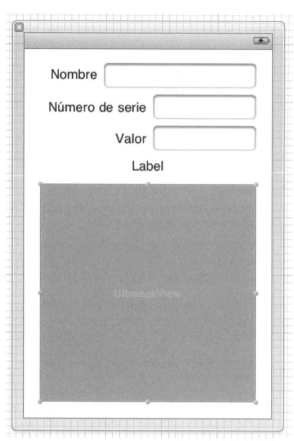

Once you have finished localizing this XIB file, you will want to test it. There is a little Xcode glitch to be aware of: sometimes Xcode just ignores a resource file's changes when you build an application. To ensure your application is being built from scratch, first delete the application from your device or simulator. Then, choose Clean from the Product menu. This will force the application to be entirely re-compiled, re-bundled, and re-installed.

Homepwner's detail view will not appear in Spanish until you change the language settings on the device. In Settings, change the language settings to Español and then relaunch your application. Select a possession row, and you will see the interface in Spanish.

NSLocalizedString and Strings Tables

In many places in your applications, you create **NSString** instances dynamically or display string literals to the user. To display translated versions of these strings, you must create a strings table. A strings table is a file containing a list of key-value pairs for all of the strings your application uses and their associated translations. It's a resource file that you add to your application, but you don't need to do a lot of work to get data from it.

Whenever you have a string in your code, it appears like this:

```
@"Hello!"
```

To internationalize a string in your code, you replace literal strings with the macro **NSLocalizedString()**.

```
NSString *translatedString =
    NSLocalizedString(@"Hello!", @"The greeting for the user");
```

This function takes two arguments: a key (which is required) and a comment (which is not). The key is the lookup value in a strings table. At runtime, **NSLocalizedString()** will look through the strings tables bundled with your application for a table that matches the user's language settings. Then, in that table, the function gets a translation that matches the key. (The function doesn't use the second argument; you will see what it's for in a moment.)

Now you're going to internationalize the string "Homepwner" that is displayed in the navigation bar. In ItemsViewController.m, locate the **init** method and change the line of code that sets the title of the navigationItem.

```
- (id)init
{
    self = [super initWithStyle:UITableViewStyleGrouped];

    if (self) {
        UIBarButtonItem *bbi = [[UIBarButtonItem alloc]
                          initWithBarButtonSystemItem:UIBarButtonSystemItemAdd
                                               target:self
                                               action:@selector(addNewPossession:)];
        [[self navigationItem] setRightBarButtonItem:bbi];
        [bbi release];

        [[self navigationItem] setTitle:
                    NSLocalizedString(@"Homepwner", @"Name of application")];

        [[self navigationItem] setLeftBarButtonItem:[self editButtonItem]];
    }

    return self;
}
```

Once you have a file that has been internationalized with **NSLocalizedString()**, you can generate strings tables with a command-line application.

Open Terminal.app and navigate to the location of ItemsViewController.m. My command looks like this:

```
cd /iphone/Homepwner/Homepwner/
```

At which point, I can use the terminal command ls to print out the directory contents and see ItemsViewController.m in that list.

To generate the strings table, enter the following into Terminal and hit return:

```
genstrings ItemsViewController.m
```

This creates a file named Localizable.strings in the same directory as ItemsViewController.m. Drag this file into the project navigator. When the application is compiled, this resource will be copied into the main bundle.

Oddly enough, Xcode sometimes has a problem with strings tables. Open the Localizable.strings file in the editor area. If you see a bunch of upside-down question marks, you need to reinterpret this file as Unicode (UTF-16). Show the utilities area and select the file inspector. Locate the area named Text Settings and change the pop-up menu next to Text Encoding to Unicode (UTF-16) (Figure 18.5). It will ask if you want to reinterpret or convert. Choose Reinterpret.

Figure 18.5   Changing encoding of a file

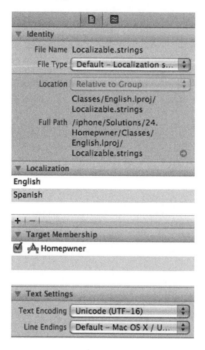

The file should look like this:

```
/* Name of application */
"Homepwner" = "Homepwner";
```

Notice that the comments in your strings table are the second arguments you supplied to **NSLocalizedString()**. Even though the function doesn't require them, they will make your localizing life easier.

Now that you've created Localizable.strings, localize it the same way you did the XIB file. (Strings tables are resources, too!) Select the file in the project navigator and click the plus button in the utilities area. Add the Spanish localization and then open the Spanish version of Localizable.strings. The string on the lefthand side is the *key* that is passed to **NSLocalizedString()**, and the string on the righthand side is what is returned. Change the text on the righthand side to the Spanish translation shown below.

```
/* Name of application */
"Homepwner" = "Dueño de casa"
```

Build and run the application again. The title of the navigation bar will appear in Spanish. If it doesn't, you might need to delete the application, clean your project, and rebuild. (Or check your user language setting.)

Challenge: Another Localization

Practice makes perfect. Localize Homepwner for another language.

For the More Curious: NSBundle's Role in Internationalization

The real work of adding a localization is done for you by the class **NSBundle**. For example, when a **UIViewController** is initialized, it is given two arguments: the name of a XIB file and an **NSBundle** object. The bundle argument is typically nil, which is interpreted as the application's *main bundle*. (The main bundle is another name for the application bundle – all of the resources and the executable for the application. When an application is built, all of the lproj directories are copied into this bundle.)

When the view controller loads its view, it asks the bundle for the XIB file. The bundle, being very smart, checks the current language settings of the device and looks in the appropriate lproj directory. The path for the XIB file in the lproj directory is returned to the view controller and loaded.

NSBundle knows how to search through localization directories for every type of resource using the instance method **pathForResource:ofType:**. When you want a path to a resource bundled with your application, you send this message to the main bundle. Here's an example using the resource file myImage.png:

```
NSString *path = [[NSBundle mainBundle] pathForResource:@"myImage"
                                        ofType:@"png"];
```

The bundle first checks to see if there is a myImage.png file in the top level of the application bundle. If so, it returns the full path to that file. If not, the bundle gets the device's language settings and looks in the appropriate lproj directory to construct the path. If no file is found, it returns nil.

This is why you must delete and clean an application when you localize a file. The previous un-localized file will still be in the root level of the application bundle because Xcode will not delete a file from the bundle when you re-install. Even though there are lproj folders in the application bundle, the bundle finds the top-level file first and returns its path.

19

Settings

Many applications include preferences that users can set. Whether users are picking the size of the text or storing usernames, there is a standard way of enabling iOS application preferences. In this chapter, you will use the **NSUserDefaults** class to add a preference to your Whereami application. This preference will specify the map type of the **MKMapView**.

Updating Whereami

Every **MKMapView** has a mapType property that specifies whether it shows roads, satellite imagery, or both. You will allow the user to change this property by adding a **UISegmentedControl** that toggles the map type. The user's choice will be saved as a preference for the next time the application is launched.

Open the Whereami project. Then open MainWindow.xib and add a **UISegmentedControl** to the interface. Change its style and number of segments as shown in Figure 19.1.

Figure 19.1 UISegmentedControl attributes

Then, create an action method and outlet for this control, as shown in Figure 19.2.

Figure 19.2   Adding to Whereami's interface

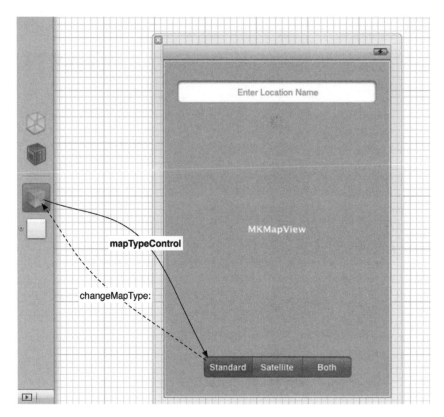

In WhereamiAppDelegate.m, implement this method to change the map type.

```
- (IBAction)changeMapType:(id)sender
{
    switch([sender selectedSegmentIndex])
    {
        case 0:
        {
            [worldView setMapType:MKMapTypeStandard];
        }break;
        case 1:
        {
            [worldView setMapType:MKMapTypeSatellite];
        }break;
        case 2:
        {
            [worldView setMapType:MKMapTypeHybrid];
        }break;
    }
}
```

Build and run the application and change the map type to make sure it works. However, if you quit the application (and kill it from the dock), it won't remember the change you made on the next launch.

NSUserDefaults

In this exercise, we will store a value to specify the map type that the user last selected so that the chosen type will automatically be displayed when the user launches the application again. This value will be stored in an instance of **NSUserDefaults**.

Every application has an instance of **NSUserDefaults** that it can access by sending the class message **standardUserDefaults** to the **NSUserDefaults** class. This instance of **NSUserDefaults** is like an **NSMutableDictionary**; you can set and remove objects in it using a key. It is also automatically read from disk when the application first accesses it and written to disk when modified.

The keys of an **NSUserDefaults** are always of type **NSString**. A key identifies a preference. An object represents the value of a preference. These objects must be property list serializable or primitives. For example, if you created a key "Text Size" and assigned the integer 16, it would mean user's preferred text size is 16 points.

But that "Text Size" key is a completely hypothetical example. There isn't a built-in key that magically resizes all of your text. In fact, there are no built-in keys at all. Instead, you create your own keys specific to your application and give them values that mean something for that application.

The keys you will create are strings and will be used both when reading the value and setting the value. You will define them as a static variable so that you can use the variable as the key instead of a hard-coded string that you may mistype. (If you mistype a variable name, the compiler will give you an error. It has no idea if you've mistyped a string.) At the top of WhereamiAppDelegate.m, declare a new static variable to hold the preference name for the map type.

```
NSString * const WhereamiMapTypePrefKey = @"WhereamiMapTypePrefKey";

@implementation WhereamiAppDelegate
```

Notice that the variable name and the key are the name of the application, the name of the preference, and the words PrefKey. This is the typical pattern for naming preference keys.

To add or change the value of a preference in an **NSUserDefaults**, you use **setObject:forKey:** just like you would with an **NSMutableDictionary**. In addition, **NSUserDefaults** has some convenience methods for putting primitives into preferences, like **setInteger:forKey:**.

In WhereamiAppDelegate.m, add the following line of code to the end of **changeMapType:**.

```
- (IBAction)changeMapType:(id)sender
{
    [[NSUserDefaults standardUserDefaults]
                setInteger:[sender selectedSegmentIndex]
                    forKey:WhereamiMapTypePrefKey];

    switch([sender selectedSegmentIndex])
    {
        case 0:
        {
            [worldView setMapType:MKMapTypeStandard];
        }break;
        case 1:
        {
            [worldView setMapType:MKMapTypeSatellite];
        }break;
        case 2:
```

```
        {
            [worldView setMapType:MKMapTypeHybrid];
        }break;
    }
}
```

Now, whenever the user changes the map type, that value will be written to the **NSUserDefaults**, which will then be saved to disk. When the **NSUserDefaults** saves its data to disk, it saves it to the Library/Preferences directory. The name of that file will be the bundle identifier for your application.

When your application firsts asks for the **standardUserDefaults**, it will load this file from disk, and all of the saved preferences will be available to your application. In WhereamiAppDelegate.m, update the method **application:didFinishLaunchingWithOptions:** to read in this value and set the map type accordingly.

```
- (BOOL)application:(UIApplication *)app
    didFinishLaunchingWithOptions:(NSDictionary *)launchOptions
{
    NSInteger mapTypeValue = [[NSUserDefaults standardUserDefaults]
                                 integerForKey:WhereamiMapTypePrefKey];

    // Update the UI
    [mapTypeControl setSelectedSegmentIndex:mapTypeValue];

    // Update the map
    [self changeMapType:mapTypeControl];
```

Build and run Whereami and change the map type. Exit the application by pressing the Home button and kill it from the dock. Then, relaunch it, and the map will display the type of map you previously selected.

When your application first launches, the value for the key WhereamiMapTypePrefKey does not exist; it defaults to 0. For this application, that works fine, but some preferences may need a temporary, non-zero default value (i.e., a "factory setting") for the application to run correctly. These temporary defaults are placed in the *registration domain* of **NSUserDefaults**. Any preferences set by the user are stored in a different domain, the *application domain*.

By default, the application domain is empty: there are no keys and no values. The first time a user changes a setting, a value is added to the application domain for the specified key. When you ask the **NSUserDefaults** for the value of a preference, it first looks in the application domain. If there is a value for that key, then the user has set a preference, and the **NSUserDefaults** returns that value. If not, the **NSUserDefaults** looks in the registration domain and finds the temporary default.

The application domain is always saved to disk; that's why it remembers user preferences on the next launch. The registration domain is not, and its values must be set every time the application launches. To set the values of the registration domain, you create an **NSDictionary** with a key-value pair for each preference you plan on using in your application. Then, you send the dictionary as an argument to the message **registerDefaults:** of NSUserDefaults.

Typically, you send the **registerDefaults:** message before any object is able to access the instance of **NSUserDefaults**. This means before the instance of the application delegate is created. What comes before the creation of the **WhereamiAppDelegate**? The creation of the **WhereamiAppDelegate** *class*. Like any object, a class also must be initialized before it can receive messages. So, after a class is created but before it receives its first message, it is sent the message **initialize**.

In `WhereamiAppDelegate.m`, override the class method **initialize** of **NSObject** to register defaults, including setting the map type preference to 1.

```
+ (void)initialize
{
    NSDictionary *defaults = [NSDictionary
                             dictionaryWithObject:[NSNumber numberWithInt:1]
                                           forKey:WhereamiMapTypePrefKey];
    [[NSUserDefaults standardUserDefaults] registerDefaults:defaults];
}
```

Delete the application from your device to remove the previously saved preferences. Then, build and run again. The first time the application launches, the default satellite map will be displayed. If you change the map type, the preference is added to the application domain, and your application will use that value from then on. The default value in the registration domain will be ignored.

NSUserDefaults is a simple class but a useful one. In addition to storing preferences, many developers use **NSUserDefaults** to store little pieces of information that are important but don't really need to be kept in distinct files. For example, if you want to display an alert to a user every 3rd time the application is launched, you could store the number of times the application has been launched in the **NSUserDefaults**.

For the More Curious: The Settings Application

Every iOS device has a Settings application. Applications that register some or all of their preferences with Settings get an entry in this application where those preferences can be changed. However, most applications do not use Settings to store their preferences: why leave the application, find Settings, change a value, and then re-open the application when you could have your own built-in interface?

But, in case it's something you want to do, here's how. To register for an entry in Settings, you add a `Settings.bundle` to your application. This bundle contains a property list that has an entry for each preference you want to expose in the Settings application. (There is a template for this bundle when you create a new file.)

Each entry contains a key that is a string that matches the name of the preference keys you use with **NSUserDefaults**. Additionally, you set a *preference specifier* key with one of the pre-defined constants. These constants indicate the type of control that will appear for this preference in the Settings application. They are things like text fields, switches, and sliders. You also add a key for a default value. Some preference specifiers require you to add additional keys. For example, a slider preference will need a minimum and a maximum value.

If you choose to use a settings bundle, you must take care to respect the changes made in the Settings application when transitioning between application states. If your application is terminated and then the user changes a value in Settings, those changes will be written to disk, and the next time your application launches, it will get the correct values. However, most iOS applications are not terminated when the user presses the Home button. Thus, when your application returns from being suspended, you should check to see if any of the preferences were changed while it was suspended.

An application returning from the suspended state that has had preferences changed will be notified via the **NSNotificationCenter**. You can register for the `NSUserDefaultsDidChangeNotification` notification to be informed of these changes. (You typically register for this notification when the application first launches.)

20

Touch Events and UIResponder

In your Hypnosister project from Chapter 6, you created a **UIScrollView** that handled touch events to scroll a view and even handled a multi-touch event to zoom. The **UIScrollView** class makes scrolling and zooming easy to implement. But what if you want to do something else, something special or unique, with touch events?

In this chapter, you are going to create a view that lets the user draw lines by dragging across the view (Figure 20.1). Using multi-touch, the user will be able to draw more than one line at a time. Double-tapping will clear the screen and allow the user to begin again.

Figure 20.1   A drawing program

Touch Events

As a subclass of **UIResponder**, your view can override four methods to handle the four distinct touch events:

- a finger or fingers touches the screen

```
- (void)touchesBegan:(NSSet *)touches
         withEvent:(UIEvent *)event;
```

- a finger or fingers move across the screen (This message is sent repeatedly as a finger moves.)

```
- (void)touchesMoved:(NSSet *)touches
         withEvent:(UIEvent *)event;
```

- a finger or fingers is removed from the screen

```
- (void)touchesEnded:(NSSet *)touches
         withEvent:(UIEvent *)event;
```

- a system event, like an incoming phone call, interrupts a touch before it ends

```
- (void)touchesCancelled:(NSSet *)touches
           withEvent:(UIEvent *)event;
```

When a touch event occurs, that event is added to a queue of events that the **UIApplication** object manages. In practice, the queue rarely fills up, and events are delivered immediately. (If your touches are sluggish, then one of your methods is hogging the CPU, and events are waiting in line to be delivered. Chapter 21 will show you how to catch these problems.)

Delivering a touch event means sending one of the **UIResponder** messages to the view the event occurred on. In these methods, there is always a **UIEvent** instance you have access to. The **UIEvent** can tell you the type of event and when this event took place. It can also tell you all of the active touches in an application. For touch events, however, you typically do not use the event object; you use **UITouch** objects instead.

When the user touches the screen, an instance of **UITouch** is created and associated with that finger. The **UITouch** knows where that finger is on the screen. As that finger moves, the same **UITouch** object is updated so that it always holds the current position of that finger on the screen. When the finger leaves the screen, the **UITouch** is discarded. (**UITouch** instances also keep track of things like the previous location of the finger and how many times this finger tapped the screen.)

As these touch events occur, the appropriate **UIResponder** messages are sent to the touched view, and the **UITouch** objects involved with those events are passed as arguments. Because more than one finger can trigger the same event at the same time, the argument passed to the view is a set of those touches. For example, if two fingers touch a view at the same time, the view will be sent **touchesBegan:withEvent:** and the first argument will be an **NSSet** that contains two **UITouch** instances. However, if two fingers touch the same view one after the other, you will get two separate **touchesBegan:withEvent:** messages, and each **NSSet** will contain one **UITouch**.

When a touch moves or ends, **touchesMoved:withEvent:** or **touchesEnded:withEvent:** will be sent to the view that the touch *originated* on. Thus, once a touch begins its life, it is tied to the view that it first touched. Also, the **NSSet** that is passed to these methods only contains the touches that triggered the event. For example, if there are two touches on the view but only one of them moved, only the moving touch will be in the set delivered via **touchesMoved:withEvent:**.

Creating the TouchTracker Application

Now let's get started with your application. In Xcode, create a new Window-based Application iPhone project and name it TouchTracker.

First, you will need a model object that describes a line. Create a new **NSObject** and name it **Line**. In Line.h, declare two CGPoint instance variables and two properties:

```
#import <Foundation/Foundation.h>

@interface Line : NSObject {
    CGPoint begin;
    CGPoint end;
}
@property (nonatomic) CGPoint begin;
@property (nonatomic) CGPoint end;
@end
```

In Line.m, synthesize the properties:

```
#import "Line.h"

@implementation Line

@synthesize begin, end;

@end
```

Next, create a new **NSObject** called **TouchDrawView**. In TouchDrawView.h, change the superclass to **UIView**. Also, declare two collection objects: an array to hold complete lines and a dictionary to hold lines that are still being drawn. We'll talk about why we use two different collection objects when you write the code to use them.

```
#import <Foundation/Foundation.h>
#import <UIKit/UIKit.h>

@interface TouchDrawView : UIView
{
    NSMutableDictionary *linesInProcess;
    NSMutableArray *completeLines;
}
- (void)clearAll;
@end
```

In your Hypnosister project, you instantiated your custom view programmatically. In TouchTracker, you will instantiate a custom view from a XIB file. Open MainWindow.xib.

From the object library, drag an instance of **UIView** onto the window. In the identity inspector, set its class to **TouchDrawView**, as shown in Figure 20.2.

Figure 20.2   Identity inspector

Views created programmatically are sent **initWithFrame:**, views that are unarchived from a XIB file are sent **initWithCoder:**. Thus, for **TouchDrawView**, you will override **initWithCoder:** instead of **initWithFrame:**.

In TouchDrawView.m, take care of the creation and destruction of the two collections:

```
#import "TouchDrawView.h"
#import "Line.h"

@implementation TouchDrawView

- (id)initWithCoder:(NSCoder *)c
{
    self = [super initWithCoder:c];

    if (self) {
        linesInProcess = [[NSMutableDictionary alloc] init];

        // Don't let the autocomplete fool you on the next line,
        // make sure you are instantiating an NSMutableArray
        // and not an NSMutableDictionary!
        completeLines = [[NSMutableArray alloc] init];

        [self setMultipleTouchEnabled:YES];
    }

    return self;
}
```

Notice that you explicitly enabled multi-touch events by sending the message **setMultipleTouchEnabled:**. Without this, only one touch at a time can be active on a view. If another finger touches the view, it will be ignored, and the view will not be sent **touchesBegan:withEvent:** or any of the other **UIResponder** messages.

In the **dealloc** method, release the objects you created.

```
- (void)dealloc
{
    [linesInProcess release];
    [completeLines release];
    [super dealloc];
}
```

Now override the **drawRect:** method to create lines using functions from Core Graphics:

```
- (void)drawRect:(CGRect)rect
{
    CGContextRef context = UIGraphicsGetCurrentContext();
    CGContextSetLineWidth(context, 10.0);
    CGContextSetLineCap(context, kCGLineCapRound);

    // Draw complete lines in black
    [[UIColor blackColor] set];
    for (Line *line in completeLines) {
        CGContextMoveToPoint(context, [line begin].x, [line begin].y);
        CGContextAddLineToPoint(context, [line end].x, [line end].y);
        CGContextStrokePath(context);
    }
```

```
    // Draw lines in process in red
    [[UIColor redColor] set];
    for (NSValue *v in linesInProcess) {
        Line *line = [linesInProcess objectForKey:v];
        CGContextMoveToPoint(context, [line begin].x, [line begin].y);
        CGContextAddLineToPoint(context, [line end].x, [line end].y);
        CGContextStrokePath(context);
    }
}
```

Finally, write a method that will clear the collections and redraw the view in TouchDrawView.m.

```
- (void)clearAll
{
    // Clear the collections
    [linesInProcess removeAllObjects];
    [completeLines removeAllObjects];

    // Redraw
    [self setNeedsDisplay];
}
```

Turning Touches into Lines

A line (remember 9th grade geometry class?) is defined by two points. Our **Line** stores these points as properties named begin and end. When a touch begins, you'll create a line and set both begin and end to the point where the touch began. When the touch moves, you will update end. When the touch ends, you will have your complete line.

There are two collection objects that hold **Line** instances. Lines that have been completed are stored in the completeLines array. Lines that are still being drawn, however, are stored in an **NSMutableDictionary**. Why do we need a dictionary? We've enabled multi-touch, so a user can draw more than one line at a time. This means we have to keep track of which touch events go with which line. For instance, imagine the user touches the screen with two fingers creating two instances of **Line**. Then one of those fingers moves. The **TouchDrawView** is sent a message for the event, but how can it know which line to update?

This is where the dictionary comes in: when a touch begins, we will grab the address of the **UITouch** object that is passed in and wrap it in an **NSValue** instance. A new **Line** will be created and added to the dictionary, and the **NSValue** will be its key. As we receive more touch events, we can use the address of the **UITouch** that is passed in to access and update the right line (Figure 20.3).

Figure 20.3   Object diagram for TouchTracker

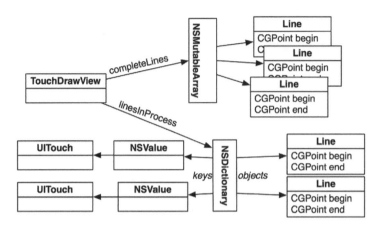

Now let's return to the methods for handling touch events. First, in TouchDrawView.m, override **touchesBegan:withEvent:** to create a new **Line** instance and store it in an **NSMutableDictionary**.

```
- (void)touchesBegan:(NSSet *)touches
        withEvent:(UIEvent *)event
{
    for (UITouch *t in touches) {

        // Is this a double tap?
        if ([t tapCount] > 1) {
            [self clearAll];
            return;
        }

        // Use the touch object (packed in an NSValue) as the key
        NSValue *key = [NSValue valueWithPointer:t];

        // Create a line for the value
        CGPoint loc = [t locationInView:self];
        Line *newLine = [[Line alloc] init];
        [newLine setBegin:loc];
        [newLine setEnd:loc];

        // Put pair in dictionary
        [linesInProcess setObject:newLine forKey:key];

        // There is a memory leak in this method
        // You will find it using Instruments in the next chapter
    }
}
```

Next, in TouchDrawView.m, override **touchesMoved:withEvent:** to update the end point of the line associated with the moving touch.

```
- (void)touchesMoved:(NSSet *)touches
        withEvent:(UIEvent *)event
```

```
{
    // Update linesInProcess with moved touches
    for (UITouch *t in touches) {
        NSValue *key = [NSValue valueWithPointer:t];

        // Find the line for this touch
        Line *line = [linesInProcess objectForKey:key];

        // Update the line
        CGPoint loc = [t locationInView:self];
        [line setEnd:loc];
    }
    // Redraw
    [self setNeedsDisplay];
}
```

When a touch ends, you need to finalize the line. However, a touch can end for two reasons: the user lifts the finger off the screen (**touchesEnded:withEvent:**) or the operating system interrupts your application (**touchesCancelled:withEvent:**). A phone call, for example, will interrupt your application.

In many applications, you'll want to handle these two events differently. However, for TouchTracker, you will write one method to handle both cases. Declare a new method in TouchDrawView.h.

```
- (void)endTouches:(NSSet *)touches;
```

In TouchDrawView.m, implement **endTouches:**.

```
- (void)endTouches:(NSSet *)touches
{
    // Remove ending touches from dictionary
    for (UITouch *t in touches) {
        NSValue *key = [NSValue valueWithPointer:t];
        Line *line = [linesInProcess objectForKey:key];

        // If this is a double tap, 'line' will be nil,
        // so make sure not to add it to the array
        if (line) {
            [completeLines addObject:line];
            [linesInProcess removeObjectForKey:key];
        }
    }
    // Redraw
    [self setNeedsDisplay];
}
```

Finally, override the two methods from **UIResponder** to call **endTouches:** in TouchDrawView.m.

```
- (void)touchesEnded:(NSSet *)touches
        withEvent:(UIEvent *)event
{
    [self endTouches:touches];
}

- (void)touchesCancelled:(NSSet *)touches
            withEvent:(UIEvent *)event
{
    [self endTouches:touches];
}
```

Build and run the application. Then make beautiful line art with one or more fingers.

The Responder Chain

In Chapter 5, we talked briefly about **UIResponder** and the first responder. A **UIResponder** can receive touch events. **UIView** is one example of a **UIResponder** subclass, but there are many others, including **UIViewController**, **UIApplication**, and **UIWindow**. You are probably thinking, "But you can't touch a **UIViewController**. It's not an on-screen object!" You are right – you can't send a touch event *directly* to a **UIViewController**, but view controllers can receive events through the *responder chain*. (By the way, you get two bonus points for keeping the view controller and its view separate in your brain.)

Every **UIResponder** has a pointer called nextResponder, and together these objects make up the responder chain shown in Figure 20.4. A touch event starts at the view that was touched. The nextResponder of a view is typically its **UIViewController** (if it has one) or its superview (if it doesn't). The nextResponder of a view controller is typically its view's superview. The top-most superview is the window (**UIWindow** inherits from **UIView**). The window's nextResponder is the singleton instance of **UIApplication**. If the application doesn't handle the event, then it is discarded. (Note that the window and application don't do anything with an event unless you subclass them.)

Figure 20.4   Responder chain

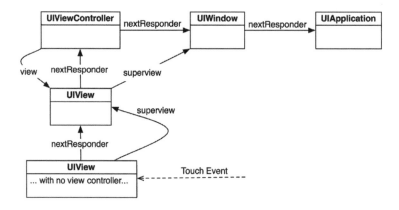

How does a **UIResponder** *not* handle an event? It forwards the same message to its nextResponder. That's what the default implementation of methods like **touchesBegan:withEvent:** do. So if a method is not overridden, its next responder will attempt to handle the touch event.

You can explicitly send a message to a next responder, too. Let's say there is a view that tracks touches, but if a double tap occurs, its next responder should handle it. The code would look like this:

```
- (void)touchesBegan:(NSSet *)touches withEvent:(UIEvent *)event
{
    UITouch *touch = [touches anyObject];
    if ([touch tapCount] == 2) {
        [[self nextResponder] touchesBegan:touches withEvent:event];
        return;
    }
}
```

```
        ... Go on to handle touches that aren't double taps
}
```

Challenge: Saving and Loading

Save the lines when the application terminates. Reload them when the application resumes.

Challenge: Circles

Use two fingers to draw circles. Try having each finger represent one corner of the bounding box around the circle. You can simulate two fingers on the simulator by holding down the option button. (Hint: This is much easier if you track touches that are working on a circle in a separate dictionary.)

For the More Curious: UIControl

The class **UIControl** is the superclass for several classes in Cocoa Touch, including **UIButton** and **UISlider**. We've seen how to set the targets and actions for these controls. Now we can take a closer look at how **UIControl** overrides the same **UIResponder** methods you implemented in this chapter.

In **UIControl**, each possible *control event* is associated with a constant. Buttons, for example, typically send action messages on the UIControlEventTouchUpInside control event. A target registered for this control event will only receive its action message if the user touches the control and then lifts the finger off the screen inside the frame of the control. Essentially, it is a tap.

For a button, however, you can have actions on other event types. For example, you might trigger a method if the user removes the finger *inside or outside* the frame. Assigning the target and action programmatically would look like this:

```
[rButton addTarget:tempController
            action:@selector(resetTemperature:)
  forControlEvents:UIControlEventTouchUpInside | UIControlEventTouchUpOutside];
```

Now consider how **UIControl** handles UIControlEventTouchUpInside.

```
// Not the exact code. There is a bit more going on!
- (void)touchesEnded:(NSSet *)touches withEvent:(UIEvent *)event
{
    // Reference to the touch that is ending
    UITouch *touch = [touches anyObject];

    // Location of that point in this control's coordinate system
    CGPoint touchLocation = [touch locationInView:self];

    // Is that point still in my viewing bounds?
    if (CGRectContainsPoint([self bounds], touchLocation))
    {
        // Send out action messages to all targets registered for this event!
        [self sendActionsForControlEvents:UIControlEventTouchUpInside];
    } else {
        // The touch ended outside the bounds, different control event
        [self sendActionsForControlEvents:UIControlEventTouchUpOutside];
    }
}
```

So how do these actions get sent to the right target? At the end of the **UIResponder** method implementations, the control sends the message **sendActionsForControlEvents:** to itself. This method looks at all of the target-action pairs the control has, and if any of them are registered for the control event passed as the argument, those targets are sent an action message.

However, a control never sends a message directly to its targets. Instead, it routes these messages through the **UIApplication** object. Why not have controls send the action messages directly to the targets? Controls can also have nil-targeted actions. If a **UIControl**'s target is nil, the **UIApplication** finds the *first responder* of its **UIWindow** and sends the action message to it.

21

Instruments

In Chapter 4, you learned about using the debugger to find and fix problems in your code. Now we're going to look at other tools available to iOS programmers and how to integrate them into application development.

The Static Analyzer

There is a memory leak in your TouchTracker application. When the user double-taps, the screen clears. At this point, all instances of **Line** should be deallocated, but they aren't. In the first part of this chapter, you'll examine this leak with Xcode's static analyzer.

When you build an application, you can ask Xcode to analyze your code. The static analyzer then makes educated guesses about what would happen if that code were to be executed and informs you of potential problems, like a memory leak. It does this without executing the code or building the application.

When the static analyzer checks the code, it examines each function and method individually by iterating over every possible *code path*. A method can have a number of control statements (if, for, switch, etc.). The conditions of these statements will dictate which code is actually executed. A code path is one of the possible paths the code will take given these control statements. For example, a method that has a single if statement has two code paths: one if the condition fails and one if the condition succeeds.

Open TouchTracker.xcodeproj.

To start the static analyzer, click and hold the Run button in the top-left corner of the workspace. In the pop-up window that appears, choose Analyze (Figure 21.1). Alternatively, you can use the keyboard shortcut: Command-Shift-B.

Figure 21.1   Using the static analyzer

Analysis results appear in the issue navigator. In this case, the analyzer found the leak in TouchDrawView.m and tells you the line where the leaked object is allocated, as shown in Figure 21.2. (If you don't see line numbers in the gutter, you can turn them on by selecting Preferences from the Xcode menu. Choose the Text Editing tab and click the checkbox Show Line Numbers.)

Figure 21.2   Analyzer results

```
56  - (void)touchesBegan:(NSSet *)touches withEvent:(UIEvent *)event
57  {
58      for (UITouch *t in touches)          [!] Potential leak of an object allocated on line 71 and stored into 'newLine'
59      {
60          // Is this a double-tap?
61          if ([t tapCount] > 1) {
62              [self clearAll];
63              return;
64          }
65
66          // Use the touch object (packed in an NSValue) as the key
67          NSValue *key = [NSValue valueWithPointer:t];
68
69          // Create a line for the value
70          CGPoint loc = [t locationInView:self];
71          Line *newLine = [[Line alloc] init];
72          [newLine setBegin:loc];
73          [newLine setEnd:loc];
74
75          // Put pair in dictionary
76          [linesInProcess setObject:newLine forKey:key];
77      }
```

The analyzer will also show us how it came to this conclusion. Click on the inline analyzer result (the result in the source file) to reveal the expanded analysis (Figure 21.3).

Figure 21.3   Expanded analysis

```
56  - (void)touchesBegan:(NSSet *)touches withEvent:(UIEvent *)event
57  {
58      for (UITouch *t in touches)
59      {                                    [!] 2. Object allocated on line 71 and stored into 'newLine' is not referenced later in this execution path and has a retain count of +1 (object leaked)
60          // Is this a double-tap?
61          if ([t tapCount] > 1) {
62              [self clearAll];
63              return;
64          }
65
66          // Use the touch object (packed in an NSValue) as the key
67          NSValue *key = [NSValue valueWithPointer:t];
68
69          // Create a line for the value
70          CGPoint loc = [t locationInView:self];
71          Line *newLine = [[Line alloc] init];   [!] 1. Method returns an Objective-C object with a +1 retain count (owning reference)
72          [newLine setBegin:loc];
73          [newLine setEnd:loc];
74
75          // Put pair in dictionary
76          [linesInProcess setObject:newLine forKey:key];
77      }
```

When you expand the analyzer's results, the arrows show the code path that generated the issue. Take a closer look at the code path shown with the darker arrows. It begins at the for loop and then assumes the if statement failed, thus skipping its body. Execution continues until the new **Line** is allocated. The analyzer highlights this allocation as the first event in the issue: the **alloc** method "returns an Objective-C object with a +1 retain count."

Then, the dimmer arrow runs from the allocation back to the for loop. This shows that when execution returns to the beginning of the for loop, the pointer newLine is not referenced again before it is lost. Therefore, the object it points to is leaked.

You can close the expanded analysis by clicking on the analysis result in the issue navigator. We will fix this leak at the end of the chapter; for now, leave it in.

In addition to memory leaks, the analyzer can also find logic errors. In TouchDrawView.m, implement the following method:

```
- (int)numberOfLines
{
    int count;

    // Check that they are non-nil before we add their counts...
    if (linesInProcess && completeLines)
        count = [linesInProcess count] + [completeLines count];

    return count;
}
```

Analyze the code. The analyzer reports a logic error in the issue navigator. View the extended analysis to see the code path that generates the error: when the if statement fails, the value of count is never given a value. Thus, the caller will receive garbage when this method returns. (The solution, of course, is to assign 0 to count when it is declared.)

When you analyze your code (which you will do on a regular basis because you are a smart programmer), you'll see issues other than those described here. Many times, we see novice programmers shy away from analyzer issues because of the technical language. Don't do this. Take the time to expand the analysis and understand what the analyzer is trying to tell you. It will be worth it for the development of your application and for your development as a programmer.

Instruments

The static analyzer is useful for catching issues that can be recognized at compile time. However, some problems can't be recognized until runtime. This is where Instruments excels. The Instruments tool monitors your application while it is running and can find real issues as they are happening. Instruments is made up of several plug-ins that enable you to inspect things like what objects are allocated, where the CPU is spending its time, file I/O, network I/O, and others. Each plug-in is known as an Instrument. Together, they help you track down inefficiencies in your application and optimize your code.

The Allocations Instrument

Now let's see how we would find the same memory leak in TouchTracker using the Allocations instrument.

When you use Instruments to monitor your application, you are *profiling* the application. While you can profile the application running on the simulator, you will get more accurate data on a device.

To profile an application, click and hold the Run button in the top left corner of the workspace. In the pop-up menu that appears, select Profile (Figure 21.4).

Figure 21.4   Profiling an application

Instruments will launch and ask which instrument to use. Choose Allocations and click Profile.

Figure 21.5 Choosing an instrument

(There is a Leaks instrument, but it is simply a subset of Allocations. Once you understand the more complicated Allocations instrument, using Leaks is easy.)

TouchTracker will launch, and a window will open in Instruments (Figure 21.6). The interface may be overwhelming at first, but, like Xcode's workspace window, it will become familiar with time and use. First, make sure you can see everything by turning on all of the areas in the window. In the View control at the top of the window, click all three buttons to reveal the three main areas. The window should look like Figure 21.6.

Figure 21.6 Allocations instrument

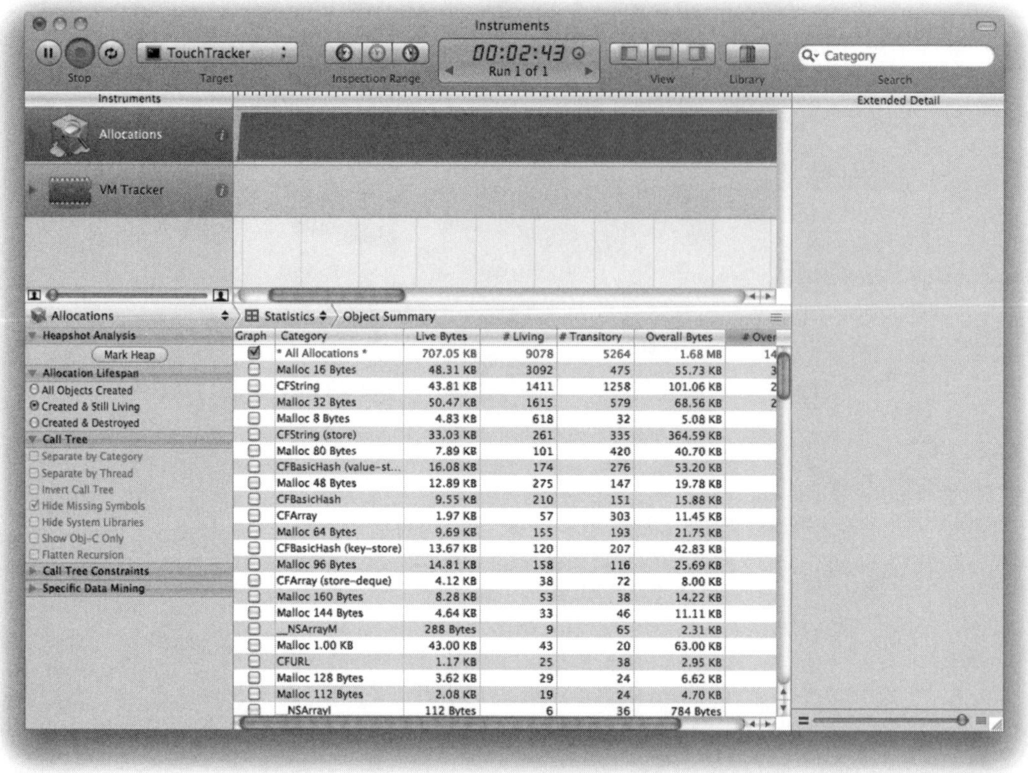

This table shows every memory allocation in the application, but we're only interested in allocations of **Line** objects. You can filter this table to show only allocations of type **Line** by typing `Line` in the Category search box in the top right corner of the window.

Then, in TouchTracker, draw some lines. Those instances will appear in the Object Summary table at the bottom of the window (Figure 21.7).

Figure 21.7 Allocated Lines

Graph	Category	Live Bytes	# Living	# Transitory	Overall Bytes	# Overall	# Allocations (Net / Overall)
	Line	192 Bytes	6	0	192 Bytes	6	

The # Living column shows you how many objects of this type are currently allocated. Live Bytes shows how much memory these living instances take up. The # Overall column shows you how many **Line**s have been created during the course of the application – even if they have since been deallocated.

As you would expect, the number of lines living and the number of lines overall are equal at the moment. Now, double-tap the screen in TouchTracker and erase your lines. In Instruments, notice that the number of living lines does not go down. The **Line**s you just cleared should be deallocated, but they are not.

Let's see what else the Allocations instrument can tell us about our leaky lines. In the table, select the row that says Line. An arrow will appear in the Category column; click that arrow to see more details about these allocations (Figure 21.8).

Figure 21.8   Line summary

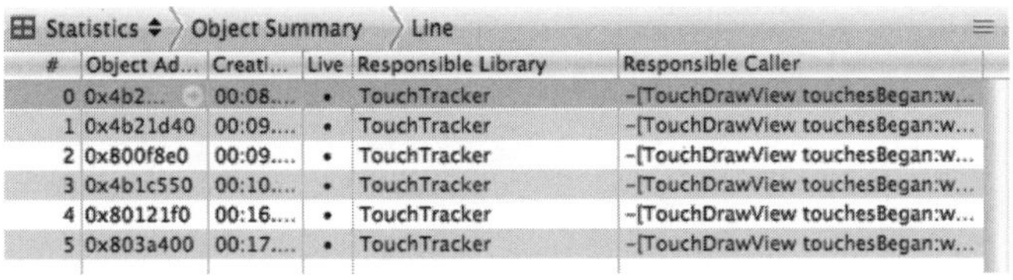

#	Object Ad...	Creati...	Live	Responsible Library	Responsible Caller
0	0x4b2...	00:08...	•	TouchTracker	–[TouchDrawView touchesBegan:w...
1	0x4b21d40	00:09....	•	TouchTracker	–[TouchDrawView touchesBegan:w...
2	0x800f8e0	00:09....	•	TouchTracker	–[TouchDrawView touchesBegan:w...
3	0x4b1c550	00:10....	•	TouchTracker	–[TouchDrawView touchesBegan:w...
4	0x80121f0	00:16....	•	TouchTracker	–[TouchDrawView touchesBegan:w...
5	0x803a400	00:17....	•	TouchTracker	–[TouchDrawView touchesBegan:w...

Each row in this table shows a single instance of **Line** that exists in the application. Select one of the rows and check out the stack trace that appears in the Extended Detail area on the right side of the Instruments window (Figure 21.9). This stack trace shows you where that instance of **Line** was created. Grayed-out items in the trace are system library calls. Items in black text are your code. Find the topmost item that is your code (-[TouchDrawView touchesBegan:withEvent:]) and double-click it.

Figure 21.9   Stack trace

The source code for this implementation will replace the table of **Line** instances (Figure 21.10). The relevant lines of code are highlighted, including where the **Line** instance is created and where it is added to the linesInProcess, which retains it. Here's where we notice that the **Line** instance is not released in the scope of this method. Also, note that Allocations only shows you a leak if you're looking for one. Unlike the static analyzer, it won't say, "Psst – you've got a leak here."

Figure 21.10   Source code in Instruments

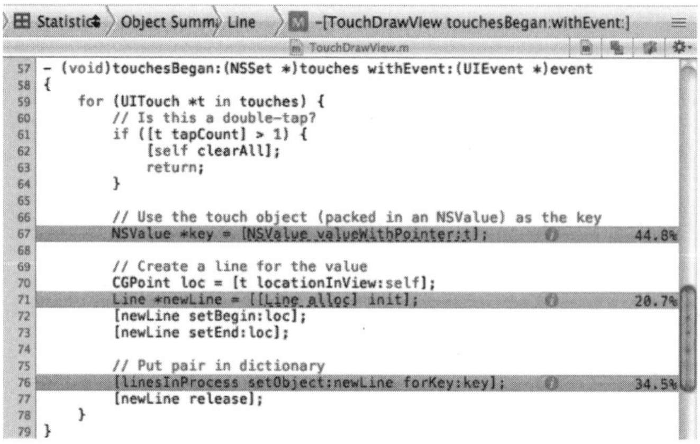

Click on the small Xcode icon in the bar above the source to open this file in Xcode. Fix the leak by releasing the line after it has been added to the dictionary.

```
- (void)touchesBegan:(NSSet *)touches
          withEvent:(UIEvent *)event
{
    for (UITouch *t in touches) {
        if ([t tapCount] > 1) {
            [self clearAll];
            return;
        }
        NSValue *key = [NSValue valueWithPointer:t];
        CGPoint loc = [t locationInView:self];

        Line *newLine = [[Line alloc] init];
        [newLine setBegin:loc];
        [newLine setEnd:loc];

        [linesInProcess setObject:newLine forKey:key];

        [newLine release];
    }

}
```

Settings in Allocations

Now that we've fixed our leak in TouchTracker, let's look at other options in the Allocations instrument. Close the Instruments window (without saving – you don't need to store the results). In Xcode, click the profile button again to build and profile the application. When Instruments launches and asks which instrument to use, choose Allocations again.

Some settings in Instruments can only be changed while Instruments is not currently profiling. In the top left corner of the Instruments window, click the red Stop button to stop profiling. Then, select the info icon next to Allocations. In the pop-up window that appears, check the box for Record reference counts and then click the x icon where the info icon was (Figure 21.11).

Figure 21.11   Enable recording of reference counts

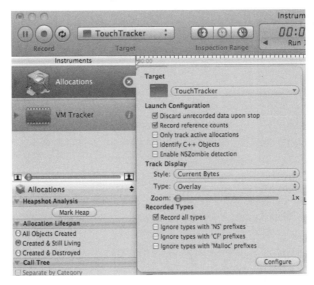

The Record reference counts option instructs Instruments to note every **alloc**, **retain**, **autorelease**, **release**, and **dealloc** message sent to every object. Click the red Record button again to start profiling with this option turned on. (Instruments can't build an application itself, so it always uses the most recent build from Xcode.)

Draw some lines in TouchTracker and then double-tap to delete them. In Instruments, filter the allocations to see just those for **Line**. No instances appear in the table because, by default, Allocations does not show objects that no longer exist. To see all objects dead or alive, find the Allocation Lifespan category on the left side of the window and then select the All Objects Created option (Figure 21.12).

Figure 21.12   Showing all objects

The **Line** instances will now show up in the table: there are 0 instances of **Line** living, and there are however many you drew before clearing overall. You've definitely fixed that leak.

Now select the **Line** row and click the arrow next to it. Then, from this table, select one of the **Line** instances and click its arrow. This new table shows you the reference count history of an individual **Line** object (Figure 21.13).

Figure 21.13   Object's lifespan

#	Category	Event Type	RefCt	Timestamp	Address	Size	Responsible Li...	Responsible Caller
0	Line	Malloc	1	00:59.938.257	0x8007da0	32	TouchTracker	–[TouchDrawView touch...
1	Line	Retain	2	00:59.938.297	0x8007da0	0	TouchTracker	–[TouchDrawView touch...
2	Line	Release	1	00:59.938.304	0x8007da0	0	TouchTracker	–[TouchDrawView touch...
3	Line	Retain	2	01:00.127.439	0x8007da0	0	TouchTracker	–[TouchDrawView endTo...
4	Line	Release	1	01:00.127.443	0x8007da0	0	TouchTracker	–[TouchDrawView endTo...
5	Line	Release	0	01:08.933.142	0x8007da0	0	TouchTracker	–[TouchDrawView clearAll]
6	Line	Free	0	01:08.933.142	0x8007da0	–32	TouchTracker	–[TouchDrawView clearAll]

Notice the bar right above the table shows a drill-down of the tables you've seen. You can return to the list of all **Line** objects by clicking on Object Summary.

Heapshot Analysis

The last item we'll examine in the Allocations instrument is Heapshot Analysis. First, clear the search box so that you aren't filtering results anymore. Then, find the Heapshot Analysis category on the left side of the Instruments window and click Mark Heap. A category named Baseline will appear in the table. You can click the disclosure button next to this category to see all of the allocations that took place before you marked the heapshot. Now, draw more lines in TouchTracker and click Mark Heap again. Another category will appear named Heapshot 1. Click the disclosure button next to Heapshot 1 (Figure 21.14).

Figure 21.14   Heapshot

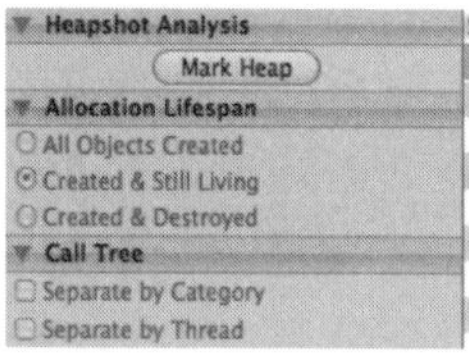

Heapshot Analysis	Snapshot		Timestamp	Heap Growth	# Persistent	
(Mark Heap)	▶ – Baseline –		12:39.600.430	764.62 KB	9167	
▼ Allocation Lifespan	▼ Heapshot 1		13:30.441.108	1.43 KB	24	
○ All Objects Created	▶ < non–object >			1.09 KB	14	
⊙ Created & Still Living	▶ GSEvent			128 Bytes	1	
○ Created & Destroyed	▶ Line			96 Bytes	3	
▼ Call Tree	▶ CFBasicHash (value–store)			48 Bytes	3	
□ Separate by Category	▶ CFBasicHash			48 Bytes	1	
□ Separate by Thread	▶ CFBasicHash (key–store)			32 Bytes	2	

Every allocation that took place after the first heapshot is in this category. You can see the **Line** instances that you just created, as well as a few objects that were used to handle other code during this time. You can take as many heapshots as you like; they are very useful for seeing what objects get allocated for a specific event. Double-tap the screen in TouchTracker to clear the lines and notice that the objects in this heapshot disappear.

To return to the full object list where we started, select the pop-up button in the bar above the table that currently says Heapshots and change it to Statistics.

Time Profiler Instrument

Now that you have hunted down wasted memory in TouchTracker, let's look for wasted CPU cycles using the Time Profiler instrument.

First, add the following CPU cycle-wasting code to the end of your **drawRect:** method:

```
float f = 0.0;
for (int i = 0; i < 1000; i++) {
    f = f + sin(sin(time(NULL) + i));
}
NSLog(@"f = %f", f);
```

Build and profile the application. When Instruments asks which instrument to use, choose Time Profiler (Figure 21.15). When **Instruments** launches the application and its window appears, make sure that all three areas are visible by clicking the buttons in the View control to blue.

Figure 21.15   Time Profiler instrument

Touch and hold your finger on the TouchTracker screen. Move your finger around but keep it on the screen. This sends **touchesMoved:withEvent:** over and over to the **TouchDrawView**. Each **touchesMoved:withEvent:** message causes **drawRect:** to be sent, which in turn causes the silly sin code to run repeatedly.

As you move your finger, watch the table in Instruments shuffle around its items. Then click the pause button (to the left of the Stop button) and examine the table's contents. Each row is one function or method call. In the left column, the amount of time spent in that function (expressed in milliseconds and as a percentage of the total run time) is displayed (Figure 21.16). This gives you an idea of where your application is spending its execution time.

Figure 21.16 Time Profiler results

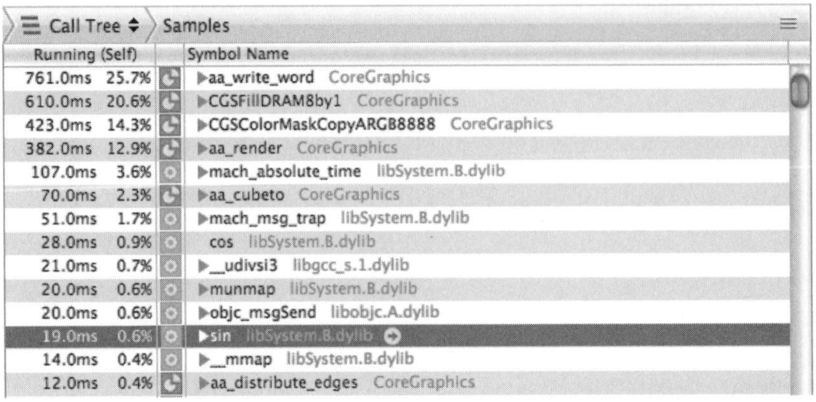
Call Tree ⇕ › Samples

Running (Self)		Symbol Name
761.0ms	25.7%	▶aa_write_word CoreGraphics
610.0ms	20.6%	▶CGSFillDRAM8by1 CoreGraphics
423.0ms	14.3%	▶CGSColorMaskCopyARGB8888 CoreGraphics
382.0ms	12.9%	▶aa_render CoreGraphics
107.0ms	3.6%	▶mach_absolute_time libSystem.B.dylib
70.0ms	2.3%	▶aa_cubeto CoreGraphics
51.0ms	1.7%	▶mach_msg_trap libSystem.B.dylib
28.0ms	0.9%	cos libSystem.B.dylib
21.0ms	0.7%	▶__udivsi3 libgcc_s.1.dylib
20.0ms	0.6%	▶munmap libSystem.B.dylib
20.0ms	0.6%	▶objc_msgSend libobjc.A.dylib
19.0ms	0.6%	▶sin libSystem.B.dylib
14.0ms	0.4%	▶__mmap libSystem.B.dylib
12.0ms	0.4%	▶aa_distribute_edges CoreGraphics

There is no rule that says, "If X percentage of time is spent in this function, your application has a problem." Instead, use Time Profiler if you notice your application acting sluggish while testing it as a user. For example, you should notice that drawing in TouchTracker is less responsive since we added the wasteful `sin` code.

We know that when drawing a line, two things are happening: **`touchesMoved:withEvent:`** and **`drawRect:`** are being sent to the **`TouchDrawView`** view. In TimeProfiler, we can check to see how much time is spent in these two methods relative to the rest of the application. If an inordinate amount of time is being spent in one of these methods, we know that's where the problem is.

(Keep in mind that some things just take time. Redrawing the entire screen every time the user's finger moves, as is done in TouchTracker, is an expensive operation. If it was hindering the user experience, you could find a way to reduce the number of times the screen is redrawn. For example, you could redraw only every tenth of a second regardless of how many touch events were sent.)

Time Profiler shows you nearly every function and method call in the application. If you want to focus on certain parts of the application's code, you can prune down its results. For example, sometimes the **`mach_msg_trap`** function will be very high on the sample list. This function is where the main thread sits when it is waiting for input. It is not a bad thing to spend time in this function, so you might want to eliminate the time spent in this function from the total amount of time shown in Time Profiler.

Use the search box in the top right corner of the Instruments window to find **`mach_msg_trap`**. Then, select it from the table. On the left side of the screen, click the Symbol button under Specific Data Mining. The **`mach_msg_trap`** function appears in the table under Specific Data Mining, and the pop-up button next to it displays Charge. Click on Charge and change it to Prune. Then, clear the text from the search box. Now, the list is adjusted so that any time spent in **`mach_msg_trap`** is ignored. You can click on Restore while **`mach_msg_trap`** is selected in the Specific Data Mining table to add it back to the total time.

Figure 21.17   Pruning a symbol

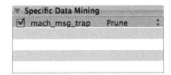

Other options for reducing the list of symbols in Time Profiler include showing only Objective-C calls, hiding system libraries, and charging calls to callers. The first two are obvious, but let's look more closely at charging calls to their caller. Select the row that holds **mach_absolute_time**. (If you are running on the simulator, select **_nanotime** instead.) Then, click the Symbol button. This function is removed from the main table, added to the Specific Data Mining table and listed as a Charge. This says that all of the time spent in this function will be attributed to the function or method that called it.

Notice in the main table that **mach_absolute_time** has been replaced with the function that calls it, **gettimeofday**. If you charge **gettimeofday**, it will be replaced with its caller, **time**. If you charge **time**, **drawRect:** will move to near the top of the list, since it now is now charged with **time**, **gettimeofday**, and **mach_absolute_time**.

Some common function calls always use a lot of CPU time. Most of the time, these are harmless and unavoidable. For example, the **objc_msgSend** function is the central dispatch function for any Objective-C message. It occasionally creeps to the top of the list when you are sending lots of messages to objects. Usually, it's nothing to worry about. However, if you are spending more time dispatching messages than actually doing work in the triggered methods *and* your application isn't performing well, you have a problem that needs solving.

As a real world example, an overzealous Objective-C developer might be tempted to create classes for things like vectors, points, and rectangles. These classes would likely have methods to add, subtract, or multiply instances as well as accessor methods to get and set instance variables. When these classes are used for drawing, the code has to send a lot of messages to do something simple, like creating two vectors and adding them together. The messages add excessive overhead considering the simplicity of the operation. Therefore, the better alternative is to create data types like these as structures and access their memory directly. (This is why CGRect and CGPoint are structures and not Objective-C classes.)

This should give you a good start with the Instruments application. The more you play with it, the more adept at using it you will become. One final word of warning before you invest a significant amount of your development time using Instruments: if there is no performance problem, don't fret over every little row in Instruments. It is a tool for diagnosing existing problems, not for finding new ones. Write clean code that works first; then, if there is a problem, you can find and fix it with the help of Instruments.

Don't forget to remove the CPU cycle-wasting code in **drawRect:**!

Xcode Schemes

In Chapter 4, we talked about how a workspace is a collection of projects, and a project is a collection targets and files. A target has a number of build settings and phases that reference files from its project.

(We'll talk more about those shortly.) When built, a target creates a product, which is usually an application. A *scheme* contains one or more targets *and* specifies what to do with the product or products (Figure 21.18).

Figure 21.18   Xcode containers

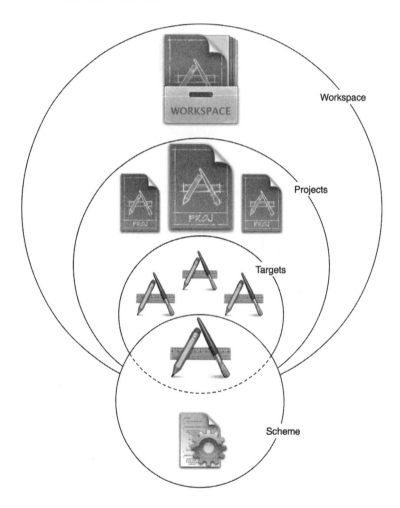

When you create a new project, a scheme with the same name as the project is created for you. This project has a TouchTracker scheme, and this scheme contains the TouchTracker target, which is responsible for building the TouchTracker iOS application.

To view the details of a scheme, click the Scheme pop-up menu at the top left of the Xcode window and select Edit Scheme.... The *scheme editor* will drop down into the workspace (Figure 21.19).

Figure 21.19   Editing a scheme

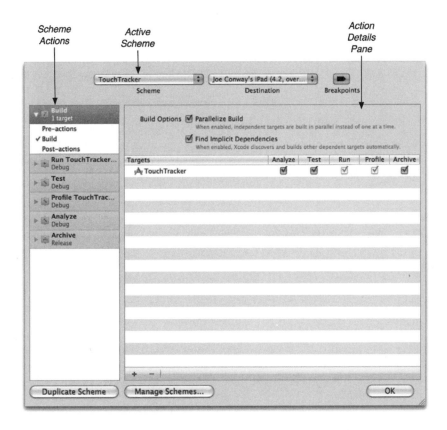

On the left side of the scheme editor is the list of actions that every scheme can do. (Notice that these scheme actions are also the choices you see when you click and hold the Run button in the Xcode workspace – with the exception of Archive.) Selecting a scheme action here shows its options in the details pane. Take a moment to look over the actions and the available options. Notice that some actions have multiple tabs that categorize their options.

Creating a new scheme

As projects become larger and more complicated, they require more specific testing and debugging. This can result in more time fiddling with the options for scheme actions. To avoid constant fiddling, we typically create new schemes for common situations. For example, if we have an application that consumes a lot of memory, we might want to routinely run the Allocations instrument on it. Instead of having Instruments ask which instrument to use when we profile the application, we can set up a new scheme that always runs Allocations.

Let's set up this scheme for the TouchTracker target. From the Scheme pop-up menu, select New Scheme.... When the sheet drops down, enter Allocations into the name and make sure TouchTracker is selected as the target (Figure 21.20). Click OK.

Figure 21.20   Creating a new scheme

Reopen the scheme editor sheet either by selecting Edit Scheme... from the Scheme pop-up menu or using the keyboard shortcut Command-Shift-<. Then click the Scheme pop-up menu in the scheme editor and select Allocations. Select the Profile action from the left table. On the detail pane, change the Instrument pop-up to Allocations and click OK (Figure 21.21).

Figure 21.21   An allocations-only scheme

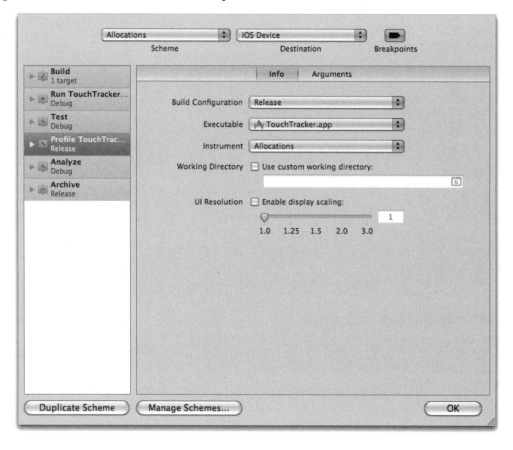

To use your new scheme, click the Scheme pop-up menu back on the workspace window. Here you can choose which scheme to use and a destination device for that scheme. Choose one of the destination options under the Allocations heading (Figure 21.22). Then, profile your application. Instruments will launch your application and automatically start the Allocations instrument.

Figure 21.22   Choosing a scheme

Switch back to the default TouchTracker scheme and profile again. This time, Instruments will again ask you to choose an instrument.

Here's a handy scheme tip: hold down the option key when selecting a scheme action from the Run button. This automatically opens the scheme editor and allows you to quickly review and change the settings of the selected scheme before performing the action. In fact, holding the option key down will open the scheme editor whether you select the action from the Run pop-up button, from the Product menu, or use a keyboard shortcut.

Build Settings

Every target includes *build settings* that describe how it should be built. Every project also has build settings that serve as defaults for all the targets within the project. Let's take a look at the project build settings for TouchTracker. Select the project from the project navigator and then select the TouchTracker project in the editor area.

Click the Build Settings tab at the top of the editor area. These are the project-level build settings – the default values that targets will inherit. There is a search box in the top-right corner of the editor area that you can use to search for a specific setting. Start typing iOS Deployment Target in the box, and the list will adjust to show this setting (which specifies the lowest version of the OS that can run the application).

Next to the search box are two sets of options. The first set, Basic or All, adjusts the settings shown. To see the difference between the second pair, Combined and Levels, let's look at the target's build settings.

In the left table of the editor area, select the TouchTracker target. Then select the Build Settings tab. These are the build settings for this specific target. Find the iOS Deployment Target setting again and click on Levels.

Figure 21.23   Build Settings Levels

Setting	Resolved	TouchTracker	TouchTracker	iOS Default
▼ Architectures				
Additional SDKs				
▶ Architectures	Optimized (armv7)	Optimized (armv7)	Standard (armv6 ar...	armv6
Base SDK	Latest iOS (iOS 4.3)		Latest iOS (iOS 4.3)	iOS 4.3

When viewing the build settings with this option, you can see each setting's value at the three different levels: OS, project, and target. (Figure 21.23). The far right column shows the iOS Default settings; these serve as the project's defaults, which it can override. The next column to the left shows the project's settings, and the one after that shows the currently selected target's settings. The Resolved column shows which setting will actually be used; it is always be equal to the left-most specified value. You can click in each column to set the value for that level.

Each target and project has multiple *build configurations*. A build configuration is a set of build settings. When you create a project, there are two build configurations: debug and release. The build settings for the debug configuration make it easier to debug your application, while the release settings turn on optimizations to speed up execution.

Let's take a look at the build settings and configurations for TouchTracker. Select the project from the project navigator and the TouchTracker project in the editor area. Then, select Info from the tabs on top of the editor area (Figure 21.24).

Figure 21.24   Build Configurations list

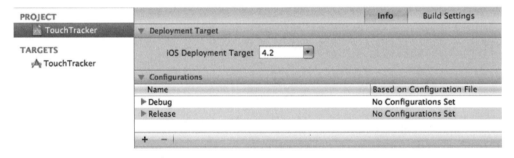

The Configurations section shows you the available build configurations in the project and targets. You can add and remove build configurations with the buttons at the bottom of this section.

When performing a scheme action, the scheme will use one of these configurations when building its targets. You can specify the build configuration that the scheme uses in the scheme editor in the option for Build Configuration in the Info pane.

Enough talk – time to do something useful. Let's change the value of the target build setting Preprocessor Macros. Preprocessor macros allow you to compile code conditionally. They are either defined or not defined at the start of a build. If you wrap a block of code in a preprocessor directive, it will only be compiled if that macro has been defined. The Preprocessor Macros setting lists preprocessor macros that are defined when a certain build configuration is used by a scheme to build a target.

Select the TouchTracker target, and in its Build Settings pane, search for the Preprocessor Macros build setting. Double-click on the value column for the Debug configuration under Preprocessor Macros. In the table that appears, add a new item: VIEW_DEBUG, as shown in Figure 21.25.

Figure 21.25   Changing a build setting

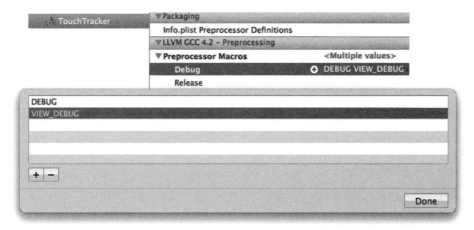

Adding this value to this setting says, "When you are building the TouchTracker target with the debug configuration, a preprocessor macro VIEW_DEBUG is defined."

Let's add some debugging code to TouchTracker that will only be compiled when the target is built with the debug configuration. **UIView** has a private method **recursiveDescription** that prints out the entire view hierarchy of an application. However, you cannot call this method in an application that you deploy to the App Store, so you will only allow it to be called if VIEW_DEBUG is defined.

In TouchTrackerAppDelegate.m, add the following code to **application:didFinishLaunchingWithOptions:**.

```
- (BOOL)application:(UIApplication *)application
    didFinishLaunchingWithOptions:(NSDictionary *)launchOptions
{
#ifdef VIEW_DEBUG
    NSLog(@"%@", [[self window] recursiveDescription]);
#endif
    [[self window] makeKeyAndVisible];
    return YES;
}
```

You can leave this code in for all builds. Because the preprocessor macro will not be defined for a release build, the code will not be compiled when you build for the App Store.

Now let's test out this code. Hold down the Option key and run the application. When the scheme editor drops down, make sure that the debug configuration is selected. Check out the console and you will see the view hierarchy of your application, starting at the window. (Don't worry about the warning that this line of code generates.)

22

Core Animation Layer

Animation is a hallmark of the iOS interface. When used properly it gives the user visual cues about the application's workflow. The classes and functions needed to animate an application's interface are in the Core Animation API. To use any part of Core Animation, you need to add the QuartzCore framework to your project.

Open your HypnoTime project and select the project from the project navigator. Then, select the HypnoTime target and the Build Phases pane. Add `QuartzCore.framework` to Link Binary With Libraries, as shown in Figure 22.1.

Figure 22.1 QuartzCore.framework

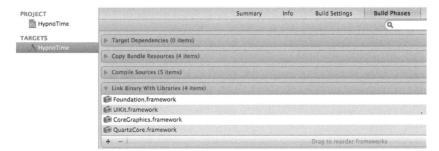

There are two classes that make Core Animation work: **CALayer** and **CAAnimation**.

At its core, an instance of **CALayer** is a buffer containing a bitmap. When you draw a layer (or a stack of layers), the rendering is hardware-accelerated. This makes drawing a layer to the screen incredibly fast. Like views, layers are arranged hierarchically – each layer can have sublayers.

A **CAAnimation** object causes a change over time. Typically, it changes one property (like `opacity`) of a layer.

In this chapter, we will focus on **CALayer**, and in the next chapter, we'll focus on **CAAnimation**.

Layers and views

In conversation, we talk about a view as though it is an object that is drawn to the screen – and this works well for discussing views and understanding higher level concepts. However, it is technically inaccurate. A view doesn't know how to draw to the screen; it only knows how to draw to an instance of **CALayer**.

Thus, the idea of layers may be new, but you've been using layers the entire time. When you instantiate a view, it creates a layer, and when the view draws, it is drawing on its layer. We call layers created by views *implicit layers*. Because every view has a layer, there is a matching layer hierarchy that mimics the view hierarchy (Figure 22.2).

After the views draw on their layers, the layers are copied to the screen. When we talk about copying a bunch of layers to the screen in a particular order and respecting each pixel's opacity, we use the word *composite*. Thus, the full description is "Each view renders its layer, and then all the layers are composited to the screen."

Figure 22.2   View and corresponding layer hierarchy

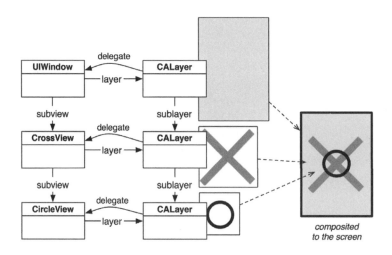

Notice in Figure 22.2 that each view has a layer and each view is its layer's delegate. We'll come back to the delegate relationship later in the chapter.

So what's the reason behind having views *and* layers? Remember that **UIView** is a subclass of **UIResponder**. A view is really an abstraction of a visible object that can be interacted with on the screen, wrapped into a tidy class. A layer, on the other hand, is all about the drawing.

Creating a CALayer

Not all layers are implicit layers. You can create a layer by sending **alloc** to the class **CALayer**. Layers created this way are called *explicit layers*. In this section, you're going to create a layer and then make it a sublayer of the layer of your **HypnosisView** (Figure 22.3).

Figure 22.3 Object diagram

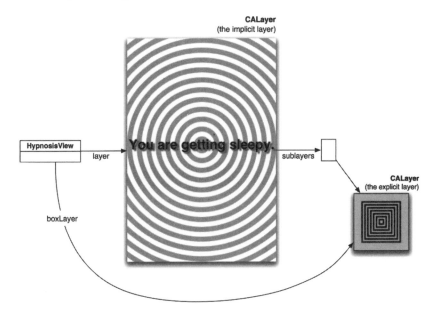

In HypnosisView.h, import the QuartzCore framework and add an instance variable to hold on to the layer object you are about to create:

```
#import <UIKit/UIKit.h>
#import <QuartzCore/QuartzCore.h>

@interface HypnosisView : UIView {
    CALayer *boxLayer;
    UIColor *stripeColor;
    float xShift, yShift;
}

@end
```

The designated initializer for a **CALayer** is simply **init**. After you instantiate a layer, you set its size, position (relative to its superlayer), and contents. In HypnosisView.m, change the **initWithFrame:** method to create a new layer and add it as a sublayer to **HypnosisView**'s layer.

```
- (id)initWithFrame:(CGRect)r
{
    self = [super initWithFrame:r];

    if (self) {
        stripeColor = [[UIColor lightGrayColor] retain];

        // Create the new layer object
        boxLayer = [[CALayer alloc] init];

        // Give it a size
        [boxLayer setBounds:CGRectMake(0.0, 0.0, 85.0, 85.0)];
```

```
        // Give it a location
        [boxLayer setPosition:CGPointMake(160.0, 100.0)];

        // Make half-transparent red the background color for the layer
        UIColor *reddish = [UIColor colorWithRed:1.0 green:0.0 blue:0.0 alpha:0.5];

        // Get a CGColor object with the same color values
        CGColorRef cgReddish = [reddish CGColor];
        [boxLayer setBackgroundColor:cgReddish];

        // Make it a sublayer of the view's layer
        [[self layer] addSublayer:boxLayer];

        [boxLayer release];
    }

    return self;
}
```

Build and run the application. You will see a semi-transparent red block appear on the view, as shown in Figure 22.4.

Figure 22.4   Red layer

Notice that layers interpret their size and position differently than views do. With a **UIView**, we typically define the frame of the view to establish its size and position. The origin of the frame rectangle is the upper-left corner of the view, and the size stretches right and down from the origin.

For a **CALayer**, instead of defining a frame, you set the bounds and position properties of the layer. The default setting for position is the *center* of the layer in its superlayer. (The anchorPoint property determines where the position lies inside the layer's bounds, and its default value is (0.5, 0.5), otherwise known as the center.) Therefore, if you change the size of the layer but leave the position constant, the layer will remain centered on the same point.

Even though a layer doesn't have a frame property, you can still get and set its "frame" by sending it the messages **frame** and **setFrame:**. When a layer is sent the message **frame**, it computes a rectangle from its position and bounds properties. Similarly, when sending a layer the message **setFrame:**, it does some math and then sets the bounds and position properties accordingly.

However, it is better to think of layers in terms of their position and bounds properties. The mental math to animate a layer is much simpler if you stick to setting the bounds and position properties directly.

Layer Content

A layer is simply a bitmap, and its *contents* can be set programmatically or with an image. To set the contents programmatically, you either subclass **CALayer** or assign a delegate to an instance of **CALayer**. The delegate then implements drawing routines. (This is how implicit layers work; the view is its layer's delegate.)

We will discuss drawing to a layer programmatically at the end of this chapter. For now, you're going to set the contents of the layer using an image file.

In HypnosisView.m, add the following code to the **initWithFrame:** method:

```
- (id)initWithFrame:(CGRect)r
{
    self = [super initWithFrame:r];

    if (self) {
        stripeColor = [[UIColor lightGrayColor] retain];

        boxLayer = [[CALayer alloc] init];
        [boxLayer setBounds:CGRectMake(0.0, 0.0, 85.0, 85.0)];
        [boxLayer setPosition:CGPointMake(160.0, 100.0)];

        UIColor *reddish = [UIColor colorWithRed:1.0 green:0.0 blue:0.0 alpha:0.5];
        CGColorRef cgReddish = [reddish CGColor];
        [boxLayer setBackgroundColor:cgReddish];

        // Create a UIImage
        UIImage *layerImage = [UIImage imageNamed:@"Hypno.png"];

        // Get the underlying CGImage
        CGImageRef image = [layerImage CGImage];

        // Put the CGImage on the layer
        [boxLayer setContents:(id)image];

        // Inset the image a bit on each side
        [boxLayer setContentsRect:CGRectMake(-0.1, -0.1, 1.2, 1.2)];

        // Let the image resize (without changing the aspect ratio)
        // to fill the contentRect
        [boxLayer setContentsGravity:kCAGravityResizeAspect];

        [[self layer] addSublayer:boxLayer];
        [boxLayer release];
```

```
    }

    return self;
}
```

In this code, we create an image and then get the underlying **CGImage** to use with Core Graphics drawing. Then we set the image as the layer's contents and make adjustments for how the contents appear within the layer.

Notice the use of **CGImageRef** and **CGColorRef** in this method. Why doesn't Core Animation use **UIImage** and **UIColor**?

The QuartzCore framework (which supplies the classes **CALayer** and **CAAnimation**) and Core Graphics framework (which supplies CGImageRef) exist on both iOS and on the Mac. UIKit (where we get **UIImage** and anything else prefixed with UI) only exists in iOS. To maintain its portability, QuartzCore must use CGImageRef instead of **UIImage**. Fortunately, UIKit objects have methods to easily access their Core Graphics counterparts, like **UIImage**'s **CGImage** method you used in the previous code.

Build and run the application. Now your layer has an image for its contents, as shown in Figure 22.5.

Figure 22.5   Layer with image

Because layers exist in a hierarchy, they can have sublayers, and each layer has a pointer back to its parent layer called superlayer. When a layer is composited to the screen, it is copied to the screen, and then each sublayer is composited atop it. Therefore, a layer always draws on top of its superlayer.

In a view hierarchy, sibling views (views with the same parent) will typically not have overlapping bounds. For instance, imagine a view with two subviews that are buttons. What would be the point of them overlapping and obscuring each other? It would only confuse and frustrate the user trying to tap one or the other.

The layer hierarchy, however, is a different story. Siblings are far more likely to overlap because layers are about visual effects and drawing, not user interaction. Which sibling is composited over the other? Each layer has a property called zPosition. If two layers are siblings and they overlap, then the layer with the higher zPosition is composited on top of the layer with the lower zPosition. (A sublayer *always* draws on top of its superlayer, regardless of zPosition.)

A layer's zPosition defaults to 0 and can be set to a negative value.

```
[underLayer setZPosition:-5];
[overLayer setZPosition:5];
[parentLayer addSublayer:underLayer];
[parentLayer addSublayer:overLayer];

// overLayer is composited on top of underLayer!
```

When the Z-axis is discussed, some developers imagine that perspective is applied, and they expect a layer to appear larger as its zPosition increases. However, Core Animation layers are presented orthographically; they do not appear as different sizes based on their zPositions.

Figure 22.6   Perspective vs. Orthographic

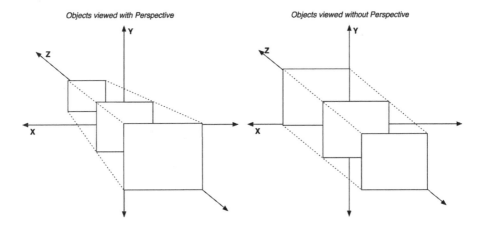

Implicitly Animatable Properties

Several of the properties of **CALayer** are *implicitly animatable*. This means that changes to these properties are automatically animated when their setters are called. The property position is an implicitly animatable property. Sending the message **setPosition:** to a **CALayer** doesn't just move the layer to a new position; it animates the change from the old position to the new one.

In this section, you will have the application respond to user taps: the boxLayer will move to wherever the user starts a touch. This change in position will be animated because position is an implicitly animatable property.

In HypnosisView.m, implement **touchesBegan:withEvent:** to change the layer's position.

```
- (void)touchesBegan:(NSSet *)touches
           withEvent:(UIEvent *)event
{
    UITouch *t = [touches anyObject];
    CGPoint p = [t locationInView:self];
    [boxLayer setPosition:p];
}
```

Build and run the application. The layer will move smoothly from its current position to where you tap. All you had to do to get this animation was send **setPosition:**. Pretty cool, huh?

If the user drags rather than taps, let's have the layer follow the user's finger. In HypnosisView.m, implement **touchesMoved:withEvent:** to send **setPosition:** to the layer. method:

```
- (void)touchesMoved:(NSSet *)touches
           withEvent:(UIEvent *)event
{
    UITouch *t = [touches anyObject];
    CGPoint p = [t locationInView:self];
    [boxLayer setPosition:p];
}
```

Build and run the application. This is not so cool. Notice how the animation makes the layer lag behind your dragging finger, making the application seem sluggish.

Why the poor response? An implicitly animatable property changes to its destination value over a constant time interval. However, changing a property while it is being animated starts another implicit animation. Therefore, if a layer is in the middle of traveling from point A to point B, and you tell it to go to point C, it will never reach B; and that little change of direction coupled with the timer restarting makes the animation seem choppy. (Figure 22.7)

Figure 22.7   Animation missing waypoints

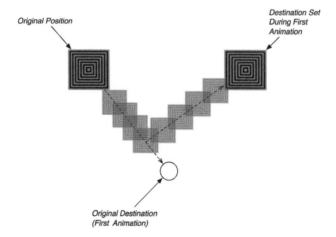

To disable an implicit animation, you can use an *animation transaction*. Animation transactions allow you to batch animations and set their parameters, like the duration and animation curve. To begin a transaction, you send the message **begin** to the class **CATransaction**. To end a transaction, you send

commit to **CATransaction**. Within the **begin** and **commit** block, you can set properties of a layer and also set values for the transaction as a whole.

Animation transactions can be used for lots of things, but here we'll use it to disable the animation of the layer's change in position. In HypnosisView.m, edit **touchesMoved:withEvent:**.

```
- (void)touchesMoved:(NSSet *)touches
           withEvent:(UIEvent *)event
{
    UITouch *t = [touches anyObject];
    CGPoint p = [t locationInView:self];
    [CATransaction begin];
    [CATransaction setDisableActions:YES];
    [boxLayer setPosition:p];
    [CATransaction commit];
}
```

Build and run the application. Now the dragging should feel much more responsive.

For the More Curious: Programmatically Generating Content

In this chapter, you set a layer's contents with an image file. Now let's look at setting a layer's contents programmatically. There are two ways of drawing to a layer that use Core Graphics: subclassing and delegation.

In practice, subclassing is the last thing you want to do. The only reason to subclass **CALayer** to provide custom content is if you need to draw differently depending on some state of the layer. If this is the approach you wish to take, you must override the method **drawInContext:**.

```
@implementation LayerSubclass

- (void)drawInContext:(CGContextRef)ctx
{
    UIImage *layerImage = nil;
    if (hypnotizing)
        layerImage = [UIImage imageNamed:@"Hypno.png"];
    else
        layerImage = [UIImage imageNamed:@"Plain.png"];

    CGRect boundingBox = CGContextGetClipBoundingBox(ctx);
    CGContextDrawImage(ctx, boundingBox, [layerImage CGImage]);
}
@end
```

Delegation is the more common way to programmatically draw to a layer. This is how implicit layers work, but you can also give an explicit layer a delegate. (However, it is not a good idea to assign a **UIView** as the delegate of an explicit layer. It is already the delegate of another layer, and bad things will happen.)

A layer sends the message **drawLayer:inContext:** to its delegate object when it is being displayed. The delegate can then perform Core Graphics calls on this context.

```
@implementation Controller

- (void)drawLayer:(CALayer *)layer inContext:(CGContextRef)ctx
{
    if (layer == hypnoLayer)
    {
        UIImage *layerImage = [UIImage imageNamed:@"Hypno.png"];
        CGRect boundingBox = CGContextGetClipBoundingBox(ctx);
        CGContextDrawImage(ctx, boundingBox, [layerImage CGImage]);
    }
}
@end
```

For both subclassing and delegation, you must send an explicit **setNeedsDisplay** to the layer in order for these methods to be invoked. Otherwise, the layer thinks it doesn't have any content and won't draw.

For the More Curious: Layers, Bitmaps, and Contexts

A layer is simply a bitmap – a chunk of memory that holds the red, green, blue, and alpha values of each pixel. When you send the message **setNeedsDisplay** to a **UIView** instance, that method is forwarded to the view's layer. After the run loop is done processing an event, every layer marked for re-display prepares a **CGContextRef**. Drawing routines called on this context generate pixels that end up in the layer's bitmap.

How do drawing routines get called on the layer's context? After a layer prepares its context, it sends the message **drawLayer:inContext:** to its delegate. The delegate of an implicit layer is its view, so in the implementation for **drawLayer:inContext:**, the view sends **drawRect:** to itself. Therefore, when you see this line at the top of your **drawRect:** implementations,

```
- (void)drawRect:(CGRect)r
{
    CGContextRef ctx = UIGraphicsGetCurrentContext();
}
```

you are getting a pointer to the layer's context. All of the drawing in **drawRect:** is filling the layer's bitmap, which is then copied to the screen.

Need to see this for yourself? Set an Xcode breakpoint in **HypnosisView**'s **drawRect:** and check out the stack trace in the debug navigator, as shown in Figure 22.8.

Figure 22.8   Stack trace in drawRect:

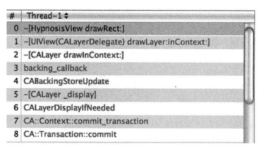

A few paragraphs up, we said that the pixels generated by drawing routines "end up in the layer's bitmap." What does that mean? When you want to create a bitmap context in Cocoa Touch (as you did when you created the thumbnails for the possessions), you typically do something like this:

```
// Create context
UIGraphicsBeginImageContextWithOptions(size, NO, [[UIScreen mainScreen] scale]);
    ... Do drawing here ...

// Get image result
UIImage *result = UIGraphicsGetImageFromCurrentImageContext();

// Clean up image context
UIGraphicsEndImageContext();
```

A bitmap context is created and drawn to, and the resulting pixels are stored in a **UIImage** instance.

The UIGraphics suite of functions provides a convenient way of creating a bitmap **CGContextRef** and writing that data to a **UIImage** object:

```
// Create a color space to use for the context
CGColorSpaceRef colorSpace = CGColorSpaceCreateDeviceRGB();

// Create a context of appropriate width and height
// with 4 bytes per pixel - RGBA
CGContextRef ctx =
    CGBitmapContextCreate(NULL, width, height, 8, width * 4,
                colorSpace, kCGImageAlphaPremultipliedLast);

// Make this context the current one
UIGraphicsPushContext(ctx);

... Do drawing here ...

// Get image result
CGImageRef image = CGBitmapContextCreateImage(ctx);
UIImage *result = [[[UIImage alloc] initWithCGImage:image] autorelease];

// Clean up image context - make previous context current if one exists
UIGraphicsPopContext();
CGImageRelease(image);
CGContextRelease(ctx);
CGColorSpaceRelease(colorSpace);
```

A layer creates the same kind of context when it needs to redraw its contents. However, a layer does it a little differently. See the NULL as the first parameter to **CGBitmapContextCreate**? That is where you pass a data buffer to hold the pixels generated by drawing routines in this context. By passing NULL, we say, "Core Graphics, figure out how much memory is needed for this buffer, create it, and then dispose of it when the context is destroyed." A **CALayer** already has a buffer (its contents), so it would call the function as follows:

```
CGContextRef ctx =
    CGBitmapContextCreate(myBitmapPixels, width, height, 8, width * 4,
                colorSpace, kCGImageAlphaPremultipliedLast);
```

Then, when this context is drawn to, all of the resulting pixels are immediately written to the bitmap that is the layer.

Challenge: Dynamic Layer Content

Give boxLayer a delegate to draw its content. When the layer is near the top of the screen, draw the Hypno.png image to the layer in the delegate method with full opacity. As the layer approaches the bottom of the screen, draw the image more transparently.

This is a very difficult challenge, so you can have three hints:

1. The delegate of boxLayer cannot be **HypnosisView**.

2. You must send **setNeedsDisplay** to the layer every time it changes position.

3. To set the opacity of drawing in a context, use the function **CGContextSetAlpha**.

Happy coding!

23

Controlling Animation with CAAnimation

An animation object drives change over time. An animation object is an instruction set ("Move from point A to point B over 2 seconds") that can be added to a **CALayer** instance. When an animation object is added to a layer, that layer begins following the instructions of the animation. Many properties of **CALayer** can be animated by animation objects: opacity, position, transform, bounds, and contents are just a few.

Animation Objects

While you have not yet used animations objects explicitly, all animation in iOS is driven by them, including the animations you saw in the last chapter. The abstract superclass for all animation objects is **CAAnimation**. **CAAnimation** is responsible for handling timing; for instance, it has a duration property that specifies the length of the animation. As an abstract superclass, you do not use **CAAnimation** objects directly. Instead, you use one of its concrete subclasses shown in Figure 23.1.

Figure 23.1   Inheritance

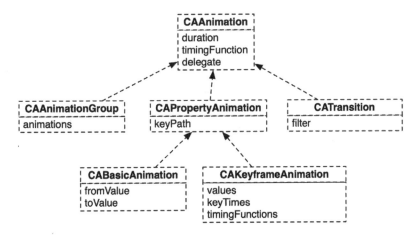

CAPropertyAnimation is a subclass of **CAAnimation** that extends the ability of its superclass by adding the ability to change the properties of a layer. Each property animation has a *key path* of type **NSString**. This string is the name of an animatable property of a **CALayer**. Many of **CALayer**'s properties are animatable. Check the documentation for a list. Search for "animatable properties" and look under the Core Animation Programming Guide (Figure 23.2).

Figure 23.2   Animatable properties in the documentation

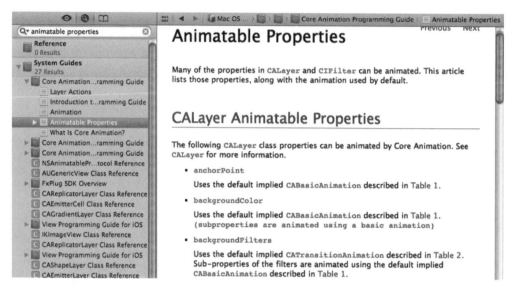

Typically, the key path matches the name of the property. For example, a property animation that will animate a layer's opacity property will have a key path of opacity.

Sometimes a property whose type is a structure (like position, whose type is CGPoint) can have each of its members accessed by a key path. (The available options for this are in the documentation under Core Animation Extensions To Key-Value Coding.)

However, like **CAAnimation**, **CAPropertyAnimation** is an abstract superclass. To create an animation object that modifies a property of a layer, you use one of the two concrete subclasses of **CAPropertyAnimation**: **CABasicAnimation** and **CAKeyframeAnimation**. Most of the time you will spend with Core Animation will involve these two classes.

CABasicAnimation is the simpler of the two classes. It has two properties: fromValue and toValue, and it inherits **CAAnimation**'s duration property. When a basic animation is added to a layer, the property to be animated is set to the value in fromValue. Over the time specified by duration, the value of the property is interpolated linearly from fromValue to toValue, as shown in Figure 23.3.

Figure 23.3   Interpolating a CABasicAnimation that animates the position of a layer

Here's an example of an animation object that acts on a layer's opacity property.

```
// Create an animation that will change the opacity of a layer
CABasicAnimation *fader = [CABasicAnimation animationWithKeyPath:@"opacity"];

// It will last 2 seconds
[fader setDuration:2.0];

// The layer's opacity will start at 1.0 (completely opaque)
[fader setFromValue:[NSNumber numberWithFloat:1.0]];

// And will end at 0.0 (completely transparent)
[fader setToValue:[NSNumber numberWithFloat:0.0]];

// Add it to the layer
[rexLayer addAnimation:fader forKey:@"BigFade"];
```

The key, "BigFade" in this case, is ignored by the system. However, you could use it to access the animation later if, for example, you needed to cancel it mid-fade.

In this code, the fromValue and toValue take **NSNumber**s as arguments. The type of these properties however, is id because animation objects need to be able to support different data types. For example, an animation that changes the position of a layer would need values that are of type CGPoint.

However, you can't just pass any object for any property; **CABasicAnimation** expects the appropriate object based on the key path. For scalar values, like opacity, you can wrap a number in an **NSNumber** instance. For properties represented by structures, like position, you wrap the structures in instances of **NSValue**.

```
CABasicAnimation *mover = [CABasicAnimation animationWithKeyPath:@"position"];
[mover setDuration:1.0];
[mover setFromValue:[NSValue valueWithCGPoint:CGPointMake(0.0, 100.0)]];
[mover setToValue:[NSValue valueWithCGPoint:CGPointMake(100.0, 100.0)]];
```

The difference between **CABasicAnimation** and **CAKeyframeAnimation** is that a basic animation only interpolates two values while a keyframe animation can interpolate as many values as you give it. These values are put into an **NSArray** in the order in which they are to occur. This array is then set as the values property of a **CAKeyframeAnimation** instance.

```
CAKeyframeAnimation *mover = [CAKeyframeAnimation animationWithKeyPath:@"position"];
NSArray *vals = [NSMutableArray array];
```

```
[vals addObject:[NSValue valueWithCGPoint:CGPointMake(0.0, 100.0)]];
[vals addObject:[NSValue valueWithCGPoint:CGPointMake(100.0, 100.0)]];
[mover setValues:vals];
[mover setDuration:1.0];
```

Each value in the `values` property is called a *keyframe*. Keyframes are the values that the animation will interpolate; the animation will take the property it is animating through each of these keyframes over its duration. A basic animation is really a keyframe animation that is limited to two keyframes. (In addition to allowing more than two keyframes, **CAKeyframeAnimation** adds the ability to change the timing of each of the keyframes, but that's more advanced than what we want to talk about right now.)

There are two more **CAAnimation** subclasses, but they are used less often. A **CAAnimationGroup** instance holds an array of animation objects. When an animation group is added to a layer, the animations run concurrently.

```
CABasicAnimation *mover = [CABasicAnimation animationWithKeyPath:@"position"];
[mover setDuration:1.0];
[mover setFromValue:[NSValue valueWithCGPoint:CGPointMake(0.0, 100.0)]];
[mover setToValue:[NSValue valueWithCGPoint:CGPointMake(100.0, 100.0)]];

CABasicAnimation *fader = [CABasicAnimation animationWithKeyPath:@"opacity"];
[fader setDuration:1.0];
[fader setFromValue:[NSNumber numberWithFloat:1.0]];
[fader setToValue:[NSNumber numberWithFloat:1.0]];

CAAnimationGroup *group = [CAAnimationGroup animation];
[group setAnimations:[NSArray arrayWithObjects:fader, mover, nil]];
```

CATransition animates layers as they are transitioning on and off the screen. On Mac OS X, **CATransition** is made very powerful by Core Image Filters. In iOS, it can only do a couple of simple transitions like fading and sliding. (**CATransition** is used by **UINavigationController** when pushing a view controller's view onto the screen.)

Spinning with CABasicAnimation

In this section, you are going to use an animation object to spin the implicit layer of the time field in HypnoTime's **CurrentTimeViewController** whenever it is updated (Figure 23.4). (Recall that an implicit layer is a layer created by a view when the view is instantiated. The time field is a **UILabel**, which is a subclass of **UIView**, so it has an implicit layer that we can animate.)

Figure 23.4   Current time mid-spin

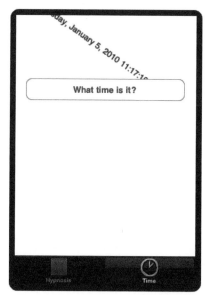

Open `HypnoTime.xcodeproj`.

The Core Animation code you will write in this exercise will be in `CurrentTimeViewController.m`. So import the header from the QuartzCore framework at the top of this file.

#import <QuartzCore/QuartzCore.h>

@implementation CurrentTimeViewController

In order to spin the `timeLabel`, you need an animation object that will apply a 360-degree rotation over time to a layer. So we need to determine four things:

- Which type of animation object suits this purpose?

- What key path handles rotation?

- How long should the animation take to complete?

- What values should the animation interpolate?

To answer the first question, think about the number of keyframes an animation would need to make a complete revolution. It only needs two: a non-rotated value and a fully-rotated value, so **CABasicAnimation** can handle this task.

To determine the key path, we use the property of **CALayer** that deals with rotation. This property is its `transform`, the transformation matrix that is applied to the layer when it draws. The `transform` of a layer can rotate, scale, translate, and skew its frame. (For more details, go to Core Animation Extensions To Key-Value Coding in the documentation.) This exercise only calls for rotating the layer, and, fortunately, you can isolate the rotation of the `transform` in a key path (Figure 23.5). Therefore, the key path of the basic animation will be `transform.rotation`.

Figure 23.5   Core Animation Extensions to Key-Value Coding documentation

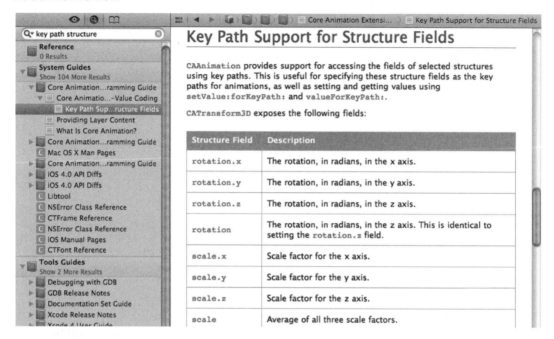

Let's make the duration of this animation one second. That's enough time for the user to see the spin but not so much time that they get bored waiting for it to complete.

Lastly, we need the values of the two keyframes: the `fromValue` and the `toValue`. The documentation says that the `transform.rotation` is in radians, so that's how we'll pass these values. A little geometry research tells us that no rotation is `0` radians and a full rotation is `2 * PI` radians. When using a **CABasicAnimation**, if you do not supply a `fromValue`, the animation assumes that `fromValue` is the current value of that property. The default value of the `transform` property is the identity matrix – no rotation. This means you only have to supply the final keyframe to this animation object.

In `CurrentTimeViewController.m`, edit the method **showCurrentTime:** to create the animation object.

```
- (IBAction)showCurrentTime:(id)sender
{
    NSDate *now = [NSDate date];
    static NSDateFormatter *formatter = nil;
    if (!formatter) {
        formatter = [[NSDateFormatter alloc] init];
        [formatter setDateStyle:NSDateFormatterShortStyle];
    }
    [timeLabel setText:[formatter stringFromDate:now]];

    // Create a basic animation
    CABasicAnimation *spin =
            [CABasicAnimation animationWithKeyPath:@"transform.rotation"];

    // fromValue is implied
    [spin setToValue:[NSNumber numberWithFloat:M_PI * 2.0]];
```

```
        [spin setDuration:1.0];
}
```

Now that you have an animation object, it needs to be applied to a layer for it to have any effect. **CALayer** instances implement the method **addAnimation:forKey:** for this purpose. This method takes two arguments: an animation object and a key. Once again: this key is *not* the key path; it is simply a human-readable name for this animation.

In **showCurrentTime:**, add your animation object to the layer to start the animation.

```
- (IBAction)showCurrentTime:(id)sender
{
    NSDate *now = [NSDate date];
    static NSDateFormatter *formatter = nil;
    if (!formatter) {
        formatter = [[NSDateFormatter alloc] init];
        [formatter setDateStyle:NSDateFormatterShortStyle];
    }
    [timeLabel setText:[formatter stringFromDate:now]];

    CABasicAnimation *spin =
                [CABasicAnimation animationWithKeyPath:@"transform.rotation"];

    [spin setToValue:[NSNumber numberWithFloat:M_PI * 2.0]];
    [spin setDuration:1.0];

    // Kick off the animation by adding it to the layer
    [[timeLabel layer] addAnimation:spin
                            forKey:@"spinAnimation"];
}
```

Build and run the application. The label field will spin 360 degrees when the user updates it – either by switching to the Time tab or tapping the button.

Note that the animation object exists independently of the layer it is applied to. This animation object could be added to any layer to rotate it 360 degrees. You can create animation objects and keep them around for later use in the application; however, make sure you retain them if you plan to do this. The animation object returned from **animationWithKeyPath:** is autoreleased.

Timing functions

You may notice that the label field's layer starts and stops suddenly; it would look nicer if it gradually accelerated and decelerated. This sort of behavior is controlled by the animation's timing function, which is an instance of the class **CAMediaTimingFunction**. By default, the timing function is linear – the values are interpolated linearly. Changing the timing function changes how these animations are interpolated. It doesn't change the duration or the keyframes.

In **showCurrentTime:**, change the timing function to "ease" in and out of the animation.

```
- (IBAction)showCurrentTime:(id)sender
{
    NSDate *now = [NSDate date];
    static NSDateFormatter *formatter = nil;
    if (!formatter) {
        formatter = [[NSDateFormatter alloc] init];
        [formatter setDateStyle:NSDateFormatterShortStyle];
    }
```

```
    [timeLabel setText:[formatter stringFromDate:now]];

    // Create a basic animation
    CABasicAnimation *spin =
            [CABasicAnimation animationWithKeyPath:@"transform.rotation"];

    [spin setToValue:[NSNumber numberWithFloat:M_PI * 2.0]];
    [spin setDuration:1.0];

    // Set the timing function
    CAMediaTimingFunction *tf = [CAMediaTimingFunction
                    functionWithName:kCAMediaTimingFunctionEaseInEaseOut];
    [spin setTimingFunction:tf];

    [[timeLabel layer] addAnimation:spin
                        forKey:@"spinAnimation"];
}
```

Build and run the application and see how the animation changes.

There are four timing functions, you have seen linear and kCAMediaTimingFunctionEaseInEaseOut. The other two are kCAMediaTimingFunctionEaseIn (accelerates gradually, stops suddenly) and kCAMediaTimingFunctionEaseOut (accelerates suddenly, stops slowly). You can also create your own timing functions with **CAMediaTimingFunction**. See the doc for details.

Animation completion

Sometimes you want to know when an animation is finished. For instance, you might want to chain animations or update another object when an animation completes. How can you know when an animation is complete? Every animation object can have a delegate, and the animation object sends the message **animationDidStop:finished:** to its delegate when an animation stops.

Edit CurrentTimeViewController.m so that it logs a message to the console whenever an animation stops.

```
- (void)animationDidStop:(CAAnimation *)anim finished:(BOOL)flag
{
    NSLog(@"%@ finished: %d", anim, flag);
}

- (IBAction)showCurrentTime:(id)sender
{
    NSDate *now = [NSDate date];
    static NSDateFormatter *formatter = nil;
    if (!formatter) {
        formatter = [[NSDateFormatter alloc] init];
        [formatter setDateStyle:NSDateFormatterShortStyle];
    }
    [timeLabel setText:[formatter stringFromDate:now]];

    CABasicAnimation *spin =
            [CABasicAnimation animationWithKeyPath:@"transform.rotation"];
    [spin setToValue:[NSNumber numberWithFloat:M_PI * 2.0]];
    [spin setDuration:1.0];
    [spin setDelegate:self];

    CAMediaTimingFunction *tf = [CAMediaTimingFunction
                    functionWithName:kCAMediaTimingFunctionEaseInEaseOut];
```

```
    [spin setTimingFunction:tf];

    [[timeLabel layer] addAnimation:spin
                              forKey:@"spinAnimation"];
}
```

Build and run the application. Notice the log statements when the animation is complete. If you press the button several times quickly, the animation in progress will be interrupted by a new one. The interrupted animation will still send the message **animationDidStop:finished:** to its delegate; however, the finished flag will be NO.

Bouncing with a CAKeyframeAnimation

For practice with **CAKeyframeAnimation**, you are going to make the time label grow and shrink to give it a bouncing effect (Figure 23.6).

Figure 23.6   Current time mid-bounce

Remove (or comment out) the spin animation and replace it with a nice bounce. The method **showCurrentTime:** should look like this:

```
- (IBAction)showCurrentTime:(id)sender
{
    NSDate *now = [NSDate date];
    static NSDateFormatter *formatter = nil;
    if (!formatter) {
        formatter = [[NSDateFormatter alloc] init];
        [formatter setDateStyle:NSDateFormatterShortStyle];
    }
    [timeLabel setText:[formatter stringFromDate:now]];

    // Create a key frame animation
    CAKeyframeAnimation *bounce =
```

```
                    [CAKeyframeAnimation animationWithKeyPath:@"transform"];

    // Create the values it will pass through
    CATransform3D forward = CATransform3DMakeScale(1.3, 1.3, 1);
    CATransform3D back = CATransform3DMakeScale(0.7, 0.7, 1);
    CATransform3D forward2 = CATransform3DMakeScale(1.2, 1.2, 1);
    CATransform3D back2 = CATransform3DMakeScale(0.9, 0.9, 1);
    [bounce setValues:[NSArray arrayWithObjects:
                        [NSValue valueWithCATransform3D:CATransform3DIdentity],
                        [NSValue valueWithCATransform3D:forward],
                        [NSValue valueWithCATransform3D:back],
                        [NSValue valueWithCATransform3D:forward2],
                        [NSValue valueWithCATransform3D:back2],
                        [NSValue valueWithCATransform3D:CATransform3DIdentity],
                        nil]];
    // Set the duration
    [bounce setDuration:0.6];

    // Animate the layer
    [[timeLabel layer] addAnimation:bounce
                        forKey:@"bounceAnimation"];
}
```

Build and run the application. The time field should now scale up and down and up and down when it is updated. The constant `CATransform3DIdentity` is the *identity matrix*. When the transform of a layer is the identity matrix, no scaling, rotation, or translation is applied to the layer: it sits squarely within its bounding box at its position. So, this animation starts at no transformation, scales a few times, and then reverts back to no transformation.

Once you understand layers and the basics of animation, there isn't a whole lot to it – other than finding the appropriate key path and getting the timing of things right. Core Animation is one of those things you can play around with and see results immediately. So play with it!

Challenge: More Animation

When the time label bounces, it should also change its opacity. Try and match the fading of the opacity with the shrinking and growing of the label. As another challenge, after the `CurrentTimeViewController`'s view slides onto the screen, have the What time is it? button slide in from the other direction.

For the More Curious: The Presentation Layer and the Model Layer

You can think of an instance of **CALayer** as having two parts: the content that gets composited onto the screen, and a set of parameters that describe how it should be composited: `opacity`, `transform`, `position`, etc. When a layer is being animated, it actually has two copies of these parameters: the model version and the presentation version. The presentation parameters are the ones that are being smoothly changed by the animation object. The model parameters are the persistent ones – the ones that will be used once the animation is over.

So, when a layer is being animated, its content is composited to the screen using the presentation parameters. When it is animation-less, the model parameters are used.

Apple calls these sets of parameters *the model layer* and *the presentation layer*.

When you ask a layer for its position, you are getting the position of the model layer. To get the presentation version, you ask for the **presentationLayer** first.

```
CGPoint whereIsItWhenAnimationStops = [layer position];
CGPoint whereIsItNow = [[layer presentationLayer] position];
```

Why is this useful? Imagine a game that has animating objects on the screen, and if the user taps one of the objects, it blows up. Only the presentation layer knows where the object currently is on the screen, which you must know in order to judge the accuracy of the user's tap.

In this chapter, our examples have had the animated objects return to their original states after the animation is complete. Often, however, you want to animate an object to a state and then have it stay there once the animation is over. To do this, you must keep the presentation and model layers clear in your mind. Not doing so leads to two common errors:

- *Your animation goes great, but at the end it snaps back to its initial position (or opacity or whatever) when you wanted it to remain where it was.* This happens because you forgot to update the model parameters to match the final state of your animation. Try using an explicit animation in **touchesBegan:withEvent:** method in HypnosisView.m. (Also comment out **touchesMoved:withEvent:**.)

  ```
  - (void)touchesBegan:(NSSet *)touches withEvent:(UIEvent *)event
  {
      UITouch *t = [touches anyObject];
      CGPoint p = [t locationInView:self];
      CABasicAnimation *ba = [CABasicAnimation animationWithKeyPath:@"position"];
      [ba setFromValue:[NSValue valueWithCGPoint:[boxLayer position]]];
      [ba setToValue:[NSValue valueWithCGPoint:p]];
      [ba setDuration:3.0];

      // Update the model layer
      [boxLayer setPosition:p];

      // Add animation that will gradually update presentation layer
      [boxLayer addAnimation:ba forKey:@"foo"];
  }
  - (void)touchesMoved:(NSSet *)touches
              withEvent:(UIEvent *)event
  {
  //    UITouch *t = [touches anyObject];
  //    CGPoint p = [t locationInView:self];
  //    [boxLayer setPosition:p];

  }
  ```

  In this animation, If you build and run now and tap the screen, you will see the boxLayer slowly move to wherever you touched the screen.

  If you comment out the line that says [boxLayer setPosition:p], you'll see that the layer bounces back to its starting position once the animation ends. For beginners, this is a very common error.

- *No animation happens. Your layer leaps directly to its final state.* When an animation begins, if there is no fromValue, the fromValue is taken from the model layer. If you update the model to the final state before starting the animation, your fromValue and toValue end up the same. Usually the fix is to give the animation an explicit fromValue.

24

Blocks and Categories

In iOS 4.0, a language-level feature called *blocks* was made available. A block is a set of instructions that can be passed around as a variable and called like a function. Blocks provide conveniences for a programmer and performance boosts for applications. If you are familiar with other high-level languages, you may know blocks as *closures* or *anonymous functions*. This chapter will briefly cover blocks and some of the common ways to use them. This chapter will also cover an Objective-C language feature called *categories*.

Colorizing TouchDrawView

Earlier, you wrote an application called TouchTracker that allowed the user to paint black lines on a white canvas. In this exercise, you will add functionality that will change the color of the lines based on their angle and length. You will implement this behavior using blocks.

Figure 24.1   TouchTracker

Open TouchTracker.xcodeproj. Each **Line** instance will have its own color instance variable. When the user shakes the device, each line will be given a new **UIColor** instance based on its angle and length. When the device rotates, the color of the lines will be inverted.

Before we get to these things, **TouchDrawView** and **Line** need to support color. In Line.h, add a new instance variable to the **Line** class and expose it as a property.

```
@interface Line : NSObject {
    CGPoint begin;
    CGPoint end;

    UIColor *color;
}
@property (nonatomic) CGPoint begin;
@property (nonatomic) CGPoint end;

@property (nonatomic, retain) UIColor *color;

@end
```

In Line.m, synthesize the property and add an **init** method to set a default color and a **dealloc** method to release it when the line is destroyed.

```
@implementation Line
@synthesize color;
- (id)init
{
    self = [super init];

    if (self) {
        [self setColor:[UIColor blackColor]];
    }

    return self;
}

- (void)dealloc
{
    [color release];
    [super dealloc];
}
```

In TouchDrawView.m, update the **drawRect:** method to use the **Line**'s color when drawing a line.

```
- (void)drawRect:(CGRect)rect {
    CGContextRef context = UIGraphicsGetCurrentContext();
    CGContextSetLineWidth(context, 10.0);
    CGContextSetLineCap(context, kCGLineCapRound);

    // [[UIColor blackColor] set];
    for (Line *line in completeLines) {
        [[line color] set];

        CGContextMoveToPoint(context, [line begin].x, [line begin].y);
        CGContextAddLineToPoint(context, [line end].x, [line end].y);
        CGContextStrokePath(context);
    }

    [[UIColor redColor] set];
```

```
    for (NSValue *v in linesInProcess) {
        Line *line = [linesInProcess objectForKey:v];
        CGContextMoveToPoint(context, [line begin].x, [line begin].y);
        CGContextAddLineToPoint(context, [line end].x, [line end].y);
        CGContextStrokePath(context);
    }
}
```

Build the application to make sure there are no errors. It should still run the same as before.

Blocks

Blocks as variables

Now that you have some experience with Objective-C and the iOS SDK, how would you add the colorize-on-shake and invert-color-on-rotate features? You would probably write a method that would loop over every line, perform some calculations with that line's data, and then set its color.

```
// A candidate for colorizeOnShake as implemented by TouchDrawView
- (void)colorizeOnShake
{
    for(Line *l in completeLines) {
        UIColor *clr = [self computeColorForLine:l];
        [l setColor:clr];
    }
    [self setNeedsDisplay];
}
```

Then, you would write a similar method for inverting the current color of a **Line**.

```
// A candidate for invertOnShake as implemented by TouchDrawView
- (void)invertOnRotate
{
    for(Line *l in completeLines) {
        // The method called to compute the color
        // is the only difference in this method
        // versus the previous one.
        UIColor *clr = [self invertedColorForLine:l];
        [l setColor:clr];
    }
    [self setNeedsDisplay];
}
```

Now, this is a fine approach, but notice the redundancy between the two methods. Imagine if you wanted to add another coloring scheme to your application; for example, a double tap could reset all of the lines to black. This method would repeat the same general form as the previous two (looping over all of the lines and giving them a color) with slightly different details (the calculations to determine the color).

It would be much cooler to write the general form once and plug in different sets of details. With blocks, you can. In TouchDrawView.m, implement a stub for the following method. This method will eventually take care of the generic part of the process.

```
- (void)transformLineColorsWithBlock:(UIColor * (^)(Line *))colorForLine
{
    // You'll fill in the body for this method in a bit.
    // The crazy syntax of the argument for this method
    // deserves some discussion first.
}
```

Scary syntax, huh? It's actually not that bad when you break it down. The method
`transformLineColorsWithBlock:` accepts one argument: a block. This block must return an instance
of `UIColor`, and its only argument is of type `Line`.

Figure 24.2   Syntax of a block

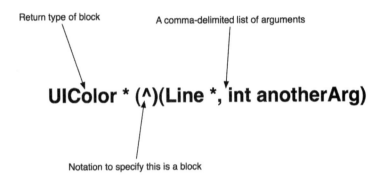

The syntax of a block is made even scarier because it is being used as an argument to a method, which
adds an additional set of parentheses around the block. You will get used to it.

The name of the block variable in the scope of this method is `colorForLine`. A block, being a piece of
executable code, can be called just like a C function. Therefore, you can run the code in this block like
so:

```
UIColor *c = colorForLine(someLine);
```

The goal of the method `transformLineColorsWithBlock:` is to change the color of every line in the
completeLines given a block that defines how they should be colored. Thus, the implementation of
this method will iterate over every `Line` in completeLines and set its color to the return value of the
block. Update this method in TouchDrawView.m.

```
- (void)transformLineColorsWithBlock:(UIColor * (^)(Line *))colorForLine
{
    for(Line *l in completeLines) {
        UIColor *c = colorForLine(l);
        [l setColor:c];
    }
    [self setNeedsDisplay];
}
```

Build your application to make sure there are no errors. It will still run the same because you have yet
to invoke this method.

Now, you will implement a method that will be invoked when the user shakes the device. It will create a block that will be sent to **transformLineColorsWithBlock:**; which executes the block for each of the completeLines. This block will do some simple geometry to compute a color for a given **Line**. You will use the difference between the x and y components of the start and end points to compute the red and green values of the color, and the length of the line for the blue component. Define this method in TouchDrawView.m.

```
- (void)colorize
{
    // Vertical means more red, horizontal means more green,
    // longer means more blue

    // A block variable named colorScheme is created here:
    UIColor * (^colorScheme)(Line *) = ^(Line *l) {
        // Compute delta between begin and end points
        // for each component
        float dx = [l end].x - [l begin].x;
        float dy = [l end].y - [l begin].y;

        // If dx is near zero, red = 1, otherwise, use slope
        float r = (fabs(dx) < 0.001 ? 1.0 : fabs(dy / dx));

        // If dy is near zero, green = 1, otherwise, use inv. slope
        float g = (fabs(dy) < 0.001 ? 1.0 : fabs(dx / dy));

        // blue = length over 300
        float b = hypot(dx, dy) / 300.0;

        return [UIColor colorWithRed:r green:g blue:b alpha:1];
    };

    // Pass this colorScheme block to the method
    // that will iterate over every line and assign
    // the computed color to that line
    [self transformLineColorsWithBlock:colorScheme];
}
```

We're back in scary syntax land, again. Let's break it down. The ultimate goal of this method is to create a block that takes a **Line** as an argument and returns a **UIColor**. This block will then be passed to the method **transformLineColorsWithBlock:**, which will execute this block for each line and set its color. Therefore, we must create a block and a block variable that holds a reference to that block.

Figure 24.3   Syntax of a block variable and block

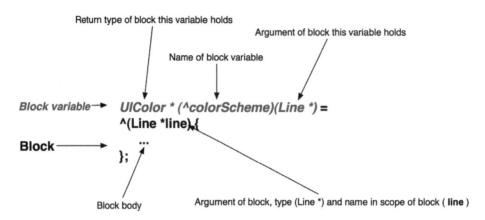

The actual block is the part that follows the assignment operator (=). A block is defined by the ^ character and parentheses that contain the arguments that must be passed to this block when it is called, followed by curly brackets where the block body is entered. Objective-C, C, and C++ code can make up the body of a block.

A block variable, which holds a reference to a block, is the part before the assignment operator. A block variable is just like any other variable: it has a type and a name. The only difference is that the variable declaration is a bit ugly. Typically, variable definitions follow the following form:

```
type varname = ...;

// Example
int counter = 0;
```

The syntax for a block variable, however, mixes the name of the variable in the middle of the type of the block. The form is the return type, followed by parentheses that contain the ^ character along with the name of the variable and another set of parentheses that contain all of the arguments for this block.

The assignment of colorScheme to the block defined in **colorize** is valid because the block it references has the same arguments and return type. (You don't have to include the return type when defining the block in this way; the compiler will figure it out.) Try changing the block to have a different argument list to see the compiler complain:

```
// The compiler will not like this: the block variable
// and defined block are of different types.
UIColor * (^colorScheme)(Line *) = ^(Line *l, int foo) {
    ...
};
```

Change the block back to the working version.

Now you have a method, **colorize**, that, when executed, will create a block that computes a color given a line. This block is sent via the message **transformLineColorsWithBlock:** to the instance of **TouchDrawView**. In TouchDrawView.m, set up **TouchDrawView** so it is sent the message **colorize** when the device is shaken by implementing the following code.

```
- (BOOL)canBecomeFirstResponder
{
    return YES;
}
- (void)didMoveToWindow
{
    [self becomeFirstResponder];
}
- (void)motionBegan:(UIEventSubtype)motion withEvent:(UIEvent *)event
{
    [self colorize];
}
```

Build and run your application. Draw some lines then shake the device. (If you are on the simulator, choose Shake Gesture from the Hardware menu.)

You may have some warnings about **colorize** or **transformLineColorsWithBlock:**. You can ignore these warnings for now; you'll fix them later. If your application is throwing an exception about unrecognized selectors, make sure you have spelled these two method names correctly in their implementation and use.

Capturing variables

So far, blocks look a lot like C function pointers. However, there is one major feature of blocks that separates it from function pointers: it captures variables. In the last section, the block created all of its variables inside its definition. What happens if you use a variable inside a block that wasn't declared in that block? For example:

```
- (void)method
{
    // A variable created in the scope of this method
    // aka, not inside aBlock
    int value = 5;

    // Create a block with no arguments or return value
    void (^aBlock)() = ^(void)
    {
        // This block simply prints out value,
        // a variable declared outside the block
        NSLog(@"%d", value);
    };

    // Call the block
    aBlock();
}
```

This, as you may expect, will print the number 5 to the console. However, so will this:

```
- (void)method
{
    int value = 5;

    void (^aBlock)() = ^()
    {
        NSLog(@"%d", value);
    };

    // Change value's value before calling block
```

```
    value = 10;

    // Call the block, value = 10 in the scope of this method
    // but the block prints 5 when invoked
    aBlock();
}
```

When a block is created, the current values of any variables it references are captured. Any time this block is executed in the future, it uses the captured values of those variables. This applies to more than just primitives – pointers to objects can be captured, too.

Let's use that knowledge. Whenever the user double-taps the screen, all lines are immediately removed from the screen. It would look nicer if these lines faded off the screen instead. The easiest way to do this is to create a full-screen layer that matches the background color of the **TouchDrawView** and animate its opacity from transparent to opaque. When the animation completes, all of the lines will be removed from the screen along with the layer, restoring the user interface to its initial state.

To focus on the interesting parts of this exercise, let's get the animation stuff out of the way. Add QuartzCore.framework to your project. Then, at the top of TouchDrawView.m, import the top-level header from this framework.

#import <QuartzCore/QuartzCore.h>

Change the implementation of **clearAll** to create a layer and apply a fade-in animation to it. In TouchDrawView.m, replace the following method:

```
- (void)clearAll
{
    // Create a new layer that obscures the whole view
    CALayer *fadeLayer = [CALayer layer];
    [fadeLayer setBounds:[self bounds]];
    [fadeLayer setPosition:
        CGPointMake([self bounds].size.width / 2.0,
                    [self bounds].size.height / 2.0)];
    [fadeLayer setBackgroundColor:[[self backgroundColor] CGColor]];

    // Add this layer to the layer hierarchy on top of
    // the view's layer
    [[self layer] addSublayer:fadeLayer];

    // Create an animation that fades this layer in over 1 sec.
    CABasicAnimation *animation = [CABasicAnimation
                            animationWithKeyPath:@"opacity"];
    [animation setFromValue:[NSNumber numberWithFloat:0]];
    [animation setToValue:[NSNumber numberWithFloat:1]];
    [animation setDuration:1];
    [fadeLayer addAnimation:animation forKey:@"Fade"];
}
```

Build and run the application. Draw some lines and then double-tap. The screen will fade to white. However, you won't be able to create any new lines (the fadeLayer is obscuring them and hasn't been removed), and the **Line**s in completeLines are still there. You will need to remove the layer from its superlayer and remove the lines from completeLines after the animation completes.

In order to do this, you could give the animation object a delegate. Then, you would implement the method **animationDidStop:finished:** to remove the layer from the screen along with all of the lines. There are two problems with this. The first is that the delegate method will be in a location other than where this animation was setup. For the purposes of code clarity, it would be nicer if you could somehow define what happens when the animation ends in the same chunk of code where the animation is kicked off.

The other problem is that, in order to remove fadeLayer from the layer hierarchy, you must keep a pointer to it (you have to send it **removeFromSuperlayer** to take it out of the layer hierarchy). Your only option, without blocks, is to create an instance variable in **TouchDrawView** that points to this layer. That's kind of a pain for what is essentially just a temporary object. Fortunately, you can solve both of these problems using a block and the class **CATransaction**.

In the Chapter 23 chapter, you used **CATransaction** to turn off implicit animations for any layer modifications occurring within the transaction. Another feature of **CATransaction** is a *completion block*. You can pass a block to a **CATransaction**, and when the animations in the transaction finish, that block will be executed.

Knowing that a block will capture its variables, you will have access to fadeLayer, completeLines, linesInProcess, and even self when the block is executed (a full second after it is created). In TouchDrawView.m's **clearAll** method, wrap the animation addition in a transaction and define the completion handler for that transaction.

```
CABasicAnimation *animation = [CABasicAnimation
                    animationWithKeyPath:@"opacity"];
[animation setFromValue:[NSNumber numberWithFloat:0]];
[animation setToValue:[NSNumber numberWithFloat:1]];
[animation setDuration:1];

[CATransaction begin];
    // Set the completion block of this transaction
    // this method requires a block that returns no
    // value and accepts no argument: (void (^)(void))
    [CATransaction setCompletionBlock:^(void)
    {
        // When the animation completes, remove
        // the fadeLayer from the layer hierarchy
        [fadeLayer removeFromSuperlayer];
        // Also remove any completed or in process
        // lines
        [linesInProcess removeAllObjects];
        [completeLines removeAllObjects];

        // Redisplay the view after lines are removed
        [self setNeedsDisplay];
    }];
    [fadeLayer addAnimation:animation forKey:@"Fade"];
[CATransaction commit];
}
```

This block will capture fadeLayer, linesInProcess, completeLines, and self. When the block executes, these variables will point at the exact same objects they point at in **clearAll**.

Build and run the application. Draw some lines and double-tap. The lines will fade out (although we know that a big layer is actually fading in on top of them). After the fade completes, the canvas will be cleared and you can go back to drawing.

How does this actually work? The compiler is smart enough to notice any references to variables when the block is defined – these values are copied into the memory for the block. For pointers to objects that are referenced, the *pointer* is copied, not the object itself. In cases where the block is kept around for use later, any objects referenced in the block are sent the message **retain**. In other words, the block takes ownership of those objects to make sure they exist when the block is executed. (See the section called "For the More Curious: Memory Management and Blocks" at the end of this chapter for more details.)

When the block is destroyed, it releases ownership of any objects it captured.

Using blocks with other built-in methods

Blocks are so useful that many built-in classes have methods that accept blocks as arguments. One example is **NSArray**'s **enumerateObjectsUsingBlock:**. When given a block, this method will loop through the array and perform that block on each element. The block that is applied to each object in the array is of the following form:

```
void (^)(id obj, NSUInteger idx, BOOL *stop)
```

The block you define, then, must have these three arguments and not return a value. You will use the **enumerateObjectsUsingBlock:** to replace the for loop in **transformLineColorsWithBlock:**. Implement this in TouchDrawView.m.

```
- (void)transformLineColorsWithBlock:(UIColor * (^)(Line *))colorForLine
{
    [completeLines enumerateObjectsUsingBlock:^(id line, NSUInteger idx, BOOL *stop) {
        [(Line *)line setColor:colorForLine(line)];
    }];
    [self setNeedsDisplay];
}
```

Notice how you are creating another block here for the argument passed to **enumerateObjectsUsingBlock:**. You don't necessarily have to declare a block variable to hold a block if you are just passing it in a message because you don't need to use that block elsewhere. Now, when this method is invoked, the objects in the array are enumerated over by this block. The block gets a reference to the object currently being enumerated (line), the index in the array of that object, and a stop flag that you can set to YES if you want to stop enumerating. For each **Line**, you call the block passed into the method and then set the color of that line given the result of the block.

Build and run the application again. The behavior should remain the same.

Another form of **enumerateObjectsUsingBlock:** exists for **NSArray** named **enumerateObjectsWithOptions:usingBlock:**. The options you can supply to this method will allow you to enumerate the array in reverse, and more importantly, enumerate the array concurrently. The runtime knows how to divvy up a number of block operations among the different CPU cores when told to.

On current iOS devices, there is only one CPU with one core. For the time being, you will see no performance boost from concurrently running a number of blocks. However, on future iOS devices, there will most likely be more than one core per CPU. Each core will be able to execute a block in parallel, speeding up the enumeration by a factor equal to the number of cores.

Keeping code compact with blocks

NSNotificationCenter also knows how to use blocks. When you have used the notification center before, you would add an observer and selector for a given notification name. Then, you would implement a method with a matching selector somewhere else in your implementation file. As you continue to write code, the method to handle that notification gets moved around, and you end up spending time looking for it when you want to update or check it. Using blocks, you can define the code that gets executed within the same chunk of code you add the notification observer.

You will add an observer that gets notified when the device orientation changes. When this happens, you will execute a block that inverts the color of all the lines. In **initWithCoder:** of TouchDrawView.m, add the following code.

```
- (id)initWithCoder:(NSCoder *)aDecoder
{
    self = [super initWithCoder:aDecoder];

    if (self) {
        linesInProcess = [[NSMutableDictionary alloc] init];
        completeLines = [[NSMutableArray alloc] init];
        [self setMultipleTouchEnabled:YES];

        [[UIDevice currentDevice] beginGeneratingDeviceOrientationNotifications];

        [[NSNotificationCenter defaultCenter]
            addObserverForName:UIDeviceOrientationDidChangeNotification
                        object:nil
                         queue:nil
                    usingBlock: ^(NSNotification * note) {
                        [self transformLineColorsWithBlock:^(Line *l) {
                            // Note that extract_invertedColor doesn't
                            // exist yet, you will implement this soon.
                            return [[l color] extract_invertedColor];
                        }];
                    }];
    }
    return self;
}
```

Whenever **TouchDrawView** is notified of an orientation change, it executes the block passed as the argument paired with **usingBlock:**. The argument to this block must be an **NSNotification** because that is what the method **addObserverForName:object:queue:usingBlock:** expects.

This block invokes the method **transformLineColorsWithBlock:** with another block. The coloring block here is defined inline (there is no variable to hold it), and it will return the inverted value of the current color of the line.

However, there is no **extract_invertedColor** for **UIColor** because you've yet to define it.

Categories

In Objective-C, classes have instance and class methods. These define the behavior of a class and its instances. Sometimes, you are using a class and you really wish "it just had a method to do this cool thing I want to do." You're in luck. You can add methods to an existing class by creating a *category* for that class.

The syntax for a category is not at all scary like blocks; in fact, it's something you've already used before. You will create a category for **UIColor** that has two new methods that an instance of **UIColor** will respond to. Create a new **NSObject** subclass. Name it UIColor+Extract.m. In UIColor +Extract.h, replace all of the code with the following:

```
#import <Foundation/Foundation.h>

#import <UIKit/UIKit.h>

@interface UIColor (Extract)

- (void)extract_getRed:(float *)r green:(float *)g blue:(float *)b;
- (UIColor *)extract_invertedColor;

@end
```

Notice you used nearly the same syntax as you would if you were declaring a new class named **UIColor**. However, there are two differences: the area for defining the superclass has been replaced with (Extract) and there is no section for instance variables. This declaration says, "I'm adding two new methods to the **UIColor** class. The name of this addition is Extract, which is just a name." Also, note that these methods are prefixed with the name of the category. Because more than one category can be added to a class, you don't want to pollute the namespace with obvious-sounding method names.

In UIColor+Extract.m, implement these two methods by replacing all of the text in the file with the following:

```
#import "UIColor+Extract.h"

@implementation UIColor (Extract)

// Note that this method uses the word "get". The
// "return values" are passed as pointers and filled
// out by the method.
- (void)extract_getRed:(float *)r green:(float *)g blue:(float *)b
{
    // Get the Core Graphics representation
    CGColorRef cgClr = [self CGColor];

    // Get each component of the color ("color channels")
    const CGFloat *components = CGColorGetComponents(cgClr);

    // Get the number of components
    size_t componentCount = CGColorGetNumberOfComponents(cgClr);

    if (componentCount == 2) {
        // A grayscale color will only have two components,
        // the grayscale value and the alpha channel
        // Assign the values pointed to by r, g, b to
        // the grayscale value
        *r = components[0];
        *g = components[0];
        *b = components[0];
    } else if (componentCount == 4) {
        // A RGB color has 4 components, r, g, b
        // and an alpha channel
        *r = components[0];
        *g = components[1];
        *b = components[2];
    } else {
        NSLog(@"Unsupported colorspace.");
        *r = *g = *b = 0;
    }
```

```
}
- (UIColor *)extract_invertedColor
{
    // Use method you just defined to get components of color
    float r = 0, g = 0, b = 0;
    [self extract_getRed:&r green:&g blue:&b];

    // Return a new UIColor instance with inverted components
    return [UIColor colorWithRed:1.0 - r
                           green:1.0 - g
                            blue:1.0 - b
                           alpha:1.0];
}
@end
```

Now, you can send the messages **getRed:green:blue:** and **invertedColor** to any instance of **UIColor**.

This approach has benefits over subclassing **UIColor**. First, if you had already been using **UIColor** in your application, you don't have to go back and change these objects to some new subclass. More importantly, however, many methods that you don't have control over may return **UIColor** instances. You would not be able to send these two new messages to those objects with a subclass.

Go back to TouchDrawView.m. At the top of this file, import the header file for this category so this file knows about these new declarations.

```
#import "TouchDrawView.h"
#import "Line.h"
#import "UIColor+Extract.h"
```

Now, when you send the message **invertedColor** to a **Line**'s color,

```
[self transformLineColorsWithBlock:^(Line *l) {
    return [[l color] extract_invertedColor];
}];
```

the method in your category will be executed. You might want to keep this category around, it is pretty useful.

Build and run the application. Draw some lines and then shake the device. Rotate it, and the colors will invert. Rotate it again, and the colors will revert back to normal.

Categories have another use: pseudo-private methods. In Objective-C, there is no such thing as a private method. If a class implements a method, you can always send that message. However, you sometimes want the ability to at least hide methods from a user of the class. For example, a method that only gets called internally by the class and requires a certain set of conditions in order to operate properly is not something you want other objects knowing about. You could, of course, leave that method declaration out of the header file, but the compiler will give you a warning when you try to use it.

To hide method declarations and hush up the compiler about undeclared methods, you can create a category at the top of an implementation file with declarations for methods you don't want used by other objects. A category used for this reason is called a *class extension* and has no name. Methods in a class extension must be implemented in the standard @implementation block of a class or the compiler will complain. Near the top of TouchDrawView.m, add the following category declaration.

```
@interface TouchDrawView ()
- (void)transformLineColorsWithBlock:(UIColor * (^)(Line *))t;
- (void)colorize;
@end

@implementation TouchDrawView
```

Now, you won't get any warnings when **TouchDrawView** uses one of these methods, but any other file that tries to use these methods will get a warning. (You may not have had any warnings to begin with depending on the order you implemented your methods.) Note that even though these methods aren't visible to other files, they can still be invoked. The compiler will just complain.

For the More Curious: Memory Management and Blocks

There are some subtle rules when it comes to managing memory for blocks. To understand how the block manages memory, you must understand the difference between the heap and the stack portions of memory.

To allocate memory from the heap, you must explicitly do so. Typically, this is done by sending the message **alloc** to a class, but it is also done when you call **malloc** or one of its friends. Sometimes, this happens in the implementation of another function or method, like **UIGraphicsBeginImageContextWithOptions** (because it calls **malloc**). When you allocate memory from the heap, it is your responsibility to clean it up. This is done by deallocating an object, freeing a malloc'ed buffer, or calling a function that frees a buffer (like **UIGraphicsEndImageContext**).

The stack operates differently than the heap. When you call a function, memory from the stack is automatically allocated. (At the lowest level, a method is really just a function, so we can use the terms interchangeably here). We call this chunk of memory a *stack frame*. A stack frame holds information that is vital to the execution of a function. For example, the memory for variables declared in a function are inside this stack frame. We call these local variables. When a function ends, that stack frame is automatically deallocated. Thus, any local variables are destroyed when the function completes.

When you define a block, it is assigned to a local variable. A newly created block then lives on the stack and consequently will be destroyed when the function it was declared in ends. However, a block sometimes needs to be called after it was created. For example, the blocks you supplied to **NSNotificationCenter** and **CATransaction** need to be executed well after the function they were declared in finishes executing. Therefore, we need some way of keeping a block around.

Interestingly enough, blocks are also objects. We can send them messages like **retain**, **release**, and **copy**.

```
void (^aBlock)() = ^(void){...};
// Retain a block - just like an Objective-C object
[aBlock retain];
// Copy a block - also like an Objective-c object
void (^anotherBlock)() = [aBlock copy];
```

You might think, then, to keep a block around, you would send it the message **retain**. However, this doesn't work the way you would expect. When a block is first created, it is a *stack-based block* – meaning its memory lives in the stack. Sending the message **retain** to a block increases its retain count, but since it still lives in the stack, it will be destroyed (regardless of its retain count) when the function it was declared in finishes.

To keep a block around, you must make a copy of it. The copy is dynamically allocated from the heap, which then gives us control over when it is deallocated. We call a block that has been moved to the heap a *heap-based block*. A heap-based block has a retain count that works in the way we expect: the object that made the copy is an owner of that block and must **release** it for it to be deallocated. Other objects may retain the copy to prevent it from being deallocated until they too release it.

Methods like **CATransaction**'s **setCompletionBlock:** will copy the block sent to it. When the transaction finishes, that block will still exist in the heap, and it will be executed. After the block is executed, the transaction releases it, and the memory is returned back to the heap. This seems pretty straightforward, but it can get tricky when you add a block to a collection object like **NSMutableArray** or **NSMutableDictionary**. Objects added to collection objects are sent the message **retain**. Because a block that only retained still lives on the stack, the block will get destroyed as soon as you leave the method it was created in. Thus, to really add a block to a collection object, you will first make a copy, then autorelease it. The collection object will retain the autoreleased copy, ensuring its existence.

```
- (NSMutableArray *)blockArray
{
    NSMutableArray *a = [NSMutableArray array];
    void (^aBlock)() = ^(void)
    {
        ...
    };
    // Copy the block to move it to the heap,
    // then autorelease it because the array
    // will retain the copy.
    [a addObject:[[aBlock copy] autorelease]];

    return a;
}
```

Earlier in this chapter, we talked about how a block will retain objects it references. This is not completely true: a stack-based block *will not* retain objects it references. Only when a block is copied to the heap will it actually retain those objects. Therefore, copying a block serves the dual purpose of ensuring not only the block exists when it is executed later, but any objects it talks to will also exist.

One thing to note about the previous chunk of code is that aBlock could potentially reference the array it belongs to in the body of the block. If this is the case, you would need to make sure that aBlock doesn't retain a, otherwise, you will get a retain cycle. There is a special modifier, __block, you can add to variables to force this non-retaining behavior.

```
- (NSMutableArray *)blockArray
{
    __block NSMutableArray *a = [NSMutableArray array];
    void (^aBlock)() = ^(void)
    {
        NSLog(@"I'm in %@!", a);
    };

    [a addObject:[[aBlock copy] autorelease]];

    return a;
}
```

This modifier has more than one use. A variable that is captured by a block is, by default, constant. You cannot change the value of a captured variable within the block. For primitives, like int, this means you cannot change the value of that integer. For pointers to objects, this means you cannot set the pointer to point at another object. You can still send messages to the object that change its instance variables, though.

If you want to allow a variable to be modified by a block (for example, a block that takes an integer that increases by one every time the block is called – a counter), you must declare that variable with the __block modifier.

```
__block int counter = 0;
void (^aBlock)() = ^(void)
{
    NSLog(@"%d", counter++);
};
aBlock(); // This will print 0
aBlock(); // This will print 1
```

Pointers to objects declared with this modifier do not get retained by the block. In other words, when a stack-based block becomes a heap-based block, the object pointed to by a __block-decorated variable is *not* retained.

The final block memory "gotcha" is related to instance variables. If you access an instance variable in a heap-based block directly, the instance variable is not retained. However, self is retained.

```
- (void)method
{
    // There is an instance variable in this class: NSString *myString;
    void (^aBlock)() = ^(void)
    {
        doSomethingWithObject(myString);
    };
    // Upon copy, *self* is retained by the block.
    void (^bCopy)() = [aBlock copy];

    // Send the copy somewhere...
}
```

If, however, you have a local variable that points at an instance variable, the previous rules apply.

```
- (void)method
{
    // There is an instance variable in this class: NSString *myString;
    NSString *var = myString;
    void (^aBlock)() = ^(void)
    {
        doSomethingWithObject(var);
    };
    // Upon copy, *var* is retained by the block.
    void (^bCopy)() = [aBlock copy];

    // Send the copy somewhere...
}
```

When you are first learning blocks, most of the information covered in this section will probably fly right over your head. However, as you become more comfortable with blocks and use them as they are intended, you will need to know these gruesome details.

For the More Curious: Pros and Cons of Callback Options

A callback, as you may remember from Chapter 4, is a chunk of code you supply in advance of an event occurring. When that event goes down, the chunk of code gets executed. While blocks have many more uses, you have seen in this chapter that they can be used as another approach to callbacks. Other approaches to callbacks you have seen are delegation, target-action pairs, and notifications. Each one has benefits and drawbacks compared to the others. This section will expand on these benefits and drawbacks so that you can pick the appropriate one for your own implementations.

First, let's note that each of these approaches to callbacks are design patterns that transcend their implementations in Cocoa Touch. For example, the target-action pair design pattern is implemented by **UIControl**, but this does not mean you have to use **UIControl** to use the design pattern. You could create your own class that kept a pointer to a target object and a SEL for the message that object would be sent when some event occurred.

Callbacks have two major components: the process of registering it and the code for the callback. When registering a callback using delegation, target-actions or notifications, you register a pointer to an object. This is the object that will receive messages when events occur. Additionally, both target-actions and notifications require a SEL that will be the message that is sent to the object. Delegation, on the other hand, uses pre-defined methods from a delegate protocol to decide the messages that get sent.

Figure 24.4 Callback design patterns

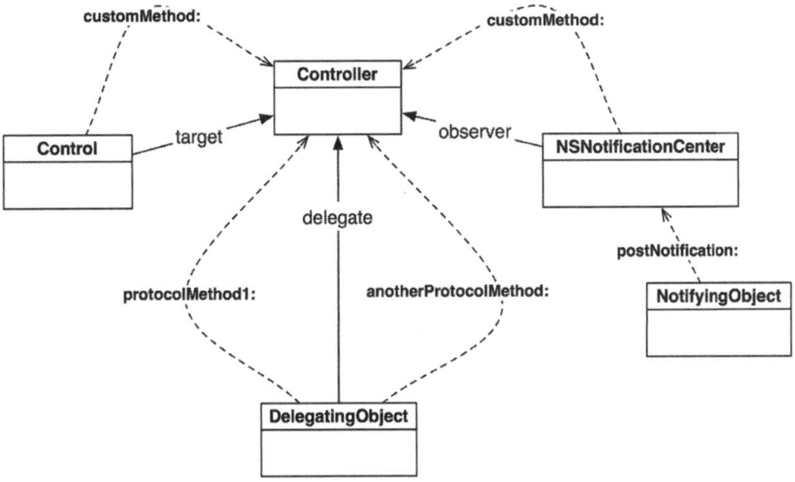

In these three callback design patterns, the code for the callback is in a distinct method implementation. Overall, each of these approaches is pretty similar, but there are certain situations that work better when using one or the other.

You use target-action when you have a close relationship between the two objects (like a view controller and one of its views) and when there may be many instances of object that call back. For example, a single interface controlled by one controller may have many buttons. If those buttons only knew how to send one message (e.g., **buttonTapped:**), there would be mass confusion in the implementation of that method ("Uhhh... which button are you again?").

Delegation is used when an object receives many events and it wants the same object to handle each of those events. You've seen many examples of this throughout this book, because delegation is a very common design pattern in Cocoa Touch. Because delegation uses a protocol that defines all of the messages that will be sent, you do not have control over the names of these methods, but you do not have to register them individually like with target-action pairs.

Notifications are used when you want multiple objects to invoke their callback for the same event and/ or when two objects are not related. Consider an application that had two view controllers that were in a tab bar controller together. They don't have pointers to each other, not like two view controllers in a navigation controller stack, but one of them is interested in what is going on in the other. Instead of giving them pointers to each other, which can be messy for a variety of reasons, one of view controllers can be kind and post notifications to the notification center. The other could register as an observer for that type of notification. Similarly, another view controller could come along and register for the same notification, and both observers would be updated.

Blocks are the outliers when it comes to callbacks because they are not an object-oriented approach. Blocks are useful when the callback is going to happen only once or when the callback is just a quick and simple task (like updating a progress bar). For example, in this chapter, you supplied a block for the completion of an animation. This animation was only going to run once, and therefore the block would only be called once.

One of the reasons blocks are better suited for this one-shot behavior is because they will retain any objects they reference. If a block was to stay around forever, the objects it references would also stay around forever. Of course, you can destroy the block when it is no longer needed, but what if that block is owned by an object that the block references? The object retains the block, the block retains the object, and now you can't deallocate them without some extra work. Since the blocks stick around just for the one event, they will retain what they need until they no longer need it.

Another reason blocks are well-suited for this situation goes along with the reason why they are good for quick and simple tasks: you can define the block's code at the same point where the block is registered as a callback. This keeps your code nice and clean.

An approach to callbacks we have not discussed is subclassing. In some languages, delegation is not feasible because of the structure of the language. In these languages, classes like **CLLocationManager** would be abstract classes – ones that were meant to be subclassed. Any time you wanted to use an instance of **CLLocationManager**, you would subclass it and write the code for what happens when an event occurs in the implementation of this subclass. The subclass would probably have an instance variable for the object it was going to tell about these events, and that object would declare and define these methods. This gets ugly pretty quickly, and thus, in Cocoa Touch, you do not see this pattern because we have better alternatives.

25

Web Services and
UIWebView

In this chapter, you will lay the foundation of an application that reads the RSS feed from the Big Nerd Ranch Forums (Figure 25.1). These posts will be listed in a table view. Selecting a post from the table will display that post from the site.

Figure 25.1   Nerdfeed

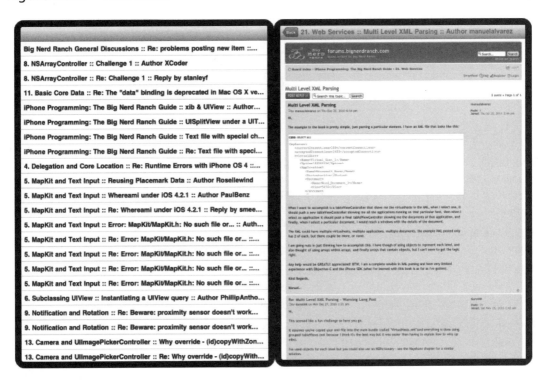

Getting Nerdfeed to the point shown in Figure 25.1 consists of two main parts: collecting data from a web service and using the **UIWebView** class to display web content. Figure 25.2 shows an object diagram for Nerdfeed.

Figure 25.2   Nerdfeed Object Diagram

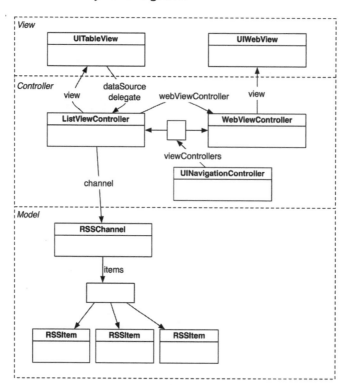

Web Services

Your handy web browser uses the HTTP protocol to communicate with a web server. In the simplest interaction, the broswer sends a request specifying some URL to the server. The server responds by sending back the requested page (typically HTML and images), which the browser formats and displays.

In more complex interactions, browser requests can include other parameters, like form data. The server processes these parameters and returns a customized, or dynamic, webpage.

Web browsers are widely used and have been for a long time. So the technologies surrounding HTTP are stable and well-developed: HTTP traffic passes neatly through most firewalls, web servers are very secure and have great performance, and web application development tools have become easy to use.

You can write a client application for iOS that leverages the HTTP infrastructure to talk to a web-enabled server. Because the HTTP protocol doesn't care about what data it transports, your client application can exchange requests and responses that contain complex data. This data is typically in XML or JSON (JavaScript Object Notation) format. (If you control the web server as well as the client, you can use any format you like; if not, you have to build your application to use whatever the server supports.)

The server side of this application is a *web service*. Using a web service from your iOS application typically requires

- formatting the data to be sent as XML or JSON

- sending that data in an HTTP request

- receiving the HTTP response

- parsing and processing the received XML or JSON data

Starting the Nerdfeed application

Create a new Window-based Application for the iPad Device Family. Name this application Nerdfeed, as shown in Figure 25.3. (If you don't have an iPad to deploy to, you can use the iPad simulator.)

Figure 25.3   Creating an iPad Window-based Application

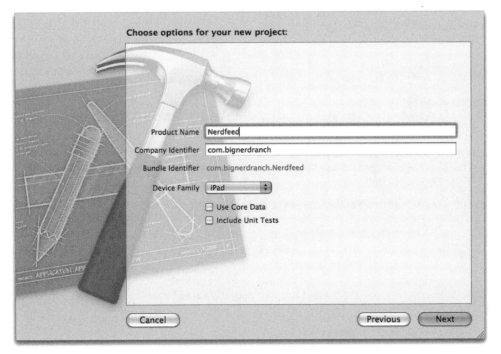

Let's knock out the basic UI before focusing on web services. Create a new **NSObject** subclass and name it **ListViewController**. In ListViewController.h, change the superclass to **UITableViewController**.

@interface ListViewController : **UITableViewController**

In ListViewController.m, write stubs for the required data source methods so we can build and run as we go through this exercise.

```
- (NSInteger)tableView:(UITableView *)tableView
 numberOfRowsInSection:(NSInteger)section
{
    return 0;
}

- (UITableViewCell *)tableView:(UITableView *)tableView
        cellForRowAtIndexPath:(NSIndexPath *)indexPath
{
    return nil;
}
```

In NerdfeedAppDelegate.m, create an instance of **ListViewController** and set it as the root view controller of a navigation controller. Make that navigation controller the root view controller of the window.

```
#import "NerdfeedAppDelegate.h"
#import "ListViewController.h"

@implementation NerdfeedAppDelegate
@synthesize window;

- (BOOL)application:(UIApplication *)application
    didFinishLaunchingWithOptions:(NSDictionary *)launchOptions
{
    ListViewController *lvc =
        [[ListViewController alloc] initWithStyle:UITableViewStylePlain];
    [lvc autorelease];

    UINavigationController *masterNav =
        [[UINavigationController alloc] initWithRootViewController:lvc];
    [masterNav autorelease];

    [[self window] setRootViewController:masterNav];

    [[self window] makeKeyAndVisible];

    return YES;
}
```

Build and run the application. You should see an empty **UITableView** and a navigation bar.

Fetching data from a URL

The Nerdfeed application will fetch data from a web server using three handy classes: **NSURL**, **NSURLRequest**, and **NSURLConnection** (Figure 25.4).

Figure 25.4   Relationship of web service classes

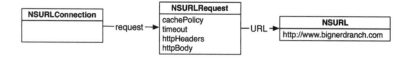

Each of these classes has an important role in communicating with a web server:

- An **NSURL** instance contains the location of a web application in URL format. For many web services, the URL will be composed of the base address, the web application you are communicating with, and any arguments that are being passed.

- An **NSURLRequest** instance holds all the data necessary to communicate with a web server. This includes an **NSURL** object, as well as a caching policy, a limit on how long you will give the web server to respond, and additional data passed through the HTTP protocol. (**NSMutableURLRequest** is the mutable subclass of **NSURLRequest**.)

- An **NSURLConnection** instance is responsible for actually making the connection to a web server, sending the information in its **NSURLRequest**, and gathering the response from the server.

In this exercise, you will be making a web service request to the `smartfeed` service hosted at `http://forums.bignerdranch.com`. You will pass a number of arguments to this service that determine the format of the data that is returned. This data will be XML that describes the most recent posts at our developer forums.

The form of a web service request varies depending on who implements the web service; there are no set-in-stone rules when it comes to web services. You will need to find the documentation for the web service to know how to format a request. As long as a client application sends the server what it wants, you have a working exchange.

The Big Nerd Ranch Forum's RSS feed wants a URL that looks like this:

```
http://forums.bignerdranch.com/smartfeed.php?limit=NO_LIMIT&count_limit=20
&sort_by=standard&feed_type=RSS2.0&feed_style=COMPACT
```

You can see that the base URL is `forums.bignerdranch.com`, the web application is `smartfeed`, and there are five arguments. These arguments are required by the `smartfeed` web application.

This is a pretty common form for a web service request. Generally, a request URL looks like this:

```
http://baseURL.com/serviceName?argumentX=valueX&argumentY=valueY
```

At times, you will need to make a string "URL-safe." For example, space characters and quotes are not allowed in URLs; They must be replaced with escape-sequences. Here is how that is done.

```
NSString *search = @"Play some \"Abba\"";
NSString *escaped =
    [search stringByAddingPercentEscapesUsingEncoding:NSUTF8StringEncoding];

// escaped is now "Play%20some%20%22Abba%22"
```

When the request to the Big Nerd Ranch forums is processed, the server will return XML data that contains the last 20 posts. The **ListViewController**, who made the request, will populate its table view with the titles of the posts.

In `ListViewController.h`, add an instance variable for the connection and one for the data that is returned from that connection. Also add a new method declaration.

```
@interface ListViewController : UITableViewController
{
    NSURLConnection *connection;
    NSMutableData *xmlData;
}
- (void)fetchEntries;
@end
```

Working with NSURLConnection

An **NSURLConnection** instance can communicate with a web server two ways: synchronously or asynchronously. Because passing data to and from a remote server can take some time, synchronous connections are generally frowned upon because they stall your application until the connection completes. This chapter will teach you how to perform an asynchronous connection with **NSURLConnection**.

When an instance of **NSURLConnection** is created, it needs to know the location of the web application and the data to pass to that web server. It also needs a delegate. When told to start communicating with the web server, **NSURLConnection** will initiate a connection to the location, begin passing it data, and possibly receive data back. It will update its delegate each step of the way with useful information.

In ListViewController.m, implement the **fetchEntries** method to create an **NSURLRequest** that connects to http://forums.bignerdranch.com and asks for the last 20 posts in RSS 2.0 format. Then, create a connection object that transfers this request to the server.

```
- (void)fetchEntries
{
    // Create a new data container for the stuff that comes back from the service
    [xmlData release];
    xmlData = [[NSMutableData alloc] init];

    // Construct a URL that will ask the service for what you want -
    // note we can concatenate literal strings together on multiple
    // lines in this way - this results in a single NSString instance
    NSURL *url = [NSURL URLWithString:
            @"http://forums.bignerdranch.com/smartfeed.php?"
            @"limit=NO_LIMIT&count_limit=20&sort_by=standard&"
            @"feed_type=RSS2.0&feed_style=COMPACT"];


    // For Apple's Hot News feed, replace the line above with
    // NSURL *url = [NSURL URLWithString:@"http://www.apple.com/pr/feeds/pr.rss"];

    // Put that URL into an NSURLRequest
    NSURLRequest *req = [NSURLRequest requestWithURL:url];

    // Create a connection that will exchange this request for data from the URL
    connection = [[NSURLConnection alloc] initWithRequest:req
                                                 delegate:self
                                          startImmediately:YES];
}
```

Kick off the exchange whenever the **ListViewController** is created. In ListViewController.m, override **initWithStyle:**.

```
- (id)initWithStyle:(UITableViewStyle)style
{
    self = [super initWithStyle:style];

    if (self) {
        [self fetchEntries];
    }

    return self;
}
```

Build the application to make sure there are no syntax errors. This code, as it stands, will make the connection to the web service and retrieve the last 20 posts. However, there is one problem: you don't see those posts anywhere. You need to implement delegate methods for **NSURLConnection** to collect the XML data returned from this request.

Figure 25.5 NSURLConnection flow chart

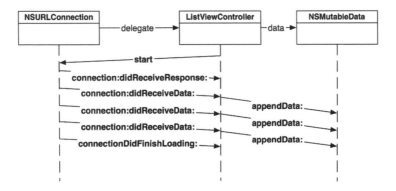

The delegate of an **NSURLConnection** is responsible for overseeing the connection and for collecting the data returned from the request. (This data is typically an XML or JSON document; for this web service, it is XML.) However, the data returned usually comes back in pieces, and it is the delegate's job to collect the pieces and put them together.

In ListViewController.m, implement **connection:didReceiveData:** to put all of the data received by the connection into the instance variable xmlData.

```
// This method will be called several times as the data arrives
- (void)connection:(NSURLConnection *)conn didReceiveData:(NSData *)data
{
    // Add the incoming chunk of data to the container we are keeping
    // The data always comes in the correct order
    [xmlData appendData:data];
}
```

When a connection has finished retrieving all of the data from a web service, it sends the message **connectionDidFinishLoading:** to its delegate. In this method, you are guaranteed to have the complete response from the web service request and can start working with that data. For now, implement **connectionDidFinishLoading:** in ListViewController.m to just print out the string representation of that data to the console to make sure good stuff is coming back.

```
- (void)connectionDidFinishLoading:(NSURLConnection *)conn
{
    // We are just checking to make sure we are getting the XML
    NSString *xmlCheck = [[[NSString alloc] initWithData:xmlData
                                            encoding:NSUTF8StringEncoding]
                                            autorelease];

    NSLog(@"xmlCheck = %@", xmlCheck);
}
```

There is a possibility that a connection will fail. If an instance of **NSURLConnection** cannot make a connection to a web service, it sends its delegate the message **connection:didFailWithError:**. Note that this message gets sent for a *connection* failure, like having no Internet connectivity or if the server doesn't exist. For other types of errors, such as data sent to a web service in the wrong format, the error information is returned in **connection:didReceiveData:**.

In ListViewController.m, implement **connection:didFailWithError:** to inform your application of a connection failure.

```
- (void)connection:(NSURLConnection *)conn
  didFailWithError:(NSError *)error
{
    // Release the connection object, we're done with it
    [connection release];
    connection = nil;

    // Release the xmlData object, we're done with it
    [xmlData release];
    xmlData = nil;

    // Grab the description of the error object passed to us
    NSString *errorString = [NSString stringWithFormat:@"Fetch failed: %@",
                            [error localizedDescription]];

    // Create and show an alert view with this error displayed
    UIAlertView *av = [[UIAlertView alloc] initWithTitle:@"Error"
                                           message:errorString
                                           delegate:nil
                                 cancelButtonTitle:@"OK"
                                 otherButtonTitles:nil];
    [av show];
    [av autorelease];
}
```

Try building and running your application. You should see the XML results in the console shortly after you launch the application. If you put your device in Airplane Mode (or if it is not connected to a network), you should see a friendly error message when you try to fetch again. (For now, you will have to restart the application from Xcode in order to refetch the data after you've received the error.)

Parsing XML

The XML that comes back from the server looks something like this:

```
<?xml version="1.0" encoding="utf-8"?>
<rss version="2.0" xmlns:atom="http://www.w3.org/2005/Atom">
```

```
<channel>
  <title>forums.bignerdranch.com</title>
  <description>Books written by Big Nerd Ranch</description>
      ...
  <item>
    <title>Big Nerd Ranch General Discussions :: Big Nerd Ranch is awesome!</title>
    <link>http://forums.bignerdranch.com/viewtopic.php?f=4&t=532&p=1517#p1517</link>
    <author>no_email@example.com (bignerd)</author>
    <category>Big Nerd Ranch General Discussions</category>
    <comments>http://forums.bignerdranch.com/posting.php?mode=reply&f=4</comments>
    <pubDate>Mon, 27 Dec 2010 11:27:01 GMT</pubDate>
  </item>
  ...
  </channel>
</rss>
```

(If you aren't seeing anything like this in your console, verify that you typed the URL correctly.)

Let's break down the XML the server returned. The top-level element in this document is an rss element. It contains a channel element. That channel element has some metadata that describes it (a title and a description). Then, there is a series of item elements. Each item has a title, link, author, etc. and represents a single post on the forum.

In a moment, you will create two new classes, **RSSChannel** and **RSSItem**, to represent the channel and item elements. The **ListViewController** will have an instance variable for the **RSSChannel**, which will hold an array of **RSSItem**s. Each **RSSItem** will be displayed as a row in the table view. Both **RSSChannel** and **RSSItem** will retain some of their metadata as instance variables, as shown in Figure 25.6.

Figure 25.6 Model object graph

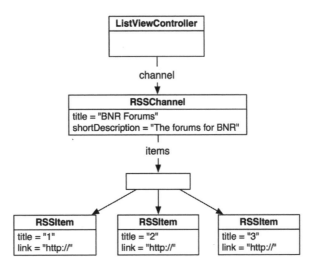

To parse the XML, you will use the class **NSXMLParser**. An **NSXMLParser** instance takes a chunk of XML data and reads it line by line. As it finds interesting information, it sends messages to its delegate, like, "I found a new element tag," or "I found a string inside of an element." The delegate object is responsible for interpreting what these messages mean in the context of the application.

In ListViewController.m, delete the code you wrote in **connectionDidFinishLoading:** to log the XML. Replace it with code to kick off the parsing and set the parser's delegate to point at the instance of **ListViewController**.

```
- (void)connectionDidFinishLoading:(NSURLConnection *)conn
{
    // Create the parser object with the data received from the web service
    NSXMLParser *parser = [[NSXMLParser alloc] initWithData:xmlData];

    // Give it a delegate
    [parser setDelegate:self];

    // Tell it to start parsing - the document will be parsed and
    // the delegate of NSXMLParser will get all of its delegate messages
    // sent to it before this line finishes execution - it is blocking
    [parser parse];

    // The parser is done (it blocks until done), you can release it immediately
    [parser release];

    // Get rid of the XML data as we no longer need it
    [xmlData release];
    xmlData = nil;

    // Get rid of the connection, no longer need it
    [connection release];
    connection = nil;

    // Reload the table.. for now, the table will be empty.
    [[self tableView] reloadData];
}
```

The delegate of the parser, **ListViewController**, will receive a message when the parser finds a new element, another message when it finds a string within an element, and another when an element is closed.

For example, if a parser saw this XML:

```
<title>Big Nerd Ranch</title>.
```

it would send its delegate three consecutive messages: "I found a new element: 'title'," then, "I found a string: 'Big Nerd Ranch'," and finally, "I found the end of an element: 'title'." These messages are found in the NSXMLParserDelegate protocol:

```
// The "I found a new element" message
  - (void)parser:(NSXMLParser *)parser        // The parser
 didStartElement:(NSString *)elementName      // Name of the element found
    namespaceURI:(NSString *)namespaceURI
   qualifiedName:(NSString *)qualifiedName
      attributes:(NSDictionary *)attributeDict;

// The "I found a string" message
  - (void)parser:(NSXMLParser *)parser        // Parser that is sending message
 foundCharacters:(NSString *)string;          // The contents of element (string)
```

```
// The "I found the end of an element" message
- (void)parser:(NSXMLParser *)parser                    // The parser
 didEndElement:(NSString *)elementName                  // Name of the element found
  namespaceURI:(NSString *)namespaceURI
 qualifiedName:(NSString *)qName;
```

The namespaceURI, qualifiedName, and attributes arguments are for more complex XML, and we'll return to them at the end of the chapter.

It is up to the **ListViewController** to make sense of that series of messages, and it does this by constructing an object tree that represents the XML feed. In this case, after the XML is parsed, there will be an instance of **RSSChannel** that contains a number of **RSSItem** instances. Here are the steps to constructing the tree:

- When the parser reports it found the start of the channel element, create an instance of **RSSChannel**.

- When the parser finds a title or description element and it is currently inside a channel element, set the appropriate property of the **RSSChannel** instance.

- When the parser finds an item element, create an instance of **RSSItem** and add it to the items array of the **RSSChannel**.

- When the parser finds a title or link element and it is currently inside a item element, set the appropriate property of the **RSSItem** instance.

This list doesn't seem too daunting. However, there is one issue that makes it difficult: the parser doesn't remember anything about what it has parsed. A parser may report, "I found a title element." Its next report is "Now I've found the string inside an element." At this point, if you asked the parser which element that string was inside, it couldn't tell you. It only knows about the string it just found. This leaves the burden of tracking state on the parser's delegate, and maintaining the state for an entire tree of objects in a single object is cumbersome.

Instead, you will spread out the logic for handling messages from the parser among the classes involved. If the last found element is a channel, then that instance of **RSSChannel** will be responsible for handling what the parser spits out next. The same goes for **RSSItem**; it will be responsible for grabbing its own title and link strings.

"But the parser can only have one delegate," you say. And you're right; it can only have one delegate *at a time*. We can change the delegate of an **NSXMLParser** whenever we please, and the parser will keep chugging through the XML and sending messages to its current delegate. The flow of the parser and the related objects is shown in Figure 25.7.

Figure 25.7   Flow diagram of XML being parsed into a tree, creating the
tree

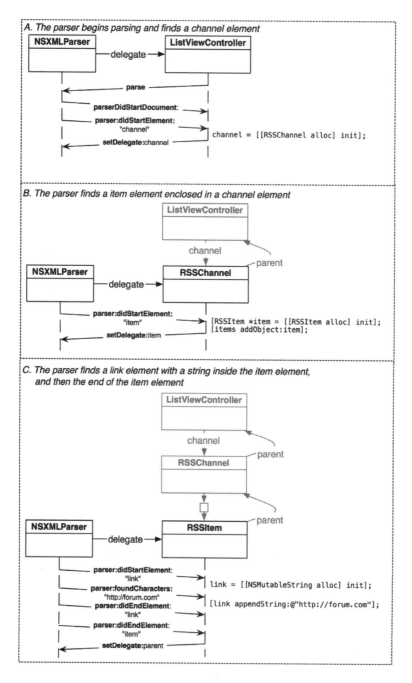

When the parser finds the end of an element, it tells its delegate. If the delegate is the object that
represents that element, that object returns control to the previous delegate (Figure 25.8).

Figure 25.8   Flow diagram of XML being parsed into a tree, back up the tree

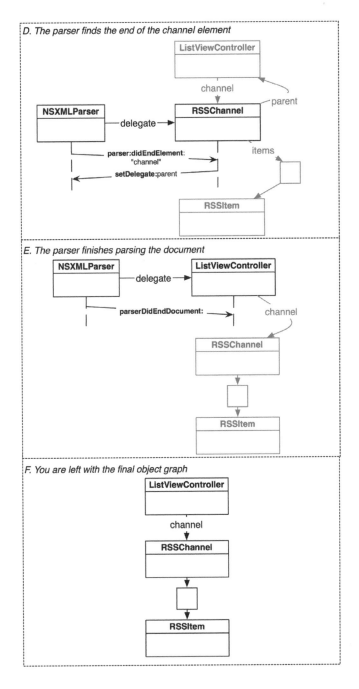

Now that we have a plan, let's get to work. Create a new **NSObject** subclass named **RSSChannel**. A channel object needs to hold some metadata, an array of **RSSItem** instances, and a pointer back to the previous parser delegate. In RSSChannel.h, add these instance variables and properties:

```
@interface RSSChannel : NSObject
{
    NSString *title;
    NSString *shortDescription;
    NSMutableArray *items;

    id parentParserDelegate;
}
@property (nonatomic, assign) id parentParserDelegate;

@property (nonatomic, retain) NSString *title;
@property (nonatomic, retain) NSString *shortDescription;
@property (nonatomic, readonly) NSMutableArray *items;

@end
```

In RSSChannel.m, synthesize the properties and override **init** and **dealloc**.

```
@implementation RSSChannel
@synthesize items, title, shortDescription, parentParserDelegate;

- (id)init
{
    self = [super init];

    if (self) {
        // Create the container for the RSSItems this channel has;
        // we'll create the RSSItem class shortly.
        items = [[NSMutableArray alloc] init];
    }

    return self;
}

- (void)dealloc
{
    // items is owned by this instance, must release
    [items release];

    // These ivars have the retain property attribute, must be released
    [title release];
    [shortDescription release];

    [super dealloc];
}
@end
```

Back in ListViewController.h, add an instance variable to hold an **RSSChannel** object and have the class conform to the NSXMLParserDelegate protocol.

```
// a forward declaration; we'll import the header in the .m
@class RSSChannel;

@interface ListViewController : UITableViewController <NSXMLParserDelegate>
{
```

```
    NSURLConnection *connection;
    NSMutableData *xmlData;

    RSSChannel *channel;
```

In `ListViewController.m`, implement an `NSXMLParserDelegate` method to catch the start of a channel element. Also, at the top of the file, import the header for **RSSChannel**.

```
#import "RSSChannel.h"

@implementation ListViewController

- (void)parser:(NSXMLParser *)parser
    didStartElement:(NSString *)elementName
      namespaceURI:(NSString *)namespaceURI
     qualifiedName:(NSString *)qualifiedName
        attributes:(NSDictionary *)attributeDict
{
    NSLog(@"%@ found a %@ element", self, elementName);
    if ([elementName isEqual:@"channel"]) {

        // If the parser saw a channel, create new instance, store in our ivar
        [channel release];
        channel = [[RSSChannel alloc] init];

        // Give the channel object a pointer back to ourselves for later
        [channel setParentParserDelegate:self];

        // Set the parser's delegate to the channel object
        [parser setDelegate:channel];
    }
}
```

Build and run the application. (Ignore the compiler warning for now.) You should see a log message that the channel was created. If you don't see this message, double-check that the URL you typed in **fetchEntries** is correct.

Now that the channel is sometimes the parser's delegate, it needs to implement `NSXMLParserDelegate` methods to handle the XML. The **RSSChannel** instance will catch the metadata it cares about along with any `item` elements.

The channel is interested in the `title` and `description` metadata elements, and you will store those strings that the parser finds in the appropriate instance variables. When the start of one of these elements is found, an **NSMutableString** instance will be created. When the parser finds a string, that string will be concatenated to the mutable string.

In `RSSChannel.h`, declare that the class conforms to `NSXMLParserDelegate` and add an instance variable for the mutable string.

```
@interface RSSChannel : NSObject <NSXMLParserDelegate>
{
    NSMutableString *currentString;
```

In `RSSChannel.m`, implement one of the `NSXMLParserDelegate` methods to catch the metadata.

```
- (void)parser:(NSXMLParser *)parser
    didStartElement:(NSString *)elementName
      namespaceURI:(NSString *)namespaceURI
     qualifiedName:(NSString *)qualifiedName
```

```
            attributes:(NSDictionary *)attributeDict
{
    NSLog(@"\t%@ found a %@ element", self, elementName);

    if ([elementName isEqual:@"title"]) {
        currentString = [[NSMutableString alloc] init];
        [self setTitle:currentString];
    }
    else if ([elementName isEqual:@"description"]) {
        currentString = [[NSMutableString alloc] init];
        [self setShortDescription:currentString];
    }
}
```

Note that currentString points at the same object as the appropriate instance variable – either title or shortDescription (Figure 25.9).

Figure 25.9   Two variables pointing at the same object

This means that when you append characters to the currentString, you are also appending them to the title or to the shortDescription.

In RSSChannel.m, implement the **parser:foundCharacters:** method.

```
- (void)parser:(NSXMLParser *)parser foundCharacters:(NSString *)str
{
    [currentString appendString:str];
}
```

When the parser finds the end of the channel element, the channel object will return control of the parser to the **ListViewController**. Implement this method in RSSChannel.m.

```
- (void)parser:(NSXMLParser *)parser
 didEndElement:(NSString *)elementName
  namespaceURI:(NSString *)namespaceURI
 qualifiedName:(NSString *)qName
{
    // If we were in an element that we were collecting the string for,
    // this appropriately releases our hold on it and the permanent ivar keeps
    // ownership of it. If we weren't parsing such an element, currentString
    // is nil and this message does nothing.
    [currentString release];
    currentString = nil;

    // If the element that ended was the channel, give up control to
    // who gave us control in the first place
    if ([elementName isEqual:@"channel"])
        [parser setDelegate:parentParserDelegate];
}
```

Let's double-check our work so far. In ListViewController.m, add the following log statement to **connectionDidFinishLoading:**.

```
- (void)connectionDidFinishLoading:(NSURLConnection *)conn
{
    NSXMLParser *parser = [[NSXMLParser alloc] initWithData:xmlData];
    [parser setDelegate:self];
    [parser parse];
    [parser release];


    [xmlData release];
    xmlData = nil;

    [connection release];
    connection = nil;

    [[self tableView] reloadData];
    NSLog(@"%@\n %@\n %@\n", channel, [channel title], [channel shortDescription]);
}
```

Build and run the application. At the end of the console, you should see the log statement with valid values for the three strings. The data isn't correct yet, but there should still be three blocks of text separated by a new line.

Now, you will need to write the code for the leaves of the object tree represented by the XML – the **RSSItem** instances. Create a new **NSObject** subclass. Name it **RSSItem**. In RSSItem.h, give the item instance variables for its metadata and for parsing.

```
@interface RSSItem : NSObject <NSXMLParserDelegate>
{
    NSString *title;
    NSString *link;
    NSMutableString *currentString;

    id parentParserDelegate;
}
@property (nonatomic, assign) id parentParserDelegate;

@property (nonatomic, retain) NSString *title;
@property (nonatomic, retain) NSString *link;


@end
```

In RSSItem.m, synthesize these properties and set up the parsing code similar to what you did for **RSSChannel**. For the properties that retain their objects, add **release** messages in **dealloc**.

```
@implementation RSSItem

@synthesize title, link, parentParserDelegate;

- (void)parser:(NSXMLParser *)parser
    didStartElement:(NSString *)elementName
      namespaceURI:(NSString *)namespaceURI
     qualifiedName:(NSString *)qualifiedName
        attributes:(NSDictionary *)attributeDict
{
    NSLog(@"\t\t%@ found a %@ element", self, elementName);

    if ([elementName isEqual:@"title"]) {
        currentString = [[NSMutableString alloc] init];
```

```
        [self setTitle:currentString];
    }
    else if ([elementName isEqual:@"link"]) {
        currentString = [[NSMutableString alloc] init];
        [self setLink:currentString];
    }
}

- (void)parser:(NSXMLParser *)parser foundCharacters:(NSString *)str
{
    [currentString appendString:str];
}

- (void)parser:(NSXMLParser *)parser
 didEndElement:(NSString *)elementName
  namespaceURI:(NSString *)namespaceURI
 qualifiedName:(NSString *)qName
{
    [currentString release];
    currentString = nil;

    if ([elementName isEqual:@"item"])
        [parser setDelegate:parentParserDelegate];
}

- (void)dealloc
{
    [title release];
    [link release];
    [super dealloc];
}
@end
```

Build the application to check for syntax errors.

In RSSChannel.m, put **RSSItem** into the object tree. At the top of this file, make sure to import the header for **RSSItem**.

```
#import "RSSItem.h"

@implementation RSSChannel

- (void)parser:(NSXMLParser *)parser
    didStartElement:(NSString *)elementName
      namespaceURI:(NSString *)namespaceURI
     qualifiedName:(NSString *)qualifiedName
        attributes:(NSDictionary *)attributeDict
{
    if ([elementName isEqual:@"title"]) {
        currentString = [[NSMutableString alloc] init];
        [self setTitle:currentString];
    }
    else if ([elementName isEqual:@"description"]) {
        currentString = [[NSMutableString alloc] init];
        [self setShortDescription:currentString];
    }
    else if ([elementName isEqual:@"item"]) {
        // When we find an item, create an instance of RSSItem
        RSSItem *entry = [[RSSItem alloc] init];
```

```
        // Set up its parent as ourselves so we can regain control of the parser
        [entry setParentParserDelegate:self];

        // Turn the parser to the RSSItem
        [parser setDelegate:entry];

        // Add the item to our array and release our hold on it
        [items addObject:entry];
        [entry release];
    }
}
```

Build and run the application. You should see log statements in the console that indicate the tree is being built. The last log statement in the console should have the correct data for the channel object, which looks something like this:

```
<RSSChannel: 0x4e18f80>
forums.bignerdranch.com
Books written by Big Nerd Ranch
```

Finally, you will connect the channel and its items to the table view. In `ListViewController.m`, import the header file for **RSSItem** and fill out the two data source methods you temporarily implemented earlier.

```
#import "RSSItem.h"

@implementation ListViewController

- (NSInteger)tableView:(UITableView *)tableView
 numberOfRowsInSection:(NSInteger)section
{
    return [[channel items] count];
}
- (UITableViewCell *)tableView:(UITableView *)tableView
        cellForRowAtIndexPath:(NSIndexPath *)indexPath
{
    UITableViewCell *cell = [tableView
                             dequeueReusableCellWithIdentifier:@"UITableViewCell"];
    if (cell == nil) {
        cell = [[[UITableViewCell alloc] initWithStyle:UITableViewCellStyleDefault
                                       reuseIdentifier:@"UITableViewCell"]
                                          autorelease];
    }
    RSSItem *item = [[channel items] objectAtIndex:[indexPath row]];
    [[cell textLabel] setText:[item title]];

    return cell;
}
```

Build and run the application. You should now see the titles of the last 20 posts in a table view. Also, take a good look at the console to see the flow of the parser and how the delegate role is passed around.

A quick tip on logging

In this exercise, you log a lot of data to the console. An important log statement could be easily missed. One way to catch important statements is to prefix the most important ones with an easily searchable token (like xxx), but that's a quick-and-dirty fix.

A more elegant and useful option is to define a preprocessor macro that you can use to categorize your log statements. For example, in Nerdfeed, you can generate a ton of log statements for checking the input and output of your web service requests. You can also generate a ton of log statements for checking the logic in the rest of the application. When you are debugging Nerdfeed, it would be helpful to separate the web service-related statements from the others so that you can turn them on or off as needed.

While there are many ways to do this, here is the simplest one:

```
#define WSLog NSLog
```

This statement tells the compiler, "When you come across **WSLog**, see **NSLog**." Save this statement in its own .h file and import it into your precompiled header (Nerdfeed_Prefix.pch). Then, when you want to log a web service-related statement in your code, use **WSLog** instead of **NSLog**, passing the exact same arguments. For example, in ListViewController.m, you could change the log statement in **connectionDidFinishLoading:** to the following:

```
WSLog(@"%@\n %@\n %@\n", channel, [channel title], [channel shortDescription]);
```

As long as **WSLog** is defined to **NSLog**, nothing will change. You will still see all of your log statements in the console. When you want to turn off the web service-related statements to concentrate on other areas, simply re-define **WSLog** to nothing in its header file:

```
#define WSLog
```

Now any **WSLog** calls will be invisible to the compiler, so they will not appear in the console to distract you from your non-web service debugging.

UIWebView

In addition to its title, an **RSSItem** also keeps a link that points to the web page where the post lives. It would be neat if Nerdfeed could open up Safari and navigate to that page. It would be even neater if Nerdfeed could render that webpage as a view without having to leave Nerdfeed to open Safari. Good news, it can.

Instances of **UIWebView** render web content. In fact, the Safari application on your device uses a **UIWebView** to render its web content. In this part of the chapter, you will create a view controller whose view is an instance of **UIWebView**. When one of the items is selected from the table view of **RSSItem**s, you will push the web view's controller onto the navigation stack and have it load the link stored in the **RSSItem**.

Create a new **NSObject** subclass and name it **WebViewController**. In WebViewController.h, add a property (but not an instance variable) and change the superclass to **UIViewController**:

```
@interface WebViewController : UIViewController
{

}
@property (nonatomic, readonly) UIWebView *webView;
@end
```

In WebViewController.m, override **loadView** to create an instance of **UIWebView** as the view of this view controller. Also, implement the method **webView** to return that view.

```
@implementation WebViewController

- (void)loadView
{
    // Create an instance of UIWebView as large as the screen
    CGRect screenFrame = [[UIScreen mainScreen] applicationFrame];
    UIWebView *wv = [[UIWebView alloc] initWithFrame:screenFrame];
    // Tell web view to scale web content to fit within bounds of webview
    [wv setScalesPageToFit:YES];

    [self setView:wv];
    [wv release];
}

- (UIWebView *)webView
{
    return (UIWebView *)[self view];
}
```

In `ListViewController.h`, add a new instance variable and property to **ListViewController**.

```
@class WebViewController;

@interface ListViewController : UITableViewController <NSXMLParserDelegate>
{
    NSURLConnection *connection;
    NSMutableData *xmlData;

    RSSChannel *channel;

    WebViewController *webViewController;
}
@property (nonatomic, retain) WebViewController *webViewController;
- (void)fetchEntries;
@end
```

In `ListViewController.m`, import the header file and synthesize the property.

```
#import "WebViewController.h"

@implementation ListViewController
@synthesize webViewController;
```

In `NerdfeedAppDelegate.m`, import the header for **WebViewController**, create an instance of **WebViewController**, and set it as the webViewController of the **ListViewController**.

```
#import "WebViewController.h"

@implementation NerdfeedAppDelegate

- (BOOL)application:(UIApplication *)application
    didFinishLaunchingWithOptions:(NSDictionary *)launchOptions
{
    ListViewController *lvc =
        [[ListViewController alloc] initWithStyle:UITableViewStylePlain];
    [lvc autorelease];
```

```
UINavigationController *masterNav =
    [[UINavigationController alloc] initWithRootViewController:lvc];
[masterNav autorelease];

WebViewController *wvc = [[[WebViewController alloc] init] autorelease];
[lvc setWebViewController:wvc];
```

(Notice that we are instantiating the **WebViewController** in the application delegate. In other exercises, the root view controller of a navigation controller was responsible for instantiating the next view controller to be pushed on the stack. We are instantiating the **WebViewController** in the application delegate in preparation for the next chapter where the interface will be different for the iPad and iPhone.)

When the user taps on a row in the table view, the **WebViewController** will be pushed onto the navigation stack, and the link for the selected **RSSItem** will be loaded in its web view. To have a web view load a web page, you send it the message **loadRequest:**. The argument is an instance of **NSURLRequest** that contains the URL you wish to navigate to. In ListViewController.m, implement the following table view delegate method:

```
- (void)tableView:(UITableView *)tableView
            didSelectRowAtIndexPath:(NSIndexPath *)indexPath
{
    // Push the web view controller onto the navigation stack - this implicitly
    // creates the web view controller's view the first time through
    [[self navigationController] pushViewController:webViewController animated:YES];

    // Grab the selected item
    RSSItem *entry = [[channel items] objectAtIndex:[indexPath row]];

    // Construct a URL with the link string of the item
    NSURL *url = [NSURL URLWithString:[entry link]];

    // Construct a requst object with that URL
    NSURLRequest *req = [NSURLRequest requestWithURL:url];

    // Load the request into the web view
    [[webViewController webView] loadRequest:req];

    // Set the title of the web view controller's navigation item
    [[webViewController navigationItem] setTitle:[entry title]];
}
```

Build and run the application. You should be able to select one of the posts, and it should take you to a new view controller that displays the web page for that post.

For the More Curious: NSXMLParser

NSXMLParser is the built-in XML parser in the iOS SDK. While there are plenty of parsers you can pick up on the Internet, adding a third party dependency is sometimes difficult. Many developers, seeing that **NSXMLParser** is not a tree-based parser (it doesn't create an object graph out of the box), go searching for an alternative parser. However, in this chapter, you've learned how to make **NSXMLParser** into a tree-based parser.

Other than tree-based parsing, some developers may be concerned about parsing more complicated XML. To parse simple XML, all you need are the three delegate methods used in this chapter. More complex XML has element attributes, namespaces, CDATA, and a slew of other items that need to be handled. Not to worry – **NSXMLParser** can handle these, too. The NSXMLParserDelegate protocol includes many more methods that handle nearly anything XML can throw at you. There are also arguments to the methods you have already used that can handle more complex XML. For example, in **parser:didStartElement:namespaceURI:qualifiedName:attributes:**, we only used the first two arguments. For the other arguments, consider the following XML:

```
<?xml version="1.0" encoding="utf-8"?>
<container version="2.0" xmlns:foo="BNR">
    <foo:item attribute1="one" attribute2="two"></item>
</container>
```

When the foo:item element is encountered by the parser, the values for the parameters to the delegate method are as follows:

- The element is "item." The namespace is ignored, and the name of the element is kept.

- The namespaceURI is "BNR." The element's name is item, and it is in the foo namespace, which has a value of "BNR."

- The qualifiedName is "foo:item."

- Attributes is a dictionary that contains two keys, "attribute1" and "attribute2." Their values are "one" and "two," respectively.

One thing **NSXMLParser** can't do is resolve XPaths. You have to use another library to handle this. (For more information, check out the Tree-Based XML Programming Guide in the Apple documentation.)

For the More Curious: The Request Body

When **NSURLConnection** talks to a web server, it uses the HTTP protocol. This protocol says that any data you send or receive must follow the HTTP specification. The actual data transferred to the server in this exercise is shown in Figure 25.10.

Figure 25.10   HTTP Request Format

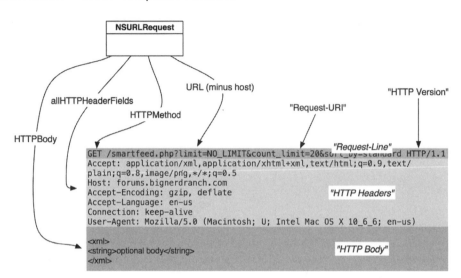

Fortunately, **NSURLRequest** has a number of methods that allow you to specify a piece of the request and then properly format it for you.

Any service request has three parts: a request-line, the HTTP headers, and the HTTP body, which is optional. The request-line (which Apple calls a status line in its API) is the first line of the request and tells the server what the client is trying to do. In this request, the client is trying to GET the resource at smartfeed.php?limit=NO_LIMIT&etc. (It also specifies the HTTP specification version that the data is in.)

The command, GET, is an HTTP method. While there are a number of supported HTTP methods, you typically only see GET and POST. The default of **NSURLRequest**, GET, indicates that the client wants something *from* the server. The thing that it wants is called the Request-URI (smartfeed.php? limit=NO_LIMIT&etc).

In the early days of the web, the Request-URI would be the path of a file on the server. For example, the request http://www.website.com/index.html would return the file index.html, and your browser would render that file in a window. Today, we also use the Request-URI to specify a service that the server implements. For example, in this chapter, you accessed the smartfeed.php service, supplied parameters to it, and were returned an XML document. You are still GETting something, but the server is more clever in interpreting what you are asking for.

In addition to getting things from a server, you can send it information. For example, many web servers allow you to upload photos. A client application would pass the image data to the server through a service request. In this situation, you use the HTTP method POST, which indicates to the server that you are including the optional HTTP body. The body of a request is data you can include with the request – typically XML, JSON or Base-64 encoded data.

When the request has a body, it must also have the Content-Length header. Handily enough, **NSURLRequest** will compute the size of the body and add this header for you.

```
NSURL *someURL = [NSURL URLWithString:@"http://www.photos.com/upload"];
UIImage *image = [self profilePicture];
NSData *data = UIImagePNGRepresentation(image);

NSMutableURLRequest *req =
    [NSMutableURLRequest requestWithURL:someURL
                            cachePolicy:NSURLRequestReloadIgnoringCacheData
                        timeoutInterval:90];

// This adds the HTTP body data and automatically sets the Content-Length header
[req setHTTPBody:data];

// This changes the HTTP Method in the request-line
[req setHTTPMethod:@"POST"];

// If you wanted to set the Content-Length programmatically...
[req setValue:[NSString stringWithFormat:@"%d", [data length]]
    forHTTPHeaderField:@"Content-Length"];
```

For the More Curious: Credentials

When you try to access a web service, it will sometimes respond with an *authentication challenge*, which means "Who the heck are you?" You then need to send a username and password (a *credential*) before the server will send its genuine response.

There are objects that represent these ideas. When the challenge is received, your connection delegate is sent a message that includes an instance of **NSURLAuthenticationChallenge**. The sender of that challenge conforms to the NSURLAuthenticationChallengeSender protocol. If you want to continue to get the data, you send back an instance of **NSURLCredential**, which typically looks something like this:

```
- (void)connection:(NSURLConnection *)conn
 didReceiveAuthenticationChallenge:(NSURLAuthenticationChallenge *)challenge
{
    // Have I already failed at least once?
    if ([challenge previousFailureCount] > 0) {

        // Why did I fail?
        NSError *failure = [challenge error];
        NSLog(@"Can't authenticate: %@", [error localizedDescription]);

        // Give up
        [[challenge sender] cancelAuthenticationChallenge:challenge];
        return;
    }

    // Create a credential
    NSURLCredential *newCred =
            [NSURLCredential credentialWithUser:@"sid"
                                       password:@"MomIsCool"
                                    persistence:NSURLCredentialPersistenceNone];

    // Supply the credential to the sender of the challenge
    [[challenge sender] useCredential:newCred
            forAuthenticationChallenge:challenge];
}
```

If you are dealing with a more secure and sophisticated web service, it may want a certificate (or certificates) to confirm your identity. Most, however, will just want a username and a password.

Credentials can have persistence. There are three possibilities:

- NSURLCredentialPersistenceNone says to the URL loading system, "Forget this credential as soon as you use it."

- NSURLCredentialPersistenceForSession says to the URL loading system, "Forget this credential when this application terminates."

- NSURLCredentialPersistencePermanent says to the URL loading system, "Put this credential in my keychain so that other applications can use it."

Challenge: More Data

Create a **UITableViewCell** subclass that has three labels. Parse the author and category elements into the **RSSItem** and display the title, author, and category for each row.

Challenge: More UIWebView

A **UIWebView** keeps its own history. You can send the messages **goBack** and **goForward** to a web view, and it will traverse through that history. Create a **UIToolbar** instance and add it to the **WebViewController**'s view hierarchy. This toolbar should have back and forward buttons that will let the web view move through its history. Bonus: use two other properties of **UIWebView** to enable and disable the toolbar items.

26
UISplitViewController

The iPhone and iPod touch have a limited amount of screen real estate. Given their small screen size, when presenting a drill-down interface, we use a **UINavigationController** to swap between a list of items and a detailed view for an item.

The iPad, on the other hand, has plenty of screen space to present both views using a built-in class called **UISplitViewController**. **UISplitViewController** is an iPad-only class that presents two view controllers in a master-detail relationship. The master view controller occupies a small strip on the left hand side of the screen, and the detail view controller occupies the rest of the screen.

In this chapter, you will have Nerdfeed present its view controllers in a split view controller when running on an iPad (Figure 26.1). We will also make Nerdfeed a universal application, and it will continue to use a **UINavigationController** when run on the iPhone.

Figure 26.1   Nerdfeed with UISplitViewController

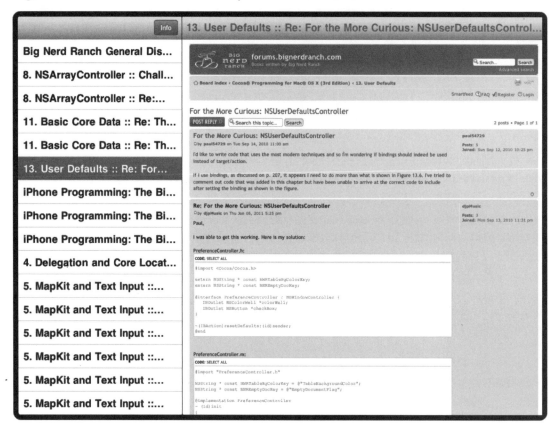

Splitting Up Nerdfeed

Creating a **UISplitViewController** is simple since you have already learned about navigation controllers and tab bar controllers. When you initialize a split view controller, you pass it an array of view controllers just like with a tab bar controller. However, a split view controller's array is limited to two view controllers: a master view controller and a detail view controller. The order of the view controllers in the array determines their roles and position in the split view; the first entry is the master view controller, and the second is the detail view controller.

Open Nerdfeed.xcodeproj in Xcode. Then, open NerdfeedAppDelegate.m.

In **application:didFinishLaunchingWithOptions:**, check if the device is an iPad before instantiating a **UISplitViewController**. The **UISplitViewController** class does not exist on the iPhone, and trying to create an instance of **UISplitViewController** will cause an exception to be thrown.

```
- (BOOL)application:(UIApplication *)application
    didFinishLaunchingWithOptions:(NSDictionary *)launchOptions
{
    ListViewController *lvc =
        [[ListViewController alloc] initWithStyle:UITableViewStylePlain];
    [lvc autorelease];

    UINavigationController *masterNav =
        [[UINavigationController alloc] initWithRootViewController:lvc];
    [masterNav autorelease];

    WebViewController *wvc = [[[WebViewController alloc] init] autorelease];
    [lvc setWebViewController:wvc];

    // Check to make sure we're running on the iPad.
    if ([[UIDevice currentDevice] userInterfaceIdiom] == UIUserInterfaceIdiomPad) {

        // webViewController must be in a navigation controller, you'll see why later.
        UINavigationController *detailNav =
            [[UINavigationController alloc] initWithRootViewController:wvc];
        [detailNav autorelease];

        // Put nav controller with list and nav controller with web view in an array
        // first view controller is the "Master" and second is the "Detail"
        NSArray *vcs = [NSArray arrayWithObjects:masterNav, detailNav, nil];

        UISplitViewController *svc =
            [[[UISplitViewController alloc] init] autorelease];

        // Set the delegate of the split view controller to the detail view controller
        // We'll need this later
        [svc setDelegate:wvc];

        // Set the split view controller's viewControllers array
        [svc setViewControllers:vcs];

        // Set the root view controller of the window to the split view controller
        [[self window] setRootViewController:svc];
    } else {
        // On non-iPad devices, go with the old version and just add the
        // single nav controller to the window
        [[self window] setRootViewController:masterNav];
    }
    [[self window] makeKeyAndVisible];

    return YES;
}
```

By placing the **UISplitViewController** code within an if statement in this method, we are laying the groundwork for making Nerdfeed a universal application. Also, now you can see why we created the instance of **WebViewController** here instead of following the typical pattern of creating the detail view controller inside the implementation for the root view controller. A split view controller must have both the master and the detail view controller when it is created. The diagram for Nerdfeed's split view controller is shown in Figure 26.2.

Figure 26.2   Controller diagram

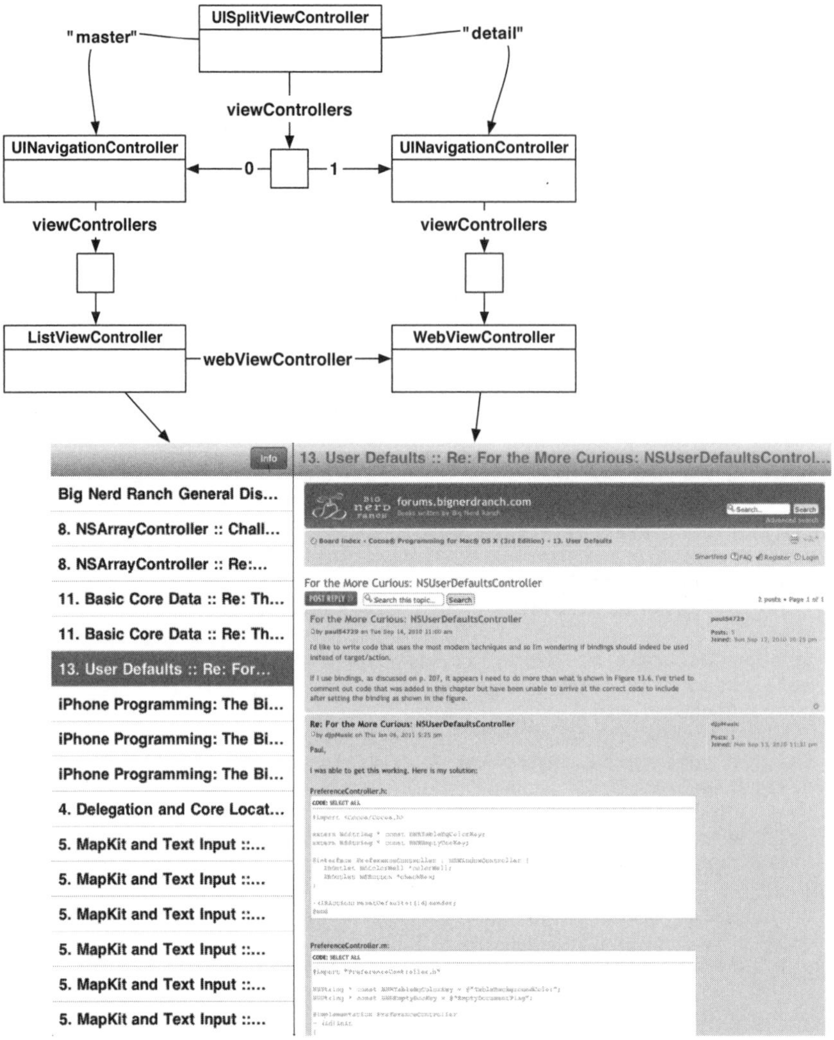

However, if you build and run right now, you won't see anything more than a navigation bar on top of a blank screen. The blank screen is your web view controller. It's blank because you haven't selected a row. You haven't selected a row because the list view controller is not on screen. Why is there no list view controller? A **UISplitViewController** only shows the detail view controller in portrait mode; there isn't enough space to show the master view controller, too. The split view controller will only display both when in landscape mode.

Unfortunately, your split view controller will not rotate to landscape mode by default. The **UISplitViewController** is a subclass of **UIViewController**, so it implements the method **shouldAutorotateToInterfaceOrientation:**. When the device rotates, the split view controller is sent this message. The method needs to return YES to allow the rotation and show the master view controller.

Overriding a method requires creating a new subclass, but before we do anything so drastic, let's look more closely at the implementation of **shouldAutorotateToInterfaceOrientation:** in **UISplitViewController**. It looks a bit like this:

```
- (BOOL)shouldAutorotateToInterfaceOrientation:(UIInterfaceOrientation)io
{
    if ([[self viewControllers] count] == 2) {
        UIViewController *master = [[self viewControllers] objectAtIndex:0];
        UIViewController *detail = [[self viewControllers] objectAtIndex:1];
        return [master shouldAutorotateToInterfaceOrientation:io]
            && [detail shouldAutorotateToInterfaceOrientation:io];
    }
    return NO;
}
```

This implementation asks the master and the detail view controller whether it should allow rotation. It sends the same message to both view controllers, and if both return YES, it rotates. So to get the **UISplitViewController** to allow rotation what we really need to do is modify the implementation of this method in the **UISplitViewController**'s two view controllers.

In ListViewController.m, override this method to return YES if Nerdfeed is running on the iPad:

```
- (BOOL)shouldAutorotateToInterfaceOrientation:(UIInterfaceOrientation)io
{
    if ([[UIDevice currentDevice] userInterfaceIdiom] == UIUserInterfaceIdiomPad)
        return YES;
    return io == UIInterfaceOrientationPortrait;
}
```

Do the same in WebViewController.m:

```
- (BOOL)shouldAutorotateToInterfaceOrientation:(UIInterfaceOrientation)io
{
    if ([[UIDevice currentDevice] userInterfaceIdiom] == UIUserInterfaceIdiomPad)
        return YES;
    return io == UIInterfaceOrientationPortrait;
}
```

Build and run the application. You should be able to rotate to landscape mode and, after the web service request finishes, see the list on the lefthand side.

But we're not done yet. If you tap a row in the list view controller, the web view controller doesn't appear in the detail panel like you want. Instead, it is pushed onto the master panel and replaces the list view controller. (Our master panel thinks it's an iPhone.) To address this problem, you will check if the **ListViewController** is a member of a split view controller and, if it is, take a different action when a row is tapped.

You can send the message **splitViewController** to any **UIViewController**, and if that view controller is part of a split view controller, it will return a pointer to the split view controller (Figure 26.3). Otherwise, it returns nil. View controllers are smart: a view controller will return this pointer if it is a member of the split view controller's array or if it belongs to another controller that is a member of a split view controller's array (as is the case with both **ListViewController** and **WebViewController**).

Figure 26.3 UIViewController's splitViewController property

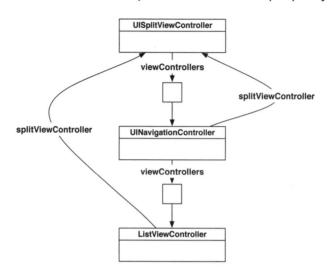

In ListViewController.m, locate the method **tableView:didSelectRowAtIndexPath:**. At the top of this method, make the check before you push the **WebViewController** onto the navigation stack.

```
- (void)tableView:(UITableView *)tableView
    didSelectRowAtIndexPath:(NSIndexPath *)indexPath
{
    if (![self splitViewController])
        [[self navigationController] pushViewController:webViewController
                                    animated:YES];

    RSSItem *entry = [[channel items] objectAtIndex:[indexPath row]];

    NSURL *url = [NSURL URLWithString:[entry link]];
    NSURLRequest *req = [NSURLRequest requestWithURL:url];

    [[webViewController webView] loadRequest:req];

    [[webViewController navigationItem] setTitle:[entry title]];
}
```

Now, if the **ListViewController** is not in a split view controller, we assume the device is not an iPad and have it push the **WebViewController** onto the navigation controller's stack. If **ListViewController** is in a split view controller, then we leave it to the **UISplitViewController** to place the **WebViewController** on the screen.

Build and run the application again. Rotate to landscape and tap on one of the rows. The web page will now load in the detail panel.

Master-Detail Communication

In Chapter 14, we discussed different options for allowing view controllers to send messages to each other. Using instance variables is the simplest option, and that's what we've done in Nerdfeed – we gave the **ListViewController** a pointer to the **WebViewController**. In this simple application, this approach works fine. Now let's make Nerdfeed a little more complex and write a delegate protocol instead.

Right now, the detail view controller displays the **WebViewController** when a row in the master view controller is selected. In a moment, you're going to create another view controller called **ChannelViewController** that will display metadata about the RSS feed. You will also create an Info button on the **ListViewController**'s navigation bar. Then the user will be able choose what to display in the detail panel: tap a row and see a post's detail view or tap the Info button and see the metadata about the RSS feed.

But, first, let's look at the big picture. The **ListViewController** will need to send messages to two different view controllers: the **WebViewController** and the **ChannelViewController**. Instead of giving the **ListViewController** another instance variable for the **ChannelViewController**, you're going to write a protocol that both detail view controllers will conform to. Then you can generalize the message that the **ListViewController** sends the two view controllers as a method in that protocol (Figure 26.4).

Figure 26.4   Master view controller delegating to detail view controllers

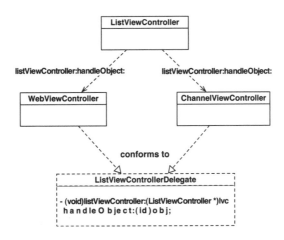

This protocol's one method will be named **listViewController:handleObject:**. The **ListViewController** will send this message to the **WebViewController** when a row in the table is tapped or to the **ChannelViewController** when the Info button is tapped. Notice that the second label and argument type of this method are very general so that it can be used with a range of classes. When the **ListViewController** sends this message to the **WebViewController**, it will pass an **RSSItem** object. When the **ListViewController** sends this message to the **ChannelViewController**, it will pass an **RSSChannel** object.

In ListViewController.h, create the ListViewControllerDelegate protocol at the end of the file.

```
- (void)fetchEntries;
@end
```

```
// A new protocol named ListViewControllerDelegate
@protocol ListViewControllerDelegate
```

```
// Classes that conform to this protocol must implement this method:
- (void)listViewController:(ListViewController *)lvc handleObject:(id)object;
```

@end

First, let's update **WebViewController**. In WebViewController.h, declare that this class conforms to ListViewControllerDelegate.

```
// Must import this file as it is where ListViewControllerDelegate is declared
#import "ListViewController.h"
```

```
@interface WebViewController : UIViewController <ListViewControllerDelegate>
{

}
@property (nonatomic, readonly) UIWebView *webView;
@end
```

When one of the rows is tapped in the table view, the **ListViewController** will send the message from the ListViewControllerDelegate protocol to the **WebViewController**. The object passed as the argument will be the **RSSItem** that corresponds to the selected row. In WebViewController.m, implement **listViewController:handleObject:**.

```
#import "RSSItem.h"
```

```
@implementation WebViewController
```

```
- (void)listViewController:(ListViewController *)lvc handleObject:(id)object
{
    // Cast the passed object to RSSItem
    RSSItem *entry = object;

    // Make sure that we are really getting a RSSItem
    if (![entry isKindOfClass:[RSSItem class]])
        return;

    // Grab the info from the item and push it into the appropriate views
    NSURL *url = [NSURL URLWithString:[entry link]];
    NSURLRequest *req = [NSURLRequest requestWithURL:url];
    [[self webView] loadRequest:req];

    [[self navigationItem] setTitle:[entry title]];
}
```

Notice that the code creating and loading the request is the same code that we are currently running in **ListViewController**.

Next, in ListViewController.m, modify the **tableView:didSelectRowAtIndexPath:** method to send **listViewController:handleObject:** to the **WebViewController**.

```
- (void)tableView:(UITableView *)tableView
    didSelectRowAtIndexPath:(NSIndexPath *)indexPath
{
    if (![self splitViewController])
```

```
        [[self navigationController] pushViewController:webViewController
                                    animated:YES];

    RSSItem *entry = [[channel items] objectAtIndex:[indexPath row]];

    [webViewController listViewController:self handleObject:entry];
}
```

Build and run the application. The behavior of the application should remain the same, but now we're sending a generalized message to the web view controller.

Now that **WebViewController** conforms to our protocol and implements the required method, we can turn to creating the **ChannelViewController** class.

Create an **NSObject** subclass and name it **ChannelViewController**. In ChannelViewController.h, change its superclass to **UITableViewController**, have it conform to the ListViewControllerDelegate protocol, and add an instance variable for the **RSSChannel** object.

```
#import "ListViewController.h"

@class RSSChannel;

@interface ChannelViewController :
    UITableViewController <ListViewControllerDelegate>
{
    RSSChannel *channel;
}

@end
```

In ChannelViewController.m, implement the data source methods to display the metadata in a table:

```
#import "RSSChannel.h"

@implementation ChannelViewController

- (NSInteger)tableView:(UITableView *)tableView
 numberOfRowsInSection:(NSInteger)section
{
    return 2;
}

- (UITableViewCell *)tableView:(UITableView *)tableView
        cellForRowAtIndexPath:(NSIndexPath *)indexPath
{
    UITableViewCell *cell =
                [tableView dequeueReusableCellWithIdentifier:@"UITableViewCell"];

    if (!cell)
        cell = [[[UITableViewCell alloc] initWithStyle:UITableViewCellStyleValue2
                                    reuseIdentifier:@"UITableViewCell"]
                                    autorelease];

    if ([indexPath row] == 0) {
        // Put the title of the channel in row 0
        [[cell textLabel] setText:@"Title"];
        [[cell detailTextLabel] setText:[channel title]];
    } else {
        // Put the description of the channel in row 1
```

```
        [[cell textLabel] setText:@"Info"];
        [[cell detailTextLabel] setText:[channel shortDescription]];
    }

    return cell;
}

- (BOOL)shouldAutorotateToInterfaceOrientation:(UIInterfaceOrientation)io
{
    if ([[UIDevice currentDevice] userInterfaceIdiom] == UIUserInterfaceIdiomPad)
        return YES;
    return io == UIInterfaceOrientationPortrait;
}

- (void)dealloc
{
    [channel release];
    [super dealloc];
}
@end
```

Then, implement the method from the `ListViewControllerDelegate` protocol in the same file, `ChannelViewController.m`.

```
- (void)listViewController:(ListViewController *)lvc handleObject:(id)object
{
    // Make sure the ListViewController gave us the right object
    if (![object isKindOfClass:[RSSChannel class]])
        return;

    // Get rid of our old channel if there is one, take ownership of the new one
    [object retain];
    [channel release];
    channel = object;

    [[self tableView] reloadData];
}
```

Now, you need to show this view controller and get the channel object to it. In `ListViewController.m`, add a **UIBarButtonItem** to the **ListViewController**'s navigationItem.

```
- (id)initWithStyle:(UITableViewStyle)style
{
    self = [super initWithStyle:style];

    if (self) {
        UIBarButtonItem *bbi =
            [[UIBarButtonItem alloc] initWithTitle:@"Info"
                                             style:UIBarButtonItemStyleBordered
                                            target:self
                                            action:@selector(showInfo:)];

        [[self navigationItem] setRightBarButtonItem:bbi];
        [bbi release];

        [self fetchEntries];
    }
    return self;
}
```

When this button is tapped, the detail view controller in the split view will be replaced with an instance of **ChannelViewController**. In ListViewController.m, implement the action method to create an instance of **ChannelViewController**. Then check for a split view controller and set the split view controller's viewControllers array.

```objc
#import "ChannelViewController.h"

@implementation ListViewController

- (void)showInfo:(id)sender
{
    // Create the channel view controller
    ChannelViewController *channelViewController = [[[ChannelViewController alloc]
                            initWithStyle:UITableViewStyleGrouped] autorelease];

    if ([self splitViewController]) {
        UINavigationController *nvc = [[[UINavigationController alloc]
                    initWithRootViewController:channelViewController] autorelease];

        // Create an array with our nav controller and this new VC's nav controller
        NSArray *vcs = [NSArray arrayWithObjects:[self navigationController],
                                        nvc,
                                        nil];

        // Grab a pointer to the split view controller
        // and reset its view controllers array.
        [[self splitViewController] setViewControllers:vcs];

        // Make detail view controller the delegate of the split view controller
        [[self splitViewController] setDelegate:channelViewController];

        // If a row has been selected, deselect it so that a row
        // is not selected when viewing the info
        NSIndexPath *selectedRow = [[self tableView] indexPathForSelectedRow];
        if (selectedRow)
            [[self tableView] deselectRowAtIndexPath:selectedRow animated:YES];
    } else {
        [[self navigationController] pushViewController:channelViewController
                                        animated:YES];
    }

    // Give the VC the channel object through the protocol message
    [channelViewController listViewController:self handleObject:channel];
}
```

Notice that here again you have left a non-split view controller, non-iPad option in an else clause that pushes the **ChannelViewController** onto the navigation controller's stack.

Build and run the application. After the RSS feed loads, tap the Info button. The detail view controller will display the metadata for the channel. However, if you tap on a post after you've loaded the metadata, nothing will happen – you can't get back to a web view. This is because the split view controller no longer has a navigation controller that holds the web view controller. The old one was only retained by the split view controller, and we replaced it with a navigation controller holding the channel view controller in **showInfo:**. We have to create another navigation controller that holds the web view controller and give it to the split view controller.

In ListViewController.m, modify the **tableView:didSelectRowAtIndexPath:** to place a navigation controller with the **WebViewController** in the split view controller.

```
- (void)tableView:(UITableView *)tableView
    didSelectRowAtIndexPath:(NSIndexPath *)indexPath
{
    if (![self splitViewController])
        [[self navigationController] pushViewController:webViewController
                                              animated:YES];
    else {
        // We have to create a new navigation controller, as the old one
        // was only retained by the split view controller and is now gone
        UINavigationController *nav =
        [[UINavigationController alloc] initWithRootViewController:webViewController];

        NSArray *vcs = [NSArray arrayWithObjects:[self navigationController],
                                                 nav,
                                                 nil];
        [nav release];

        [[self splitViewController] setViewControllers:vcs];

        // Make the detail view controller the delegate of the split view controller
        [[self splitViewController] setDelegate:webViewController];
    }

    RSSItem *entry = [[channel items] objectAtIndex:[indexPath row]];
    [webViewController listViewController:self handleObject:entry];
}
```

Build and run the application. You should be able to move back and forth between the two detail view controllers.

The **ListViewController** doesn't know how to show a post in a web view or show the info for the **RSSChannel**. So it needs to delegate those behaviors to other objects. **ListViewController** does know about the ListViewControllerDelegate protocol, by which it can send messages to a conforming detailed view controller to handle things it can't.

Even though the **ListViewController** never sets either of the detail view controllers as its delegate, this is still delegation. Delegation is a design pattern, not a naming convention. For another example, the table view-data source relationship is still delegation, even though the variable the table view sends messages to is called a dataSource.

Displaying the Master View Controller in Portrait Mode

While in portrait mode, the master view controller is missing in action. It would be nice if you could see the master view controller to select a new post from the list without having to rotate the device. **UISplitViewController** lets you do just that by supplying its delegate with a **UIBarButtonItem**. Tapping this button shows the master view controller in a **UIPopoverController**.

In your code, whenever a detail view controller was given to the split view controller, that detail view controller was set as the split view controller's delegate. When rotating to portrait mode, the detail view controller will get a pointer to the **UIBarButtonItem**.

In WebViewController.m, implement the following delegate method to place the bar button item in the **WebViewController**'s navigation item.

```
- (void)splitViewController:(UISplitViewController *)svc
      willHideViewController:(UIViewController *)aViewController
          withBarButtonItem:(UIBarButtonItem *)barButtonItem
       forPopoverController:(UIPopoverController *)pc
{
    // If this bar button item doesn't have a title, it won't appear at all.
    [barButtonItem setTitle:@"List"];

    // Take this bar button item and put it on the left side of our nav item.
    [[self navigationItem] setLeftBarButtonItem:barButtonItem];
}
```

Notice that we explicitly set the title of the button. If the button doesn't have a title, it won't appear at all. (If the master view controller's navigationItem has a title, then the button will be set to that title. But that's not true in Nerdfeed.)

Build and run the application. Rotate to portrait mode, and you will see the bar button item appear on the left of the navigation bar. Tap that button, and the master view controller's view will appear in a **UIPopoverController**.

This bar button item is why we always had you put the detail view controller inside a navigation controller. You don't have to use a navigation controller to put a view controller in a split view controller, but it makes using the bar button item much easier. (If you don't use a navigation controller, you can instantiate your own **UINavigationBar** or **UIToolbar** to hold the bar button item and add it as a subview of the **WebViewController**'s view.)

There are three small issues left to address with your List button. First, when the device is rotated back to landscape mode, the button is still there. To remove it, the delegate needs to respond to another message from the **UISplitViewController**. Implement this delegate method in WebViewController.m.

```
- (void)splitViewController:(UISplitViewController *)svc
      willShowViewController:(UIViewController *)aViewController
   invalidatingBarButtonItem:(UIBarButtonItem *)button
{
    // Remove the bar button item from our navigation item
    // We'll double check that its the correct button, even though we know it is
    if (button == [[self navigationItem] leftBarButtonItem])
        [[self navigationItem] setLeftBarButtonItem:nil];
}
```

Build and run the application. The List button will now appear and disappear as you rotate between portrait and landscape modes.

The second issue is that the **ChannelViewController** also needs to show the List button. In ChannelViewController.m, implement the two UISplitViewControllerDelegate methods.

```
- (void)splitViewController:(UISplitViewController *)svc
      willHideViewController:(UIViewController *)aViewController
          withBarButtonItem:(UIBarButtonItem *)barButtonItem
       forPopoverController:(UIPopoverController *)pc
{
    [barButtonItem setTitle:@"List"];

    [[self navigationItem] setLeftBarButtonItem:barButtonItem];
}
```

```
- (void)splitViewController:(UISplitViewController *)svc
     willShowViewController:(UIViewController *)aViewController
  invalidatingBarButtonItem:(UIBarButtonItem *)button
{
    if (button == [[self navigationItem] leftBarButtonItem])
        [[self navigationItem] setLeftBarButtonItem:nil];
}
```

Build and run the application. Now the List button will also appear on the navigation bar when the **ChannelViewController** is on the screen.

Since both **WebViewController** and **ChannelViewController** can be the delegate for a **UISplitViewController**, it's best to declare that they conform to the UISplitViewControllerDelegate protocol.

In WebViewController.h, add this declaration:

```
@interface WebViewController : UIViewController
            <ListViewControllerDelegate, UISplitViewControllerDelegate>
```

And do the same in ChannelViewController.h.

```
@interface ChannelViewController : UITableViewController
            <ListViewControllerDelegate, UISplitViewControllerDelegate>
```

Build and run the application. The behavior will be the same, but there won't be any warnings.

Finally, if you are in portrait mode and switch between the **ChannelViewController** and the **WebViewController**, the List button disappears. To keep the button on the screen, the **ListViewController** needs to take the button from the current detail view controller and give it to the new detail view controller.

At the top of ListViewController.m, create a category to implement a new private method:

```
@interface ListViewController ()
- (void)transferBarButtonToViewController:(UIViewController *)vc;
@end

@implementation ListViewController
```

Then, implement this method in ListViewController.m.

```
- (void)transferBarButtonToViewController:(UIViewController *)vc
{
    // Get the navigation controller in the detail spot of the split view controller
    UINavigationController *nvc = [[[self splitViewController] viewControllers]
                                                         objectAtIndex:1];

    // Get the root view controller out of that nav controller
    UIViewController *currentVC = [[nvc viewControllers] objectAtIndex:0];

    // If it's the same view controller, let's not do anything
    if (vc == currentVC)
        return;

    // Get that view controller's navigation item
    UINavigationItem *currentVCItem = [currentVC navigationItem];
```

```
    // Tell new view controller to use left bar button item of current nav item
    [[vc navigationItem] setLeftBarButtonItem:[currentVCItem leftBarButtonItem]];

    // Remove the bar button item from the current view controller's nav item
    [currentVCItem setLeftBarButtonItem:nil];
}
```

Whenever the user switches between the two different views, you will invoke this method. Because this method references the current detail view controller, it must be called before the split view controller is updated with a new set of view controllers. In ListViewController.m, invoke this method near the top of **showInfo:**.

```
- (void)showInfo:(id)sender
{
    ChannelViewController *channelViewController =
        [[[ChannelViewController alloc]
                            initWithStyle:UITableViewStyleGrouped] autorelease];

    if ([self splitViewController])
    {
        [self transferBarButtonToViewController:channelViewController];

        UINavigationController *nvc =
            [[UINavigationController alloc]
                initWithRootViewController:channelViewController];
```

Now do the same going the other way. In ListViewController.m, locate the **tableView:didSelectRowAtIndexPath:** method and add the following code:

```
- (void)tableView:(UITableView *)tableView
    didSelectRowAtIndexPath:(NSIndexPath *)indexPath
{
    if (![self splitViewController])
        [[self navigationController] pushViewController:webViewController
                                              animated:YES];
    else {
        [self transferBarButtonToViewController:webViewController];

        UINavigationController *nav =
            [[UINavigationController alloc] initWithRootViewController:webViewController];
```

Build and run the application. The List button should now always appear in portrait mode – no matter what the user does – and never appear in landscape mode.

Universalizing Nerdfeed

When first creating Nerdfeed, we chose to go with an iPad-only application. Now, you're going to turn it into a universal application. Select the Nerdfeed project from the project navigator. In the editor area, choose the Nerdfeed target and then the Summary tab.

Figure 26.5   Universalizing Nerdfeed

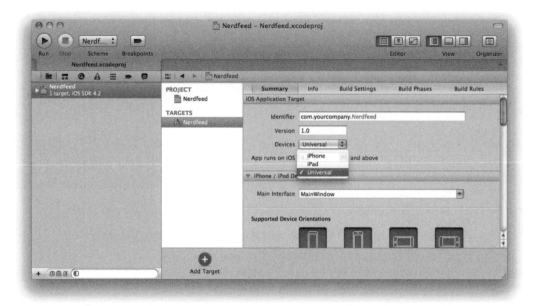

From the Devices pop-up menu, choose Universal. A sheet will appear asking if you want to copy and convert MainWindow.xib. Choose No.

Figure 26.6   Changing simulators

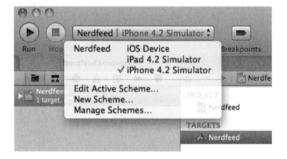

That's all there is to it – the application is now universal. You can test it by building and running again on one simulator and then the other.

There are two reasons the universalization process was so easy for Nerdfeed. Remembering these reasons will help you when you're writing your own applications.

• As we built Nerdfeed, we were mindful of the device differences in the classes we used. For example, knowing that a **UISplitViewController** doesn't exist on the iPhone or iPod touch, we made sure that there was an alternative interface on those devices. In general, when using an Apple-provided class, you should read the discussion in the documentation about that class. It will give you tips about the availability of the class and its methods on the different devices.

- Nerdfeed is still a relatively simple application. It is always easier to universalize an application early in development. As an application grows, its details get buried in the massive pile of code. Finding and fixing issues as you're writing code is much easier than coming back later. Details are harder to find, and there is the risk of breaking what already works.

27

Media Playback and Background Execution

Many applications on a mobile device need audio and video playback. In this chapter, you will learn how to use the most common audio and video playback routines the iOS SDK offers. In addition, we will look at background processes and multitasking.

Figure 27.1   MediaPlayer

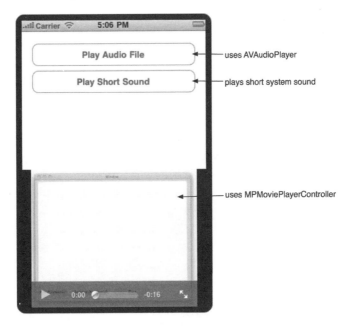

Creating the MediaPlayer Application

Create an iPhone Window-based Application in Xcode. Name this project MediaPlayer.

MediaPlayer will have a very simple interface so that you can concentrate on the guts of media playback. The application will display two buttons that will initiate different types of audio playback, and it will also display a movie. The object diagram for this application is shown in Figure 27.1.

Figure 27.2   MediaPlayer object diagram

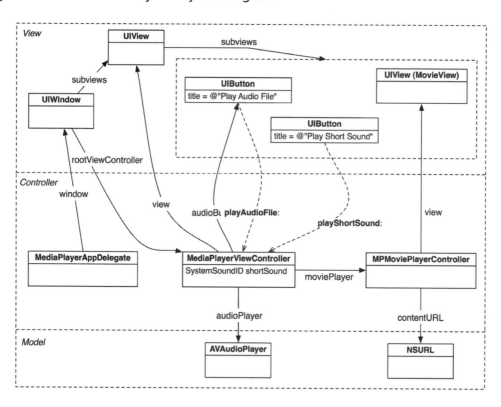

Create a new **UIViewController** subclass (File → New → New File...) and check With XIB for user interface. Name this subclass MediaPlayerViewController. In MediaPlayerAppDelegate.m, import the header file for **MediaPlayerViewController**, create an instance of the view controller, and set it to be the window's rootViewController.

```
#import "MediaPlayerAppDelegate.h"
#import "MediaPlayerViewController.h"

@implementation MediaPlayerAppDelegate
@synthesize window;

- (BOOL)application:(UIApplication *)application
    didFinishLaunchingWithOptions:(NSDictionary *)launchOptions
{
    MediaPlayerViewController *vc = [[MediaPlayerViewController alloc] init];
    [[self window] setRootViewController:vc];
    [vc release];

    [[self window] makeKeyAndVisible];

    return YES;
}
```

The application needs two buttons for playing audio. One button's title will change during runtime, and both buttons need action methods. In MediaPlayerViewController.h, declare an instance variable for the button with the title that will change and the two action methods.

```
@interface MediaPlayerViewController : UIViewController
{
    IBOutlet UIButton *audioButton;
}
- (IBAction)playAudioFile:(id)sender;
- (IBAction)playShortSound:(id)sender;
@end
```

Save this file and then open MediaPlayerViewController.xib.

Click the View object in the outline view to open it. Drag two **UIButton** objects onto the view and title them as shown in Figure 27.3. Then, make the action connections from the buttons back to the **MediaPlayerViewController**. Finally, connect the audioButton outlet to the button labeled Play Audio File.

Figure 27.3 MediaPlayerViewController.xib connections

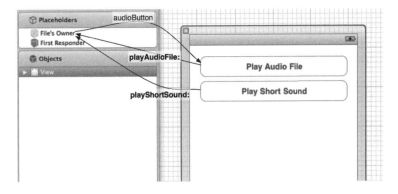

In order to build and run the application without warnings, you will need stub methods for the IBActions you declared. In MediaPlayerViewController.m, implement them as follows.

```
- (IBAction)playAudioFile:(id)sender
{
    NSLog(@"playAudioFile!");
}
- (IBAction)playShortSound:(id)sender
{
    NSLog(@"playSound!");
}
```

If you want to check your connections, you can build and run the application. The log messages should show up on the console.

System Sounds

Audio files come in different formats. The format describes the organization of the audio data within the file. Some files, like MP3 and M4A, have been compressed and require a decoder for playback. Compressed files are much smaller in size but require more work by the processor to play.

The extra work it takes to decode a compressed file can affect application performance, and compression doesn't save much disk space if the recording is short. Thus, short sound effect files are not compressed. These sounds are typically used as an interface element. They are not critical to an application but add to the atmosphere you are trying to create.

The AudioToolbox framework gives you the ability to register short sound effects on the system sound server. Sounds registered with the system sound server are called *system sounds*. System sounds must

- be a sound file less than 30 seconds in length

- have data in linear PCM or IMA4 format

- be packaged as one of the following three types: Core Audio Format (.caf), Waveform audio format (.wav), or Audio Interchange File Format (.aiff)

Add the AudioToolbox framework to your project so that you can register and play system sounds. Then, in MediaPlayerViewController.h, declare a **SystemSoundID** instance variable. Because this type is declared in AudioToolbox framework, you will also need to import AudioToolbox's top-level header file.

```
#import <AudioToolbox/AudioToolbox.h>
@interface MediaPlayerViewController : UIViewController
{
    IBOutlet UIButton *audioButton;
    SystemSoundID shortSound;
}
```

Every registered system sound is given a **SystemSoundID**, which is really just an integer that you can think of as a ticket. When you want to play a registered sound effect, you tell the sound server the number on your ticket.

Registering system sounds

The audio data for a system sound must be contained in a file located on the device. In this exercise, you will bundle a short audio clip file with the application. Locate the file Sound12.aif and add it to the project navigator. (This file and other resources can be downloaded from http://www.bignerdranch.com/solutions/iOSProgramming.zip.)

To register this sound, you call the function **AudioServicesCreateSystemSoundID** and pass the full path of the file as a **CFURLRef** object. How do we get the **CFURLRef**? First, you grab the full file path using **NSBundle**'s **pathForResource:ofType:** method. The object returned from this method, however, is of type **NSString**. To get from an string to a URL, you use **NSURL**'s **fileURLWithPath:** to create an **NSURL** instance. Finally, you cast the **NSURL** instance to its toll-free bridged counterpart: **CFURLRef**.

In MediaPlayer, you are going to do this when the application launches, so add this code to **MediaPlayerViewController**'s **init** method. In MediaPlayerViewController.m, edit **init** to get a path to the Sound12.aif file and register its contents as a system sound.

```
- (id)init
{
    self = [super initWithNibName:@"MediaPlayerViewController" bundle:nil];

    if (self) {
        // Get the full path of Sound12.aif
        NSString *soundPath = [[NSBundle mainBundle] pathForResource:@"Sound12"
                                                              ofType:@"aif"];
        // If this file is actually in the bundle...
        if (soundPath) {
            // Create a file URL with this path
            NSURL *soundURL = [NSURL fileURLWithPath:soundPath];

            // Register sound file located at that URL as a system sound
            OSStatus err = AudioServicesCreateSystemSoundID((CFURLRef)soundURL,
                                                            &shortSound);
            if (err != kAudioServicesNoError)
                NSLog(@"Could not load %@, error code: %d", soundURL, err);
        }
    }

    return self;
}
- (id)initWithNibName:(NSString *)nibNameOrNil bundle:(NSBundle *)nibBundleOrNil
{
    return [self init];
}
```

Notice the &shortSound passed to the **AudioServicesCreateSystemSoundID** function. This function has an error code as a return value. Only one value can be returned from a function, so the **SystemSoundID** cannot be returned to the caller. Instead, to get that value from the function, you pass the address of a **SystemSoundID** variable to the function. This function then writes the value of the **SystemSoundID** to that location in memory. This is called *passing by reference* and allows the function to change the value of a variable.

Playing system sounds

Back in the MediaPlayerViewController.m, implement the method **playShortSound:**.

```
- (IBAction)playShortSound:(id)sender
{
    AudioServicesPlaySystemSound(shortSound);
}
```

Build and run your application. You should hear a pleasant noise every time you tap the Play Short Sound button. (Make sure your volume is turned up.)

Most of the time, you will keep a system sound available the entire time an application is running. However, if you want to dispose of a short sound to free up memory while an application is running, you can call the C function **AudioServicesDisposeSystemSoundID**.

```
    AudioServicesDisposeSystemSoundID(aSystemSound);
```

On the iPhone (but not the iPad or iPod touch), you can use system sounds to vibrate the device. Add the following line of code to MediaPlayerViewController.m to trigger vibration.

```
- (IBAction)playShortSound:(id)sender
{
    AudioServicesPlaySystemSound(shortSound);
    AudioServicesPlaySystemSound(kSystemSoundID_Vibrate);
}
```

Build and run the application on an iPhone and tap the short sound button. It will play the sound and vibrate in your hand.

Compressed Audio Files

To play a compressed audio format or any file that is longer than 30 seconds, you use the class **AVAudioPlayer**. In addition to playing longer compressed audio, this class also gives you more control over audio playback.

The **AVAudioPlayer** class is defined in the AVFoundation framework. Add the AVFoundation framework to your project and import its header file into MediaPlayerViewController.h. Declare an instance variable of type **AVAudioPlayer**.

```
#import <AVFoundation/AVFoundation.h>

@interface MediaPlayerViewController : UIViewController <AVAudioPlayerDelegate>
{
    IBOutlet UIButton *audioButton;
    SystemSoundID shortSound;

    AVAudioPlayer *audioPlayer;
```

In this exercise, you will use an instance of this class to play an MP3 file. Locate the file Music.mp3 and add it to the project navigator. (This file and other resources can be downloaded from http://www.bignerdranch.com/solutions/iOSProgramming.zip.)

Once again, you will use **NSBundle**'s **pathForResource:ofType:** to get the path of the file as an **NSString** and then use **NSURL**'s **fileURLWithPath:** to create an **NSURL** instance. In MediaPlayerViewController.m, add the following code to the top of **init**.

```
- (id)init
{
    self = [super initWithNibName:@"MediaPlayerViewController" bundle:nil];

    if (self) {

        NSString *musicPath = [[NSBundle mainBundle] pathForResource:@"Music"
                                                           ofType:@"mp3"];
        if (musicPath) {
            NSURL *musicURL = [NSURL fileURLWithPath:musicPath];
            audioPlayer = [[AVAudioPlayer alloc] initWithContentsOfURL:musicURL
                                                         error:nil];
            [audioPlayer setDelegate:self];
        }

        NSString *soundPath = [[NSBundle mainBundle] pathForResource:@"Sound12"
                                                           ofType:@"aif"];
```

Finally, in MediaPlayerViewController.m, have the associated button begin playback of the audioPlayer.

```
- (IBAction)playAudioFile:(id)sender
{
    if ([audioPlayer isPlaying]) {
        // Stop playing audio and change text of button
        [audioPlayer stop];
        [sender setTitle:@"Play Audio File"
                forState:UIControlStateNormal];
    }
    else {
        // Start playing audio and change text of button so
        // user can tap to stop playback
        [audioPlayer play];
        [sender setTitle:@"Stop Audio File"
                forState:UIControlStateNormal];
    }
}
```

Build and run the application. Tap the Play Audio File and listen for the music.

With **AVAudioPlayer**, you have more control over the audio playback, and you can halt its playback whenever you choose. You can also implement delegate methods for an **AVAudioPlayer** that will allow you to control what happens when the audio player finishes playing or when it gets interrupted. For instance, when the audio player finishes, you want the title of the button that plays the audio file to revert to Play Audio File.

In MediaPlayerViewController.m, implement **audioPlayerDidFinishPlaying:successfully:** to change the title of the button. .

```
- (void)audioPlayerDidFinishPlaying:(AVAudioPlayer *)player
                      successfully:(BOOL)flag
{
    [audioButton setTitle:@"Play Audio File"
                forState:UIControlStateNormal];
}
```

Build and run the application. Let the audio file finish on its own and watch the playback button return to its original state.

Audio playback can be interrupted. For example, playback will be interrupted when a phone call occurs. When the iPhone interrupts an **AVAudioPlayer** instance from playing, it pauses the music for you. At this moment, you can also perform additional tasks, like updating the user interface, with the delegate method **audioPlayerBeginInterruption:**.

Another delegate method, **audioPlayerEndInterruption:**, is sent to the **AVAudioPlayer**'s delegate when the interruption ends. In the case of a phone call, this message is sent to the delegate if the user ignores the call. Implement this method in MediaPlayerViewController.m.

```
- (void)audioPlayerEndInterruption:(AVAudioPlayer *)player
{
    [audioPlayer play];
}
```

Playing Movie Files

MPMoviePlayerController is responsible for playing movies on iOS. The YouTube application uses the same class to play its movies, so you've probably seen the interface in Figure 27.4 before.

Figure 27.4   MPMoviePlayerController in action

Playing a movie file on iOS is fairly restricted. You are limited to two formats:

- H.264 (Baseline Profile Level 3.0)

- MPEG-4 Part 2 video (Simple Profile)

(Fortunately, iTunes has an option to convert video files into these formats. In iTunes, select a movie file and choose Create iPod or iPhone Version from the Advanced menu.)

Instances of **MPMoviePlayerController** can also play streaming video from a URL somewhere off in Internet land. However, you should seriously consider the problems of this approach on a mobile device. If you have the choice, either bundle a movie file with the application or have your application download the video to the application sandbox after launching. If you do not have the choice, be aware that Apple can reject your application if a video file is too large to be transported over the network in an appropriate amount of time. For example, your application can be rejected if it claims to support the original iPhone (using the Edge network) and streams video at more than 1MB per second.

In order to use **MPMoviePlayerController**, you need yet another framework – the MediaPlayer framework. Add the MediaPlayer framework to your project and import the appropriate header file at the top of MediaPlayerViewController.h. While you're there, create an instance variable in **MediaPlayerViewController** for the movie player.

```
#import <MediaPlayer/MediaPlayer.h>

@interface MediaPlayerViewController : UIViewController <AVAudioPlayerDelegate>
{
    MPMoviePlayerController *moviePlayer;
```

In this exercise, you will bundle the Layers.m4v movie with the application. Locate this file and add it to the project navigator. (This file and other resources can be downloaded from http://www.bignerdranch.com/solutions/iOSProgramming.zip.)

To load the movie, add the following code to the top of **init** in MediaPlayerViewController.m.

```
- (id)init
{
    self = [super initWithNibName:@"MediaPlayerViewController" bundle:nil];

    if (self) {

        NSString *moviePath = [[NSBundle mainBundle] pathForResource:@"Layers"
                                                              ofType:@"m4v"];
        if (moviePath) {
            NSURL *movieURL = [NSURL fileURLWithPath:moviePath];
            moviePlayer = [[MPMoviePlayerController alloc]
                                    initWithContentURL:movieURL];
        }

        NSString *musicPath = [[NSBundle mainBundle] pathForResource:@"Music"
                                                              ofType:@"mp3"];
```

Every **MPMoviePlayerController** has a view that displays the movie and the player controls. In MediaPlayerViewController.m, override **viewDidLoad** to add the moviePlayer's view to the **MediaPlayerViewController**'s view.

```
- (void)viewDidLoad
{
    [[self view] addSubview:[moviePlayer view]];
    float halfHeight = [[self view] bounds].size.height / 2.0;
    float width = [[self view] bounds].size.width;
    [[moviePlayer view] setFrame:CGRectMake(0, halfHeight, width, halfHeight)];
}
```

Build and run the application. The movie player will appear in the bottom half of the screen. You can tap the play button within that view to begin playback. You can also tap the full-screen button to present that video in full-screen mode.

Note that only one instance of **MPMoviePlayerController** can operate within an application. Therefore, you should not create multiple instances of **MPMoviePlayerController**. If your application intends to present a movie in multiple places, you should either reuse a single movie player controller or destroy the movie player controller and recreate another elsewhere.

MPMoviePlayerViewController

If you wish to present a full-screen only video, you can use the class **MPMoviePlayerViewController** (notice the addition of "View" in the class name). This class inherits from **UIViewController** and manages a view that presents a movie. Instantiating an **MPMoviePlayerViewController** is just like instantiating an **MPMoviePlayerController**:

```
MPMoviePlayerViewController *playerViewController =
    [[MPMoviePlayerViewController alloc] initWithContentURL:movieURL];
```

To present the full-screen video on top of an existing view controller, you send the message **presentMoviePlayerViewControllerAnimated:** to a view controller that is currently on the screen.

```
[viewController presentMoviePlayerViewControllerAnimated:playerViewController];
```

Alternatively, you can add an **MPMoviePlayerViewController** to a tab bar or navigation controller.

Note that, internally, an **MPMoviePlayerViewController** uses an **MPMoviePlayerController**. Therefore, creating an instance of **MPMoviePlayerViewController** will invalidate any existing movie player controllers as you can only have one movie player at a time.

Preloading video

When you instantiate an **MPMoviePlayerController**, it immediately begins loading the video you ask it to. This loading happens on another thread so that your application does not halt while the video loads. A video loaded from disk will most likely be ready to play immediately, but one being streamed from the Internet may take some time to load. You may not want to display an unloaded video right away.

To know when a video has loaded, you can register for a notification when the movie player's load state changes. The loadState property of a movie player tells you whether the movie is playable, stalled, or has enough data to play without interruption.

```
[[NSNotificationCenter defaultCenter]
    addObserver:self
        selector:@selector(displayPreloadedVideo:)
            name:MPMoviePlayerLoadStateDidChangeNotification
        object:moviePlayer];
```

```
- (void)displayPreloadedVideo:(NSNotification *)note
{
    MPMoviePlayerController *mp = [note object];
    if ([mp loadState] == MPMovieLoadStatePlaythroughOK)
        [[self view] addSubview:[mp view]];
}
```

An instance of **MPMoviePlayerController** posts notifications for other events, too. Check out the documentation for the class to see all available notification names.

Now you can play any sort of media you like! Remember that audio and video files are relatively large compared to other resources you might have in an application. Gratuitous use of these types of resources may increase an application bundle's size and the amount of time it takes to download.

Background Processes

An application can play audio even when it's not the active application. Let's modify the MediaPlayer application so that it continues playing audio even when its been put in the background state.

By default, when the user presses the Home button, an application is put into the background state and then transitioned to the suspended state shortly thereafter. Audio playback cannot continue in the suspended state because no code can be executed when an application is suspended. If your application needs to continue executing code once it is no longer active, it can request to stay in the background state instead of transitioning to the suspended state.

To delay being transitioned to the suspended state, you add a key-value pair to the application's Info property list. To get to an application's info property list, select the project from the project navigator and then select the target and the Info pane.

In MediaPlayer's Info property list, add a new row by selecting the last row and clicking the plus button (+) next to it. In the Key column of the new row, enter UIBackgroundModes. The Key column will automatically update to display Required background modes, and its value will become an array that has a single item.

Click the disclosure tab next to the text Required background modes, and the items in the array will appear beneath it. There is currently one empty item. Enter "audio" in the Value column, and it will automatically update to display App plays audio (Figure 27.5).

458

Figure 27.5   Info property list with background audio mode

Key	Type	Value
Summary	Info	Build Settings	Build Phas
▼ Custom iOS Target Properties		
Key	Type	Value
Localization native development region	String	English
Bundle display name	String	${PRODUCT_NAME}
Executable file	String	${EXECUTABLE_NAME}
Icon file	String	
Bundle identifier	String	com.yourcompany.${PRODUCT_NAME:rfc1034id}
InfoDictionary version	String	6.0
Bundle name	String	${PRODUCT_NAME}
Bundle OS Type code	String	APPL
Bundle creator OS Type code	String	????
Bundle version	String	1.0
Application requires iPhone environmer	Boolean	YES
Main nib file base name	String	MainWindow
▼ Required background modes	Array	(1 item)
Item 0	String	App plays audio

MediaPlayer is now registered for background audio and will continue playing audio when it is put into the background state. However, the application will only continue playing audio of a certain *audio session category*. Every application has a single instance of **AVAudioSession** that manages the category of audio it plays. This category determines many things about how the application interacts with the system in terms of audio, including whether an application can continue playing audio in the background. (For more information about audio session categories, see the Audio Session Programming Guide in the documentation.)

To change the audio session's category, you send it the message **setCategory:error:** with one of the defined constants. The category that allows an application to continue playing audio in the background is AVAudioSessionCategoryPlayback. In MediaPlayerViewController.m, add the following code to **init**.

```
if (musicPath) {
    NSURL *musicURL = [NSURL fileURLWithPath:musicPath];
    [[AVAudioSession sharedInstance]
            setCategory:AVAudioSessionCategoryPlayback error:nil];
    audioPlayer = [[AVAudioPlayer alloc] initWithContentsOfURL:musicURL
                                                 error:nil];
    [audioPlayer setDelegate:self];
}
```

Build and run the application. (Do this on the device; background processes won't work on the simulator). Tap the button titled Play Audio File and then press the Home button. Notice how the track keeps playing even if you open another application. When the track ends, the application will transition to the suspended state.

Guidelines for background execution

An application operating in the background is under stricter rules than an application in the foreground. Here are some general guidelines that an application should follow when it is operating in the background:

- *Do not* use OpenGL ES or shared system resources (like the address book). The operating system will terminate your application if it notices you doing either of these things.

- *Do not* update your views. The user can't see them anyway.

- *Do* release unneeded memory, similar to when responding to a low-memory warning.

- *Do* throttle back the application's workload. For example, an application that plays audio in the background should perform just the tasks needed to play the audio and nothing else.

An application that runs in the background is still subject to termination by the operating system when memory gets low. The operating system will first issue a low-memory warning to all applications in the active or background state. If memory remains low, the OS will start purging suspended applications. If that doesn't free up enough memory, then background applications are terminated.

When an application running in the background is terminated, its delegate is gracefully sent the message `applicationWillTerminate:` and given a moment to perform any final tasks. However, it is safer to save any application information in the method `applicationDidEnterBackground:`, like we did in Chapter 15.

Other forms of background execution

In addition to audio playback, there are two types of standard background execution: voice over internet protocol (VOIP) and location updates. You can add `location` or `voip` to the Required background modes array in the info property list to configure your application to support these modes. VOIP is its own, very complicated process that is outside the scope of this book, but let's take a moment to look at location updates and the various possibilities for using them in the background.

An application that is in the background (for any reason) will continue to receive location updates. As the location is updated, the delegate of the `CLLocationManager` is sent `locationManager:didUpdateToLocation:fromLocation:` as normal. You can specify that an application wants to remain in the background specifically for location updates by adding the `location` key to its UIBackgroundModes. An application that registers `location` as a background mode will remain in background mode as long as a `CLLocationManager` is actively updating its location.

However, continually updating the location while running in the background is a big drain on the battery. If your application doesn't require precise updates at frequent intervals, you can instead monitor for significant location changes. A significant location change occurs when the device switches to a new cell phone tower. (Cell phone towers in metropolitan areas are typically a quarter- to half-mile apart and two miles apart in more rural areas.)

An added benefit of monitoring for significant location changes is that even if your application is suspended, the operating system will briefly wake your application up in the background. When it is awoken, the location manager's delegate is sent the appropriate message so your application can handle the change in location.

To enable significant location changes, send the message `startMonitoringSignificantLocationChanges` to an instance of `CLLocationManager` when it is instantiated.

```
CLLocationManager *manager = [[CLLocationManager alloc] init];
[manager startMonitoringSignificantLocationChanges];
```

At times, you may want your application to stay in the background (and not get suspended) for a reason other than one of the three standard background modes. For example, an application downloading a file from the Internet may want to finish downloading that file before it is suspended. In this case, you can request to stay in the background for longer. You can ask the operating system for additional time to complete a background task with the **UIApplication**'s method **beginBackgroundTaskWithExpirationHandler:**.

As an example, let's say you were downloading a large image from NASA's public domain images. Once this download started, you would like it to complete even if the user exits the application. Thus, when you begin the web service request to fetch this image, you would register a background task:

```
NSString *path = @"http://grin.hq.nasa.gov/IMAGES/MEDIUM/GPN-2000-000946.jpg";
NSURL *url = [NSURL URLWithString:path];
NSURLRequest *req = [NSURLRequest requestWithURL:url];
NSURLConnection *conn = [[NSURLConnection alloc] initWithRequest:req
                                                 delegate:self
                                          startImmediately:YES];
[self setConnection:connection];
[conn release];

UIBackgroundTaskIdentifier downloadImageTask =
    [[UIApplication sharedApplication] beginBackgroundTaskWithExpirationHandler:
    ^(void)
    {
        [[self connection] cancel];
        [self setConnection:nil];

        [[UIApplication sharedApplication] endBackgroundTask:downloadImageTask];
        downloadImageTask = UIBackgroundTaskInvalid;
    }];
```

endBackgroundTask: When you start a background task, you are returned a UIBackgroundTaskIdentifier that uniquely defines it. There are two possible outcomes of registering for additional execution time in the background: the task completes in the time allotted or time runs out and you must deal with the consequences. If time runs out, the block you supply to **beginBackgroundTaskWithExpirationHandler:** is invoked. Regardless of which event occurs, you must send the message **endBackgroundTask:** to the instance of **UIApplication** and pass the UIBackgroundTaskIdentifier for that task.

Thus, the expiration block must always send this message to the application. Furthermore, you must send this message when the task completes. For **NSURLConnection**, you simply call this code when the connection finishes or fails.

```
- (void)connection:(NSURLConnection *)conn didFailWithError:(NSError *)error
{
    [self setConnection:nil;

    [[UIApplication sharedApplication] endBackgroundTask:downloadImageTask];
    downloadImageTask = UIBackgroundTaskInvalid;
}
- (void)connectionDidFinishLoading:(NSURLConnection *)conn
{
    [self setConnection:nil];
```

```
    [[UIApplication sharedApplication] endBackgroundTask:downloadImageTask];
    downloadImageTask = UIBackgroundTaskInvalid;
}
```

The operating system may or may not give you additional time to complete the task depending on system constraints, and the amount of time is never guaranteed. You should also never use this method to attempt to keep your application in the background just for the sake of keeping it in the background. It is rare that an application would need to use this method of background execution, but if you are absolutely sure your application does, consult the Executing Code in the Background section of the *iOS Application Programming Guide*.

Low-level APIs

In this section, you have been exposed to the simplest, highest-level API for sound and video. If you plan to do a lot of audio work (either recording or playing), you should go deeper and learn about audio queues, which are part of the AudioToolbox framework. You may also want to study Core Audio, the framework upon which all of this is built. In addition, as of iOS 4, you can use the Core Video framework for low-level video management.

Challenge: Audio Recording

You can also record audio with the iOS SDK. Using the class **AVAudioRecorder**, record audio data and then play it back with a new button. (Remember, you can't write data to the application bundle.)

28

Bonjour and Web Servers

In this chapter, you're going to start an exercise involving two applications:

- a Desktop web server (CocoaServer)

- an iOS client application (Notified)

You will create both applications and have them discover each other using Bonjour. You will also enable them to communicate via HTTP. In the next chapter, you will add the ability to send push notifications from the Desktop server to the iOS client. (That's why our client application is called Notified.)

This is ambitious stuff. There is a lot of code and information in the next two chapters. You will need to keep track of separate projects in Xcode for the server and client. We'll do our best to keep everything clear. Stick with us, and the results will be worth it.

Bonjour

Bonjour is a protocol that allows a server to broadcast its presence and advertise its services on a local area network. It also allows other machines on the network to browse for services they are interested in connecting to.

When a server publishes a service, it announces to everyone on the local area network, "I'm a server. You want to connect to me because I know how to do this really cool thing." For example, a printer could use Bonjour to advertise its service on a network. When you connect to a printer, "the really cool thing" it can do is receive page data and print it.

There is a distinction to be made between the "server" and the "service." A *server* refers to a process running on a machine that you connect to; servers exist independently of Bonjour. A *service* is a term that is specific to Bonjour, and it refers to the advertisement of a server on the local area network. Thus, Bonjour is a way for clients to find servers.

You can think of this relationship by picturing a gas station. The server is the gas station, and if you already know where this gas station is, you can go there to buy fuel. However, not everyone will know about this gas station, so it puts a sign out front that advertises that it is a gas station. This sign is the Bonjour service. If the sign is taken down, you can still buy fuel from the gas station, but people may not be able to find it.

Every type of service has a name. For example, a web server is advertised as the service type "_http._tcp." and a printer is advertised as "_printer._tcp.". Client applications can scan the local area network for a type they are interested in and find all servers that are advertising that service type. Thus, the gas station's service type might be "fuel." People looking for fuel would look around for a "fuel" sign and find this gas station. A server can publish multiple services with different service types. For example, the gas station could also sell 128 oz. soft drinks, and it would put another sign out front to advertise that.

Creating CocoaServer

We'll get started with Bonjour by creating the server application. From the File menu, select New and New Project.... Then select Application from the Mac OS X heading. Choose the Cocoa Application template and click Next (Figure 28.1).

Figure 28.1   Creating CocoaServer

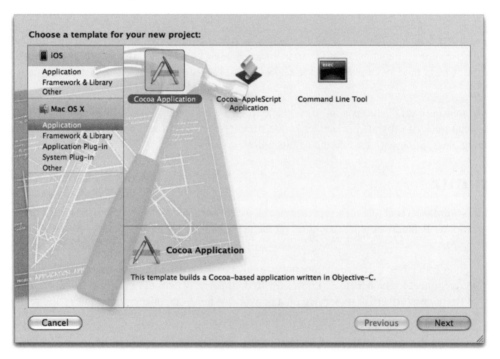

On the next pane, name the product CocoaServer and configure the rest of the items as shown in Figure 28.2.

Figure 28.2   Configuring CocoaServer

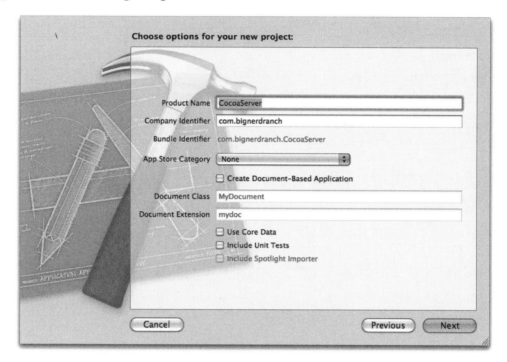

Now we will set up a bare-bones interface for our server. Every Cocoa application has a main XIB file called MainMenu.xib. Find and select this file in the project navigator. Like MainWindow.xib of an iOS application, MainMenu.xib has an application delegate object and a window object. Click on Window - Cocoa Server in the outline view to open the window object in the canvas area.

Next, reveal the object library in the utilities area. Find the Label object, drag it onto the window, and enter Server is not active as its text. Then, find and drag a table view onto the window. (Remember, you can search for these items in the search bar at the bottom of the object library.) Your window should look like the one in Figure 28.3.

Figure 28.3   Configured window in MainMenu.xib

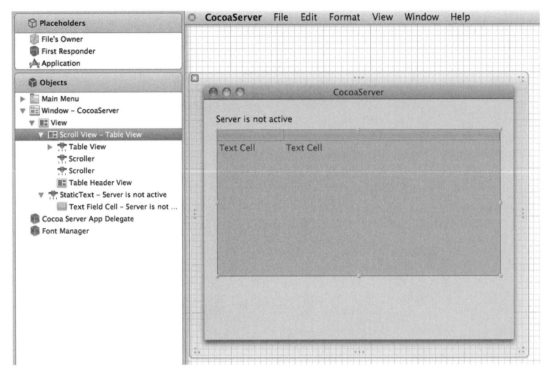

This table view is an instance of **NSTableView**. **NSTableView** works differently than **UITableView**. First, a Cocoa table view can have more than one column. (For this application, however, you will only need one.) Second, an **NSTableView** is displayed within an **NSScrollView**. If you click once on the **NSTableView** object, you actually select the scroll view. You have to click twice to select the table view. (Clicking three times gets you the **NSTableColumn**. If you're not sure what object you've selected, you can always confirm its class in the identity inspector.)

Click twice on the **NSTableView** and open the attribute inspector to see the table view's properties. Change the number of columns to 1. Then, create and hook up the outlets, as shown in Figure 28.4. (Make sure that you are connecting the outlets to the **CocoaServerAppDelegate**, not the Font Manager object that is next to it. You can hover over the objects while viewing them in the dock to see their name, or you can expand the dock into the outline view to see the class names.)

Figure 28.4   XIB connections in MainMenu.xib

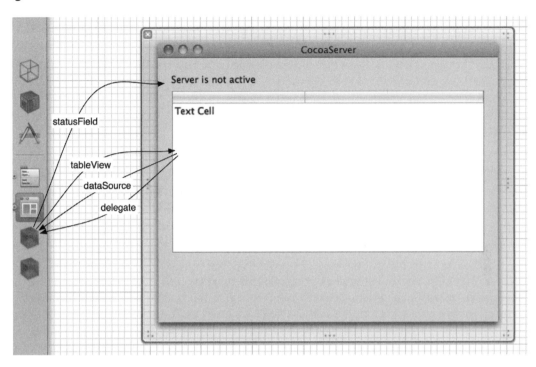

After adding the outlets, `CocoaServerAppDelegate.h` should now look like this:

```
@interface CocoaServerAppDelegate : NSObject <NSApplicationDelegate>
{
    NSWindow *window;

    IBOutlet NSTableView *tableView;
    IBOutlet NSTextField *statusField;
}
```

Publishing a Bonjour service

Now you are going to have CocoaServer publish a single Bonjour service named "CocoaHTTPServer." This service will advertise an HTTP server that receives HTTP requests from clients. Each request will contain the client's device name, and this name will be added to CocoaServer's table view.

To publish a service with Bonjour, you must first create and configure an instance of **NSNetService** and assign it a delegate.

In `CocoaServerAppDelegate.h`, add two new instance variables and three protocols.

```
@interface CocoaServerAppDelegate : NSObject
    <NSApplicationDelegate, NSNetServiceDelegate,
    NSTableViewDataSource, NSTableViewDelegate>
{
    NSWindow *window;
```

```
    IBOutlet NSTableView *tableView;
    IBOutlet NSTextField *statusField;

    NSNetService *service;
    NSMutableArray *registeredUsers;
}
```

In `CocoaServerAppDelegate.m`, instantiate the two instance variables, set the delegate, and publish the service.

```
- (void)applicationDidFinishLaunching:(NSNotification *)aNotification
{
    registeredUsers = [[NSMutableArray alloc] init];

    // Create a service object that will advertise the server's existence
    // on the local network
    service = [[NSNetService alloc] initWithDomain:@""
                                              type:@"_http._tcp."
                                              name:@"CocoaHTTPServer"
                                              port:10000];
    [service setDelegate:self];
    [service publish];
}
```

Let's look more closely at the initialization method of the **NSNetService**. The *domain* of an **NSNetService** published on the local area network is the empty string. (To publish a service only on your own computer so that your applications can find each other, use the string local., including the dot.)

The *type* of the service is how clients search for the service and connect to it. There are two parts to the type string: the application protocol and the transport protocol. The application protocol of our service is http, and the transport protocol is tcp. Thus, a client will connect to this service using HTTP over TCP. Both of the protocols must be prefixed with an underscore (_) and suffixed with a dot (.). The type is how the service advertises the "really cool thing" it does; printers, for example, use the type "_printer._tcp.".

The application protocol defines the format of the data that will be sent to the server. A HTTP server expects data that conforms to the HTTP protocol, and a printer server expects data that conforms to the network printing protocol. The transport protocol indicates the type of connection that should be made – TCP streaming connections or connectionless UDP communication. You can make up your own application protocols if you are defining a new data format, but the transport protocol will typically be TCP or UDP.

The *name* of the service uniquely identifies it among other services that have the same type on the same network. Thus, while many services may broadcast that they support HTTP over TCP, only one can be named CocoaHTTPServer. If two services have the same name and the same type, only one will be published; the other will fail. A printer, for example, might have a name that specifies its make, model, plus some unique identifier that distinguishes it from similar printers on the network.

The *port* of the service is hard-coded for now. Later in the chapter, you will have the server assign the port dynamically.

So continuing with our printer example, if an application is looking to print something, it searches the network for all _printer._tcp. services. Then, the user selects a specific printer by its unique name.

Now that you've published the **NSNetService**, let's update the user interface to announce the service's status. In `CocoaServerAppDelegate.m`, implement three delegate methods from the

NSNetServiceDelegate protocol to update the interface when the net service either publishes or fails to publish.

```
- (void)netServiceDidPublish:(NSNetService *)sender
{
    // When the service succeeds in publishing...
    [statusField setStringValue:@"Server is advertising"];
}

- (void)netServiceDidStop:(NSNetService *)sender
{
    // If the service stops for some reason...
    [statusField setStringValue:@"Server is not advertising"];
}

- (void)netService:(NSNetService *)sender didNotPublish:(NSDictionary *)errorDict
{
    // If the service fails to publish, either immediately or in the future...
    [statusField setStringValue:@"Server is not advertising"];
}
```

Build and run CocoaServer (and don't worry about the warnings for the **NSTableViewDataSource** protocol right now). The user interface will report that the server is advertising.

Browsing for services via Bonjour

Of course, Bonjour isn't much fun unless you have a client application to find the published service. Create a new iPhone Window-based Application named Notified.

Now that you have two projects for this exercise, it will become more difficult to maintain them. However, we can use Xcode *workspaces* to help organize these projects. First, close all of the projects and windows you currently have open in Xcode.

From the File menu, select New and then New Workspace.... An empty workspace will appear and prompt you to save it. Save it as NotifiedClientServer.

Locate CocoaServer.xcodeproj on the filesystem and drag its icon onto the project navigator in the NotifiedClientServer workspace. Then, do the same for Notified.xcodeproj. Make sure that CocoaServer is not highlighted when adding Notified to the project navigator. You can do this by positioning your cursor above the CocoaServer project when dragging Notified.

Now verify that you did this by correctly by closing the disclosure tab next to both projects. You should still see both project files in the project navigator when their disclosure buttons are closed (Figure 28.5).

Figure 28.5   Both projects in NotifiedClientServer workspace

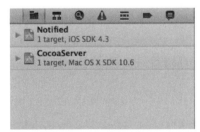

(If you made a mistake by dragging Notified's project into the CocoaServer project, you can select Notified, click the Delete button, and try again. Make sure you choose Remove References Only when prompted.)

Now that both projects are in the same workspace, you can easily navigate to their files in the same window. If you close the workspace and want to re-open it, make sure you open the NotifiedClientServer.xcworkspace file and not the individual projects.

Open MainWindow.xib from the Notified project. Add a **UILabel** to the top of the window and make its text Finding Server.... Create and connect an outlet in **NotifiedAppDelegate** for this label (Figure 28.6).

Figure 28.6   Notified's XIB

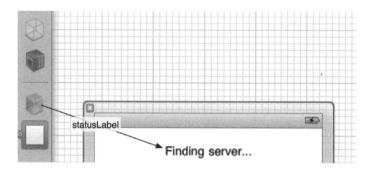

To search for Bonjour services, a client application uses an instance of **NSNetServiceBrowser**. An **NSNetServiceBrowser** can search the network for services of a particular service type. Any matching **NSNetService** on the network will be returned to the browser's delegate.

In NotifiedAppDelegate.h, add instance variables for a net service and a net service browser. Also, declare that **NotifiedAppDelegate** conforms to the NSNetServiceBrowserDelegate and NSNetServiceDelegate protocols.

```
@interface NotifiedAppDelegate : NSObject
    <UIApplicationDelegate,
        NSNetServiceBrowserDelegate, NSNetServiceDelegate>
{
    IBOutlet UILabel *statusLabel;

    NSNetService *desktopServer;
    NSNetServiceBrowser *browser;
}
```

In NotifiedAppDelegate.m, create an **NSNetServiceBrowser** and have it search for HTTP services that are broadcasting on the local network with Bonjour.

```
- (BOOL)application:(UIApplication *)application
    didFinishLaunchingWithOptions:(NSDictionary *)launchOptions
{
    // Search for all http servers on the local area network
    browser = [[NSNetServiceBrowser alloc] init];
```

```
[browser setDelegate:self];
[browser searchForServicesOfType:@"_http._tcp." inDomain:@""];
```

When a matching service is found, the browser's delegate is sent the message
netServiceBrowser:didFindService:moreComing:. The instance of **NSNetService** that represents the
found service is the second parameter. From this object, you can get the name of the service, its type,
and its domain – the same information the server specified when it published the service (Figure 28.7).

Figure 28.7   NSNetServiceBrowser finding a service

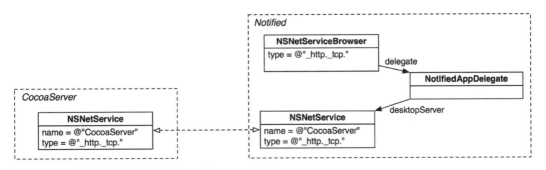

When the moreComing argument is YES, it means "I have a bunch of services I'm sending you, but I
can only send you one at a time." This is helpful information: if you want to display all the services
the browser found, you can wait until you have all of them before updating the interface. By default,
a browser will keep searching for services, and if it finds more services later, it will send this message
again. If you want the browser to stop searching, you send it the message **stop**.

When you get an **NSNetService** object back from the browser, it only has basic information about the
service. If you want to find out more, including its IP address and the port the service is running on,
you can *resolve* the service. You must resolve a service to be able to connect to it.

In NotifiedAppDelegate.m, implement **netServiceBrowser:didFindService:moreComing:** to
resolve any returned services named CocoaHTTPServer.

```
- (void)netServiceBrowser:(NSNetServiceBrowser *)aNetServiceBrowser
          didFindService:(NSNetService *)aNetService
              moreComing:(BOOL)moreServicesComing
{
    // Looking for an HTTP service, but only one with the name CocoaHTTPServer
    if (!desktopServer && [[aNetService name] isEqualToString:@"CocoaHTTPServer"]) {
        desktopServer = [aNetService retain];
        [desktopServer resolveWithTimeout:30];
        [desktopServer setDelegate:self];
        [statusLabel setText:@"Resolving CocoaHTTPServer..."];
    } else {
        NSLog(@"ignoring %@", aNetService);
    }
}
```

Notice that the **NSNetService** is retained here; it needs to stick around while it is resolving. Whether
the resolution succeeds or fails, the net service will send a message to its delegate and pass itself as an

argument. Thus, you will have a pointer to this object later and do not need to store it in an instance variable.

When an **NSNetService** is successfully resolved, it sends the message **netServiceDidResolveAddress:** to its delegate. In NotifiedAppDelegate.m, implement this method.

```
- (void)netServiceDidResolveAddress:(NSNetService *)sender
{
    [statusLabel setText:@"Resolved service..."];
}
```

If the service fails to resolve for some reason, you must release the **NSNetService** instance. Implement **netService:didNotResolve:** in NotifiedAppDelegate.m.

```
- (void)netService:(NSNetService *)sender didNotResolve:(NSDictionary *)errorDict
{
    // Couldn't figure out the address...
    [statusLabel setText:@"Could not resolve service."];
    NSLog(@"%@", errorDict);

    // Release the service object
    [desktopServer release];
    desktopServer = nil;
}
```

Before you build and run, make sure your device and computer are on the same local area network; otherwise, the device will not be able to find the server. (If you are using the simulator, then you have nothing to worry about.)

When you have a workspace with multiple projects, you can pick which target you are building and running by choosing the appropriate one from the Scheme pop-up menu.

Also when running multiple targets from Xcode, you need to be able to switch between the two processes in the debugger. You can do so by clicking the name of the application in the debugger bar and selecting the name of the other application (Figure 28.8).

Figure 28.8   Changing Debuggers

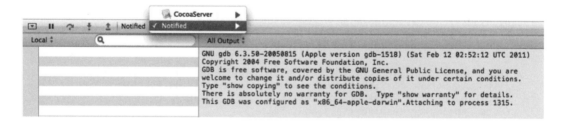

Build and run CocoaServer. Then, build and run Notified. After a moment, the status label in Notified will report that it has resolved the service.

Isn't it romantic? Your client and server have found each other. But perhaps finding someone is easy when compared with the challenge of really communicating over the long term. Bonjour is great for broadcasting and discovering services on a network, but it does not allow the client and server to exchange information. So in the next section, we will move on to enabling communication between our client and server via HTTP.

Also note that here you have used Bonjour here with a desktop server and an iOS client, but iOS devices can also publish services via Bonjour.

HTTP Communication

Now for the second part of this chapter – adding web server functionality to CocoaServer so that it can receive HTTP requests from its clients.

Writing a web server in Objective-C

CocoaServer advertises an HTTP service, so it needs to be able to accept HTTP requests. Then, clients, like Notified, can use **NSURLConnection** to exchange information with CocoaServer.

Writing a web server from scratch is not a task we can cover in this book. Instead, we have modified some of Apple's sample code to lay the foundation of a web server in Objective-C. This code is available at http://www.bignerdranch.com/solutions/iOSProgramming.zip in the solution directory for the CocoaServer project.

The web server code is encapsulated in two classes: **TCPServer** and **HTTPServer**. Find TCPServer.h, TCPServer.m, HTTPServer.h, and HTTPServer.m and drag them into the CocoaServer project navigator. Make sure to copy the files to the project's directory when prompted.

If you are really curious, you can check out the code in these files. It is pretty advanced stuff, though. After the next chapter, the code will make more sense, so consider waiting till then to poke around.

In CocoaServerAppDelegate.h, import the header for **HTTPServer** and declare an instance variable of that type.

```
#import "HTTPServer.h"

@interface CocoaServerAppDelegate : NSObject
    <NSApplicationDelegate, NSNetServiceDelegate,
    NSTableViewDataSource, NSTableViewDelegate>
{
    HTTPServer *server;
```

In CocoaServerAppDelegate.m, instantiate a server object and have it start accepting connections.

```
- (void)applicationDidFinishLaunching:(NSNotification *)aNotification
{
    server = [[HTTPServer alloc] init];
    [server setDelegate:self];

    NSError *err = nil;
    [server start:&err];

    if (err) {
        NSLog(@"Server failed to start: %@", err);
        return;
    }
```

When the server starts, it will pick an open port to accept connections on. The **NSNetService** needs to broadcast that same port so clients will know which port to connect on. In

CocoaServerAppDelegate.m, update the **applicationDidFinishLaunching:** method to provide the port dynamically:

```
service = [[NSNetService alloc] initWithDomain:@""
                                          type:@"_http._tcp."
                                          name:@"CocoaHTTPServer"
                                          port:[server port]];
[service setDelegate:self];
[service publish];
}
```

Build CocoaServer to make sure there are no syntax errors.

Getting address data from the server

Now let's take care of the client's needs. For this exercise, Notified must

- get address data (IP address and port) from the resolved net service

- use that data to construct a request URL

- create a POST request that contains the name of its device

- send the request to CocoaServer using **NSURLConnection**

When an **NSNetService** is resolved, it stores the IP address and port of the server it came from. Sending the message **addresses** to that object returns an array of **NSData** instances. (Typically, a server only has one address so there is only one object in this array.) The data wrapped in the **NSData** instances is a low-level C sockaddr_in structure, which holds the IP address and port of a host.

To use and access this structure, import two files from the system libraries at the top of NotifiedAppDelegate.m.

```
#import <netinet/in.h>
#import <arpa/inet.h>
```

In NotifiedAppDelegate.h, declare a method to create and return a string with the server's address.

```
- (NSString *)serverHostName;
```

Implement this method in NotifiedAppDelegate.m.

```
- (NSString *)serverHostName
{
    NSArray *addresses = [desktopServer addresses];

    NSData *firstAddress = [addresses objectAtIndex:0];

    // The binary data in the NSData object is a sockaddr_in - which
    // represents a network host
    const struct sockaddr_in *addy = [firstAddress bytes];

    // Convert 4-byte IP address in network byte order to a C string
    // of the format: xxx.xxx.xxx.xxx
    char *ipAddress = inet_ntoa(addy->sin_addr);

    // Convert the 2-byte port number from network to host byte order
```

```
    UInt16 port = ntohs(addy->sin_port);

    return [NSString stringWithFormat:@"%s:%u", ipAddress, port];
}
```

Byte ordering

Everyone agrees that a 32-bit number is made up of 4 bytes. There are, however, two different ways of ordering those bytes: *big-endian* (where the significant byte comes first) and *little-endian* (where the least significant byte comes first). Your Intel Mac is big-endian. If you have an older Mac with a PowerPC chip, it is little-endian. Usually this difference (which affects not just 32-bit words, but 16-bit and 64-bit words as well) can be ignored because the system is internally consistent. However, once you send a multi-byte word to another machine, you must worry about whether it will be interpreted correctly.

It was decided that the Internet would be big-endian. We refer to this as *network byte order*. The endianness of the local machine is referred to as *host byte order*. In the code above, you received the port number as two bytes in network byte order. To convert it to host byte order, you used the **ntohs** function:

```
UInt16 port = ntohs(addy->sin_port);    // Network to Host a Short int
```

If you're sure your machine is big-endian, should you leave this line out? No. First of all, it won't hurt anything if your host byte order is already equivalent to network byte order. Secondly, your code could find itself on another machine one day, and you can't know what that machine's host byte order will be.

Making service requests

Add another method to NotifiedAppDelegate.h.

- (void)postInformationToServer;

In this method, you will make an HTTP request to the resolved server using **NSURLConnection**. The body of this request will contain an XML-serialized **NSDictionary** with a name key.

CocoaServer will only process POST requests that include register as the service name. The form of the request URL that CocoaServer will support looks something like this:

```
http://10.0.0.1:40000/register
```

(The exact request will depend on your network configuration and the port the server picks.)

In Chapter 25, you passed information in the URL string as arguments to the service. As you can see, the request URL for this exercise doesn't have any arguments. Instead, you're going to send information in the HTTP body of the request. (If you need a review of HTTP request structure, flip back to the section called "For the More Curious: The Request Body" in Chapter 25.)

The information that the client will send the server is its device name, which you will put in an **NSDictionary**. However, you can't pass a dictionary object in an HTTP request, so you will use the class **NSPropertyListSerialization** to represent the dictionary in XML. (**NSDictionary** is a property list serializable object, and **NSPropertyListSerialization** can turn any property list serializable object into XML. It can also turn XML back into an object.)

In `NotifiedAppDelegate.m`, implement **postInformationToServer**. Notice the use of the message **serverHostName** to construct the request URL.

```
- (void)postInformationToServer
{
    [statusLabel setText:@"Sending data to server..."];

    // Create a dictionary with relevant information
    NSDictionary *d = [NSDictionary dictionaryWithObjectsAndKeys:
                                [[UIDevice currentDevice] name], @"name", nil];

    // Create XML representation of this dictionary
    NSData *data = [NSPropertyListSerialization
                            dataWithPropertyList:d
                                    format:NSPropertyListXMLFormat_v1_0
                                   options:0
                                     error:nil];

    // Make a connection to the provider to post the information to it - the URL
    // is the address and port of the resolved service
    NSString *urlString = [NSString stringWithFormat:@"http://%@/register",
                                        [self serverHostName]];

    // The request will use this URL, be a POST, and have the dictionary as its data
    NSMutableURLRequest *req = [NSMutableURLRequest requestWithURL:
                                        [NSURL URLWithString:urlString]];
    [req setHTTPMethod:@"POST"];
    [req setHTTPBody:data];

    NSURLConnection *connection = [[NSURLConnection alloc] initWithRequest:req
                                                        delegate:self];
    [connection start];
}
```

Now implement the **NSURLConnection** delegate methods to update Notified's user interface with the status of the connection.

```
- (void)connectionDidFinishLoading:(NSURLConnection *)connection
{
    [statusLabel setText:@"Data sent to server."];
    [connection release];
}

- (void)connection:(NSURLConnection *)connection didFailWithError:(NSError *)error
{
    [statusLabel setText:@"Connection to server failed."];
    NSLog(@"%@", error);

    [connection release];
}
```

In `NotifiedAppDelegate.m`, send the **postInformationToServer** message when the net service is resolved.

```
- (void)netServiceDidResolveAddress:(NSNetService *)sender
{
    [statusLabel setText:@"Resolved service..."];
    server = sender;
```

```
    [self postInformationToServer];
}
```

Build Notified to make sure there are no syntax errors.

Receiving service requests

Now that Notified can make the appropriate request, CocoaServer must be able to receive it. To do this, CocoaServer must

- test the received request for correctness

- retrieve the device name from the request

- update its table with the received device name

First, here's a brief overview of the web server classes you added to the CocoaServer project. The **TCPServer** class listens for and accepts new socket connections. When a new connection comes in, **HTTPServer**, a subclass of **TCPServer**, creates an instance of another class called **HTTPConnection**. The **HTTPConnection** object reads the data (in our case, a web service request) that is being passed through the connection. Then, the **HTTPConnection** creates an instance of another class, **HTTPServerRequest**, that encapsulates the request. Finally, the **HTTPServerRequest** is passed to the server's delegate to be handled.

When a client application sends a web service request to this server, **CocoaServerAppDelegate** will be sent the message **HTTPConnection:didReceiveRequest:**. (**CocoaServerAppDelegate** is the delegate of the **HTTPServer** and therefore the delegate of the **HTTPConnection** object that the **HTTPServer** creates.)

In CocoaServerAppDelegate.m, implement the **HTTPConnection:didReceiveRequest:** method for **HTTPConnection**. This method will check the contents of a request, ensure it meets the server's requirements, and then respond to the client.

```
- (void)HTTPConnection:(HTTPConnection *)conn
    didReceiveRequest:(HTTPServerRequest *)mess
{
    BOOL requestWasOkay = NO;

    // The HTTPServerRequest contains the message object
    // that holds the request from the client
    CFHTTPMessageRef request = [mess request];

    // Get the HTTP method of that request
    NSString *method = [(NSString *)CFHTTPMessageCopyRequestMethod(request)
                            autorelease];

    // We only care about POST requests
    if ([method isEqualToString:@"POST"]) {
        //Get the Request-URI
        NSURL *requestURL = [(NSURL *)CFHTTPMessageCopyRequestURL(request)
                            autorelease];

        // We only care about "register" service requests - the requestURL
        // will have a slash in front of it
        if ([[requestURL absoluteString] isEqualToString:@"/register"]) {
```

```
                    // This method is not yet implemented, but it will return YES
                    // if the data in the request was appropriate
                    requestWasOkay = [self handleRegister:request];
            }
    }

    CFHTTPMessageRef response = NULL;
    if (requestWasOkay) {
            // If the client gave us what we wanted, then tell them they did
            // a good job by returning status code 200 - this is the response
            // an NSURLConnection receives
            response = CFHTTPMessageCreateResponse(NULL,
                                                   200,
                                                   NULL,
                                                   kCFHTTPVersion1_1);

    } else {
            // If the client gave us bad data, then tell them they did
            // with a bad request status code
            response = CFHTTPMessageCreateResponse(NULL,
                                                   400,
                                                   NULL,
                                                   kCFHTTPVersion1_1);
    }

    // Must set the content-length of a response
    CFHTTPMessageSetHeaderFieldValue(response,
                                     (CFStringRef)@"Content-Length",
                                     (CFStringRef)@"0");

    // By setting the response of the HTTPServerRequest,
    // it automatically dispatches it to the requesting client
    // and we can release it
    [mess setResponse:response];

    CFRelease(response);
}
```

Now in CocoaServerAppDelegate.h, declare a new method:

```
- (BOOL)handleRegister:(CFHTTPMessageRef)request;
```

In **handleRegister:**, you will pull the HTTP body out of the request and turn it back into an **NSDictionary** object on the server using **NSPropertyListSerialization**. This dictionary will be added to the list of registeredUsers. The method returns YES to its caller, **HTTPConnection:didReceiveRequest:**, if it was able to get a device name from the request body. In CocoaServerAppDelegate.m, implement **handleRegister:**.

```
- (BOOL)handleRegister:(CFHTTPMessageRef)request
{
    // Get the data from the service request
    NSData *body = [(NSData *)CFHTTPMessageCopyBody(request) autorelease];

    // We know that it is a dictionary (if it's not, this method will return nil)
    NSDictionary *bodyDict = [NSPropertyListSerialization
                                  propertyListFromData:body
                                      mutabilityOption:NSPropertyListImmutable
                                                format:nil
                                      errorDescription:nil];
```

```
        // Get the "name" object from this dictionary
        // and make sure the object exists
        NSString *name = [bodyDict objectForKey:@"name"];
        if (name) {
            // Take the whole dictionary and add it to the registeredUsers,
            // update the table that will eventually show the users
            [registeredUsers addObject:bodyDict];
            [tableView reloadData];
            return YES;
        }
        return NO;
}
```

Finally, in CocoaServerAppDelegate.m, implement the two data source methods for **NSTableView** to show the list of registered users. (Notice that these data source methods are different than the ones in iOS.)

```
- (id)tableView:(NSTableView *)aTableView
    objectValueForTableColumn:(NSTableColumn *)aTableColumn
                          row:(NSInteger)rowIndex
{
    NSDictionary *entry = [registeredUsers objectAtIndex:rowIndex];
    return [NSString stringWithFormat:@"%@", [entry objectForKey:@"name"]];
}

- (NSInteger)numberOfRowsInTableView:(NSTableView *)aTableView
{
    return [registeredUsers count];
}
```

Build and run CocoaServer and leave it running. Then build and run Notified. (Make sure that CocoaServer is still running and that the device and computer are on the same network.) After a moment, you should see your device appear in the list of devices in CocoaServer.

For the More Curious: TXTRecords

While Bonjour does not allow a client and server to exchange information, a service published via Bonjour can include additional information that can be read by clients. For example, a printer could tell clients that it is in the third-floor library, or a workstation could display the rules for using it. Every **NSNetService** has a *TXT Record* for this purpose.

You can create a TXT Record with an **NSDictionary**. This dictionary has some restrictions – its keys can only be **NSStrings**, and its values must be **NSData** objects that encapsulate an **NSString** or binary data. Once you have a valid dictionary, you pass it to the class method **dataFromTXTRecordDictionary:** of **NSNetService** and set it as an **NSNetService**'s TXTXRecordData.

```
- (void)setMessage:(NSString *)str forNetService:(NSNetService *)service
{
    // Pack the string into an NSData
    NSData *stringData = [str dataUsingEncoding:NSUTF8StringEncoding];

    // Put the data in a dictionary
    NSDictionary *txtDict = [NSDictionary dictionaryWithObject:stringData
                                                        forKey:@"message"];

    // Pack the dictionary into an NSData
```

```
    NSData *txtData = [NSNetService dataFromTXTRecordDictionary:txtDict];

    // Put that data into the net service
    [service setTXTRecordData:txtData];
}
```

A TXT record isn't available to a client until it has resolved the net service. Once resolved, the client can pull the data out and convert it back into an **NSDictionary**.

```
- (void)netServiceDidResolveAddress:(NSNetService *)ns
{
    // Try to get the TXT Record
    NSData *data = [ns TXTRecordData];

    // Is there TXT data?
    if (data) {

        // Convert it into a dictionary
        NSDictionary *txtDict = [NSNetService dictionaryFromTXTRecordData:data];

        // Get the data that the publisher put in under the message key
        NSData *mData = [txtDict objectForKey:@"message"];

        // Is there data?
        if (mData) {

            // Make a string
            NSString *message = [[NSString alloc] initWithData:mData
                                            encoding:NSUTF8StringEncoding];
            NSLog(@"%@ says: %@", ns, message);
            [message release];
        }
    }
}
```

29

Push Notifications and Networking

On an iOS device, only one application can run in the foreground at a time. Sometimes, you want an application that isn't currently running to notify you when something happens: an opponent in a game makes a move, a buddy sends you a message in a chat program, or you have 5 minutes to get to your next meeting.

Push notifications are one approach to solving this problem. A push notification is a message sent from Apple's servers to a device. The user sees a pop-up window on screen with the name of the application that has been notified, a message, and possibly an alert sound or icon badge.

It's not a coincidence that it is difficult to find a working implementation of push notifications on the Net – this stuff isn't easy. You have to create an SSL certificate, provision the application, and write the network code to connect to Apple's server.

But, in this chapter, we're going to get it all done using the applications you created in Chapter 28. You will update CocoaServer to send push notifications and update Notified to receive them. Push notifications also require a middle man (Apple's push notification server) and a device token, which uniquely identifies an iOS device. Figure 29.1 gives you an idea of the relationships between the three players.

Figure 29.1   Flow of a push notification

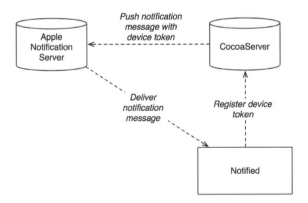

Preparing Client for Push Notifications

To get Notified ready to receive push notifications, we must register for notifications with the Apple push notification server and then create a provisioning profile that allows for push notifications.

Registering for notifications

Registering for notifications does two things: it sets the types of notification the application will accept, and it retrieves the required device token from Apple's server.

There are three types of notifications: alerts, badges, and alert sounds. (Badges are small numeric icons that appear on an application's icon. You've probably seen them on the Mail and App Store icons when you have unread mail or application updates to download.) When an application registers for push notifications, it chooses the types of notifications it wishes to receive. When a notification is delivered, the operating system only delivers the types that the application has registered for.

Reopen NotifiedClientServer.xcworkspace. In NotifiedAppDelegate.m, register for all notification types at the top of **application:didFinishLaunchingWithOptions:**.

```
- (BOOL)application:(UIApplication *)application
    didFinishLaunchingWithOptions:(NSDictionary *)launchOptions
{
    // Register (every time the app launches) for notifications
    [[UIApplication sharedApplication] registerForRemoteNotificationTypes:
                                    UIRemoteNotificationTypeAlert
                                  | UIRemoteNotificationTypeBadge
                                  | UIRemoteNotificationTypeSound];
```

In addition to setting the valid notification types for this application, this code will make a network connection to Apple's push notification servers to retrieve a *device token*. The device token is a 32-byte string of binary data that uniquely identifies the registering device. You can think of it like a phone number that Apple dials each time it wants to deliver a notification. Once Apple has generated the device token, it is returned to your device and delivered to the registering application via the application delegate method **application:didRegisterForRemoteNotificationsWithDeviceToken:**. (The device token will be the same each time you register, but re-registering keeps the servers up-to-date.)

In NotifiedAppDelegate.h, add an instance variable to hold this token.

```
@interface NotifiedAppDelegate : NSObject
    <UIApplicationDelegate, NSNetServiceBrowserDelegate, NSNetServiceDelegate>
{
    NSData *pushToken;
```

In NotifiedAppDelegate.m, implement the delegate method.

```
- (void)application:(UIApplication *)application
    didRegisterForRemoteNotificationsWithDeviceToken:(NSData *)deviceToken
{
    // We'll keep this token and then attempt to send it to the server
    pushToken = [deviceToken retain];

    // Shortly, we'll change the implementation of this method to send the device
    // token along with the device name to the server
```

```
    [self postInformationToServer];
}
```

Notice that this method triggers the **postInformationToServer** method that you wrote in Chapter 28. Now this message is sent at two separate times: when the device token is retrieved and when the net service is resolved. You'll see why this is important in a moment.

If the application fails to register with Apple, a different delegate method is called. Typically, this occurs when there is no network connection available. Implement this method in NotifiedAppDelegate.m.

```
- (void)application:(UIApplication *)application
    didFailToRegisterForRemoteNotificationsWithError:(NSError *)error
{
    [statusLabel setText:@"Failed to register with Apple"];
    NSLog(@"%@", error);
}
```

Provisioning for push notifications

For the registration to succeed, the application has to be provisioned for push notifications. This requires generating a push notification certificate and embedding it in a provisioning profile that the application uses. You are going to create a new provisioning profile for Notified. Then, when Notified is built, it will use the developer certificate from this profile to sign the application code. When the application registers for push notifications, a value from this provisioning profile will be used to verify that it is able to receive notifications.

To generate the provisioning profile and the push notification certificate, you must be the Team Agent of your iOS developer account.

Log into the portal at developer.apple.com/ios and enter the iOS Provisioning Portal. While in the portal, you're going to create a new App ID, create and download the SSL certificate, and create and configure the new provisioning profile.

In the left navigation table, select the App IDs item and click New App ID. Name this App ID Notified and select Generate New from the pop-up menu (Figure 29.2). The Bundle Identifier item will need to be something unique. For example, mine is com.bignerdranch.Notified. You can replace the middle of the bundle identifier with your company name, and that should ensure its uniqueness. Note that you *cannot* use the wildcard character (*) for this App ID. Click Submit.

Figure 29.2   Generating an application ID

Create App ID

Description

Enter a common name or description of your App ID using alphanumeric characters. The description you specify will be used throughout the Provisioning Portal to identify this App ID.

| Notified | You cannot use special characters as @, &, *, " in your description. |

Bundle Seed ID (App ID Prefix)

Generate a new or select an existing Bundle Seed ID for your App ID.

Generate New ⬍ If you are creating a suite of applications that will share the same Keychain access, use the same bundle Seed ID for each of your application's App IDs.

Bundle Identifier (App ID Suffix)

Enter a unique identifier for your App ID. The recommended practice is to use a reverse-domain name style string for the Bundle Identifier portion of the App ID.

| com.bignerdranch.Notified| | Example: com.domainname.appname |

Cancel   Submit

Back in the list of App IDs, click the Configure button on the same row as the Notified App ID. On the page that appears, click the checkbox to enable push notifications. Then, click the Configure button for the Development Push SSL Certificate (Figure 29.3).

Figure 29.3   Enabling development notifications

| ID | **Notified** ZSH2HC58KM.com.bignerdranch.notified |

☑ **Enable for Apple Push Notification service**

Push SSL Certificate	Status	Expiration Date	Action
🖼 Development Push SSL Certificate	🌐 Configurable		Configure
🖼 Production Push SSL Certificate	🌐 Configurable		Configure

Now an overlay window with an assistant will appear and walk you through the steps of generating an SSL certificate. This certificate will be used to encrypt and decrypt push notification data. Follow the instructions in this guide, and you will eventually download a file named `aps_developer_identity.cer`. Keep this file handy; you will use it soon.

Now, select Provisioning from the left navigation table in the provisioning portal and click New Profile. Name this profile whatever you wish. Select your developer certificate (the one you have been using to sign your applications when building on the device) from the list of certificates. Choose the Notified App ID from the pop-up menu, and then select your development device from the list of devices. Click Submit.

This will take you back to the list of provisioning profiles, and your new profile will say Pending. Refresh your browser, and a Download button will appear. Download your new profile and drag it onto the Xcode window.

You will want to use this push notification-enabled profile to deploy the Notified application to your device. For that to happen, the application's bundle identifier must match the profile's App ID. In Xcode, select the Notified project from the project navigator and the Notified target from the editor area. Then, select the Info pane and locate the Bundle Identifier key (Figure 29.4). Change it to exactly match the App ID in the provisioning profile you just created. (This value is case-sensitive!)

Figure 29.4   Changing the bundle identifier

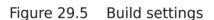

One more step and our client application will be ready to receive push notifications. In the Build Settings pane, locate the Code Signing Identity setting. Click the value column for this setting and select the Notified provisioning profile from the list. (There are a number of sub-items in this setting. Changing the top-level item should also change all of the sub-items. However, if you have previously set a sub-item's values to something other than its parent's setting, you may need to change it individually.) My Code Signing Identity setting looks like the one in Figure 29.5.

Figure 29.5   Build settings

Build and run the application on a device. (You can't test push notifications on the simulator.) The application will ask you if it is okay to accept push notifications – say yes!

Exit the application and open the Settings application. Select the Notifications item and then select Notified, which now appears in this list. This application registered for all three notification types, so there is a switch for each type. Make sure they are all switched on.

Congratulations! Notified can now receive push notifications. Now let's turn to the server side.

Delivering a Push Notification

To deliver a push notification to a device, a server you control (like CocoaServer) must send a notification package to Apple's push notification server. Then Apple's push notification server delivers the notification to the device. The server you control is called the *provider*. The notification package contains the notification the user will eventually receive along with the device token and some other administrative information. The Apple server then uses the device token to route the notification to the correct device.

Getting the token to the provider

Before the provider can send the notification package to Apple's push notification server, it needs to know the device token. You're going to have Notified send CocoaServer its device token in an HTTP request. You've already implemented everything you need to do this in Chapter 28. All that remains is adding the device token to the HTTP request.

Open NotifiedAppDelegate.m and find the **postInformationToServer** method. In this method, Notified connects to CocoaServer, constructs an HTTP request, and sends the request to CocoaServer. Recall that the **postInformationToServer** message is now sent to the **NotifiedAppDelegate** twice: once when it resolves the net service and again when it retrieves the device token from Apple's server. As it stands now, whichever event happens first will trigger the code in **postInformationToServer**. But that's not what we want. We want **postInformationToServer** to be executed only after *both* events have occurred. We only want to send the HTTP request after we're sure we have a server and a token.

In NotifiedAppDelegate.m, update **postInformationToServer** to test for both the server and the token before continuing. Then, add the device token as the body of the HTTP request.

```
- (void)postInformationToServer
{
    // We make sure we have both before we make the connection
    if (desktopServer && pushToken) {

        [statusLabel setText:@"Sending data to server..."];

        NSArray *addresses = [server addresses];
        NSData *firstAddress = [addresses objectAtIndex:0];
        const struct sockaddr_in *addy = [firstAddress bytes];
        char *ipAddress = inet_ntoa(addy->sin_addr);
        UInt16 port = ntohs(addy->sin_port);


        // Now, we are adding the token to the dictionary that will be the
        // body of the request
        NSDictionary *d =
```

```
    [NSDictionary dictionaryWithObjectsAndKeys:pushToken, @"token",
                      [[UIDevice currentDevice] name], @"name", nil];

NSData *data = [NSPropertyListSerialization
                     dataWithPropertyList:d
                               format:NSPropertyListXMLFormat_v1_0
                              options:0
                                error:nil];

NSString *urlString = [NSString stringWithFormat:@"http://%s:%u/register",
                                              ipAddress, port];

NSMutableURLRequest *req
  = [NSMutableURLRequest requestWithURL:[NSURL URLWithString:urlString]];

[req setHTTPMethod:@"POST"];
[req setHTTPBody:data];

NSURLConnection *connection = [[NSURLConnection alloc] initWithRequest:req
                                          delegate:self];
[connection start];

// This curly brace ends the if statement - it wasn't here before
}
}
```

Now the provider needs to be able to receive tokens from HTTP requests. Open CocoaServerAppDelegate.m and modify the **handleRegister:** method to collect and keep the token a client passes.

```
- (BOOL)handleRegister:(CFHTTPMessageRef)request
{
    NSData *body = [(NSData *)CFHTTPMessageCopyBody(request) autorelease];

    NSDictionary *bodyDict = [NSPropertyListSerialization
                                propertyListFromData:body
                                    mutabilityOption:NSPropertyListImmutable
                                              format:nil
                                    errorDescription:nil];

    // Grab the "token" and "name" objects from this dictionary
    // and make sure they are there
    NSData *token = [bodyDict objectForKey:@"token"];
    NSString *name = [bodyDict objectForKey:@"name"];
    if (token && name) {

        // Make sure we haven't already recorded this device token
        BOOL unique = YES;
        for(NSDictionary *d in registeredUsers) {
            if ([[d objectForKey:@"token"] isEqual:token])
                unique = NO;
        }

        if (unique) {
            // If we haven't recorded this token, then it's a new one and
            // we'll keep it - refresh the table
            [registeredUsers addObject:bodyDict];
            [tableView reloadData];
        }
```

```
      return YES;
   }
   return NO;
}
```

Also, update the data source method in `CocoaServerAppDelegate.m` to show the device token in the server's table view:

```
- (id)tableView:(NSTableView *)aTableView
    objectValueForTableColumn:(NSTableColumn *)aTableColumn
                        row:(NSInteger)rowIndex
{
    NSDictionary *entry = [registeredUsers objectAtIndex:rowIndex];
    return [NSString stringWithFormat:@"%@ (%@)",
                          [entry objectForKey:@"name"],
                          [entry objectForKey:@"token"]];
}
```

Build and run CocoaServer. Then, build and run Notified on a device that is on the same local area network. After a moment, you should see the device name and token in the table view of CocoaServer.

Keep in mind that there are other ways to get a device token to the provider; an HTTP request is just the way that works best for this exercise.

Sending Push Notifications

Now that CocoaServer has the device token of its client application, it can send a notification package to Apple's push notification server. The first step in this process is connecting to the notification server with **NSStream**. Once we have a connection, we'll pack up and send the notification data that will eventually be sent to the device.

Connecting to Apple's server with NSStream

Apple requires that the data sent to its server from the provider be encrypted. This is where the SSL certificate you downloaded comes into play – the provider must encrypt its outgoing data with this certificate.

Locate the `aps_developer_identity.cer` file that you downloaded earlier. Double-click on it to add it to your Login keychain. In Keychain Access, you should see this certificate and its private key (Figure 29.6). Remember that the certificate that signs your application for deployment is different than the certificate used to encrypt data.

Figure 29.6   SSL certificate in Keychain Access

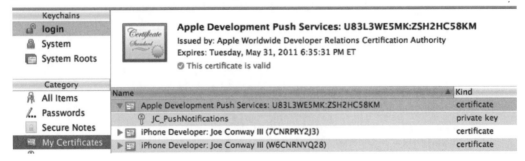

To make it easy for CocoaServer to find this certificate, you will bundle it with the application. Drag aps_developer_identity.cer to CocoaServer's project navigator and check the box to copy it to the project's directory. Now, when CocoaServer is built, it will have access to this certificate.

Using NSStream

The provider will make a connection to Apple's push notification server and secure the data it sends by signing it with this certificate. This connection to the notification server should stay open even if you aren't currently sending push notifications; if you close and re-open the connection multiple times, Apple may think you are trying to flood the server and reject your connection. Therefore, when CocoaServer starts, you will initiate a connection to the notification server and keep it open.

In CocoaServerAppDelegate.h, declare three new methods and two new instance variables.

```
    NSOutputStream *writeStream;
    NSInputStream *readStream;
}
- (void)configureStreams;
- (NSArray *)certificateArray;
- (void)connectToNotificationServer;
```

The implementation of **connectToNotificationServer** will open a *streaming connection* to the notification server. A streaming connection is kept alive, and the two connected machines are free to send data to each other whenever they please.

Let's get some network theory out of the way. In Unix (on which iOS is built), we use *file descriptors* to transfer data. We can think of a file descriptor as a wormhole. We put data into it, and that data appears at the other end. Data arrives the same way. The operating system handles where that data goes to or comes from; we just interface with our end of the file descriptor. The other side of a file descriptor may be connected to a file on the filesystem or to the network hardware that talks to the Internet. This is low-level stuff, and a number of abstractions have been built on top of it to make our lives easier. You don't have to know about file descriptors to load a file, but that's what is happening underneath the hood.

When a file descriptor is used to channel data to and from the network hardware, we call it an *internet socket* (or more commonly, just a *socket*). When you put data into an internet socket, it ends up on another machine. When that machine sends back data, you can read that data from a socket. Thus, a streaming connection is really just two sockets: one that you put data on and one that you take data from.

In **connectToNotificationServer**, you're going to create your sockets and connect them using the C-level Core Foundation framework. The function **CFStreamCreatePairWithSocketToHost** returns two stream objects of type **CFWriteStreamRef** and **CFReadStreamRef**.

These Core Foundation classes are toll-free bridged with the two classes from Apple's streaming API: **NSOutputStream** and **NSInputStream**. You will use instances of these classes to manage your connected sockets.

In CocoaServerAppDelegate.m, implement **connectToNotificationServer**.

```
- (void)connectToNotificationServer
{
    // Connect to push notification server, we get back two stream objects
```

489

```
    // that will allow us to write to and read from that server
    CFStreamCreatePairWithSocketToHost(NULL,
                                       (CFStringRef)@"gateway.sandbox.push.apple.com",
                                       2195,
                                       (CFReadStreamRef *)(&readStream),
                                       (CFWriteStreamRef *)(&writeStream));
    // Open up the streams
    [readStream open];
    [writeStream open];

    // Make sure that opening didn't fail
    if ([readStream streamStatus] != NSStreamStatusError
    && [writeStream streamStatus] != NSStreamStatusError) {
        [self configureStreams];
    }
    else {
        NSLog(@"Failed to connect to Apple.");
    }
}
```

You can see in the **CFStreamCreatePairWithSocketToHost** function that the host name of the development push notification server is gateway.sandbox.push.apple.com and it accepts connections on port 2195.

Since these streams need to encrypt their data, you must load the certificate into memory and hand it to them. First, add Security.framework to your project. Then, at the top of CocoaServerAppDelegate.m, import the top-level header for this framework.

```
#import <Security/Security.h>
```

Next, in CocoaServerAppDelegate.m, implement **certificateArray** to load the certificate from the bundle, establish its private key (also called its *identity*) from the Keychain, and then return an array containing the certificate and its key.

```
- (NSArray *)certificateArray
{
    // Get the path of the certificate in the bundle
    NSString *certPath =
        [[NSBundle mainBundle] pathForResource:@"aps_developer_identity"
                                        ofType:@"cer"];

    // Pull the data from the filesystem and create a SecCertificate object
    NSData *certData = [NSData dataWithContentsOfFile:certPath];
    SecCertificateRef cert = SecCertificateCreateWithData(NULL, (CFDataRef)certData);

    // Create the identity (private key) which requires
    // that the certificate lives in the keychain
    SecIdentityRef identity;
    OSStatus err = SecIdentityCreateWithCertificate(NULL, cert, &identity);
    if (err) {
        NSLog(@"Failed to create certificate identity: %d", err);
        return nil;
    }

    // Put the key and certificate into an array
    return [NSArray arrayWithObjects:(id)identity, (id)cert, nil];
}
```

Figure 29.7 Stream behavior

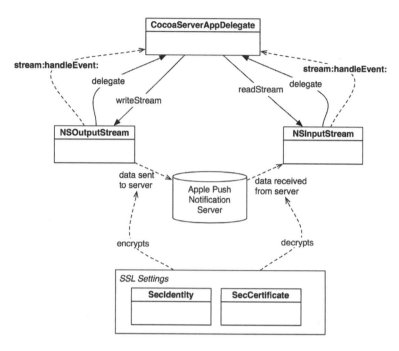

Now, the implementation of **configureStreams** will configure the streams with the encryption certificate. In the same method, you will give the streams delegates and schedule them into the run loop so that they are monitored for data (Figure 29.7). Implement this method in CocoaServerAppDelegate.m.

```
- (void)configureStreams
{
    NSArray *certArray = [self certificateArray];
    if(!certArray)
        return;

    // Give the streams their SSL settings so they can encrypt/decrypt
    // data to/from the server
    NSDictionary *sslSettings =
        [NSDictionary dictionaryWithObjectsAndKeys:[self certificateArray],
                                (id)kCFStreamSSLCertificates,
                                (id)kCFStreamSocketSecurityLevelNegotiatedSSL,
                                (id)kCFStreamSSLLevel, nil];

    [writeStream setProperty:sslSettings
                forKey:(id)kCFStreamPropertySSLSettings];

    [readStream setProperty:sslSettings
                forKey:(id)kCFStreamPropertySSLSettings];

    // Give streams a delegate so we can monitor them
    [readStream setDelegate:self];
    [writeStream setDelegate:self];
```

```
// Schedule the streams into the run loop so that they can do their work
[writeStream scheduleInRunLoop:[NSRunLoop currentRunLoop]
                       forMode:NSDefaultRunLoopMode];
[readStream scheduleInRunLoop:[NSRunLoop currentRunLoop]
                      forMode:NSDefaultRunLoopMode];
}
```

Once the streams have been opened and scheduled into the run loop, they will start telling their delegate (the **CocoaServerAppDelegate**) what's going on in their lives. For example, a read stream might say, "I have some new data sitting on the socket. Would you like to read it?" A write stream might say, "I just sent a bunch of data, and now I'm ready for more." Also, if a stream encounters a problem, it will report an error to its delegate.

In CocoaServerAppDelegate.h, declare that **CocoaServerAppDelegate** conforms to the NSStreamDelegate protocol.

```
@interface CocoaServerAppDelegate : NSObject
    <NSApplicationDelegate, NSNetServiceDelegate,
    NSTableViewDataSource, NSTableViewDelegate,
    NSStreamDelegate>
```

Then, in CocoaServerAppDelegate.m, implement the event-handling delegate method.

```
- (void)stream:(NSStream *)aStream handleEvent:(NSStreamEvent)eventCode
{
    switch(eventCode)
    {
        case NSStreamEventHasBytesAvailable:
        {
            NSLog(@"%@ has bytes", aStream);
        } break;
        case NSStreamEventOpenCompleted:
        {
            NSLog(@"%@ is open", aStream);
        } break;
        case NSStreamEventHasSpaceAvailable:
        {
            NSLog(@"%@ can accept bytes", aStream);
        }break;
        case NSStreamEventErrorOccurred:
        {
            NSLog(@"%@ error: %@", aStream, [aStream streamError]);
        } break;
        case NSStreamEventEndEncountered:
        {
            NSLog(@"%@ ended - probably closed by server", aStream);
        } break;
    }
}
```

Finally, at the end of **applicationDidFinishLaunching:**, kick off the whole process of connecting to the Apple push notification server.

```
service = [[NSNetService alloc] initWithDomain:@""
                                          type:@"_http._tcp."
                                          name:@"CocoaHTTPServer"
                                          port:[server port]];

[service setDelegate:self];
```

```
    [service publish];

    [self connectToNotificationServer];
}
```

Build and run CocoaServer. Mac OS X will ask if it is okay to use the private key to securely speak with the notification server. Select Always Allow. After a moment, your console should report that both streams have opened and that the write stream can accept bytes. The console will look something like this:

```
<SSCFInputStream: 0x10044d580> is open
<NSCFOutputStream: 0x10044d650> is open
<NSCFOutputStream: 0x10044d650> can accept bytes
```

You now have an encrypted connection to the push notification server. In the next section, you'll format and send the notification data.

Providing data to the notification server

Once you have a connection to the notification server, you can send it notifications to forward to devices. There are two formats for the notification data sent to the server: simple and enhanced. We will use the enhanced format because it can inform the provider of any error in the data and it allows the provider to include an expiration date for the notification.

The data will be a packed binary buffer, so we will use an instance of **NSMutableData** to put together this information (Figure 29.8). The first byte of the data is called the *command* and it is either 1 or 0. If the notification data is in the enhanced format, the command is 1, otherwise, it's 0.

Figure 29.8   Enhanced notification format

Next is a 32-bit value that identifies this notification. If there is an error delivering the notification, your application will be given back this identifier along with the error so you can decide what to do next.

Another 32-bit integer follows the identifier, and it specifies an expiration date. If a push notification cannot be delivered to a device (most likely because it does not have an Internet connection), the notification server will try to re-send it later. The expiration date says, "If you still haven't delivered this notification by this time, then just trash it." The value of expiration date is the number of seconds past the epoch (Jan 1, 1970) at which the server should trash the notification. If you wanted, for example, to have the notification expire in a day, you will call the function **time** to get the current number of seconds since the epoch and then add a day's worth of seconds to that value.

Next comes the device token: first a 16-bit integer to specify the length of the device token data (which at this point is always 32 bytes, but in the future may vary) and then the token data itself. The token data information is the same value the iOS application receives after it registers. It allows the push notification server to route the notification to the correct device.

Last is the actual notification *payload* (and a 16-bit integer before it to specify its size). The payload is the notification data that will make it to the device. It can include alert text, the name of a sound file to play, or a badge number to place on the application's icon. This data will be binary-encoded JSON. JSON is like XML; it is a platform-independent mark-up language used to transport data. There is no built-in JSON generator in the iOS SDK, but constructing it by hand for simple things like delivering a notification is easy enough.

In the JSON payload, there are a few reserved keys. The first is aps, which is the top-level container for standard notification key-values. The standard notification keys are alert, sound, and badge. Therefore, a simple notification that sends an alert to a device looks like this:

```
{
    "aps":
    {
        "alert":"Here's a simple message"
    }
}
```

If you want to include a sound file to play with the alert, you would add the name of that file to the aps container.

```
{
    "aps":
    {
        "alert":"Here's a simple message",
        "sound":"Sound12.aif"
    }
}
```

The alert can also be a container if you need to add supported customizations to your notification, like localizing the text or providing a special launch image for a notified application. You can check the documentation for all of these keys. Furthermore, you can specify your own keys outside of the aps container for use by your application. These keys will be available to the iOS application when it is awoken by a notification, but they will not be visible to the user.

However, you should never rely on the delivery of a push notification. Therefore, do not relay critical information in customizations of a notification; instead, indicate to the application that it should fetch critical information from the server. Also, do not include confidential information, like passwords or credit card numbers, in the payload.

Time to make the data. In CocoaServerAppDelegate.h, declare a new method to construct the notification data.

```
- (NSData *)notificationDataForMessage:(NSString *)msgText token:(NSData *)token;
```

Implement this method in CocoaServerAppDelegate.m.

```
- (NSData *)notificationDataForMessage:(NSString *)msgText token:(NSData *)token
{
    // To signify the enhanced format, we use 1 as the first byte
    uint8_t command = 1;

    // This is the identifier for this specific notification
    static uint32_t identifier = 5000;
```

```
    // The notification will expire in one day
    uint32_t expiry = htonl(time(NULL) + 86400);

    // Find the binary lengths of the data we will send
    uint16_t tokenLength = htons([token length]);

    // Must escape text before inserting in JSON
    NSMutableString *escapedText = [[msgText mutableCopy] autorelease];

    // Replace \ with \\
    [escapedText replaceOccurrencesOfString:@"\\"
                                 withString:@"\\\\"
                                    options:0
                                      range:NSMakeRange(0, [escapedText length])];

    // Replace " with \"
    [escapedText replaceOccurrencesOfString:@"\""
                                 withString:@"\\\""
                                    options:0
                                      range:NSMakeRange(0, [escapedText length])];

    // Construct the JSON payload to deliver to the device
    NSString *payload =
            [NSString stringWithFormat:@"{\"aps\":{\"alert\":\"%@\"}}", escapedText];

    // We'll have to encode this into a binary buffer, so NSString won't fly
    const char *payloadBuffer = [payload UTF8String];

    // Note: sending length to an NSString will give us the number
    // of characters, not the number of bytes, but strlen
    // gives us the number of bytes. (Some characters
    // take up more than one byte in Unicode)
    uint16_t payloadLength = htons(strlen(payloadBuffer));

    // Create a binary data container to pack all of the data
    NSMutableData *data = [NSMutableData data];

    // Add each component in the right order to the data container
    [data appendBytes:&command length:sizeof(uint8_t)];

    [data appendBytes:&identifier length:sizeof(uint32_t)];

    [data appendBytes:&expiry length:sizeof(uint32_t)];

    [data appendBytes:&tokenLength length:sizeof(uint16_t)];
    [data appendBytes:[token bytes] length:[token length]];

    [data appendBytes:&payloadLength length:sizeof(uint16_t)];
    [data appendBytes:payloadBuffer length:strlen(payloadBuffer)];

    // Increment the identifier for the next notification
    identifier++;

    return data;
}
```

Now we need some way for the CocoaServer to specify the text of the message it sends to registered users. In the CocoaServer project, open MainMenu.xib. Add an **NSTextField** (not a label) and an **NSButton** to the interface. Then make outlets and actions and connect them as shown in Figure 29.9.

Figure 29.9   Finished CocoaServer XIB

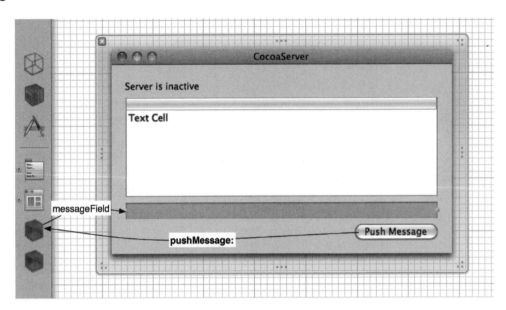

In `CocoaServerAppDelegate.m`, implement **pushMessage:** so that it sends the contents of the `messageField` to the device that is currently selected in the table view.

```
- (IBAction)pushMessage:(id)sender
{
    // If you haven't selected a row, there is no one to send
    // the message to
    NSInteger row = [tableView selectedRow];
    if (row == -1)
        return;

    // Pull the message out of the text view and the token
    // of the device we are going to talk to
    NSString *msgText = [messageField stringValue];
    NSData *token = [[registeredUsers objectAtIndex:row] objectForKey:@"token"];

    NSData *data = [self notificationDataForMessage:msgText token:token];

    // Send this data out to Apple's server
    [writeStream write:[data bytes] maxLength:[data length]];
}
```

Notice the use of **write:maxLength:** at the end of this method. To send data to a server with **NSOutputStream**, you send it this message. The **write:maxLength:** method takes a buffer of bytes and the length of that buffer as arguments. It returns the actual number of bytes written (or -1 if there was an error).

When you write to a stream, the data is essentially "queued up" for transfer. The stream will make the transfer when it can. In this case, the stream is scheduled into the main run loop. Therefore, when the main run loop is not processing another event, it will spend time flushing the output to the network interface. When the data has made its way out to the Internet, the write stream indicates to its delegate that it is ready to accept bytes again by sending the message `stream:handleEvent:` with `NSStreamEventHasSpaceAvailable` as the event type.

Now it's time to see what you have wrought. Build and run CocoaServer. Then, build and run Notified. After the device appears in CocoaServer's table view, exit Notified by pressing the Home button. In CocoaServer, select the device in the table view, enter a message into the text field, and press Push Message. Wait a moment for the notification server to do its part, and then check your device for the notification. How awesome is that?

Detecting errors in notification delivery

If there is an error delivering an enhanced notification, the server will respond with an error. This data will be 6 bytes long. The first byte is a command and will always be the value 8. The second byte is a status code that indicates the type of the error. (You can see all of the status codes in the documentation.) The final 4 bytes is the identifier of that notification.

When a read stream has data available, it sends the message `stream:handleEvent:` to its delegate. Then, you send the message `read:maxLength:` to the stream that has the data, passing an allocated buffer to hold the result of the read along with the size of that buffer. The **NSInputStream** will take the bytes off the stream and put them into the buffer until it reaches the number of bytes you specified. The value returned by this method is a number. A positive number indicates the number of bytes that were actually transferred to the buffer. The value is 0 if there are no bytes left to read and -1 if there was an error.

Typically, when you read from an input stream, you pick a reasonable size (based on the size of the data you are planning to receive) for a buffer, read that many bytes, and then repeat until the buffer returns 0.

We know that a notification delivery error is always 6 bytes. Thus, we can read 6 bytes at a time from the stream. In `CocoaServerAppDelegate.m`, locate the method `stream:handleEvent:` and add the following code:

```
case NSStreamEventHasBytesAvailable:
{
    if (aStream == readStream)
    {
        // If data came back from the server, we have an error
        // Let's fetch it out
        NSUInteger lengthRead = 0;
        do
        {
            // Error packet is always 6 bytes
            uint8_t *buffer = malloc(6);
            lengthRead = [readStream read:buffer maxLength:6];

            // First byte is command (always 8)
            uint8_t command = buffer[0];

            // Second byte is the status code
            uint8_t status = buffer[1];

            // This will be the notification identifier
            uint32_t *ident = (uint32_t *)(buffer + 2);
```

```
                    NSLog(@"ERROR WITH NOTIFICATION: %d %d %d",
                            (int)command, (int)status, *ident);

                    free(buffer);
                } while(lengthRead > 0);
            }
        } break;
```

Now, if there is an issue with your notification data, the console will show you why.

More on reading from a stream

This stream-reading technique is sufficient for our application because we know the exact size of the data we will get back from the server. In general, however, you have to take more precautions. Sometimes, you will get more than one packet, a partial packet, or a combination of the two (e.g., one and a half packets). Sometimes, data of variable sizes will be sent. The solution to these problems is creating a packet format that both the client and server agree upon. Take a look at the notification data you prepare for the notification server: it has a format that is set-in-stone and you always pass the size of the variable parts of that data. By being a notification provider, you have agreed to this format.

A typical format uses the first byte as a command that indicates the format of the data. Since you always receive at least one byte when the stream informs its delegate that it has bytes available, you can safely read this byte and determine what to do next. Many formats use the next chunk of bytes to indicate the length of the rest of the packet. So, the stream will check the command and say, "Oh, this is a Message command, so I know that the next 2 bytes will be the length of the packet. I'll read those two bytes to figure out how large the packet is."

The delegate will then attempt to read that many bytes from the stream. If there are exactly that many bytes left in the read stream, you have a single and complete packet from the server and can use that data in your application.

In practice, though, that doesn't always happen. If the data you read is not the exact length you are expecting, you will have to store that data for later. Let's consider two examples:

- You read the first three bytes of a stream, and they indicate that there are 40 more bytes in the packet. You allocate a buffer that is 40 bytes and attempt to read 40 bytes from the stream – but the stream only has 32 bytes available. In this situation, you keep that data around. Then, the next time a stream informs its delegate that bytes are available, you immediately lop off the first 8 bytes and append them to the stored data. Now, you have a complete packet.

- You read the first three bytes and again know that there are 40 bytes left in the packet. But, there are actually 60 bytes available. The first 40 bytes are a complete packet – you can use that data immediately. However, the last 20 bytes belong to another packet. So, you grab the first byte to determine the format. Let's assume the same format, so you check the next two bytes for the length and see that the packet is 36 bytes. You keep the extra bytes around, and the next chunk of data that comes in will be appended to it.

Additional Client-side Notification Handling

Now that you've pulled off the basics of push notifications, let's look at three additions to notification handling in the client application: pushing sounds and badges, receiving notifications while running, and using notification data when not running.

498

Sounds and badges

When Notified registers for notifications, it specifies that it can also receive sound and badge notifications. A sound notification's JSON payload contains the filename of a sound, and the notified application will search its application bundle for a matching file and play it if it exists. This sound file must follow the same rules as a system sound: less than 30 seconds and in a raw data format. Locate Sound12.aif that you used in Chapter 27 and add it to the Notified project in the project navigator.

In the CocoaServer project, update the method **notificationDataForMessage:token:** in CocoaServerAppDelegate.m to badge the application and have it play the alert sound.

```
// Find the binary lengths of the data we will send
uint16_t tokenLength = htons([token length]);

// Construct the JSON payload to deliver to the device
NSString *payload = [NSString stringWithFormat:
        @"{\"aps\":{\"alert\":\"%@\",\"sound\":\"Sound12.aif\",\"badge\":1}}",
        escapedText];

// We'll have to encode this into a binary buffer, so NSString won't fly
const char *payloadBuffer = [payload UTF8String];
```

The notification payload expanded looks like this:

```
{
    "aps":
    {
        "alert":"Message",
        "sound":"Sound12.aif",
        "badge":1
    }
}
```

Build and run CocoaServer and Notified. Close Notified by pressing the Home button. Deliver a notification from CocoaServer. Shortly, you will see the alert – and hear a sound and see a badge on the application icon.

After you have badged an application, you typically want to remove that badge after the user launches the application. In NotifiedAppDelegate.m, implement the following delegate method to clear the badge.

```
- (void)applicationDidBecomeActive:(UIApplication *)application
{
    // When the user opens the application, clear the badge since we've seen the
    // notification
    [[UIApplication sharedApplication] setApplicationIconBadgeNumber:0];
}
```

When a provider badges an application, the last notification sent determines the badge value that appears on the icon. So if a notification payload does not contain a badge value, any existing badge value is cleared.

Build and run Notified, close it, and push another notification from CocoaServer. Relaunch Notified and exit it again to see its icon. Notice that the badge has disappeared.

Accessing data in notifications

Earlier in the chapter, we mentioned that, while you can send custom data in the alert of the JSON payload of a notification, you shouldn't send anything critical. For instance, imagine a basic chess application where you play remote opponents. It would be great to notify the user when an opponent has moved, but you wouldn't pass the actual move in the notification. Instead, you would announce that a move has been made. When the application is launched, it will check the server for the latest move. Of course, it should do that anyway. The notification only serves as a convenient interrupt so the user doesn't have to keep launching the application to see if that slow &*%#@ has moved yet.

Remember, delivery of push notifications is not guaranteed, so you don't want to base your application's logic (or your user's experience) on them. Returning to the game example, if you did pass the opponent's move in a push notification, and the user chose to ignore the notification, then that data would be lost.

Given that caveat, there is some data that it makes sense to pass in a notification – data the application can use to set its context after launching. If the user is launching the application from a particular notification, you could pass data that tells the application to open in the context most related to the event the notification announced.

In the chess example, say the application supports multiple games. A move, and thus a notification, would be associated with a particular game. You could pass data in the notification so that if the application is launched from the alert window, it will open directly to the game in question. Very slick. But it's not the end of the world if the notification is not delivered or if the user ignores the notification.

Our Notified application has very little context. So to demonstrate how to access data passed in a notification, we're just going to have the text of the alert appear in the Notified interface.

When an application that is not currently running receives a push notification, the user typically sees a pop-up window and gets a chance to launch the application. What happens if the application receiving the notification is currently running? The notification is still delivered, but the pop-up window does not appear. To get the data out of the notification, you must implement the UIApplicationDelegate method **application:didReceiveRemoteNotification:** to receive it.

Open Notified's MainWindow.xib and add a **UITextView** to the window. Create and connect an outlet for it, as shown in Figure 29.10.

Figure 29.10   Finished iOS XIB

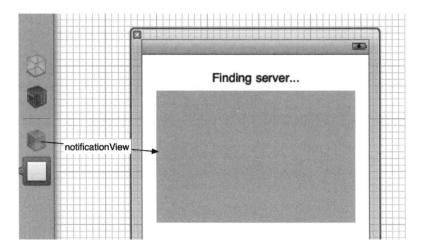

When an iOS application is informed of a notification, it gets a dictionary that the JSON payload has been parsed into. Therefore, there will be a top-level aps dictionary that contains an alert string. In NotifiedAppDelegate.m, implement **application:didReceiveRemoteNotification:** to fill out the notificationView with the alert from the notification.

```
- (void)application:(UIApplication *)application
    didReceiveRemoteNotification:(NSDictionary *)userInfo
{
    // If we get a notification while the app is running, we'll just get the alert
    // and display it to the user
    [notificationView setText:[[userInfo objectForKey:@"aps"]
                                        objectForKey:@"alert"]];
}
```

Build and run Notified and keep it running. Then push another notification from CocoaServer. After a moment, the notification message will appear in the text view.

When an application is not running, the user can launch it from the alert window. If your application wants to use the data from the notification once it is launched from the alert window, you can retrieve it from the launchOptions dictionary of **application:didFinishLaunchingWithOptions:**. Add the following code to the top of this method in NotifiedAppDelegate.m.

```
- (BOOL)application:(UIApplication *)application
    didFinishLaunchingWithOptions:(NSDictionary *)launchOptions
{
    // If the user chooses to launch the application in response to a notification,
    // get the notification information to use in the app
    NSDictionary *remoteDict =
        [launchOptions
          objectForKey:UIApplicationLaunchOptionsRemoteNotificationKey];
    if (remoteDict)
        [self application:application didReceiveRemoteNotification:remoteDict];
```

Build and run Notified. Exit the application and kill it from the dock. Then send another notification and tap the View button. The text of the alert will appear in the **UITextView** once Notified has relaunched.

The Production Server and Moving Forward

When you deploy an application to the App Store, you need to use a different SSL certificate and talk to a different notification server. The process for generating that certificate is the same; in the developer portal, just configure the Production section of the App ID. In your server, you must point the connection to another instance of the notification server. The hostname of this server is gateway.push.apple.com, and the port is still 2195.

Also, CocoaServer isn't exactly a production server: it isn't optimized to handle many service requests at once.

Finally, all of the networking APIs and classes used in CocoaServer work in iOS as well. An iOS application can get instances of **NSInputStream** and **NSOutputStream** after calling **CFStreamCreatePairWithSocketToHost** and use those to exchange data with other machines.

For the More Curious: The Feedback Service

Not every user will keep your application forever. If a user uninstalls your application, you should no longer send notifications to that device. To determine if a user has uninstalled your application, Apple has a feedback server that spits out device tokens for uninstalled applications. You simply hook a read stream to this server, and it will fire device tokens at you.

This read stream needs to be configured with the same SSL certificate used to push notifications. The host for the feedback service is located at feedback.push.apple.com, port 2196 (The development server is feedback.sandbox.push.apple.com). When a user uninstalls an application, the data you receive on the read stream will be 38 bytes long.

The first four bytes will be a time_t value that gives you the number of seconds since the epoch that Apple realized the user had uninstalled the application. If this value is greater than the last time the application sent your server its device token, then you know that the user no longer has your application installed. (If it is less than that, then they have re-installed the application.) Therefore, you typically note the time that you receive a device token so you can make this comparison later.

The rest of the packet from the feedback server will be the token of the device that uninstalled the application. The first two bytes of this part of the packet will be the length of the device token, which for now is 32 bytes. Then, the next 32 bytes are the device token itself. When you receive this data from the server, you should remove that device token from your list of registered devices.

30

Afterword

Welcome to the end of the book! You should be very proud of all your work and all that you have learned. Now, there's good news and bad news:

- *The good news:* The stuff that leaves programmers befuddled when they come to the iOS platform is behind you now. You are an iOS developer.

- *The bad news:* You are probably not a very good iOS developer.

What to do next

It is now time to make some mistakes, read some really tedious documentation, and be humbled by the heartless experts who will ridicule your questions. Here's what we recommend:

Write apps now. If you don't immediately use what you have learned, it will fade. Exercise and extend your knowledge. Now.

Go deep. This book has consistently favored breadth over depth; any chapter could have been expanded into an entire book. Find a topic that you find interesting and really wallow in it – do some experiments, read Apple's docs on the topic, read a posting on a blog or on StackOverflow.

Connect. There is an iOS Developer Meetup in most cities, and the talks are surprisingly good. There are discussion groups online. If you are doing a project, find people to help you: designers, testers (AKA guinea pigs), and other developers.

Make mistakes and fix them. You will learn a lot the days you say, "This has become a ball of crap! I'm going to throw it away and write it again with an architecture that makes sense." Polite programmers call this *refactoring*.

Give back. Share the knowledge. Answer a dumb question with grace. Give away some code.

Shameless plugs

You can find us both on Twitter, where we keep you informed about programming and entertained about life: @joeconwaybnr and @aaronhillegass.

Keep an eye out for future guides from Big Nerd Ranch. We also offer week-long courses for developers. And if you just need some code written, we do contract programming. For more information, visit our website at http://www.bignerdranch.com/.

It is you, dear reader, who makes our lives of writing, coding, and teaching possible. So thank you for buying our book.

Index

Symbols

`#import`, 56
`#pragma mark`, 302
`%@` prefix, 38
`.h` files, 43
`.m` files, 46
`@` prefix
   for hard-coded strings, 38
   and Objective-C keywords, 43
`@class`, 118
`@implementation`, 46
`@interface`, 43, 397
`@optional`, 84
`@protocol`, 84
`@selector()`, 210
`_cmd`, 272
`__block`, 402

A

accelerometer, 149-156
`accelerometer:didAccelerate:`, 149, 151, 152
accessor methods, 45-48, 67-72
accessory indicator (of `UITableViewCell`), 182
action methods, 17-20, 341, 342
active state, 266, 500
`addAnimation:forKey:`, 381
`addObject:`, 33, 37, 40
`addSubview:`, 119
`alloc`, 32, 33, 61
allocation, 59-61
Allocations instrument, 345-352
analyzing (code), 343-345
angled brackets, 114
animation transactions, 370
`animationDidStop:finished:`, 382
animations
   (see also `CALayer`, layers)
   `CABasicAnimation`, 376, 377, 379-381, 384
   `CAKeyframeAnimation`, 377, 383, 384
   choosing, 379
   classes of, 363, 375-378
   and data types, 377
   identity matrices in, 384
   implicit, 369-371

   key paths of, 375, 379
   keyframes in, 378-380
   keys for, 381
   reusing, 381
   timing functions of, 381, 382
`animationWithKeyPath:`, 381
anonymous functions (see blocks)
anti-aliasing, 157
API Reference, 103-108
APIs
   (see also frameworks)
   Core Animation, 363, 368, 376
   Core Audio, 462
   Core Foundation, 234-236
   Core Video, 462
   private, 311
App ID, 24
Apple documentation, 103-108
application bundle, 257, 276, 277, 325, 452, 458
application delegate, 6, 11, 12, 15
application dock, 266
application domain, 330
application sandbox, 257-260, 276
application states, 265-268, 272, 273, 458-462
`application:didReceiveRemoteNotification:`, 500
`applicationDidBecomeActive:`, 272
`applicationDidEnterBackground:`, 267, 268, 273
applications
   (see also `UIApplication`)
   allowing orientations, 169
   build settings for, 359-361
   building, 21, 77, 91-95, 322
   cleaning, 322
   data storage, 257, 258
   data storage options, 314
   debugging (see debugginguniversal applications)
   deploying, 23, 24
   directories in, 257-260
   icons for, 24-27
   launch images for, 27
   profiling, 346, 347
   and run loop, 65
   running on simulator, 21
   size limits, 458
   templates for, 77

build settings, 359-361
bundles
    application, 257, 276, 277, 325, 458
    identifier, 24
    NSBundle, 325
byte ordering, 475

C

CAAnimation, 363
    (see also animations)
CAAnimationGroup, 378
CABasicAnimation, 376, 377, 379-381
CAKeyframeAnimation, 377, 383, 384
CALayer
    (see also animations, layers)
    addAnimation:forKey:, 381
    animatable properties of, 369-371
    bitmap context for, 372
    contents, 367
    creating, 364-366
    delegate, 371
    described, 363
    designated initializer, 365
    drawInContext:, 371, 372
    presentationLayer, 384
    properties, 366-370, 375, 376, 379
    setPosition:, 369
    subclassing, 371
    superlayer, 368
    zPosition, 368, 369
callbacks, 83, 403
CAMediaTimingFunction, 381
camera
    (see also images)
    recording video, 238-240
    taking pictures, 226-231
canBecomeFirstResponder, 154
CAPropertyAnimation, 375
categories
    for "private methods", 399, 400, 444
    syntax of, 397-399
    vs. subclassing, 399
CATransaction, 370
CATransform3DIdentity, 384
CATransition, 378
cells (see table view cells, **UITableViewCell**)
CFReadStreamRef, 489

CFRelease, 235
CFStreamCreatePairWithSocketToHost, 489
CFStringRef, 234, 235
CFUUIDCreate, 235
CFUUIDCreateString, 235
CFUUIDRef, 234-236
CFWriteStreamRef, 489
CGBitmapContextCreate, 373
CGContextRef
    drawing to, 286
    inside **drawRect:**, 116, 121
    and layers, 372, 373
CGImage, 367
CGPoint, 117, 376, 377
CGRect, 117
CGSize, 117, 286
@class, 118
class extensions, 399
class methods, 53-55
classes
    (see also individual class names)
    allocating from heap, 59, 61
    creating, 41
    inheritance of, 40, 44
    name prefixes for, 79
    overview, 31, 32
    properties (see properties)
    reusing, 176
    size in memory, 75
    subclassing, 40-56
    superclasses, 40, 43, 51
CLLocation, 81, 82
CLLocationManager, 80-82, 460
CLLocationManagerDelegate, 83
closures (see blocks)
_cmd, 272
Cocoa Touch, 78
    in Cocoa Touch, 78
code snippet library, 186-188
command-line tool, 35
compile-time errors, 56, 93, 94
compiling, 93
connection:didFailWithError:, 412
connection:didReceiveData:, 411, 412
connectionDidFinishLoading:, 411-414
connections inspector, 19
console, 22, 38
contentMode (**UIImageView**), 224, 225

declarations
  forward, 118
  instance variable, 44
  method, 45, 49, 50, 54, 55
  overview, 43
  protocol, 85, 103
decodeObjectForKey:, 263
delegate (property), 81, 86, 442
  (see also delegation)
delegation
  as approach to callbacks, 403
  choosing a delegate, 150
  and controller objects, 85
  creating a delegate protocol, 437-442
  creating a protocol, 253, 254
  delegate, 81, 86, 442
  and layers, 371
  and memory management, 85
  overview, 82, 83
  protocols used for, 83-85
  swapping delegates, 415
deleteRowsAtIndexPaths:withRowAnimation:,
198
dequeueReusableCellWithIdentifier:, 284
description, 39
description (**NSObject**), 41, 48
designated initializers, 49-53
detail view controllers, 432
developer certificates, 23
device tokens, 482, 483, 486-488, 493
devices
  checking for camera, 228, 229
  deploying apps to, 23
  deploying to, 24
  determining type of, 243
  orientation of, 151, 160, 163
  provisioning, 23, 24
  Retina display, 25
dictionaries
  and blocks, 401
  described, 232
  memory management of, 271
  using, 234-236
  and web server requests, 475-479
  writing to filesystem, 275
didReceiveMemoryWarning, 143
directories
  application, 257-260

Documents/, 258, 259
Library/Caches/, 258
Library/Preferences/, 257
lproj, 319, 325
temporary, 258
dirty rectangle, 117
dismissModalViewControllerAnimated:, 249,
251
dismissPopoverAnimated:, 246
dock
  for applications, 266
  in editor area, 5
documentation, using, 103-108
Documents/ (directory), 258, 259
domain, application, 330
domain, registration, 330
dot-notation, xvii
drawLayer:inContext: (**CALayer**), 371, 372
drawRect:, 116, 120, 121, 126, 280, 372
drill-down interface
  with **UINavigationController**, 203
  with **UISplitViewController**, 431

E

editButtonItem, 210
editing (**UITableView**,
UITableViewController), 191, 196
editor area, 5
encodeInt:forKey:, 262
encodeObject:forKey:, 262
encodeWithCoder:, 260-262
endEditing:, 221, 237
entities (Core Data), 292-297, 307-311
enumerateObjectsUsingBlock: (**NSArray**), 396
errors
  compile-time, 93, 94
  connection, 412
  linker, 94, 95
  and **NSError**, 274, 275
  run-time, 56, 57
event loop, 125
exceptions, 56
explicit layers, 371
  (see also **CALayer**)

F

fast enumeration, 57

M

.m files, 46
M4A, 452
`mach_msg_trap`, 354
macros, preprocessor, 360, 361
`main`, 36
main bundle, 257, 276, 277, 325, 452, 458
`mainBundle`, 194, 277
`MainWindow.xib`, 6
`malloc`, 59
MapKit (framework), 97, 99
MapKit annotation, 99
maps
    (see also `MKAnnotation`, `MKMapView`)
    changing type of, 327, 328
    zooming, 103-108
mapType (`MKMapView`), 327, 328
`mapView:didUpdateUserLocation:`, 106
masks, autoresize, 164, 165, 167-169
master view controllers, 432, 442
MediaPlayer (framework), 456
MediaPlayer application
    in background, 458
    playing audio, 452-455
    playing video, 455-458
    recording audio, 462
mediaTypes, 238
memory leaks
    avoiding with `autorelease`, 64, 65
    defined, 59
    finding with Allocations instrument, 345-352
    finding with static analyzer, 343-345
    fixing, 63-70
memory management
    basics of, 59-73
    and blocks, 400-402
    C functions, 235
    and controller objects, 86
    data segment, 74
    and delegates, 85
    dictionaries, 232, 271
    lazy allocation of views, 143
    and notifications, 160
    `NSMutableArray`, 66
    optimizing with Allocations instrument, 345-352
    and properties, 71

and retain cycles, 125
rules for, 73
stack, 400
stack frame, 74
structures, 111, 235
and `UITableViewCell`, 185
memory warnings, 143, 231, 271, 460
messages, 33-35
    (see also methods)
methods
    (see also accessor methods, individual method names)
    (see also categories)
    accessor, 45-48
    action, 17-20, 341, 342
    class, 53-55
    convenience, 54, 55, 64, 67, 73
    data source, 180
    declaring, 45, 49, 50, 54
    defined, 32
    designated initializer, 49-53
    implementing, 46, 47, 49, 51
    initializer, 49-53
    making calls to illegal, 248
    names of, 34
    overriding, 41, 48, 49, 51-53
    parameters of, 50
    private, 399, 444
    protocol, 84
    stepping through, 88-90
    vs. messages, 34
    writing new, 49
MKAnnotation (protocol), 108-111
`MKAnnotationView`, 98, 108
MKCoordinateRegion, 107, 108
`MKMapView`, 98, 99, 102-108, 327
MKMapViewDelegate, 103-106
`MKReverseGeocoder`, 114
`MKUserLocation`, 107
MobileCoreServices, 240
`.mobileprovision` files, 24
modal view controllers
    defined, 229
    dismissing, 249, 250
    and non-disappearing parent view, 251
    styles of, 250
    transitions for, 254
modalPresentationStyle, 250

proximity monitoring, 170
push notifications
    accessing data in, 500-502
    aps container in, 494
    badges in, 482, 499
    certificates for, 483-486, 488, 490
    delivering to device, 486-497
    described, 481
    device tokens for, 482, 483, 486-488, 493
    errors in delivering, 497, 498
    expiration dates for, 493
    limitations of, 494, 500
    and notification server, 486, 488-497
    package formats for, 493-495
    payload in, 494
    provisioning for, 483-486
    receiving in running app, 500
    registering for, 482, 483
    setting app context with, 500
    sounds in, 499
    types of, 482
    unregistering a device for, 502
pushViewController:animated:, 217-219

Q

QuartzCore, 363, 368
Quiz application, 2-29
quotation marks, 114

R

RandomPossessions application
    creating command-line tool, 35-39
    creating **Possession** class, 41-56
read:maxLength:, 497
receiver, 33
reference counting, 61, 63
registerDefaults:, 330
registration domain, 330
relationships (Core Data), 295-297, 312, 313
release, 62-70
reloadData, 198
removeObserver:, 160
reordering controls, 200
required methods (protocols), 84
resignFirstResponder, 112, 221
resizing views, 164, 165, 167-169
resources

defined, 25, 276
    localizing, 319-322
responder chain, 340
responders (see first responder, **UIResponder**)
respondsToSelector:, 84
retain, 62, 63
retain counts, 61-64, 73, 125
retain cycles, 125
Retina display, 25, 29, 156-158
reuseIdentifier (**UITableViewCell**), 186
reusing
    animation objects, 381
    classes, 176
    table view cells, 185, 186
root object (in archiving), 260
rootViewController (of window), 131, 207
rootViewController
(**UINavigationController**), 204-206
rotation, 161-169, 434
rows (of a table view)
    adding, 197
    deleting, 198, 199
    moving, 199-201
run loop, 65, 125
run-time errors, 56, 57

S

sandbox, application, 257-260, 276
schemes, 24, 355-359, 472
screenshots, 28
scrolling, 121, 122
sections (of table view), 182, 191
Security (framework), 490
SEL, 210
selector, 33, 210
self, 51, 55
sendAction:to:from:forEvent:, 342
sendActionsForControlEvents:, 342
setAutoresizingMask:, 167-169
setCategory:error:, 459, 460
setCompletionBlock: (**CATransaction**), 401
setEditing:animated:, 196, 210
setMultipleTouchEnabled:, 336
setNeedsDisplay, 125, 372
setObject:forKey:, 232-234
setPosition:, 369
setProximityMonitoringEnabled:, 170

parsing, 413-423
property lists, 275

Z
ZeroConf standard, 463
zooming (maps), 103-108
zooming (views), 122, 123
zPosition, 368, 369

TRAINING

ACHIEVE NERDVANA

Since 2001, Big Nerd Ranch has offered intensive computer programming courses taught by our expert instructors in a retreat environment. It is at our Ranch where we think our students flourish. Classes, accommodations and dining all take place within the same building, freeing you to learn, code and discuss with your programming peers and instructors. At Big Nerd Ranch, we take care of the details; your only job is to learn.

Our Teachers

Our teachers are leaders in their respective fields. They offer deep understanding of the technologies they teach, as well as a broad spectrum of development experience, allowing them to address the concerns you encounter as a developer. Big Nerd Ranch instructors provide the necessary combination of knowledge and outstanding teaching experience, enabling our students to leave the Ranch with a vastly improved set of skills.

The Big Nerd Way

We have developed "The Big Nerd Ranch Way". This methodology guides the development and presentation of our classes. The style is casual but focused, with brief lectures followed by hands-on exercises designed to give you immediate, relevant understanding of each piece of the technology you are learning.

Your Stay At The Ranch

One fee covers tuition, meals, lodging and transportation to and from the airport. At the Big Nerd Ranch, we remove the distractions inherent in standard corporate training by offering classes in quiet, comfortable settings in Atlanta, Georgia and Frankfurt, Germany.

Available Classes

Advanced Mac OS X
Android
Beginning Cocoa
Beginning iOS (iPhone/iPad)
Beginning Ruby on Rails
Cocoa Commuter Class in Spanish
Cocoa I
Cocoa II
Commuter iOS Class
Django
iOS (iPhone/iPad)
OpenGL
Python Mastery
Ruby on Rails I
Ruby on Rails II

Interested in a class?

Register online at www.bignerdranch.com or call 404.478.9005 for more information.
Full class schedule, pricing and availability also online.

ON-SITE TRAINING

OUR NERDS, YOUR LOCATION

Through our on-site training program you can affordably and conveniently have our renowned classes come to you. Our expert instructors will help your team advance through nerd-based instructional support that is fresh, engaging and allows for unencumbered hands-on learning.

Clients around the globe have praised our on-site instruction for some of the following reasons:

Flexibility

- *Classes can be booked when the timing is right for your team.*
- *We can tailor our existing syllabi to ensure our training meets your organization's unique needs.*
- *Post-class mentorship is available to support your team as they work on especially challenging projects.*

Affordability

- *No need for planes, trains and automobiles for all of your staff; our Nerds come to you.*
- *Train up to 22 students at a significant discount over open-enrollment training.*

Nerd Know-how

- *Our instructors are highly practiced in both teaching and programming. They move beyond theory by bringing their real-life experiences to your team.*
- *On-site training includes post-class access to our Nerds, our extensive Alumni Network, and our Big Nerd Ranch Forums. Learning support doesn't end just because your class does.*

For your on-site training, we provide an instructor, all Big Nerd Ranch copyrighted class materials, gifts, certificates of completion and access to our extensive Alumni Network. You'll provide the classroom set up, computers and related devices for all students, a projector and a screen.

Ready to book an on-site training course?

For a free Big Nerd Ranch on-site proposal, please contact us at 404.478.9005.

CONSULTING

BiG nerD ranch

ACHIEVE NERDVANA IN-HOUSE & ON-SITE

When you contract with Big Nerd Ranch, we'll work directly with you to turn your needs into a full-fledged desktop and/or mobile solution. Our developers and designers have consistently created some of the iPhone App Store's most intriguing applications.

Management Philosophy

Big Nerd Ranch holistically manages every client relationship. Our goal is to communicate and educate our clients from project initiation to completion, while ultimately helping them gain a competitive advantage in their niche marketplace.

Project Strategy

We take a detail-oriented approach to all of our project estimations. We'll work with you to define a strategy, specify product offerings and then build them into software that stands alone.

Our Process

Our consulting process is broken down into three distinct phases: Requirements, Execution and Monitoring/Controlling. Bring your business case to us and we'll develop a plan for a user interface and database design. From there, we'll develop a quote and begin the design and implementation process. Our Nerds will perform many tests, including debugging and performance tuning, ensuring the app does what you want it to do. Finally, we'll beta test your app and get it ready for submission and deployment in the iTunes store and/or the Android Market. Once your app is finished, the Nerds will work with you on subsequent version updates and can even help with the marketing of your app.

Testimonials

"tops has worked closely with Big Nerd Ranch for over eight years. Consistently they have delivered high-quality code for our projects; clean and poetic. Thanks to their contributions, we have become a leader in our field."

Dr. Mark Sanchez
President/Founder
tops Software
topsortho.com

"From the simplest GUI design gig to jobs that plumb the darkest corners of the OS, Big Nerd Ranch should be the first contact in your virtual Rolodex under Mac/iPhone consulting. It's no exaggeration to say that Aaron Hillegass literally wrote the book on Cocoa programming, and you couldn't possibly do better than to bring his and his team's expertise to bear on your application. I've yet to work with a consulting firm that is as competent and communicative as Big Nerd Ranch. Simply put, these guys deliver."

Glenn Zelniker
CEO
Z-Systems Audio Engineering
www.z-sys.com

"We turned to Big Nerd Ranch to develop the Teavana concept into an iPhone app. More than just a developer, they partnered with us to make the app better than we could have imagined alone. The final app was bug-free and functioned exactly as expected. I would definitely recommend Big Nerd Ranch and can't speak highly enough about their work."

Jay Allen
VP of Ecommerce
Teavana Corporation
www.teavana.com

We'd love to talk to you about your project.

Contact our consulting team today for a free consultation at consult@bignerdranch.com or visit www.bignerdranch.com/consulting for more information.